The Dynamics of Change
in Latin American Politics

PRENTICE-HALL INTERNATIONAL, INC., *London*
PRENTICE-HALL OF AUSTRALIA, PTY., LTD., *Sydney*
PRENTICE-HALL OF CANADA, LTD., *Toronto*
PRENTICE-HALL OF INDIA (PRIVATE) LTD., *New Delhi*
PRENTICE-HALL OF JAPAN, INC., *Tokyo*

The Dynamics of Change
in Latin American Politics

Edited by

JOHN D. MARTZ
University of North Carolina

PRENTICE-HALL, INC.
Englewood Cliffs, N.J.

Current printing (last digit):
12 11 10 9 8 7 6 5 4 3

Library of Congress Catalog Card No. 65-10182

Printed in the United States of America
22180-C

To MJ with love, adding the reminder that the magical number is 3½. She will understand.

Preface

Organizing a book of readings often presents the compiler with perils that exceed the possible rewards. The alleged relative ease with which selections are drawn together—assuming a reasonable knowledge of the literature—sometimes suggests a cheap way of placing one's name on the spine of a bound volume. Indeed, the function of the editor in such a work is seen by some as an exercise in intellectual prostitution. This view is perhaps understandable, yet when all is said and done, there is a definite place for readers. This particular book has been brought together in the genuine belief that, given the state of Latin American political science in the 1960's, such a volume fills a legitimate need.

With the contemporary expansion of our interest in studying Latin America with the tools and techniques of modern political science—about which the opening essay will have more to say—the importance of a book of basic readings for courses in the politics of the region is clear. The growing number of significant contributions, which are widely scattered through a variety of journals and publications beyond the resources of the average college undergraduate, further justifies the preparation of such a book.

An inevitable pitfall of such an undertaking is the matter of the actual choices, for the experienced Latin Americanist will find items he does not highly regard, while others he will search for in vain. One cannot be unduly apologetic about this, however. Even if the available literature is scarcely overflowing with brilliantly original work, much worthwhile material is extant that could not be used here. My effort has been that of selecting the items believed most representative in terms of the over-all framework discussed in the first essay. Many fine pieces could not be included, and not all of the leading Latin Americanists could be sampled. It should also be noted that, with the scope of the book specifically that of Latin American politics, selections dealing with hemispheric affairs and inter-American relations were not used.

The publishers and authors receive full appreciation for granting their kind permission to reprint their material. Let me also express my particular thanks to two colleagues in the Department of Political Science at the University of North Carolina under whom I previously had the privilege of studying, Professors Federico G. Gil and Charles B. Robson. To the former I am indebted in many ways, only one of which is his examination of the original outline. The latter has influenced me in terms of the methodology of comparative government, not to mention a number of less direct ways. Neither they nor anyone else, of course, has any share in the shortcomings of this effort, for which I alone bear the ultimate responsibility.

A word of gratitude is also due Mrs. Lee Ann Matthews, secretary of the Institute of Latin American Studies at the University of North Carolina, who was most helpful and reliable in various necessary administrative and clerical tasks. Finally and most importantly, my continuing debt for the personal forbearance as well as the critical remarks and suggestions of Mary Jeanne Reid Martz.

J.D.M.

Table of Contents

The State of Research and Study
in Latin American Politics and Government   1

PART ONE

The Setting for Change   7

1   A Proposed Framework for Latin American Politics

Kalman H. Silvert   9

2   Putting Latin American Politics in Perspective

Martin Needler   21

3   The Hacienda

Frank Tannenbaum   27

4   Latin American Constitutions: Nominal and Real

J. Lloyd Mecham   35

5   Latin American Executives: Essence and Variations

Rosendo A. Gómez   45

6   Trends in Social Thought
in Twentieth-century Latin America

Harold E. Davis   56

7   Conditions Favoring
the Rise of Communism in Latin America

Robert J. Alexander   **67**

8   Southern Dialectic

George I. Blanksten   **77**

9   *Aprismo*: Peru's Indigenous Political Theory

Harry Kantor   **86**

PART TWO

The Nature of Change   **93**

10   Nationalism in Latin America

Kalman H. Silvert   **95**

11   The Political Role
of the Latin American Middle Sectors

John J. Johnson   **104**

12   Measurement of Latin American Political Change

Russell H. Fitzgibbon
Kenneth F. Johnson   **113**

13   Toward a Theory of Power
and Political Instability in Latin America

Merle Kling   **130**

14   Violence as a Power Factor
in Latin American Politics

William S. Stokes   **140**

15   The Aspiration for Economic Development

George I. Blanksten   **150**

16   Ideologies of Economic Development
in Latin America

Albert O. Hirschman   **159**

17   The Land Reform Issue in Latin America

Thomas F. Carroll   **172**

PART THREE

The Agents of Change

18 Political Groups in Latin America

George I. Blanksten   184

19 The Party Potpourri in Latin America

Russell H. Fitzgibbon   203

20 Responsible Parties in Latin America

Federico G. Gil   214

21 Mexico's One-party System: A Re-evaluation

L. Vincent Padgett   223

22 The Confrontation with the Political University

John P. Harrison   228

23 Developing Political Orientations
of Panamanian Students

Daniel Goldrich
Edward W. Scott   237

24 Labor and Politics: Problems and Prospects

Moisés Poblete Troncoso
Ben G. Burnett   251

25 Civil-Military Relations in Latin America

L. N. McAlister   256

26 The Role of the Military
in Latin American Politics

Theodore Wyckoff   263

27 Dichotomies in the Church

John J. Kennedy   276

List of Contributors

Robert J. Alexander
Professor of History, Rutgers University. Author, *The Perón Era* (1951); *Communism in Latin America* (1957); *The Bolivian National Revolution* (1958); *Prophets of the Revolution* (1962); *Today's Latin America* (1962).

George I. Blanksten
Professor of Political Science, Northwestern University. Author, *Ecuador: Constitutions and Caudillos* (1951); *Perón's Argentina* (1953). Contributor, *Government and Politics in Latin America* (1958); *Politics of the Developing Areas* (1960).

Ben G. Burnett
Associate Professor of Political Science, Whittier College. Co-author, *The Rise of the Latin American Labor Movement* (1960).

Thomas F. Carroll
Staff member of the Food and Agriculture Organization of the United Nations. Contributor, *Latin American Issues: Essays and Comments* (1961).

Harold E. Davis
Professor of Latin American History and Government, American University. Author, *Makers of Democracy in Latin America* (1945); *Latin American Leaders* (1949); *Latin American Social Thought* (1961). Editor, *Government and Politics in Latin America* (1958).

Russell H. Fitzgibbon
Professor of Political Science, University of California, Santa Barbara. Director, Center for Latin American Studies. Author, *Cuba and the U.S.* (1935); *Latin America, Past and Present* (1946); *Uruguay: Por-*

trait of a Democracy (1954). Editor, *The Constitutions of the Americas* (1948).

Federico G. Gil

Professor of Political Science, University of North Carolina. Director, Institute of Latin American Studies. Co-author, *Governments of Latin America* (1957). Contributor, *World Pressures in American Foreign Policy* (1964); *The Political Systems of Latin America* (1964).

Daniel Goldrich

Associate Professor of Political Science, University of Oregon. Author of numerous articles in the professional journals.

Rosendo A. Gómez

Associate Professor of Government, University of Arizona. Author, *Government and Politics in Latin America* (1960, 1963).

John P. Harrison

Professor of History, University of Texas. Director, Institute of Latin American Studies. Author of numerous articles in the professional journals.

Albert O. Hirschman

Professor of International Economic Relations, Columbia University. Author, *Journeys Toward Progress: Studies of Economic Policy-making in Latin America* (1963). Editor, *Latin American Issues: Essays and Comments* (1961).

John J. Johnson

Professor of History, Stanford University. Author, *Pioneer Telegraphy in Chile* (1948); *Political Change in Latin America: The Emergence of the Middle Sectors* (1958). Editor, *The Role of the Military in Underdeveloped Countries* (1962).

Kenneth F. Johnson

Assistant Professor of Political Science, Colorado State University. Contributor to the professional journals.

Harry Kantor

Professor of Political Science, University of Florida. Author, *Ideology and Program of the Peruvian Aprista Movement* (1953). Co-author, *América Latina de Hoy* (1960).

John J. Kennedy

Professor of Government, University of Notre Dame. Author, *Catholicism, Nationalism, and Democracy in Argentina* (1958).

Merle Kling

Professor of Political Science, Washington University. Author, *A Mexican Interest Group in Action* (1961).

John D. Martz

Assistant Professor of Political Science, University of North Carolina. Author, *Central America: The Crisis and the Challenge* (1959); *Colombia: A Contemporary Political Study* (1962); *Acción Democrática: The Evolution of a Modern Political Party* (1964).

L. N. McAlister

Professor of History, University of Florida. Director, Center for Latin American Studies. Author of numerous articles in the professional journals.

J. Lloyd Mecham

Professor Emeritus of Government, University of Texas. Author, *Church and State in Latin America* (1934); *The United States and Inter-American Security, 1889–1960* (1961).

Martin Needler

Assistant Professor of Political Science, University of Michigan. Author, *Latin America in Perspective* (1963). Editor, *The Political Systems of Latin America* (1964).

L. Vincent Padgett

Professor of Political Science, San Diego State College.   Author of numerous articles in the professional journals.

Moisés Poblete Troncoso

Consultant, government of Chile, affiliated with National University in Santiago. Author, *Evolución del Derecho Social en América* (1942); *El Movimiento Obrero Latinoamericano* (1946); *El Derecho del Trabajo y la Seguridad Social en Chile* (1949). Co-author, *The Rise of the Latin American Labor Movement* (1960).

Edward W. Scott

Collaborator of Professor Goldrich as a graduate student in political science, Michigan State University.

Kalman H. Silvert

Professor of Government, Dartmouth College. Author, *A Study in Government: Guatemala—Constitutions of State and Nation* (1957); *The Conflict Society: Reaction and Revolution in Latin America* (1961). Editor, *Expectant Peoples: Nationalism and Development* (1963).

William S. Stokes

Professor of Comparative Political Institutions, Claremont Men's College. Author, *Honduras: An Area Study in Government* (1950); *Latin American Politics* (1959).

Frank Tannenbaum

Professor Emeritus of Latin American History, Columbia University. Author, *The Labor Movement* (1921); *Peace by Revolution* (1933); *Whither Latin America?* (1934); *Mexico: The Struggle for Peace and Bread* (1950); *Ten Keys to Latin America* (1963).

Theodore Wyckoff

Lieutenant Colonel, Professor of Military Science, Arizona State University. Author of numerous articles in professional and military journals.

The Dynamics of Change
in Latin American Politics

The State of Research and Study
in Latin American Politics and Government

I

In 1889 Woodrow Wilson wrote that the political institutions of the United States could be understood "only by those who know somewhat familiarly other systems of government and the main facts of general institutional history. . . .Certainly it does not now have to be argued that the only thorough method of study in politics is the comparative and historical." Today more than ever the student of Latin American politics and government is impressed with the value and utility of the comparative approach in an area where the existence of twenty nations prohibits the thorough and detailed knowledge of them by any one individual. Yet a long and slow evolution has been traced over the years of the twentieth century, during which the study of the region has been characterized by gradual shifts in emphasis and in approach.

To arrive at the present state of Latin American political studies in the United States, one of two paths may be followed. The first pursues the establishment of political science as a new and burgeoning discipline, related to yet independent of its parent, history. The second traces the broad course of Latin American studies, without initially discriminating among the several disciplines. For a number of years a history approach dominated, only recently to be challenged by the self-conscious but ambitious field of political science. Whichever path is followed, however, one reaches the present location to find political scientists attempting to analyze problems differently from in the past, employing analytical tools and techniques that are sometimes still being tested elsewhere.

A significant sign of the times, mirroring the long sway held by the historians, is the fact that many of the leading students of recent and contemporary political affairs in the hemisphere are trained historians. Moreover, a number of those now working specifically as political scientists in the universities received their initiation to Latin America as graduate students working under historians. Several of the writings included in this volume, which are regarded as primarily political in concern, were written by men who are active members of history departments.

No one denies that both historians

and political scientists are active in seeking improved knowledge and more acute insight into Latin America generally. What must be remembered here is the fact that there *is* or at least *can be* a definite distinction in procedures, and that today's trained political scientist possesses certain intellectual and analytical procedures that are important in furthering understanding. As political scientists in general have progressed in their reliance upon comparative political studies, so have those concerned with Latin America introduced new and different methods.

Until rather recently, the emphasis in comparative government was almost entirely institutional, even in the largely ignored field of Latin America. Disciplinary dissatisfaction gradually mounted, and a panel of the American Political Science Association in 1944 noted that the narrowness of descriptive analyses of foreign institutions was becoming something of an anachronism. By the 1950's, this feeling was far stronger. A characteristically pointed dissection of the more traditional, legalistically slanted studies was articulated by Roy C. Macridis, who attacked them as parochial, static, and essentially descriptive. Institutional emphases caused a neglect of informal arrangements, thus encouraging insensitivity to nonconstitutional determinants of political behavior.

So it was that, by the decade of the fifties, political scientists in the United States saw as the primary focus of comparative politics a consideration of political dynamics and the process of decision-making. New efforts and a determined grasping for effective tools became widespread, with occasional false starts inevitably encountered in the eager quest for meaningful insights. Gabriel A. Almond, a leading exponent of the movement to modernize comparative political studies, appropriately

pleaded only that "it may be said of new concepts as it was of the salvation of souls... 'there shall be weeping and gnashing of teeth, for many are called but few are chosen.' "

II

Such weeping and gnashing has by no means been absent in the ranks of Latin American political scientists. The rapid increase of popular participation in the Latin American political process has been reflected by the growing importance of informal dynamics, and the problems of comparative analysis gradually forced, first, a shift away from traditional historical studies and, second, a move from institutional analyses to those centering upon dynamic forces. In the first stage, attention turned toward comparative views of the three customary branches of government in each of the republics in question. This was an important step forward, although clearly a preliminary one.

Attention was subsequently given to the examination of such shifting, frequently unstructured elements as political parties, interest groups, labor movements, and student organizations—each of these influential in the shaping of a given polity. Even more lately has come the historico-sociological focus on the area's "middle sectors," with a set of propositions most fully developed by John J. Johnson. By the start of the 1960's, methodological approaches have included the examination of political style, and frequent reference is made to the components of a totality termed the "political culture."

As this is written, students of comparative politics are entering upon a serious exploration of the possibilities of a broad, theoretical framework applicable to all the so-called underdeveloped or developing areas, thus including Latin America. There is a growing awareness that definite distinctions exist between Western and non-Western countries. Yet it appears that no true dichotomy is possible in the case of Latin America, where patterns of social and political institutions and behavior are mixed. Even where such categories as preindustrial and partially westernized are used, Latin America stubbornly refuses to be placed in a convenient pigeonhole.

Given the rapid evolution of research, it is useful to trace its growth by noting a few of the textbooks on the region's politics and government. The first useful such volume was Austin F. MacDonald's *Latin American Politics and Government,* which first appeared in 1949. MacDonald was not unaware of the informal processes of politics, yet his chapters on the individual countries gave but a pale reflection of reality. Each republic was first discussed by sketching the events of recent political history, after which the constitution was studied in its particulars. This volume, a significant work at the time and certainly a useful contribution, nonetheless was soon to be superseded and improved upon. Toward the end of the 1950's, two texts appeared: *Governments of Latin America,* by William Whatley Pierson and Federico G. Gil, and *Government and Politics in Latin America,* edited by Harold E. Davis.

Each was, in its own way, a forward step. The Pierson and Gil volume rejected the country-by-country scheme, with its concomitant problems of duplication and rapid obsolescence. Instead, it dealt with the region's politics by topic, devoting individual chapters to political parties, economy, education, labor, the Church, and so forth. The Davis work, with contributing chapters by eleven scholars, also followed a topical approach while leaning somewhat upon the political actors and the impact of dynamic forces within society.

Two of the newest contributions have different angles of attack. The first is the pioneering work, *The Politics of the Developing Areas,* edited by Gabriel A. Almond and James S. Coleman; the second is *Political Systems of Latin America,* edited by Martin C. Needler. The former is not specifically a Latin American work, but George I. Blanksten provides a brilliant essay of nearly eighty pages in which he discusses Latin America in terms of the editors' proposed framework. The effort is primarily functional, and political operations are discussed in terms of socialization and recruitment, interest articulation, interest aggregation, and political communication.

Critics have charged either that Latin America is not appropriately studied within a scheme applicable as well to Africa and the Middle East, or that the functional approach in general is less than promising. Valid or not, such comments do not alter the intrinsic justification of the effort. The Needler book returns to the country-by-country arrangement and is authored by some dozen experts in their particular countries, with attempted points of comparability expressed through the operative constants of national politics. Thought is given to the dynamic processes and to the general political culture in terms of values, attitudes, and expectations.

The impact of the behavioral sciences upon the broad study of politics has led to bitter controversy among political scientists, and the hint of a similar dispute is arising among Latin Americanists. It is neither appropriate nor necessary to enter into the issue here, but it is relevant to observe that the limits of behavioralism in political science are somewhat less narrow than within the Latin American subfield. The sheer lack of information, of basic data and statistics, provides one inhibiting element, and another comes from the assorted problems of field research.

Two projects in particular give evidence of the first inroads of statistical or behavioral methods in the study of Latin America. One is the continuing research of Russell H. Fitzgibbon, who attempts to measure through statistical indices the degree of political change, the most recent example of which is reproduced in this work. The second project is that of Daniel Goldrich, who in recent years has conducted extensive interviews of Panamanian students in attempting to identify and assess their political awareness and partisan inclinations. A sample of the latter is also reprinted here.

The statistical difficulties encountered through the lack of basic information are large, although there is no reason to regard them as insuperable. At the same time, researchers with field experience can testify to the lack of adequate information, to the erratic responses by interview respondents, and to a general situation that for a serious student is decidedly primitive. The ingenuity of the researchers is pressed into constant use, and the very fact that so much of the field remains virgin terrain is neither cause for hesitation on their parts nor narrowminded glibness on the part of critics.

III

The progressive strides in recent years, then, are leading students of Latin American politics toward new vistas by means of methodological innovations of varying utility. If the results have been uneven in quality, there is little need for apology. The use of political science in the study of the region is young, and the inevitable pitfalls will be bridged with the passage of time. The present frontiers, including as they do the presence of behavior-

alism, of quantification, and the increasingly sophisticated use of statistics, will gradually recede. Research, furthermore, will be conducted increasingly through interviews and surveys of various sorts, while library-bound investigations will become less common, although library research in the sense of background will always be important in its own right.

In the eyes of at least a few political scientists, the dilemma facing students of Latin American politics seems to be the relative disciplinary confusion and the plethora of approaches and techniques. When there is still occasional debate concerning the connotations of the very word "science" in the title political science, it is understandable that the Latin America subfield seems highly unstructured. Proposed directions of investigation in some cases run closely parallel to one another; other times, they spray forth radially from a small core of data and knowledge in seemingly unrelated fashion.

If the choice of directions poses a dilemma, it is no less an opportunity. In reiterating that existing research is in many instances primitive, it should not be forgotten that progress is continuous. Methodological problems cannot be met and grappled with instantaneously. The coordinated use of related but varying disciplines will contribute to a forward surge, and there is as much room for a wide variety of approaches as the mind's breadth can visualize. It can scarcely be overemphasized that tolerance is necessary in the march toward greater knowledge, and there should be neither time nor energy wasted on fanatical controversy over widely differing methods.

Each individual effort has its own *raison d'être,* and the pushing back of frontiers enlarges rather than shrinks the potentialities. Far too many fields demand attention to permit abstruse methodological conflicts or semantic hair-splitting. Students and researchers should be precise, imaginative, and realistically hard-nosed in examining their own work and that of others. These requirements do not open the door for either dogmatism or rancor. Given the present absence of a highly developed, generally accepted conceptual framework, we must seek progress through all feasible paths, remembering that there is no single royal road to insight and to understanding.

A prime example of what is believed to be the apt philosophy was expressed by the French student of political parties, Maurice Duverger. He declared at the outset that he found it impossible to give a valid description of the comparative functioning of parties, yet he saw the need as essential and therefore proceeded with the task. This, it would seem, embodies the necessary *élan* for the students of Latin American politics: a realistic awareness of the formidable obstacles ahead, yet a venturesome willingness to accept the hazards in entering upon virgin territory that one day will be familiar to all.

IV

The preceding commentary is not to suggest that a new methodological scheme is offered in this volume. The very nature of a book of readings makes this patently impossible. At the same time, it is believed that a unifying theme runs through the heart of our best present studies of Latin American politics, and it is relied upon here in the form indicated by the title. Both traditionally oriented studies and examples of the most contemporary research are represented, providing a sampling of the most significant and searching inquiries extant. The broad commitment of the great majority is toward matters of change and reform.

It is perhaps a truism to speak of the mid-twentieth century as a time of revolutionary change, of Revolution with a capital "R." This thematic emphasis is inherent in contemporary Latin America, and is both convenient in organization and conducive to ordered thinking. An examination of the structure as set forth in the table of contents should suggest that change in the present context can be either revolutionary or evolutionary, violent and swift, or pacific and gradual.

Change can be studied, then, in terms of reform, of the remolding and reshaping of institutions and processes rather than the destruction of one set and the substitution of another. Given the social and economic pressures of present-day Latin America, the magnetism of sweeping revolutionary ideals in the minds of the discontented and the ambitious is understandable. This fact should be recognized, however, without accepting the deceptive notion that gradualist reform, building upon existing institutions and customs, cannot provide efficacious and lasting progress.

The theme of change is writ large, and it takes on many guises and forms. Both institutional realities and informal processes play their part, and it behooves the serious student to be aware of both. Certainly the traditions and customs inherited from a rich and turbulent past provide a substantial part of the political milieu within which rapid and meaningful change is being introduced. Thus, the thematic treatment includes the contention that change takes a variety of forms, and that institutions and past practices may be as influential as unstructured dynamic forces. First, the setting, the background for change, is a prerequisite to all further understanding, and necessarily provides the introductory material. Second, the nature of change itself is highly diversified and, as already noted, deserves attention in terms of gradualist reform as well as violent revolution. Beyond this, the growing importance of economic and social development expresses itself, although not in the narrow sense of political science. Third, the agents of change come up for study, revealing certain of the ways in which individual and collective actors both influence and are influenced by the forces of the times.

The relative lack of cohesion and a spirit of dynamism tend to result in greater and sometimes more vigorous action on the part of the associational as contrasted with the institutional groups. This is reflected by the more lengthy examination of the former in the final part of the book. The contribution of external actors is not minimized, although not dealt with here. The length and scope of these readings made it advisable to omit any section dealing with the Cold War in the hemisphere, the *Alianza para el Progreso,* or the complexities of United States-Latin American relations. These matters open up a new set of conditions and circumstances that deserve book-length treatment in their own right. It should also be noted that, given the rapidity of

change characteristic of contemporary Latin America, a number of statements of fact in several selections are no longer true.

One final comment relates to some of the underlying constants that are altered only slowly over a long period of time. Barring the truly total revolution that only rarely occurs, a set of basic essentials will remain valid for some period of time. Trends of thought, political behavior, and institutional regularities are not meaningless. Notwithstanding the vicissitudes of daily politics and the powerful forces of history sweeping the region, the basic elements of political life, both institutional and informal, will remain basic to an understanding of the region. It is with this conviction that the over-all structure as well as the detailed choice and order of selections has been put into practice. There *are* patterns of regularity, of discernible attitudes and outlook, that form the basis upon which both stability and change in Latin America are predicated. It is to these that the following sampling of research and study is directed.

PART ONE

The Setting for Change

Geographic considerations aside, there are a number of features characteristic of the Latin American political milieu, many of which are self-evidently influential in providing a foundation upon which change can be based. A broad picture of the cultural and political environment emerges from the opening pair of essays, to which a current set of observations can be added in Federico G. Gil's "Four Trends in Contemporary Latin American Politics," a paper later appearing in Spanish in the *Journal of Inter-American Studies* I, No. 4 (October 1959), 459–75.

More specifically, institutions frequently contributing to the stability— if not necessarily stagnation—of Latin American politics are the hacienda, the constitution, and the executive in the performance of its duties. While the hacienda has come to represent certain of the more regressive influences in the body politic, the myth and reality of constitutionalism have alternately strengthened and weakened the *status quo*. The extraordinary versatility with which constitutions have been employed requires an understanding of the Hispanic attitudes toward such a document. Closely related is the parallel

contrast of façade and actual content in the national executive, dominating politics in diverse ways while ordinarily remaining within the letter of the constitution. An interesting study of almost diametrically opposed usage of constitutionalism and of executive power is James L. Busey's "Foundations of Political Contrast: Costa Rica and Nicaragua," *Western Political Quarterly* XI, No. 3 (September 1958), 627–59.

The political setting, notwithstanding the rapidity of current political changes, is far from devoid of serious thinking and the study of fundamental problems. There has been no dearth of philosophic inquiry toward basic questions of freedom and order, of liberty and discipline. Furthermore, the twentieth century has seen the impact of foreign ideologies, including those of communism and fascism, while at the same time producing its own indigenous theory. If Peron's *justicialismo* bore similarities to European fascism, the conceptualization of *aprismo* was original.

Useful studies of public liberties and civic duties are found in Fredrick B. Pike, ed., *Freedom and Reform in Latin America* (South Bend, Ind.: University of Notre Dame Press, 1959), as well as Angel del Río, ed., *Responsible Freedom in the Americas* (New York: Doubleday & Company, Inc., 1955). At least two revolutionary movements of some ideological and great pragmatic significance are also worthy of examination and are discussed at length in Robert E. Scott's *Mexican Government in Transition* (Urbana, Ill.: Illinois University Press, 1959), and John D. Martz's *Acción Democrática: Evolution of a Modern Political Party* (1965). The major contribution on *aprismo* by Professor Kantor is his *The Ideology and Program of the Peruvian Aprista Movement* (Berkeley, Calif.: University of California Press, 1953).

1

A Proposed Framework
for Latin American Politics

Kalman H. Silvert

A hobby of Latin Americanists, their hands forced by the variety of their area of study, is to develop typologies within which to squeeze all twenty republics. One of the efficient ways in which to set up a distribution is in accordance with social class, a most obvious feature of Latin societies visible in clothing, speech, occupation, habitation, education, and of course, political power. The allied subjects of social class and social mobility tell us whether a society is open or closed, and thus are essential to predictions concerning stability and the probabilities for democratic processes. Social structural analysis is also indispensable for an understanding of nationalism and potentialities for economic growth.

The simplest societies in Latin America are those ordinarily called semifeudal, ruled by a small elite, the holders of major economic power, recipients of the highest social status and prestige, monopolists of the political organism. Under them can be found

a shriveled administrative and professional group charged with the operation of the cities, the public service, and the discharge of the necessary professional functions, especially law and medicine. At the bottom are the peasants, migratory or tenant farmers, sometimes the owners of their own small plots; and in the cities, those persons necessary to the more menial functions. In some countries the lowest agricultural group is divided ethnically into Indians and other persons considered Europeanized, no matter what their physical race, by virtue of their speaking a European language, their wearing of non-Indian dress, and their feeling of being a part of the national life, even though most tenuously.

Guatemala is an excellent case of a structure only slightly more complicated than that described above. Of a total population of about 3 million, perhaps only 125,000 can be counted as effective actors in the reaching of political decisions at the national level. This figure is reached by subtracting the Indian population, those rural mestizos who are not truly national in their concepts, the illiterates, persons under 18, and a part of the female population.

From Kalman H. Silvert, *The Conflict Society: Reaction and Revolution in Latin America* (New Orleans, La.: The Hauser Press, 1961). Reprinted by permission.

At the other end of the scale is Argentina. Almost a third of the 20 million Argentines live in Greater Buenos Aires, and in the country as a whole, two-thirds live in towns and cities of over 2,000 population. About a third of the Argentines are in the middle and upper occupational levels. Except for scattered and isolated Indian and mixed rural groups, the population is European. Agricultural labor is not rooted to the soil as in Peruvian and Chilean haciendas, for example; farm workers and ranch hands may and in fact do make use of the channels of social mobility, forming one of the most important mass groups supporting ex-dictator Perón and contributing to the huge increase in the city populations of the past 15 years.

Caste-like racial distinctions and a sharp cultural cut between the city and the country make popular sovereignty and the dispersion of political power at best a very limited possibility in such countries as Guatemala. The homogeneity of Argentina speeds communications, distributes aspirational goals almost universally, and promotes mass participation in politics for good or ill.

The velocity of Latin American social change, and it is in some fundamental respects the fastest moving part of the world, can create very complicated class systems. Mexico and Brazil, to take two examples among various, have what may be called double systems. There is an old and a new upper group, the former generally agrarian and clerical in orientation, the latter urban industrial and secularist. The old service middle group coexists with the new white-collar and professional elements, while the industrial blue-collar groups find little in common with depressed agrarian persons. Add the racial complication of the Indian populations of Mexico at the village cultural level, and this somewhat oversimplified picture is complete.

The most important class phenomenon from a political viewpoint is the rapid growth of middle groups. Fomented by the exploding cities, the complex skills demanded by the new industries, the expanding welfare functions of government, and the extension of the professions, the middle sectors are already the decisive voice in at least half of the Latin American countries. Their presence spells the doom of traditional *caudillismo*, but not necessarily the immediate and automatic stability and democracy which popular myth attributes to them.

Nationalism

An ordinary view of nationalism is that it is a negative sentiment, backward-looking, exclusivist, antiforeign, and at times even insane, as in Nazi Germany. A cooler reaction would be to think of nationalism within established political units as a social value elevating loyalty to the state and to the citizenry included therein to a supreme position. In the event of a clash involving, say, religious institutions or even the right of a parent to beat his child, a national society would assume ultimate adherence to the dictates of the state rather than of any intervening, buffer institutions. Some of the usual historical manifestations of nationalism are citizens' armies, such symbols as flags and anthems, a public education system, reverence for the past as well as glorification of the future, and so on. Supernationalism, the product of totalitarian systems, is the extension of this loyalty to make it fit a disintegrating situation; historical nationalism, on the other hand, is an integrative and generalizing mechanism.

The creation of new middle (as well as upper and lower) economic positions, which occurs in developing countries, forces apart the traditional social structure, introducing the middle classes which are such a dynamic part of the new Latin America. These complications are at the same time rationalized by nationalism, a loyalty pattern to cover not only the geographical areas involved, but now also the new identifications across class lines which build consistency and stability into the higher degree of interdependence that industrial urbanism always implies. Where there are middle groups, there is nationalism, the basic political value of westernism.

Despite a lack of hard data, some informed guessing may be done as to the degree to which various Latin American countries have become truly national societies. In point for this subjective evaluation are such criteria as ethnic integration of the population, political history as it may indicate cohesiveness or disorganization, complexity of the city and the occupational range of the economic apparatus, degree of autonomy or dependency of the countryside and the political power of the peasantry, if any, mobility factors, and so on. Closest to nation-state standing in Latin America are Uruguay, Argentina, Costa Rica, and Chile, and perhaps in that descending order, although to be so exact as to give rankings within the categories is to open the door to much wrangling. The next category might well include those countries moving rapidly toward nationhood with a solid social consensus approving the trend. Again in questionable descending order, these countries are Mexico, Brazil, Cuba, Venezuela, and Colombia. The third category includes those in which the upper groups are moving violently toward nationalist aspirations, but with sluggish response in the body social. They are Peru, Bolivia, Guatemala, Ecuador, El Salvador, and Panama, once again in dubious order. And lastly, slow rates of movement, with almost all social sectors stagnant, are to be found in Honduras, Paraguay,

Nicaragua, the Dominican Republic, and Haiti.

Class, Nationalism, and Democracy

The social value of nationalism is a necessary condition for democracy, but not a sufficient one. Without it, the almost universal acceptance of the rules within which democracy works and the necessary belief in the reciprocating continuity of acquiescence and opposition cannot function.

> Democracy presupposes a toughminded and tenacious acceptance of the nation as deserving a continuing loyalty which transcends loyalty to class. Democracy assumes that the proper adjustments and accommodations among classes, probably accompanied by vigorous debate and pulling and hauling, will be made peacefully within the framework provided. If loyalty to a class, whether a proletariat in the professional sense or an elite group, supersedes the common loyalty then democracy suffers accordingly.[1]

National loyalty identifications, however, are not sufficient to guarantee democracy, since the sentiment may also be employed for the implementation of totalitarian, as contrasted with authoritarian rule. Latin American dictatorships, even including the Perón one, so far have been more closely related to the works of a Cromwell or a Frederick the Great than to a Hitler or a Mussolini. Totalitarianisms are so called precisely because they seek to destroy completely the institutional buffers between the individual and the state, to erase all nonstate loyalties, and to void all doctrines propounding governmental

---

1 Russell H. Fitzgibbon, "Pathology of Democracy in Latin America," *American Political Science Review*, XLIV, No. 1 (March 1950), 122. For an excellent discussion of social structure and political change, see John J. Johnson, *Political Change in Latin America: The Emergence of the Middle Sectors* (Stanford, Calif.: Stanford University Press, 1958).

self-restraint. When scientific techniques are not well developed, then the full weight of the dictator can fall directly only on the visible elite; others escape for negative reasons, saved by the sheer impossibility of the police task. With IBM machines, radio patrol cars, and modern propaganda techniques, the state gains the power to "finger" any-one, to minimize if not erase the cush-ioning effects of religious, kin, and class shock absorbers. If nationalism implies economic development and middle classes, then it also implies stronger governments and thus possibilities for sterner autocracies as well as fuller democracies. In short, nationalism is a neutral factor, its color a reflection of other choices.

What we may call "political culture," notions of civic goodness and badness, the attitudes of innovating groups, and the pressures from the international world all contribute to throwing the choice toward more or less freedom. In Latin America, even the harshest dictators customarily attempt to clothe themselves in legal legitimacy and to talk in the name of democracy, tutelary or otherwise. This pose is not mere farce; it conditions future action most importantly.

Latin American constitutions are an excellent case in point of the orienting power of expressed traditional goals. Over 200 constitutions have been adopted in the more or less 150 years during which the Latins have been at work on organic law. Most of the changes have been in the hortatory and the distributing clauses as one or another philosophy or this or that administrative gimmick has been ex-perimented with. But the aspirations outlined in these documents have often served to condition the actions of future governments. As a Latin American jurist has said in commenting on the advanced theories contained in consti-tutional law, "After all, before you embrace a woman, you tell her you love her." Through the schools, law, the writings of impassioned leaders, Latin Americans have been told for almost two centuries that democracy is desirable. The writings of Locke, Ben-tham, and the two Mills, *The Federalist Papers,* the Constitution of the United States, and the Declaration of the Rights of Man, among many other such expressions of man's dignity, have all been imported to help in solidifying this predisposition. While the economic and social conditions in most of Latin America have not been of a type to support full-blown democracies, these political values have constantly served as a prod for the changing of the op-posed root conditions. Small wonder that the twentieth century is so often called The Age of Politics in Latin America.

It is thus no accident that included in the list of those countries which are most nearly nation-states are also to be found those usually considered most democratic. A noted American histori-an, Arthur P. Whitaker, suggests that "the countries which have approxi-mated most closely to the democratic ideal have been—Argentina, Brazil, Chile, Colombia, Costa Rica, and Uruguay." A typology developed by a political sociologist posits only two cate-gories, "Democracies and Unstable Dic-tatorships" and "Stable Dictatorships." He puts in the former Argentina, Brazil, Chile, Colombia, Costa Rica, Mexico, and Uruguay; and in the latter, all the rest of Latin America. While two cate-gories are insufficient to explain all of Latin America, the reappearance of the first seven in high position on all three listings, "The National," "The Democratic," and "Democracies and Unstable Dictatorships," clearly indicates certain factors common to all. Nationalism plus the long belief in the value of democracy may well be in combination as the common denominator.

It should not be expected that such a fundamental change as the flowering of national democracies can occur without great disturbance. . . .

The Role of the Military

The obvious part played by the military in Latin American politics is a normal concomitant of oligarchical governments. Where democracy is impossible, as in the nonnational states, then government is by definition the creature of only a part of the body social. Thus, knowledge of the law, not to speak of respect for it, must be limited and the degree of anticipated obedience to be expected is low. In carrying out its internal, political, policing functions, the military interacts with its peer groups or with those whom it desires to emulate. There is no divorce, then, between the armed forces and the social elements making up the effective political groups in the less developed nations; on the contrary, the identification is all too close.

The patterns of military-civilian relationships change with the nature of the society and the development of the political value system. The simplest relationship is, first, the traditional caudillistic form, in which the leader is almost always an officer in the armed forces and uses this power position to cement himself into office. Second, there is the modern variant of this practice, in which the military rule in trustee fashion, but are dependent upon institutional forms and maintain a degree of impersonalism, so that a *caudillo* does not emerge. The government which succeeded Perón in 1955 was of this type, a tutelary military rule which prepared the way for the holding of elections and the reinstitution of constitutional government. The Venezuelan provisional administration of Admiral Wolfgang Larrazábal, which recently ceded to the legally elected Rómulo Betancourt, also falls into this category.

A third variant is the military acting as the general orienters of policy. The Mexican situation is thus viewed by some specialists; that is, that the military defines the outside limits within which the constituted authorities may work, thus taking into its own hands only the ultimate tutelary role in partial control of the civil functionaries. The Argentine armed forces are certainly playing this role at the moment in limiting the actions of President Arturo Frondizi with respect to the unions, communism, *Peronismo,* and the Church. Closely allied to this category is the fourth variant, the situation in which no government can exist without at least the tacit consent of the military. Peru falls into this classification, as do Brazil and Guatemala, at least for the moment. Any one of these first four situations is unstable, for slipping from one to another relationship is always a possibility unless social inhibitions against military interventionism have grown strong, as in Mexico.

Fifth, we find the military acting as a veto group only insofar as their own interests are concerned, but otherwise quite powerless politically. It may be that Chile fits this classification, or it may even fall into the sixth, in which the armed forces are professional and apolitical. Uruguay is in this last, fortunate position. The final possibility is that the military should be nonexistent. Costa Rica is the lone example, the only country in Latin America which has simply abolished its armed services on the dual grounds that the good citizen himself is enough to defend the country against any neighboring enemies, and that no one is able to defend it against the mighty nuclear weapons of the world powers.

Military intervention in political affairs is a long-standing impediment to the development of responsible government, a constant invitation to the dissatisfied to seek adjudication by bullet. Even though the military, armed with their World War II weapons, have not always been on the side of the devil, by and large they are a hindrance to the development of experience in the peaceful transfer of power. They can be hemmed in effectively only by the development of a complex of parties and pressure groups to orient the collective power of the citizenry. Certainly the growing complication of Latin American governments makes it ever riskier to entrust public administration to untrained and *ad hoc* military governors.

Party Systems

Among other functions, political parties organize the electorate for their periodic interventions in decision-making. They serve to carry ideas back and forth between the government and the populace when campaigns and elections are not in process. That they also act as employment agencies is well known. Not every Latin American group bearing the title *"partido"* is really a political party by these criteria. When what is called a party merely performs policing functions for a dictatorial government and serves as a housekeeping agency for the imposition of views from the top, then we are not dealing with a functional party. Of this one-way control type are the single party "systems" of such a country as the Dominican Republic. The party is so closely identified with the administration that to be of an opposition group is to be sub-

versive or even treasonous. Venezuela has also operated so in the recent past, as have other Latin countries in their periods of harsher, caudillistic authoritarianism.

Mexico, however, offers the case of a single dominant party playing out its role without crudely repressive practices. There are opposition parties, the most important of which are the clerical PAN (National Action party) on the right, and the Communist party on the left. Membership in these opposition groups is no crime, and they legitimately serve to organize dissident opinions. But they have no ability to win an election, even though they may campaign, publish, meet, and speak without interference. The PRI (Institutional Revolutionary party), the official entity, embraces everyone from the industrialist to the government employee to the trade unionist. Sometimes it is argued that the PRI is analogous to the Democratic party of the American South, in truth representative of many factions, with the real decisions among opposing views made in the primary elections. In Mexico, the arguments take place among the leaders representing their rank-and-file supporters, and then the party makes known its official position. PRI is not monolithic; it is part of the trust arrangement in which Mexico's development is held by the military, the intellectuals, the new economic elites, the trade unions, and the middle class groups. Labor difficulties offer some hint that the PRI may eventually break into its component interest parts, but it would be a rash man indeed who would presume to predict when this split will occur.

Aside from the false and the real one-party systems named above, there are also a few two-party structures to be counted. Traditionally political development, as has been said, revolved about Conservatives and Liberals. In

Colombia, where this division still exists, we have the most consistent case of biparty politics. Uruguay, with its *Colorados* and *Blancos* ("Reds" and "Whites") has been considered by many political scientists as not a true example of a two-party structure, for the *Colorados* had won office uninterruptedly for almost a century. But in 1958 the Whites finally won a national election, and so we may presume Uruguay to be in the two-party class.

There are also mixed cases, in which two major parties contend at the national level, but a multiplicity argue over the municipal and provincial posts. Argentina is the most complicated case of this kind, for since 1945 only two major parties have presented themselves for the presidential elections; unhappily for simplicity, they have not always been the same two parties. In 1946, there was the *Peronista* party, with virtually all the opposition in a coalition opposed to him. The traditional Radical party led the opposition in the hopeless elections of 1951, but later, in 1958, the Radicals split into their two historic blocs, the Intransigent Radicals and the Radicals of the People, they being the only two serious contenders. The Conservatives, Socialists, Christian Democrats, Peronists, and Communists continue to be forces of some consequence, however, so that Argentina is on the borderline between a two-party and a multiparty system.

The electoral laws of Argentina, modeled as they are after those of the United States, including an electoral college, favor a two-party system even though social practice and the diversity of new interest groups favor a multiparty structure. Chile's laws, to take an opposite example, had until 1959 provided for an extreme form of proportional representation within the neo-parliamentary governmental organization established in the constitution of 1925. The result has been one of the most stable multiparty systems in Latin America running, from right to left, from Conservatives through Liberals to Radicals in the center, and on left to Christian Democrats, various branches of the Socialists, and the Communists. The close similarity both in Chile and Argentina to the political party spread of France and Italy is clear, and is no accident, for both countries are deeply influenced by those two European idea sources.

The multiparty system of Brazil, however, is more indigenous in origin and orientation, and also includes phenomena peculiar to the size and population of that huge country. The ideological distribution is strongly influenced by entirely internal considerations and is only peripherally liable to influence from abroad, while the extent and diversity of the country has been propitious for the development of sectional parties. Although these regional groups, or what are sometimes called "particularistic" parties, have died out almost everywhere in Latin America, including Brazil, the regional origins of a political party may have much to do with setting present-day attitudes. The province of São Paulo has been particularly noteworthy in its influence on national politics through party mechanisms.

What the parties carry along in terms of substantive programs is also considerably varied. There are the well-known "somebodyisms," the personalistic parties which identify with a charismatic individual. Thus arise the labels, *Peronismo, Batllismo, Porfirismo,* and so on, referring to the conglomeration of attitudes, ideas, and loyalties surrounding Perón in Argentina, Batlle in Uruguay, and Porfirio Díaz in Mexico, to take only three of numerous examples. An ideational tone accompanies these personalistic designations: a kind of Black Populism in the case of Perón;

secularist, middle class reform politics identified with Batlle; and the classical marriage of liberal positivism and *caudillismo* associated with Díaz. When the party is totally personalistic, a condition almost invariably associated with the fraudulent one-party systems, then the suffix *"ismo"* is not used, and only *"ista"* is employed. It would sound foolish to say *Trujillismo or Perezjimenismo* to denote the "philosophies" of Trujillo of the Dominican Republic and of ex-President Pérez Jiménez of Venezuela. For them, only *Trujillista* or *Perezjimenista* makes sense. Only the more ideological leaders can have their names enlarged with either suffix.

There is little meaningful relationship between party system and the social order, except in the most backward authoritarianisms. In those cases, it is only by classificatory generosity that one can speak of parties at all. A better clue to political development is derived from party programs and approaches, rather than from counting the number of parties and relating them systematically. A reasonable hypothesis is that the more national a country, the less personalistic will be the parties, the more they will adjust conflicting interests within their own mechanisms, the greater will be their concern with institutional self-preservation and the winning of elections as a good in itself. As is to be expected then, Argentina, Chile, Uruguay, and Costa Rica all have long histories of impersonal party politics.

Professional parties coexisting with single-interest and personalistic parties are readily observable in Brazil, Venezuela, and Cuba; these nations are among those in the second level of adjustment to nation-state status. Mexico and Colombia, bracketing the list of countries in this second level, have unique structures for Latin America, but their parties may with confidence be called impersonal and broadly based

in the interests they represent, regardless of their ideologies. In Peru, Bolivia. Guatemala, Ecuador, El Salvador, and Panama, the parties tend to be narrowly based, many are short-lived, and in numerous cases little difference can be observed between a party and the single interest it represents.

A preliminary nonpublic mediation of interest disputes is necessary so that the electorate may choose among alternatives, not at the level of detail, but of policy. Without an impersonal, political party structure aiding in the day-to-day mediation of disagreement, substantively good voting is difficult if not impossible in anything more than a town situation. The weeding out of issues to simplify national politics is a major party function, and one which has international effects. The introduction of this level of debate may slow down process of diplomatic negotiation but is necessary when a national consensus, rather than a mere executive opinion, is required for lasting agreement on substantive issues. In brief, it is intrinsically more difficult to negotiate truly important matters with democratic nation-states than with dictatorships. It is only good sense to make the effort, however, especially when we recognize that the age of *caudillos* is drawing to a troubled close, as surely it is in Latin America.

Marxism and Communism as Special Cases

Marxist thought and Communist ideology, as Western phenomena, have no market in nonnational cultures. Naturally, then, the general social and economic development of Latin America opens up possibilities for the growth of communism as it does for the evolution of middle classes. Communist parties seem especially important in situations either of rapidly developing nationalism, or in cases in which normal processes are being bottled up by intransigent opposition. Robert S. Alexander, in his *Communism in Latin America,* argues that wherever a democratic trade-union movement is allowed to flourish, the Communists lose their major source of mass support and become ineffectual. He cites Mexico as the most pertinent example, adding that in a period of national construction Communists may play a very important role, but thereafter they can be "withered away," to turn their phrase against them, by the open play of normal democratic politics.

A senate investigating subcommittee released the following figures on Communist party membership in the various Latin American countries during 1958:

Argentina	70,000 to 80,000
Bolivia	4,000
Brazil	50,000
Chile	20,000 to 25,000
Colombia	5,000
Costa Rica	300
Cuba	12,000
Dominican Republic	Negligible
Ecuador	1,000
El Salvador	500
Guatemala	1,000
Haiti	Negligible
Honduras	500
Mexico	5,000
Nicaragua	200
Panama	500
Paraguay	500
Peru	6,000
Uruguay	3,000
Venezuela	30,000 to 35,000

There might be some disagreement as to the numbers given, but nowhere do Communists comprise a truly mass party, one which could conceivably win at the polls. The confusion arises when parties of the center and the democratic left combine with Communists, either officially or informally, to attain given national objectives. This kind of alliance takes place either in times of such acute political crisis that polarization is an obvious necessity, as is the present situation in Chile; or else it occurs when the objectives are massive and all-embracing, such as the secularization and nationalization of politics, as in Guatemala during the ten-year period of Juan José Arévalo and Jacobo Arbenz from 1944 to 1954. A similar coalition occurred in Mexico during the decade of the thirties, but the period of subsequent consolidation drastically reduced the advantage of alliance with the far left, and the center-left and center have now succeeded in weaning away from the Communists much of their popular and emotional support.

There is almost no chance that Communists by themselves can win directly anywhere in Latin America. In combination with other parties lies their only chance of formal penetration into affairs of state. During the post-World War II East-West honeymoon, Communists held many and important offices in several countries, including Brazil and Chile. But in those two republics, as well as many others, the outbreak of the Cold War saw the parties outlawed and diplomatic relations broken with the Soviet Union. There has been a gradual relaxation of these legal restrictions, but communism has not regained the status it had a decade ago, The Cuban case, however, is contributing to a resurgence of "Popular Frontism" which may usher in a massive increase in real, manipulative Communist power. This danger is intense and is growing rapidly.

Outside the realm of party politics, an unsophisticated blend of economic determinism is a common way of thought among educated Latin Americans. In areas where economic necessities loom large, where the example of the external world continuously pushes toward expanded consumption, to put primary attention on economic factors as the key to social change is natural. The United States has also contributed to this kind of easy analysis by an accent on economic development and the igenuous insistence that people with full bellies don't become Communists. It is not only Communists, Trotskyists, and left Socialists who have Marxist ideas; in an amorphous way, anyone who subscribes to the absolute premise that "Money Talks" contributes to a dime-store variety of economic determinism.

Pressure Groups

Interest or pressure groups are few in Latin America. Where caudillistic one-party rule holds sway, there is insufficient complication to give much room to variegated pressure groups. And where multiparty systems operate, except in the most developed countries, the parties represent small middle and upper groups and speak in the name of the economic interests themselves.

But still, there remain some extremely important associations which can be called pressure groups. Foremost in rank is the Church, although some analysts go so far as to presume the religious institution almost an integral part of government. The intellectual ground here is very treacherous. Probably nowhere is the Church less than a veto group; that is, it may not be able to innovate policy, but it can make action against it very costly if not impossible. In Ecuador, where the Church is at its strongest, it probably transcends veto status and can institute action, as it probably also can in Colombia. In other lands where the Church has great strength, such as El Salvador and Peru, it probably cannot act in the nature of a party as it does in Ecuador and Colombia.

Legal separation of Church and state exists in Brazil, Chile, Cuba, Ecuador, El Salvador, Guatemala, Honduras, Mexico, Nicaragua, Panama, and Uruguay. The Church is established in Argentina, Bolivia, Colombia, Costa Rica, the Dominican Republic, Haiti, Paraguay, Peru, and Venezuela. But this legal categorization tells us little, for while almost all the established churches have this legal status as a holdover from the rights of the Spanish monarchy and while the purpose of establishment is to make the religious institution subservient to the state, the degree of control varies widely. There has, for instance, been active persecution of the Church in Venezuela, in contrast to an impressively strong Church in Colombia. And where legal separation exists, the same range of attitude is also to be found, from the past bitter attacks on the Church in Mexico, to the comfortable adjustment in Chile, to Church ascendency in Ecuador.

Another variable is the Church itself, which is by no means the same in its politics everywhere. The Gallican-influenced Churches of Brazil and Chile have very different political traits from the Spanish and Italian Church of Argentina. Most of the Chilean clergy now favor Christian Democracy; in the main, the Argentine clergy backed Perón for all but the last years of his regime, and still support many of the ideas of *justicialismo*. The long-range trend everywhere is for the Church to throw in with the rising middle groups, to oppose *caudillismos*, gently to support labor, and to drift slowly toward the official support of Christian Democratic parties. There is much opposition within the Church itself to certain of these temporal decisions, of course, and it would be highly incorrect to indicate that there is a general Latin political consensus in the Church.

The students, notorious political

actors that they are, also constitute a pressure group. Latin American universities, organized on the Bologna system, introduce their students immediately to subprofessional life; the social class gulf between student and professor is almost minimal, for almost all students in Latin American universities are of middle- and upper-occupational group parents; their chances to participate at reasonably elevated levels in the national life after graduation are thus high to begin with. University elections are often good indicators of public elections, a kind of academic Maine and Vermont. Political divisions among the students parallel those of the major political parties, and student political activities train youngsters for active life outside. There are few church universities of high prestige in those Latin American countries where they are allowed to exist. Although students in religious universities are also political activists, the incidents about which one reads in the newspapers almost invariably are initiated in the national universities, citadels of the new, rising, nationalistic middle youth.

Other pressure groups are what one might expect: associations of landowners, mine operators, industrialists, chambers of commerce, and prestige social clubs nudging into the political sphere. Then there are union groups, invariably politically militant if they are not subservient arms of the state. At times, they are both. Where labor is fairly free of governmental supervision, it tends to group in Socialist, Communist, and Radical camps; and in three countries—Argentina, Chile, and Uruguay—unionism also accepts anarchists. The union movement of Mexico has been closely allied to the growth of the single party, whatever its name may have been at any particular period. In the most retarded countries, unions are either *de facto* or even sometimes *de jure* illegal. Hon-

duras, for example, legalized labor organization only as recently as 1954.

Another kind of occupational pressure group is the professional association, often intimately tied in with the universities from which they depend in many countries.

Groups-in-interest are another crucial index of impersonalism and maturity in the political process. To the extent to which they exist, a policy of countervailing powers becomes a possibility, assuring the operation of lateral controls in the political system and making possible government by decisions as the result of compromise through bargaining instead of by fiat through uncontrolled self-interest.

Implications Toward the Understanding of Latin America

This hurried building of typologies is not intended to describe Latin American politics with any richness of detail, of course. But this kind of overview may suffice at least for indicating the range of difference which may be expected, as well as—more importantly—the intrinsically revolutionary nature of change occurring to one or another degree everywhere. Those countries which have had their national revolutions are still in the act of consolidating them; those countries which have not entered the stage of the national revolution are growing restive. And those caught in the midst of the process are tortured not only with the inherent pain of the change itself, but also by persistent misunderstandings at home as well as abroad. The numerous expressions of Latin resentment against the United States are but one indication, not only of mutual misunderstanding, but also of mutual frustration.

The United States is commonly accused of generally impeding social change in Latin America, of standing for "stability" instead of for social progress. This charge is by and large true, despite a few exceptions and despite the American ability to accommodate to newly national regimes once installed and shaken down. In these times it is commonplace to remark on the rolling back of colonialism and on the tide of nationalism sweeping the so-called underdeveloped world. It is equally trite to state that there is little use attempting to arrest this trend unless one is willing to apply brute force in manners which contemporary civilization finds it difficult to accept.

This survey has attempted to build various typologies demonstrating where the several Latin American republics are to be found along the path to national integration. But the metaphor is incorrect—the twenty republics are not following a single path, but rather a series of paths which appear to lead to the same functional destination, although characterized by growingly diverse national characteristics and styles. If the United States cannot anticipate the course of events and help to mold them, then for the sake of good hemispheric relations it must at least prevent itself from being cast in the role of bottleneck.

2

Putting Latin American Politics
in Perspective

Martin Needler

How does one go about *explaining* why Latin American politics takes the forms it does? There are no problems in *describing* the major features of politics in the area: the central role of the military, the prevalence of violence, the ascendancy of dominant personalities rather than the sway of impersonally functioning institutions, the widespread graft and nepotism—these are the commonplaces of commentary. There are commonplaces of interpretation, too, but their power of explanation no longer compels, if it ever did. Latin American authors themselves have traditionally been free with "racial" explanations which cite alleged deficiencies in the Indian races, or in peoples of mixed blood; these are largely out of fashion now, even in Latin America. Economic and cultural explanations, on the other hand, are still popular: the gulf separating social classes—poverty and illiteracy—lead to a politics of desperation and violence, one reads; alternatively, the colonial past, or the heritage of the Iberian

peninsula itself, can be shown to have set the patterns of violence, authoritarian rule, and revolt, which persist today.

Explanations along these lines, however, while plausible enough so long as one considers only the American republics themselves, lose their force when one tries to apply them on a wider scale. Poverty and illiteracy have all been the rule in human societies, in the stable and orderly ones, too; while on the other hand a politics of violence, a "Latin American" type of politics, is becoming visible in countries which have never known Spanish or Portuguese rule. Consider for a moment recent events in the former Belgian Congo: independence from the colonial power is followed by a struggle between federalists and unitarists; a charismatic *caudillo*, Patrice Lumumba, is captured by his rivals and predictably, the *ley fuga* is applied—he is shot "while trying to escape."

The present article will attempt an explanation of the major features of Latin American political dynamics from a rather different perspective, one which places at the forefront of the enquiry the fact that the stability of

From Martin Needler, "Putting Latin-American Politics in Perspective," *Inter-American Economic Affairs,* Vol. XVI, No. 2 (Autumn 1962). Reprinted by permission.

a system of political institutions rests on an acceptance of those institutions as legitimate.

I

In a stable polity, the maintenance of order does not rest routinely on the application of force. Force is kept in reserve, of course, to put down the occasional violations of the peace; but normally political life moves in well-marked channels, in accordance with preadjusted patterns of behavior. This is true by definition, since this is the kind of thing we have in mind in speaking of a stable political system. Now in the short run, in an immediate sense, observance of the rules of the game, willingness to stay within the marked channels, is a matter of habit. One does what is customary; one follows precedent. In the long run, however, when out-of-the-ordinary circumstances arise, when methods of handling new situations must be devised—that is, when new institutional patterns of behavior are to be created—then existent patterns are reproduced, or new patterns are created, because they conform to accepted ideas of legitimacy. These ideas will be peculiar to the time, and perhaps to the place; nevertheless, they will be accepted as natural and right. For example: a group of North Americans organized in a club or society is faced with the necessity of making some collective decision. They take a vote, and the majority preference becomes the group decision. Perfectly natural to us; yet strange and repugnant to Samoans, who allot decision-making power only to heads of extended families; or to traditionalist Indonesians, who prefer to talk things out until a consensus is reached; or even to our own ancestors of four centuries ago.

To carry the reasoning a step further: one obeys a person in authority because he has come by his office in the proper manner; in a manner which is established by precedent, of course, but which also is "right" in being based on accepted principles of legitimacy. (Whether one obeys or not will probably also depend on whether the injunction is a lawful one, that is, on whether the official is acting in the way he is supposed, on whether he is staying within the bounds of our expectations as to his behavior. For present purposes, however, I wish to stress the idea of legitimacy, especially as it applies to the right to hold an office, rather than to the behavior imputed to the office.) The present essay, then, will urge the view that the features of political life traditionally characteristic of Latin America derive from the existence of what might be called a "legitimacy vacuum"; that the Latin American states are passing through a period of transition between one set of principles of legitimacy and another; that during the period of transition some features have survived from the old way, some have developed as precursors of the new, but for the most part legitimacy does not attach to existent institutions; that in the absence of stable patterns of legitimate political behavior, no alternatives exist to the dominance of personality, the absence of public spirit, and the rule of force.

II

The central feature of the colonial legitimacy system in Latin America was that political power, like social status, depended on the acknowledgment of the rights of birth. This was clearly true at the very top rank of the political order: the monarch came into his title by inheritance. The legitimacy of the tenure of office of inferior authorities, in turn, rested on royal appointment, and so the whole structure of authority derived legitimacy from this inherited title. But social status conferred by birth constituted the normal prerequisite for the holding of high office in any case; moreover, the leading offices in the Spanish colonies were reserved for Spaniards born in the peninsula itself, rather than in the New World, throughout virtually the whole of the colonial period. The scope of one's political functions, then, was defined by the rank into which one was born.

The nature of the role ascribed to the holder of public office reflected this situation. The duties of upper officials were unspecialized and did not require tedious training or the acquisition of skills unbecoming to a gentleman. At the top of the local colonial hierarchy, administrative roles were actually not even differentiated into separate political, military, and religious categories, the colonial governor being responsible for saving souls and leading military campaigns, as much as for collecting taxes and keeping the roads in repair. The minimal technical skills that were necessary were regularly provided by the clergy, who formed an integral part of the governing system.

Authority in this system, then, came from the top down, deriving from the rights of birth, and ultimately from God's grace. To be sure, there were occasional ambiguities over the details of the rules governing the precedence of different degrees of relationship in inheriting a throne, and there were accordingly succession crises. Nevertheless, normally the inheritability of the position of supreme authority, like the criterion of status based on birth which applied to eligibility for lesser positions, made possible stability and continuity in the political order.

III

No one is "born to rule" today anywhere touched by the modern spirit. In modern political systems, supreme authority can be derived legitimately only from popular choice. Legitimacy comes now not from "above" but from "below."

A whole series of lesser principles flows from this revolution in basic political values. Popular sovereignty presupposes and reinforces juridical equality and equality at least of social opportunity. Given equality of opportunity, the criterion of public personnel policy becomes merit, not social status; while in a public service based on merit, technical specialization becomes possible (as it cannot be in a service based on class), high standards of technical proficiency can be expected, and government can take on increasingly complex functions.

If popular sovereignty thus makes the welfare state possible, it also makes it probable—following the ancient Aristotelian maxim, rediscovered by Harrington and again by Hamilton, that the distribution of property tends to follow the distribution of power. That is, a democracy is likely to redistribute property in the direction of equality (through a system of progressive taxation which supports social services benefiting especially the poorer citizens, and so on).

One is thus likely to find the institutions of the modern polity accepted as legitimate, not only because of the habitual acceptance commanded by any stably operating political order, but also because governments functioning within it—for electoral purposes, if for no other—clearly attempt to govern in the interest of as wide a segment of the population as possible; because of the general conformity of official administrative actions to rational technical criteria; and because the popular will is obviously the highest authority in the state.

IV

With the fairly clear exception of Uruguay, none of the Latin American republics has emerged altogether into the modern period in its political and social institutions. Some occupy a position not far from the pole of the colonial polity; others are clearly in steady progress towards the modern pole; all combine some features of old and new, together with key characteristics of the process of transition itself.

What has happened, in effect, is that the wars of independence succeeded in sweeping away the colonial system, in eliminating any possibility of relying on the idea that legitimate authority comes from above, from the royal succession sanctioned by the grace of God, without replacing it by the belief that legitimate authority comes from below, from the popular will. Contrast the American and French Revolutions, which had ended royal authority to replace it with new conceptions of political right, conceptions which would impel a reordering of social institutions on a basis of the principle of equality. After abortive (except, for a time, in Brazil) attempts at establishing indigenous dynasties, the newly independent republics became, regardless of what their constitutions said, turbulent oligarchies, in which the possession of power lacked that overwhelming legitimation that comes from its being derived from a great principle of right. The locus of power at a given moment was, accordingly, arbitrary and could be contested by whoever was able.

Yet often the constitution itself was nominally based upon the notion of popular sovereignty and embellished with mottoes taken from the French and American Revolutions. But the social reality, and operative social beliefs, were so strongly at variance with the doctrines expressed in the constitution, that the document necessarily failed to provide an actual working guide for the political system. To this day, of course—to the surprise of North Americans—the Latin American constitution is generally regarded as a statement of ideals, a set of aspirations, rather than a sober directive to which political reality must conform.

Politics existed, then, and, for the most part, exist today in a "legitimacy vacuum." In the absence of any compelling legitimation of the right to hold office of the present incumbents, their term lasts as long as they can maintain themselves by force of arms. In the absence of a set of operative ideals which inform the behavior patterns of everyday political life, cynicism predominates, public office is used to promote private advantage, nepotism and theft become the cardinal principles of public administration. If the chief criterion of public personnel selection under the Crown was birth, and in the democracy is merit, then in a legitimacy vacuum it is—personal loyalty. Because one's hold on power is so insecure, to remain in power becomes the all-important objective. One dare not take chances, in such a situation, by relying on strangers; positions of trust must necessarily be given to fellow partisans and, where possible, to relatives.

Where institutions carry no conviction and where the bonds of party are too often only those of self-interest, the single available alternative focus of loyalty and faith is the individual leader: and personalism is of one piece with the lack of public spirit and the absence of a doctrine of legitimacy. Militarism, too, is an unavoidable concomitant. Where authority is not respected, force must be resorted to.

Where force is used, the army necessarily has the last word. In this type of situation, the army is in politics whether it wants to be or not. Put in a different way, the army is crucial because it alone operates on a principle of authority, made necessary by the nature of its mission, which commands acquiescence.

Looked at in this light, those distinctive features of Latin American politics which have been explained racially or culturally or economically can be seen rather to be attributes of a certain stage of political evolution, a time of transition, the period of a legitimacy vacuum. Accordingly, they can be found elsewhere, where polities must pass from a set of institutions based on one principle to another set resting on a different premise. One can find a "Latin American politics" in Europe in the age of the transition from the hierarchy of reciprocal obligation of the late Middle Ages to the monarchical sovereignty of the modern period; or in Rome during the transition from republic to empire.

It has been pointed out that the violent changes of political control, which occur so frequently in the region and generally pass for revolutions, can hardly be called "revolutions" in the strict sense of an overturn of society and polity, since the changes that occur have often consisted of no more than the substitution of one group of individuals for another without far-reaching consequences for the society. To earn the title of "revolution," a shift in the locus of power should be more than a palace revolt within the ruling circle, or a *cuartelazo*. It is often said that the revolution proper involves a restructuring of society and politics, a reshuffling of the class system. This is of course true, and in this sense there can be "peaceful revolutions," just as much as there can be violent shifts of power which are not revolutions. In fact, the genuine revolutionary process,

the remaking of society, is likely to extend over a considerable period of time. In official parlance in Mexico, the Mexican Revolution which began in 1910 is regarded as still continuing.

But the changes which collectively constitute the revolutionary process do not occur at random; they aim at fulfilling the goals of the revolution, at giving its ideals concrete embodiment in new institutions and patterns of behavior. If this is so, then the distinctive feature of a revolution is that it establishes new goals for the society; it reorganizes society, but it must first reorganize the values which that society accepts; a successful revolution means the acceptance as "good" of things which were not regarded as good before, the rejection as "bad" of things previously acceptable or commendable.

This transformation of the accepted value system can clearly be seen if one looks again at the example just cited above, the Mexican Revolution of 1910, one of the few genuine revolutions-by-violence in Latin America. Prior to the revolution, the Indian was semiofficially regarded as an inferior being, to be kept out of sight as much as possible, being prohibited by Porfirio Díaz's police from entering the Alameda, the public park in the center of Mexico City, for example. After the revolution, Mexico's Indian heritage became a matter of national pride, to be stressed in her art and her history, to be studied at length in her universities, and the Indian himself became a subject of special government attention and expenditure. Prior to the revolution, foreign investment was to be favored, nurtured, and protected, as one of the cardinal principles of national policy. After the revolution, the presumption was to be against foreign investment, at least on the level of official declarations, its role in the economy to be limited progressively to a demonstrably necessary minimum.

If the revolutionary process consists

of the progressive implementation in practice of the new ideals posited by the revolution, then it is quite possible that not all the changes which occur will have been envisaged specifically by the original leadership. It is even true, moreover, that the ideals which the revolution comes to have will not be limited to those espoused by the original leaders of the revolution. In the revolutionary process, ideas which were "in the air," which were ripe for official acceptance, which embody genuine popular aspirations, will attach themselves to the ideology of the revolution, which in retrospect will have become something more than, although not opposed to, what the original leaders of the revolution contemplated.

The initiator of the Mexican Revolution, Francisco I. Madero, for example, limited his demands to political reform —"Effective Suffrage; No Re-election" is the motto which remains the official slogan of the revolution to this day— while in retrospect the major achievements of the revolution include, as well as the political reform, the reform of the landholding system, the establishment of unions, the incorporation of the Indian into national life, and the initiation of industrialization.

A clearer case, from our own day, of the autonomy of the revolutionary process, once started in motion, is that of the Bolivian Revolution of 1952. Neither of the two major structural changes wrought by the revolution to date, the land reform and the nationalization of the tin mines, was deliberately undertaken by the leadership of the National Revolutionary Movement which the revolution brought to power. The peasants seized the land, and the tin workers seized the mines; the government was left to establish a basis of legality for the *faits accomplis*.

One would probably be justified, ac-cordingly, in concluding that the authentic revolutions which occur in Latin America in the present era, though they may take place under a variety of auspices and exhibit national peculiarities, if they are to succeed and establish themselves permanently, will embody the political values generally accepted today as legitimate: the legal equality of persons, the universal right to participate through representatives in political decision-making, the individual's claim on his government for social justice.

V

If the above thesis has a meaning for the present time, it is this: that Latin American politics cannot, in the present era, become stable and peaceful, unless it is restructured on the basis of the only contemporarily available conception of legitimacy. This is, today even more than a century and a half ago, popular sovereignty and juridical and social equality. When this is accepted as the basis of institutions and policy, a breakthrough into a new world of legitimacy is achieved. This was, at bottom, the nature of the change wrought by Batlle in Uruguay and begun by Carranza and Obregón in Mexico.

Often, in superficial analyses, the requirements of stability and those of democracy and social equality are opposed to each other. But, today, the stability achieved at the expense of democratic ideals can only be an optical illusion; it lives by force and will die by force. The basis for a stability which abides can today only be a foundation of democratic legitimacy, achieved by the institution of a regime which, in the process of policy-making and in the substance of policy itself, is responsive to the popular will.

3

The Hacienda

Frank Tannenbaum

The Structure of the Hacienda

The Hacienda played a special role in Latin America. It would be no exaggeration to say that the hacienda—or the *fazenda,* as it is known in Brazil—set the tone and determined the quality of Latin American culture during the nineteenth century and until the First World War. In some instances—in Ecuador, Chile, Peru, in Argentina, and other areas as well—its influence has continued up to the present. This is not an argument for unitary causation. Other factors, such as the Spanish tradition, the presence of the Indian and the Negro, the broad influence of the Church, and the impact of the larger world, deserve consideration. But here we are dealing with those areas where over one-half of the population is rural and where the typical agricultural holding is large. The United Nations estimated in 1951 that plots of over 15,000 acres, though comprising only

From Frank Tannenbaum, "Toward an Appreciation of Latin America," *The United States and Latin America,* ed. Herbert L. Matthews for the American Assembly (2nd ed.; Englewood Cliffs, N.J.: Prentice-Hall, Inc., 1963). Reprinted by permission.

1½ per cent of all private holdings, accounted for half of all the land in agriculture in Latin America. Some of these holdings are very extensive indeed. There once were plantations in Mexico of 1,000,000 acres, and similar units still exist in Brazil and in other countries.

A few examples will make this clear. In Mexico as late as 1923, 114 owners held 25 per cent of the land. In 1958 in Argentina, 283 families owned 17 per cent of the province of Buenos Aires. In Uruguay, 787 proprietors controlled 30 per cent of the land in use. In Colombia, less than 1 per cent of the owners held 42.2 per cent of all land in use, while in Cuba in 1955, 1.5 per cent had title to 46 per cent of the acreage under cultivation.

Before entering into a discussion of the hacienda as such, it is useful to note that at least in the Andean countries, Central America, and Mexico there were two distinctive agricultural systems—the hacienda and the village community. In Guatemala, for instance, the hacienda occupied the valley, the slopes, and the rolling hills—the best agricultural lands. The Indian villages, on the other hand, were limited to the steep mountains, the inaccessible areas, and the poor soil. This was also true in Mexico and Bolivia; it is true today in Ecuador and Peru. The hacienda has the best agricultural lands, and the Indian or mestizo villages the poorest. The village may be communal, following an older Indian tradition, or it may have adopted every possible variation that lies between collective and individual ownership.

But the village is a community with its own local traditional government where the entire male population participates in the governmental process. It looks after its own public works, its policing, and its roads; it builds a common school if there is to be one and cares for the church. Each individual as he grows up takes his turn in carrying out the various tasks that the community requires. In the case of Amatanango in Chiapas in Mexico, for example, each boy begins as a messenger for the town government, in time he becomes one of the village policemen, and after satisfying all of the required offices in the civil government and in the Church, ends up as an *anciano,* one of the elders on the council governing the community. Each Indian or mestizo village has its own collective personality. Each member has a recognized place of his own and a defined relationship to all the others. He is a participant in government and Church because he has regular functions to perform in both.

This village may be next to a hacienda—and there are cases where a village has somehow survived, although surrounded by a hacienda—but generally speaking, the rural world divides sharply between the hacienda in the valley and the village on the steep mountainsides. Between these two agricultural organizations there has always been friction, the hacienda encroaching upon the village, absorbing its woods, pastures, and water supply, and the village every now and then rising in rebellion, protesting, or going to court. The story is an old one and goes back to the early days after the conquest when the Indians crowded the offices of the Spanish officials, asking for protection against the *hacendado* who was encroaching upon their lands.

After independence, the Indians were less able to find support against the neighboring hacienda. The history of rural land holdings after independence is one in which—in the name of liberalism, equality, and individual rights—the Indian was increasingly dispossessed of his lands in favor of the hacienda. Property taken from the Church by the new national governments tended to swell the size of the haciendas and the power and prestige of the *hacendados.* The little villages during the same period decreased in number, size, and significance. The relatively few and isolated areas where they increased in number, as in southern Chile, southern Brazil, and some places in Argentina, had little bearing on the general trend. The private hacienda carried everything before it.

The hacienda is not just an agricultural property owned by an individual. The hacienda is a society, under private auspices. It is an entire social system and governs the life of those attached to it from the cradle to the grave. It encompasses economics, politics, education, social activities, and industrial development. A curious phenomenon in Latin American intellectual life is that the hacienda, which is so all-embracing in its influence is, except in an occasional novel, never written about or seriously studied. It is, or was, so much part of the environment that the intellectuals, who were mostly children of the hacienda, were no more conscious of its existence than we are of the air we breathe. When the Latin American sociologist looked for something to write about, he worried about the unemployed in London, or about the new sugar and banana plantations in foreign lands. But the hacienda, which had a determining effect on the country's culture, was something he was hardly aware of.

The hacienda as a society may be described by saying that it was—and is—an economic and social system that seeks to achieve self-sufficiency and autarchy on a local scale. It seeks this not as a matter of malice, but as a matter of logic. Each unit expands until it has within its own borders all that it needs—salt from the sea, *panela* (black, unrefined sugar) from its own cane fields, corn, barley, wheat, coconuts, bananas, apples, and pears. All of this depends upon where the hacienda is located. If it can run from the seacoast to the mountain top, from the river bottom where sugar cane will grow to the snow line, it can raise all of the crops that will grow in all the climates. Not all haciendas—not any perhaps—satisfy this ideal completely, but that is the aim of hacienda organization: to buy nothing; to raise and make everything within the limits of its own boundaries. The big house is built from the timbers found on the land—and these may be, as I have seen them, mahogany. The furniture is made at home. The cloth is woven there from wool shorn off home-grown sheep. The llamas that graze in the hills, the oxen, and the horses are raised and broken where they were born. The saddles, bridles, and harnesses are made from the hides of the slaughtered animals. The wooden plow, the wagon, the windmill for the grinding of the corn, or the water mill for the grinding of cane are all fabricated locally. The table may be loaded at a meal with every kind of meat, grain, and fruit, and all of these—the table itself, the house, and the

servants as well—will have been raised, contrived, conserved, grown on the place. Even the tablecloth that covers the table, the sandals of the servants if they are not barefooted, and perhaps the Indian musician who sits behind the screen and plays his old songs on his homemade instrument are from the plantation. I know this from personal experience on a plantation in the province of Ayacucho in Peru.

The people on the plantation are born there. They cannot leave because they may be in debt, or because there is no place to go. This is home and every other place is foreign. Here too their fathers and grandfathers were born and are buried. If the place changes hands, they change with it. In 1948 the leading newspaper in La Paz, Bolivia, carried an advertisement offering for sale on the main highway a half hour from the capital of the country a hacienda with 500 acres of land, 50 sheep, much water, and 20 peons. Similar advertisements have appeared in Ecuador and Chile even more recently. The point is that what we are dealing with is a closed system—economically, socially, politically, and culturally.

The hacienda is a way of life rather than a business. It is not an investment. It was inherited. It is operated with the exenditure of as little cash as possible. If the hacienda is large, there may be a couple of hundred or more families residing within its borders. These are scattered in groups of five or ten families in different parts of the hacienda, depending on the kind of crops grown and the terrain. The laborer on the hacienda usually has a hut, which he has built, and a given amount of land, which he works himself or shares.

The hacienda provides the land, the work animals, and the seed, and the peon carries the *hacendado's* share of the crop to the granary near the big house. The hacienda will also receive annually one out of the ten or twelve sheep grazed on hacienda lands by Indians who do not live there. The size of the share is determined by the crop and the tradition of the hacienda. In addition, the Indian also owes the landlord a given number of days of work each week throughout the year. This practice varies. It might be one day's work a week for each hectare of land or so many days a week for living on the land. The families might also owe a certain amount of service in the big house. Thus the hacienda has its labor supplied to it without the use of money. If there are 200 families on the hacienda and if they each owe only one day's work a week for each of two hectares allotted to each family, the hacienda would command 400 workdays each week.

The neighboring villages provide another source of labor. These workers are also not paid in wages. Instead, the Indians are charged so much for the grazing of each animal and are required to pay the debt in labor. This is not an uncommon practice.

This labor is used by the hacienda for working the lands it tills on its own account. These lands might be in sugar cane, from which it can grind sugar, using either oxen or water power in a small, homemade *trapiche* (water- or mule-driven factory), squeeze out the juice and make *panela,* and manufacture rum as well. Or its cash crop may be coffee, cocoa, or other products which can be carried to the market on the backs of mules or men, over steep mountains and through narrow gorges to the nearest railroad station or, more recently, to the nearest automobile road or to the nearest town. The cash crop can be raised, harvested, and delivered part or all the way to the nearest market without the expenditure of any cash.

In a curious way, the hacienda is largely beyond the reach of the money economy. Internally it provides, so far as it can, for almost all of its needs. All of the buildings, the draft animals, the tools, the labor supply are derived from internal operations. The seed the hacienda supplies to the sharecroppers comes out of the storehouses in which it was deposited in the fall. If the laborers run short of food or other supplies, these can be purchased in the hacienda store—*tienda de Raya* in Mexican parlance, "company store" in ours.

The peon will pay no cash for his purchases for he has none. His account will be kept in a little book by a storekeeper, usually some distant relative or *compadre* of the *hacendado.* The debt can be liquidated by labor, but it rarely is, and serves to tie the laboring population to the hacienda, since they cannot leave without first paying off their debt. This has long been so. The system began in the colonial era, persisted all through the nineteenth century, and is still found wherever the hacienda survives. It is as hard to kill as were the company store and token coin or script in the mining and lumbering industries in the United States. Token coin has its use on the hacienda for the payment of wages for any extra labor which may be needed beyond that owed by the peons, or for tasks which for some reason lie outside the peon's traditional duties. These token coins, a piece of metal sometimes bearing the name of the hacienda, stamped with *vale un día de trabajo* (it is worth one day's work), can only be exchanged in the hacienda store.

As the hacienda satisfies its own and its community's needs with as little recourse to the market as possible, it buys little and it sells little as well. The distances, the poor roads, the primitive means of communication make the transport of goods from one part of the country to another difficult and expensive. The hacienda's relatively small income is, so to speak, net profit—taxes on land have always been low and production costs are minimal in monetary terms.

The Hacienda as a Society

The hacienda is, however, not merely an economic enterprise. It is also a social, political, and cultural institution. Socially it is a closed community living within its borders. Part of the hacienda population is located near the big house, where the store, the church, the school (if there is one), the repair shops, the granaries, the blacksmith, the carpenter, and the harness shop are also found. The grist mill and the *trapiche* (sugar mill) are also, in all likelihood, near the big house if there is water close by. The stables for the favorite horses, cows, and other animals raised for household use or consumption will be near at hand. The laborers living near the big house tend the livestock and operate the various shops and mills. This is usually the larger part of the hacienda community. The rest are scattered in small groups in different parts of the domain, tending to different functions and raising crops appropriate to the altitude and the climate. Each little ranch hamlet is isolated and far away. It may be anywhere from one to ten miles from the next hamlet, depending on the size of the hacienda. Contacts with the outside world are few indeed, and paths on the hacienda lead mainly to the center where the big house is located. Only one rarely used path leads to another hacienda, and to still another, until the neighboring town is reached, which may be 10, 20, 30, or more miles away.

Community activity takes place in front of the big house on Sundays when the peons come to church even if there is no priest in regular attendance. All burials, christenings, and marriages, when they are solemnized, are social matters involving the Church and as large a part of the hacienda community as is aware of the occasion. The important feast days are likely to be the saint's day of the owner or of some favorite member of the family. Then the entire community will turn the event into a holiday with decorations, music, dancing, and drinking. A similar day is given to celebrating the patron saint of the local church. There may be others, depending on the local Indian, mestizo, or Negro traditions. Beyond these festive occasions the hacienda community has no public functions or responsibilities. It is not a governmental unit, an organized parish, or a cooperative. If any vestige of the older Indian community survives on the hacienda, it is unrecognized by the *hacendado,* and what functions it retains must of necessity lie outside of the hacienda.

The Hacienda and Politics

There may be, and often is, a bond between the peons on the place and the *hacendado* which goes beyond the formal manager-laborer relation. The *hacendado* may have stood as godfather to many of the children born on the place. He may have a role not as employer primarily but as the head of a family of which all the laborers consider themselves members. The hacienda laborers' community may have an integrity deriving from many years of cooperation, interdependence, and mutual aid. The hacienda is an old institution. It has usually belonged to the same family over many generations, sometimes for centuries. Isolation from the larger world, time, circumstance, and the need for mutual protection have tended to bring the haciendas within the same region close to each other. By intermarriage the owner of the hacienda is likely to be related to most of the proprietors of the neighboring properties, so that the *hacendados* of a particular region comprise a large family extended over a vast area where everyone knows and is related to everyone else.

In time, one or another of these closely knit families will have acquired an ascendancy over the others and assumed a kind of traditional leadership over the region. Given the loyalty of family members to each other and the godfather relation that always exists, you have the basis for political power and regional *caciquismo*. Because of the turbulence and instability that followed independence, *caciquismo* served the important end of protecting its own. The interdependence of the regional hacienda owners became a pattern for self-protection and defense—either military or political. The rule that developed, and was logically required by the situation, was that each region followed its own leader—if necessary, against the national one. The local leaders each had a following which belonged only to them, and the national leader depended upon their support.

In that situation the power of the national leader tended to be unstable, temporary, and subject to many hazards. He really lived on borrowed strength. The power of the local *cacique* was very great and beyond the effective control of the central government. The hacienda thus supported a system of local *caciquismo,* which became a major cause of political instability. The hacienda community's fealty gave the *hacendado* a power which was immediate and direct, and a group of related and interdependent *hacendados* were able to control an entire region.

The hacienda also dominated the small neighboring city and prevented it from developing economically or politically. The complaint so often heard in the Latin American smaller town, that it has no "movement," that it is "dead," is true and no great mystery. The haciendas which surround the town buy little. Their peons have no money and the hacienda grows and manufactures very nearly all that it requires. The town has no important distributing function. The hacienda sells relatively little, considering its size and the number of people living on it. What it does sell is marketed, usually, on a wholesale basis by some agent employed by the hacienda, or by a member of the family, and is sent on, if possible to a larger city at a distance, with the result that the smaller neighboring city is bypassed. Even the mule pack carrying the hacienda goods to the city or the nearest railroad belongs to the hacienda.

The better houses in the town usually belong to the neighboring haciendas and are occupied by some members of the family, probably an old mother, or a brother who does not like to live on the hacienda or who has some professional interest. The children of the *hacendado* also are in this house during the school year. The servants in the house come from the hacienda and are a permanent part of the household, requiring no money wage. In the mountains of Peru the house has the service of one or more *pongos* (unpaid servants) who each work in the house for a week, then go back to the hacienda. This is part of their payment for the few hectares of land they till on the hacienda. In addition, the house is supplied from the hacienda with a large part of its needs—wheat, barley, rice, corn, whatever fruits are raised, and, depending on the distance, butter, cheese, and whatever else the climate will allow to be transported. As a result, the big houses in the town are not important participants in the local market.

All of this and much more has kept the town commercially inactive. If the hacienda dominates the town economically, it does so politically as well. The great family will control every local office, from the colonel of the local militia to the rural police. The tax gatherer, the mayor, the judge, the postmaster, will be related directly or through marriage or as godfathers to members of the family. And unless the president of the country feels strong enough to be indifferent to the interest and pride of the local leadership, he will not impose "foreigners" on the locality.

The Future of the Hacienda

If we summarize the role of the hacienda in the development of Latin America we will see that it has been—and continues to be, where haciendas still exist—an isolating and conservative influence. Its traditional sharecropping system prevented the use of improved machinery, methods, or seeds. It tied labor force to the property and kept mobility to a minimum. It was a dampening influence on commercial development because it bought and sold relatively little in the open market. Its huge expanse, linked only by paths leading to the big house, discouraged road-building. It established and maintained a system of dependence between the hacendado and his peons which perpetuated an authoritarian tradition of master and very humble servant (I saw in Bolivia the Indians on a plantation bend their knees and kiss the hands of the hacendado). It prevented the accumulation of capital, required no investment, called for no change, and did nothing to prevent soil erosion and improve agricultural techniques. The hacienda family controlled the local political scene and set the tone socially. It paid little taxes and neglected, or was

unable, to put all of its resources to good use.

Perhaps most serious of all is that the hacienda fostered and maintained the hacendado as a social ideal—a superior being possessed of broad acres and numerous servants, dominant, domineering, patronizing, and paternal, with no restrictions between himself and the peon on the plantation. All other elements in society—craftsmen, businessmen, entrepreneurs, and the entire middle class—were looked upon with disdain as a necessary affliction that had at best to be suffered. The hacendado was the master of all he surveyed and the world looked good to him. It gave him economic stability, social prestige, political power, affluence, and leisure. Those of his children who did not remain on the hacienda went off to the capital of the country, attended the university, and became lawyers, doctors, or literary men. Many of them combined literature with a profession. They might also meddle in politics, especially if the administration was one which their family—the extended family, the people who came from the same region, who followed the same local traditional leadership—had helped to bring into office.

Education fitted the ideal. Primary schooling for the mass of the people was a matter of indifference; higher education in the main led to a limited number of professions—medicine, law, and to a much lesser degree civil engineering. In earlier days, the university also taught theology. The emphasis more recently has been on philosophy and literature. Thus if Latin America has fallen behind the United States and western Europe in industrial expansion, in the development of politically stable and democratic government, and in the growth of an educational system adequate for modern needs, much of the fault lies with the hacienda system.

It has in fact reached an impasse from which it cannot escape. The pressure for economic, political, and social change is building so rapidly that the hacienda system canot escape the challenge, and it cannot meet it. *The hacienda has no built-in device that will allow for reform of the system,* that will enable it to transform itself so as to survive and adjust to the present. It has found no way of meeting the challenges of television and atomic energy—and,

if you like, of psychoanalysis and Karl Marx—and yet it canot remain indifferent to them.

In the two countries where the hacienda has been repudiated, Mexico and Bolivia, it was done by revolution. Revolution, too, has transferred to the government the traditional commercial plantation in Cuba. The question of whether there is another way of dealing with impending change remains to be seen. . . .

4

Latin American Constitutions:
Nominal and Real

J. Lloyd Mecham

If the drafting of democratic constitutions serves as preparation for practice in the art of popular government then, indeed, Latin Americans are well prepared. Since gaining independence the 20 republics have essayed a grand total of 186[1] *magna cartae,* or an average of 9.3 each. A breakdown per country reveals the following: Argentina 4; Bolivia 14; Brazil 5; Chile 7; Colombia 6; Costa Rica 7; Cuba 2; Dominican Republic 22; Ecuador 16; El Salvador 10; Guatemala 5; Haiti 18; Honduras 10; Mexico 5; Nicaragua 8; Panama 3; Paraguay 4; Peru 12; Uruguay 4; and Venezuela 24. To-

day 13 of the Latin American republics are governed by constitutions adopted since 1940, and only 2 antedate World War I.[2] There seems to be no end to constitution-making.

This points up an anomaly: on the one hand apparent devotion to constitutionalism as a cure for national problems, and on the other, lack of respect for constitutional mandates. Nowhere are constitutions more elaborate and less observed. Politically, Latin Americans seem to be unqualified optimists, for the long succession of constitutional failures has never dampened hopes that the perfect constitution—a cure-all for national ills—will be discovered eventually.

The Nominal Constitution

Since it is the objective of the present inquiry to show how widely government in operation departs from constitutional mandate, we first note the constitutional norm, that is, a composite or average constitution of the Latin American republics.

From J. Lloyd Mecham, "Latin American Constitutions: Nominal or Real," *Journal of Politics,* Vol. XXI, No. 2 (May 1959). Reprinted by permission.
[1] There is no agreement concerning the total number of Latin American constitutions. This is because many amended or revised constitutions were promulgated as new instruments. "It has been the habit of new political regimes to adopt new constitutions rather than to run the risk of loss of prestige by operating under the instrument identified with an opposing and defeated party." William W. Pierson and Federico G. Gil, *Governments of Latin America* (New York: McGraw-Hill Book Company, 1957), p. 160.

[2] Argentina (1853) and Colombia (1886); both extensively revised.

The composite constitution

This constitution is a lengthy instrument of about 35 pages, in contrast to 13 pages for the Constitution of the United States. Cuba's constitution is the longest with 68 pages; Mexico and Venezuela tie for second at 54 pages each. The excessive length results in part from a distrust of government, particularly the executive; hence the elaborate provisions to prevent abuse of power.

The composite constitution contains no preamble. It sets about forthrightly to declare that the nation is sovereign, independent, and unitary or federal as the case may be; that the government is republican, democratic, and representative; that sovereignty is vested in the people who express their will be suffrage which is obligatory and secret for all citizens, male and female, over 20 years of age. No literacy or property tests are required. This is universal suffrage in its most liberal sense.

The guarantees of individual liberty, the familiar rights of man, are spelled out in great detail. These include: the freedoms of speech, press, assembly, and petition; equality before the law; habeas corpus; no unreasonable searches or seizures; due process; no retroactive penalties; and no capital punishment. Religious freedom is guaranteed, and all cults receive the equal protection of the state. The minute enumeration of the inalienable rights of the individual is inspired by a desire to erect a constitutional barrier to tyranny.

The effectiveness of this barrier is weakened, however, by provisions for the suspension of the individual guarantees in times of stress. This device is called "declaration of state of siege," a temporary annulment, by presidential decree, of all constitutional guarantees and privileges. This important presidential power is restricted only by the formality of securing congressional approval before the act if the congress is in session, and after the act when that body is convened. The easy suspension of the constitutional guarantees is evidence of the fact that they are considerably less than absolute.

One of the most detailed and lengthy sections of the constitution deals with "social rights and duties," a recent addition to Latin American constitutional law. Conforming to contemporary conceptions of social justice, social rights and duties are enumerated *in extenso* under the subheads: labor, family, education, and the economic order.

Labor is declared to be both a right of the individual and a social obligation. The state recognizes a special responsibility to protect the worker. The labor section, a veritable labor code, guarantees maximum hours of work and minimum wages, equal pay for equal work without regard for sex, compensation for industrial accidents, special protection for women and children, annual holidays with pay, medical assistance, collective labor contracts, and the right to strike. A labor jurisdiction is established to which all controversies between capital and labor are to be submitted.

The social guarantees relating to the family are based on the principle that the family, motherhood, and marriage are under the protection of the state. It is the duty of the state to safeguard the social development of the family, to preserve its integrity, and to assume responsibility for neglected children. All children are equal before the law whether born in wedlock or not.

Education also receives special mention. It is the right of everyone to receive instruction and is the responsibility of the state to provide educational facilities. Primary education is obligatory; that provided by the state is free. Secondary and higher instruction imparted by the state is also gratuitous.

The guarantees relating to the economic order are inspired by considerations of social welfare and national consciousness. Thus, although the right to private property is recognized, its use and retention are conditioned by social need. Private property cannot be expropriated without just compensation. The subsoil belongs to the state which may make concessions for its exploitation. Many of the social and economic guarantees find their inspiration in the nationalistic aspiration to abolish or bring under greater control foreign enterprises.

The supreme powers of government are divided for their exercise, by application of the principle of the separation of powers, into the legislative, the executive, and the judicial. Two or more of these powers shall never be united in one person or group of persons, for by counterbalancing and checking each other they will prevent the establishment of a tyranny.

The legislative power is vested in a congress composed of two houses, a chamber of deputies and a senate. Both deputies and senators are chosen by direct popular vote, for terms of four and six years respectively. The deputies are apportioned according to population, whereas each province or principal political subdivision is arbitrarily assigned an equal number of senators. In the federal unions each state enjoys equal representation in the senate, and the federal district is given representation in both of the houses. Vacancies in the chamber of deputies are filled by alternates elected at the regular elections. In general both houses of the national legislature possess the same powers and perform the same functions. They are equal partners in the legislative process. Although each chamber possesses certain special powers these are of no particular consequence.

It should not be necessary in centralistic states to delegate powers to the national congress, for it is understood to possess the power to legislate on all subjects which are not denied to it. Why then the delegation of such obvious powers as: tariff duties, taxation, creation and abolition of public offices, and appropriations? This is because in the colonial period all of these powers belonged to the king and his viceroy; and because of the persistence of the tradition of the strong executive it is felt necessary, by these constitutional delegations, to erect barriers to the establishment of a dictatorship.

The powers of the national government in the federal states of Latin America are considerably broader than in the United States. In addition to virtually all those powers delegated to the United States Congress, the Latin American federal congress is authorized to enact general codes of civil, penal, procedural, and commercial law for the whole nation. The federal congress is also authorized by express constitutional grant to enact necessary legislation dealing with labor, education, public health, and natural resources. Most significant of all these exceptional federal powers, because of its use to convert constitutional federalism into actual centralism, is that of intervention into the affairs of the states "for the preservation of the republican representative form of government." As with respect to the declaration of a state of siege, the president plays the leading role in intervention; the congress ratifies the presidential initiative.

An interesting feature of the legislative branch found in the composite constitution, and of course unknown to the United States Constitution, is the permanent committee of congress. Composed of senators and deputies chosen by their respective chambers, this body functions during the recess of congress. Its principal task is to keep a watchful eye over the executive branch of the government, and, in the event of gross abuse of power, to summon the congress in special session. Here is another of the numerous paper barriers to dictatorship.

The executive power is exercised by the president with a council of ministers. The president is chosen by direct vote of the people (even in the federal states), serves for a term of four years, and is not eligible for re-election until after one term intervenes. There is no provision for a vice-president because this heir apparent might become the magnet for conspiracies against the constituted government.

The powers of the Latin American president are relatively greater than those of the president of the United States, for, in addition to the customary executive grants, he is authorized to directly initiate legislation in the national congress, expel foreigners on his own authority, suspend the constitutional guarantees, and in federal states impose his will on state administrations by exercise of the power of intervention. His decree-making power is so broad as to be quasi-legislative in character; indeed, the constitution authorizes the congress to delegate, in emergencies, extraordinary legislative powers to the president. Constitutional checks on dictatorship are thus cancelled out by contrary constitutional delegations. The end result is that dictatorships are possible within the terms, if not the spirit, of the constitution.

The composite constitution provides that the president shall be assisted by ministers of state, the superior chiefs of their respective departments. The number and nature of these departments are to be determined by legislation. The ministers are appointed and removed by the president. All regulations, decrees, and orders of the president must be countersigned by the minister to whose department the matter pertains.

This too is intended to operate as a check on the chief executive. It might be effective were not the minister the creature of the president. Ministers have the right to attend the congressional sessions and to participate in the debates, but without a vote. Although the congress can summon a minister for a report or questioning (called interpellation) it has no power to impose political responsibility. Thus the Latin American cabinet, although not parliamentary, is rather distinct from that of the United States.

The judicial system, independent and coordinate, is composed of a hierarchy of courts; a supreme court, appellate courts, and inferior courts or courts of first instance. In the federal unions the state constitutions provide for a separate system of courts as in each of the states of the United States. The supreme court in the unitary states exercises supervisory jurisdiction over the entire court system, and in the federal unions over all the federal courts. The justices are appointed and serve for limited terms. The Latin American countries base their legal system on the Roman law and so do not make use of trial by jury. United States influence is discovered however, in the constitutional provision conferring on the supreme court the power to declare laws unconstitutional.

In addition to the regular courts there are a number of special courts, notably the administrative tribunals and the electoral tribunals. The former have jurisdiction over suits involving the infringement of private rights by public officials, and the latter have jurisdiction over all cases involving the application of the electoral laws. The members of the electoral tribunal are recruited from the regular judiciary.

In its organization of local government the composite constitution for the unitary state provides a highly centralized system as in France. The nation is divided, principally for administrative purposes, into departments, and each department has a governor appointed by the president, and directly responsible to the minister of interior. There is no departmental assembly. Insofar as self government exists on the local level it is found in the municipalities which have their own elected mayors and councils. It should be recognized however, that neither mayor nor councilman actually has much to do. The various national ministries, particularly the *gobierno* or ministry of the interior which controls the police, absorb most of the local jurisdiction. Local self-government functions under highly restrictive limitations both in law and custom. Within the respective states of the federal unions the organization of local government conforms rather closely to that of the unitary nations.

Reflective of the prominence which the military assumes in the political life of the Latin American nations, a separate constitutional chapter is devoted to "the armed forces." In addition to national defense the military are assigned the role of "guaranteeing the constitutional powers." This provides a basis for political intervention despite the injunction that the armed forces are "essentially obedient and not deliberative." This is another of the numerous but ineffective constitutional world-barriers to the rule of force.

The constitution is easily amended. The proposed amendment must receive a two-thirds vote in two consecutive legislative sessions. The executive cannot object. This is meaningless, however, since the amendment would have little chance of adoption if the president opposed. There is no popular ratification of constitutional amendments; indeed, the original constitution itself was not popularly ratified.

Variations from the norm

Such is an average Latin American constitution. Of course there are many interesting departures from this composite instrument. Included in these exceptions to the rule are the following: the National Council of Government or plural executive in Uruguay; the unicameral congress in four of the Central American republics, also Panama and Paraguay; functional representation in the senate in Peru and Ecuador, and modified parliamentarism or ministerial responsibility in Cuba, Ecuador, Guatemala, Panama, Peru, and Uruguay.

But by no means exceptional in Latin American constitutions are unique and extraordinary provisions gauged by any constitutional standard. In the first place are those broad idealistic declarations, such as, in the Paraguayan Constitution (Art. 22), "Every Paraguayan home should be located on a piece of [privately] owned land," and "All inhabitants of the Republic [Paraguay] are obliged to earn their living by legitimate work"; also, the Venezuelan Constitution (Preliminary Declaration) consecrates "labor as the supreme virtue and as the supreme claim to human betterment." In the second place are those provisions that elaborate the obvious such as: "All usurped authority is ineffective and its acts are null" (Dominican Republic, Art. 89); and "There will be no public officials in Nicaragua the functions of which are not determined by law or regulation" (Art. 316); and "Public officials are not masters but trustees of authority" (Costa Rica, Art. 19). And in the third place there are numerous constitutional provisions which reflect an awareness of instability and inevitability of *coup d'état* and revolution, such as: "All usurped authority is ineffective and its acts are null. Every decision agreed to because of the direct or indirect application of force or the assemblage of people with a subversive attitude is similarly null" (Venezuela, Art. 87). Some constitutions even sanction the right of revolution; for example that of El Salvador (Art. 36) reads: "The right of insurrection shall in no case produce the abrogation of the laws, its effects being limited to the removal, as may be necessary, of persons discharging governmental office"; and the fundamental charter of Guatemala (Art. 2) recognizes the right of the people to "revert to rebellion" when the principle of "alternability in the exercise of the office of the President... is dared to be violated." The final article (136) in the Mexican Constitution achieves the ultimate in naiveté; it reads: "This Constitution shall not lose its force and vigor even should its observance be interrupted by rebellion. In case a government the principles of which are contrary to those it sanctions be established through any public disturbance, as soon as the people recover their liberty, its observance shall be re-established." An identical article appeared in the Mexican Constitution of 1857.

In spite of these constitutional curiosities, which in fact have been inconsequential in contributing to or detracting from the effective operation of governments, the contemporary Latin American constitutions measure up quite well, compared with other world constitutions, as advanced instruments of democratic government. Latin American framers of constitutions are generally keen scholars of political theory and bring to the constituent assemblies a high level of competence. Nor can it be fairly held that this competence is purely theoretical. One need but read carefully the debates and proceedings of constitutional conventions to realize that they reflect, not only an intimate acquaintance with the literature of political science and with constitutional development and trends around the world, but also with their own national deficiencies. Latin Americans are unsparing in self-criticism; thus there is little that a foreign political scientist can tell them of which they are unaware.

The Latin American's attitude toward constitutional law differs radically from that of the Anglo-American in that whereas to us the constitution is the fundamental law and must be observed, to the Latin American it is, in many respects, merely a declaration of ideal objectives. To us the constitution is almost sacrosanct, for we subscribe to the principle of a government of law; to the Latin American the constitution, generally a useful and convenient guide and program, must bend to the principle of a government of men.

The Operative Constitution

The foregoing, in broad outline, is the composite "paper" constitution of the Latin American republics, together with certain distinctive variations. It is now in order to describe that constitution as actually operative. With the exception of Uruguay, and the doubtful addition of Costa Rica, Chile, and Mexico, democratic government does not exist in Latin America. A majority of the countries are either undisguised personalistic dictatorships or pseudo-democracies. In either case the proud constitutional assertions that these are popular, representative, democratic states, and that all governmental authority derives from the people in whom sovereignty resides, are mere verbiage, or at best declarations of ideal aspirations.

Divergences in actual practice

Universal suffrage, provided by more than half of the constitutions, is actually exercised by only a fraction of those qualified, even in countries where voting is supposed to be compulsory. These few votes must then run the gamut of the "official count." It is a well-known fact that a requisite more important than honest voting is the honest poll of the votes. Since governments in power are usually in control of the voting and the tabulating of the vote, it is a commonplace that Latin American administrations never lose elections. On the rare occasions when this happens, as in Cuba in 1944 when Batista "allowed" the election of Dr. Grau San Martín, the shock of the unusual event reverberated throughout Latin America.

What shall we say about the observance of those fundamental guarantees of individual liberty: the freedoms of speech, press, assembly, and conscience? What of the guarantees of domicile and all of the components of what we know as due process of law? Since from the earliest days of their independence, Latin Americans have been so profoundly engrossed in the constitutionalizing of an ever expanding enumeration of civil liberties, it seems that they should, by this time, have attained a status of sanctity and respect. This however is not the case. The guarantees are respected only at governmental convenience and by sufferance. The constitutions generously supply the executives with the means to be employed in emergencies, to suspend the guarantees. This device, known as "state of siege," is abused by overuse for it is the customary resort to overwhelm opposition and entrench dictatorship. It is ironical

that democratic constitutions bestow so lavishly on the executive the means to destroy the feeble manifestations of democracy. With respect to the status of the individual guarantees, therefore, much depends on the attitude of the president.

A principle of the "paper constitution" which is transformed beyond recognition in the operating constitution is the separation of the powers. Theoretically the three powers—executive, legislative, and judicial—are separate, coordinate, and equal. Numerous safeguards, many of which are found in our own constitutions, are provided to prevent wanton exercise of authority by any one of these powers. Because of the well-founded belief that it is the executive which will be most prone to irresponsibility and be acquisitive of power, the most numerous constitutional limitations are those imposed on the presidents. Despite all this, and responsive to the strongman tradition in Latin governments, the executive overshadows the other two powers. Latin American governments are emphatically of the strong presidential type.

That the president is the dominant power in the government is never doubted. His supremacy derives from his dual position as constitutional chief executive and as extraconstitutional *caudillo,* chief or boss. From the earliest days of their independence Latin Americans have shown a strong disposition for *caudillos,* preferably for those with a military background, for the magnetic attraction of the man on horseback can always be expected to reinforce the lure of demagogues. The *caudillo* embodies the program of his political partisans; he is the platform of his pseudoparty. This is what is called *personalismo* in Latin American politics, which means placing emphasis on individuals rather than on public policies. The *caudillo* because of his hold on the popular imagination, but more significantly because of his control of the army, meets with docile acceptance. Neither the disguised dictatorship nor the pseudodemocracy is a government of laws; all are governments of men. One of the least effective of the constitutional checks on ambitious presidents is the no-re-election provision. *Caudillismo* and *personalismo* have transformed the constitutional office of the presidency beyond recognition.

In consequence of the dominance of the executive it is hardly necessary to indicate the position of the congress and the courts. Both are subordinate to the executive. Since the president usually controls the electoral machinery and since the members of congress are elected with his approval, or certainly without his disapproval, they are almost completely amenable to the executive's pleasure. Although they put on a show of heated debate, these histrionics are usually intended for the edification of a gullible public. Since most of the congressmen are the president's men and can be counted on to go down the line for him, the president gets the kind of legislation he wants. Rare indeed are the occasions when he must exercise the veto power.

Freedom and equality of the courts is also a fiction, for the judiciary, like the legislature, is subordinate to the executive, numerous constitutional provisions to bulwark the power and independence of the courts to the contrary notwithstanding. In fact, the courts of Latin America are even less effective than the legislature in limiting the authority of strong presidents. Although a number of the constitutions give to the courts the power of judicial review, rare, indeed, are the judges who will tempt fate by invalidating acts of congress or presidential decree laws. It simply is not good form or good sense.

It is not necessarily because the presidents have ways of getting rid of objectionable judges which accounts for their surrender of independence; rather it is because of a long-standing tradition of Spanish origin that there must be no interference by the judiciary with the policies of the chief executive. The old principle that the king can do no wrong is observed by the deference paid by the courts to the wishes of the president. However, routine matters in the lower courts, and other cases in which the executive manifests no interest, are usually free of political interference.

The constitutions of the centralistic states give to the president and his minister of interior sufficient power to maintain a firm grip on local government. Therefore it is seldom necessary to resort to extraconstitutional means to impose the will of the executive on all strata of local government. In the federal states however, the imposing of the will of the national government on the individual states and their subdivisions, resulting in the converting of theoretical federalism into actual centralism, is accomplished by violating the spirit, if not the letter, of the constitution. This is the notorious interventionism, a common practice in all of the so-called federal states of Latin America: Argentina, Brazil, Mexico, and Venezuela.

As if it were the manifest purpose of the federal constitution to nullify the very federalism which those instruments established, they give the federal authorities, actually the president, exceptional power to intervene in and control state governments. The power usually invoked is to preserve the republican form of government. The vagueness of the meaning of "republican form of government" gives to the president ample latitude for action, an opportunity, needless to say, which he seldom neglects, particularly when the opposition seems to have won an election, for it is intolerable that a state government should be controlled by elements distasteful to the national administration. On such occasions the election is declared to be fraudulent (as, indeed, it was) and, since for this reason the republican form of government ceased to exist, it accordingly is the duty and responsibility of the president to order an intervention. An executive decree brings the state government under federal control. An interventor appointed by the president takes full charge of state affairs supplanting both the governor and the legislature. In due time, when the president is disposed to restore autonomy to the state, his interventor supervises an election and makes certain that only officials acceptable to the national administration are successful at the polls. Certainly, if there is a constitutional principle which is rendered meaningless by actual practice, it is that the states are autonomous entities in the federal unions of Latin America.

Equally as fictitious as Latin American federalism is the constitutional mandate that the army does not deliberate, that is, intervene in politics. Any practical discussion of Latin American politics which omits reference to the political role of the army would be sadly unrealistic, for the most significant feature of Latin American politics has always been the predominance of the military authority over the civil. It is an old story dating from the independence period when the possession of governmental authority became the prize of contesting arms. None of the countries has escaped the blight of military political intervention, and today the military are in control, openly or disguised, in most of the nations of Latin America.

The very nature and purpose of the army invites political activity, for it is designed more to preserve internal order and support the regime than to defend the frontiers against foreign invaders. Several of the constitutions impose on the army the responsibility of guaranteeing the fulfillment of the constitution and the laws. The militarists do not shirk this obligation for they regard themselves as the most competent, unselfish, and patriotic interpreters of the national interest. Moreover, it is a well-established fact that a presidential candidate is severely handicapped unless he bears a military title. There is a feeling, shared by more than just the militarists, that the nature of the executive office calls for the qualities and experience generally associated with military command. Today military men preside over several of the countries. But whether the president be an army officer or a civilian he never forgets that his tenure is dependent on the continued support of the army. Accordingly, he showers favors on the officers and men to keep them happy, for dissatisfaction breeds revolt, the over-indulged resort of the political opposition. . . .

Adjusting the constitutions to reality

In view of the considerable divergences of actual practice from the constitutional norm, the question arises: how can the fundamental charters of Latin America be regarded as "acceptable examples of the constitution-makers art" since they are merely nominal or paper constitutions? Does not the fact that they are observed in the breach prove their artificiality? No, this is not necessarily so, for the validity of the cliché that Latin American constitutions are "divorced from reality" needs to be examined.

It can be conceded that these constitutions are divorced from reality in that they ostensibly establish democracies on the insecure foundation of a citizenry lacking in the tradition of freedom and undisciplined in democratic processes. However, it should be recalled that Latin American constitution-makers do not delude themselves that they are building upon achieved democracy, but rather are setting their nations upon the road to democratic achievement. When viewed in this light Latin American constitutions are actually in considerable harmony with reality.

The critics of these alleged "exotic" and "artificial" constitutions fail to develop their arguments to any reasonable conclusion. They appear to hold for the incompatibility of the Latin American and the democratic constitution. Yet it is a fair surmise that these very critics would be the last to argue for the abandonment of all democratic pretense in Latin American constitutions. This must mean then, that they believe that the materials for democratic government are at hand in Latin America, and all that is needed is a rational arrangement of these parts.

This we find impossible to accept. How indeed are these so-called artificial and exotic constitutions to be modified to conform to the realities of the Latin American scene and still retain their democratic character? What provisions which they do not already contain in profusion will curb *caudillismo,* the *cuartelazo,* and the rigging of elections? Who can suggest constitutional formulae which will broaden and strengthen the bases of popular government and usher in political, social, and economic democracy?

The simple truth of the matter is that there are no constitutional formulae which, however well-suited to any practical situation or peculiar environment, will of themselves inaugurate a democratic regime. The road to popular and responsible government is a long and difficult way. There are no easy shortcuts. Those requisites of a democratic society: fair play, tolerance, self-discipline, responsibility, human dignity, majority rule but respect for the minority, a spirit of compromise, and respect for the rule of law, are the qualities of a democratic citizen which have deep roots in his historical past. These qualities which are of the inner man and so cannot be legislated into existence have not unfortunately prospered in the soil of the Latin American's historical past. Nor after 140 years of tortured experience in self-government does the present status of democratic achievement in Latin America auger much improvement in the foreseeable future.

5

Latin American Executives:
Essence and Variations

Rosendo A. Gómez

The most widely professed fact in the field of Latin American politics is unquestionably the dominant role of the president. The task facing Latin Americanists is not the defense of this theme but the elaboration of it. One of the most confining factors—so often lamented at conferences where these matters are discussed—is the lack of information in depth concerning all of the revelancies of power structure. This is particularly evident in appraising cultural factors although it must be admitted that much excellent work is now being done. A very challenging problem in the area of comparative government is involved, a problem admitting of some of the methodological uneasiness associated with that branch of political inquiry. Obviously, in the study of Latin American politics one may proceed with greater assurance with the "variations on a theme" technique than would be possible in many other areas; however, some disillusion-

ment and appreciable inaccuracies lie in wait if one submits to this temptation too extensively.

It would appear that there are two assignments in the analysis of executive power that should be accepted and carried out, pending the results of more plodding tasks of fact-enrichment. The first assignment is to consider more sweepingly the executive power in Latin America in its relationship to the broad matter of executive power in general. The second assignment is to classify our existing observations in more meaningful ways. Both of these assignments may be described as attempts to frame hypotheses, in the future investigation of which we may channel our efforts to significant findings.

New-World Authoritarianism

At the risk of summoning the obvious, one should first consider the essence of executive power. The organization of the modern responsible executive is the outcome of a long struggle between the temptations and demands of power and the restraints, of public or self-imposed character, that have

From Rosendo A. Gómez, "Latin American Executives: Essence and Variations," *Journal of Inter-American Studies,* Vol. III, No. 1 (January 1961). Reprinted by permission.

become operable upon the holder of such power. This struggle has built our modern institutions of representative government. For all but a short modern period, authoritarianism has been the prevailing (and some would still say, the natural) pattern for the application of power. So many for so long have phrased the nature of this running battle that it encompasses the whole sweep of political literature that has become available to us—from "philosopher-kings" to Lord Acton's frequently quoted observation on the insidiousness of power. It is held to be very remarkable, indeed, as evidenced in modern democratic systems, that the executive power has been constricted to the degree observable in our time. It has involved not merely the notion of responsibility—responsibility is after all a very old idea of the portfolio of political scientists—but, more significantly, the reduction of executive power to the concept of *managership*.

The prescription for executive power in a system, and the application of it in practice, together comprise a crucial aspect of politics. Jacques Necker, who observed the organization of power in revolutionary France following the events of 1789, wrote of this:

> The executive power is the moving force of government. It .epresents, in the political system, that mysterious principle which, in moral man, unites action to the will. In the meantime, so various are its relations, so extensive is its influence, and so great the place, thus to express itself, which it occupies in the social order, that the adjustment of its limits and the accurate adaptation of its means to its ends, offer to the human mind one of the most comprehensive subjects of reflection.[1]

One finds in this description all the

ingredients that have combined to form our modern representative institutions. It is, from the political scientist's point of view, an acceptable version in capsule form of the framework within which Western democratic systems have developed. The executive power has always suggested motion and action; and the central problem, among moral men, is to adjust the limits of this raw force to the requirements of society.

The organization of executive power in the United States and Great Britain represent major examples of the delicate balancing of action and restraint. These examples have very remarkably combined power with sensitivity to mandate and opinion. By contrast, the French system has been characterized by excessive preoccupation with shackling executive power to the point where the terms "assembly government" and *"immobilisme"* are commonly used to describe that tendency. Curiously, the French and American revolutions, although often coupled together as expressions of the confidence in rational man in a revolutionary age, did not develop similar institutionalizations of executive power. In each case, the initial reaction was the same—a shift of emphasis from the *ancien régime* to assembly government. In the short space of approximately a decade, however, the United States dipped into its genius to fill the void, replacing the assembly-oriented Articles of Confederation with the strong executive of the United States Constitution; the French have struggled with the problem almost constantly and are at the moment launching an attempt at a strong executive superimposed upon the cabinet system. It is too early to say whether this development is fastened securely or whether it is dependent upon the personality of General De Gaulle for its existence. In any event, the French experience of approximately 170 years well attests to the uneasiness expressed

---

[1] Jacques Necker, *An Essay on the True Principles of Executive Power in the Great States* (London: Robinson, 1792), I, 1.

by M. Necker who watched the throes of organization.

Latin American independence from Spain was fought in the name of the same ideals that spearheaded the French and American revolutions. The presidential system was adopted throughout Latin America with high aspirations. The experience of the years since the revolutionary movement has been somewhat disenchanting. The delicate balance between action and restraint has not been found in many Latin American republics. The Latin American colonies vaulted into independence with a great strain of authoritarianism in their culture and with little opportunity to erase the past.

The delicacy of the problem of organization of executive power is clearly illustrated by the observations of some of the Latin American revolutionary leaders. Those who led the revolution had undergone intellectual ferment in the years preceding the action; they were familiar with the writings of the patron saints of the French and American struggles. What more logical thing than strong consideration of the presidential system since it was believed to be the product of revolutionary ideas? Bolívar, whose thought ranged widely, believed essentially in recognizing Latin America's authoritarian antecedents and was supposed to have said that the "new states of America, once Spanish, need kings with the title of President." Monteagudo, the brilliant Argentine journalist, who favored monarchy, wrote that Argentines were "not able to be as free as those born in that classic land, England...nor as free as the democrats of North America." Charles Darwin, from the "classic land," and not averse to adding observations on politics to his experiences, upon viewing affairs in Santa Fé province in the Argentina of 1833, wrote in his journal that "tyranny seems as yet better adapted to these countries

than republicanism." A practitioner of politics, president of Argentina from 1868 to 1874, and also a great admirer of the United States, Domingo Sarmiento, very wistfully expressed the problem: "Would that a people could be free by the same sort of *ad hominem* arguments that can bring about independence!"[2] Many decades later, this was summed up by Leo S. Rowe who pointed out that Latin American countries were still engaged in a struggle "to bring their social organization into closer harmony with their political institutions."[3]

The nature of New-World authoritarianism

The experience of the past two decades has brought to comparative government, and to social studies in general, a considerable emphasis upon authoritarianism. The spectacular and extreme versions represented by the Hitler and Mussolini systems undoubtedly gave great impetus to this emphasis. In addition to the investigation of the nature of this pattern, there have also been attempts to maintain distinctions; thus, it is necessary to realize that, while totalitarian systems are extreme examples of authoritarianism, highly authoritarian systems can exist without all of the overwhelming machinery and oppressive techniques of the totalitarian state. The concern to maintain distinctions has been deepened by the increasing and alarming tendency in these postwar years to group rather too easily or to polarize into neat, little ideological packages. In the study of Latin American systems, it is vital to distinguish degrees

---

[2] Ricardo Rojas, *El Pensamiento de Sarmiento* (Buenos Aires: Editorial Losada, 1941), p. 190.

[3] Leo S. Rowe, "The Development of Democracy on the American Continent," *American Political Science Review,* XVI, No. 1 (February 1922), 3.

of authoritarianism. Indeed, the first observation that must be made is that no Latin American system, however loftily a leader may have ascended within it, has been classifiable as a totalitarian state.

There is no doubt concerning the deeply ingrained authoritarianism of Iberian culture nor of its tenacious remnants in Latin America. But authoritarianism in the New World is significantly different from the Old-World Iberian pattern. The distinctions do not lie in such cultural trapping as Church, family, or personalism; these tend to be very much the same. The real distinctions are historical in nature, functions of time and space, rather than of basic cultural patterns.

The basic difference between Old- and New-World Iberian authoritarianism centers on a vital factor in history—*revolutionary commitment*. In critical periods when national sentiment is directed to revolution, and particularly if important institutional changes are sought, the ideals and institutions for which the revolution is fought constitute a commitment which will dictate the form, if not always the substance, of the particular nation for a long period of time. Next to natural historical growth (such as custom's place in the growth of law), this may well be the most compelling institutional and ideological determinant. If the substance is appreciable (as in the United States), a high degree of consistency to the commitment may be maintained; if the substance is meager, the form will nevertheless be employed to await the growth of substance. The Latin American republics, unlike the seats of Old-World authoritarianism such as Spain and Portugal, have a revolutionary commitment to the ideals and institutions of responsible, representative democracy of the presidential type. The consistency displayed varies consider-

ably from republic to republic, but even in republics where substance may be long in developing the revolutionary commitment is compelling and is a major institutional determinant.

One of the most common manifestations of Latin American commitment is the compulsion to seek legality by constitution, even if power be won extraconstitutionally and be maintained in this way. No Latin American president rests comfortably in power without eventually seeking constitutional status, if he ascended to power without it. Much of the addiction to constitution-making in Latin America is attributable to this compulsion.

It would appear in the face of these observations that a significant factor in comparative government is often overlooked—the environmental impact of institutions per se. Generally speaking, most students of comparative government emphasize the necessity to immerse themselves in the particular culture in order to understand properly its political institutions. A corollary of this thought is that one wastes time inspecting institutions for any value in themselves. Yet, there is danger in overemphasizing the lack of importance of institutions. For institutions per se may be influences as well as mere results. This is clear in Latin America where, if it may be argued that the presidential system was too abruptly adopted, generations of Latin Americans have stuck doggedly to the form— the commitment—until it has become a firm and continuous environmental influence.

Another distinction between Old- and New-World authoritarianism, another function of time and space, is the separation from the old order of Europe. This, of course, has created a spirit of innovation, a feeling of creativity institutionally speaking. It has accounted for a very decided sense of constructiveness, of society in motion; this sense can, of course, develop action both for progress or withdrawal. A Latin American republic is always faced with a wide range of choices and nowhere is this more evident than in the activities of the executive power.

Major Types of Latin American Executives

In the foregoing paragraphs may be found an introduction to the essence of the relationship between Latin American executive power and executive power in general. From this basis one may begin investigation of the differences in degree that have developed. The following paragraphs attempt a classification of Latin American executives based upon patterns that have been distinguishable, particularly in the last twenty-five years.

Before investigating these classifications, it would be well to stipulate two assumptions upon which the approach rests. First, it should be assumed that the Latin American presidencies are offices with historical depth in accordance with the principle of commitment mentioned above; we are not discussing useless and fleeting-institutions. Second, it is assumed that standards applied with the United States in mind are unrealistic; all executives in Latin America are to some degree illustrative of authoritarianism in the Iberian tradition; all of the ordinary evidences of *personalismo* are taken for granted as characteristic of even the most responsible presidents.

Constitutional president

Perhaps the most distinguishing feature of this type is that it has existed in greater numbers than is widely believed. One of the most commonly used terms with reference to Latin American politics is "dictator." To be

sure, there have been many dictators through the years, but there have also been a great many presidents who have taken over official duties and conducted these duties within reasonable reach of constitutional directives.

A number of conditions are necessary for satisfaction of this classification. Election must be constitutionally acceptable, a reasonable reflection of the popular will (taking into consideration the retardation in such matters as suffrage and the reality of public opinion that exists in many republics). It must be understood that this condition does not bar the eventual constitutionality of a regime established initially by *coup d'état*. Establishment of power by force may be necessary for the fulfillment of constitutional conditions. At a suitable time thereafter, however, legitimization of proper sort must follow. It is not easy to assess the propriety of these steps in all cases. When is a coup legitimized properly and when is it legitimized under intimidation, for example? There is no sure formula widely applicable. One may perhaps safely judge that the legitimization of the National Revolutionary Movement in Bolivia in 1952, when Paz Estenssoro took over the presidency reflected a genuinely popular sentiment, since he had received a plurality of votes cast in the election at issue. On the other hand, Batista legitimized himself in 1954 under strong intimidation of Cuban opposition groups that left considerable doubt as to genuineness. A government of doubtful status itself can pave the way for a constitutional regime. For example, General Odría's government, established by force in Peru in 1948, and later supposedly legitimized by an election in 1950, made its way under the shadow of a suppressed popular party (the *Apristas*); by 1956, however, this party was allowed some freedom and the election of Manuel Prado qualifies, in the main, as a constitutionally proper one.

To satisfy the requirements of this type, it is also necessary that the opposition be given freedom to contest elections reasonably effectively and to express its views regarding policy-making as well. Again, we encounter difficulty in interpretation and must resort to a realistic appraisal of local circumstances. Thus, in spite of the opposition's continuous cry of fraud and *imposición,* the *Partido Revolucionario Institucional* (PRI) in Mexico must be granted a place of legitimacy in these respects. The PRI must be viewed for what it is—a very large confederation of political groups within which the ordinary differences of politics are fought out, similar to the Democratic party in some United States southern states. There is considerable difference between the PRI and the *Colorados* of Paraguay or the *Partido Dominicano* of the Dominican Republic, to mention the other major examples of one-party domination in the Latin American area. It is a difference that touches upon aspects of the formation of opposition from effective party organization to the various phases of the electoral process, and including the effective pression of opposition in the various media of communication. A very crucial criterion is of course the application of laws affecting the freedom of expression in its many forms.

The fraternity of constitutional presidents does not include those executives who have unreasonably maneuvered constitutions to extend their tenure of office beyond the spirit of the constitution. The practice of *continuismo* is not in harmony with Latin American constitutionalism and it is particularly at variance when it involves that version by which a president-dominated constitutional assembly, after drawing up a new fundamental law, proceeds to appoint the incumbent to serve as president under the new system. This disqualification does not extend, of course, to a proper constitutional amendment relating to extension of tenure if the incumbent then is elected to the office.

Finally, it should be observed that to occupy the post of constitutional president, personalism must be confined to constitutional limits. When a president, however legitimate originally, climbs to a pedestal and creates himself as an order above the constitution, particularly if he actively sponsors a cult centered on his person, he has violated the spirit of Western constitutionalism. The constitutional president must be conscious of his heritage in this respect and exercise restraint.

There is a strong correlation between republics supplying the larger number of constitutional presidents and the political awareness evident among the great mass of people in those republics. This awareness is in turn dependent upon well-known economic and educational advantages. The most constant of these have been Chile, Costa Rica, Mexico, and Uruguay. In the second rank may be placed Argentina, Brazil, Colombia, and Cuba. Ecuador, Guatemala, Peru, El Salvador, and Venezuela have shown occasional promise; Bolivia appears to be enjoying an introduction.

Demagogic caudillo

This type has not as yet appeared in quantity, but it is a highly spectacular type that warrants attention because of the very modern touch involved. It bears some similarities to European fascism, although it is not generally as such. There are a number of distinguishing features that serve to give this type a standing of its own. Argentina affords the best example during the years that Juan Perón dominated the scene.

The first characteristic of the demagogic *caudillo* is a very close relationship with constitutionalism. It emerges in a system that has had deep commitments to constitutional presidencies in the past. The demagogic *caudillo* can easily win legitimation by elections. He rises above constitutionalism not necessarily by violation of electoral laws but chiefly on other grounds. The proper habitat of this type is the republic with a high degree of political awareness founded on an economic order of considerable productivity. A key to the power structure created is a large industrial worker's movement of such massive power that it becomes an aggressive reflection of popular support. It must be constantly wooed and rewarded even to a point beyond the attention customarily given to the military. The demagogic *caudillo* realizes the harnessing of a force which supercedes the military and which, until the structure weakens, can be used effectively to stand off strong military opposition. The maintenance of such a system of mass approval calls for extraordinary powers of organization, diversion, and communication. One of the weaknesses of the system is the difficulty of keeping mass support alive, for the mass appetite grows and becomes increasingly difficult to satisfy. Since the leader has committed himself to the role of savior of the worker and since increasing adulation of him soon transcends the more mundane spirit of the constitution, the cult of the Leader results. It is this characteristic that most closely resembles the European totalitarian systems of recent memory.

Excessive nationalism, with the implication that Latin American leadership is involved, together with heavy doses of anti-Yankeeism, is very important to the pattern. One of the distinctive touches is ideological in nature. The Leader becomes the symbol of an ideology—preferably a "new way"—like the supposedly new course by Perón's *justicialismo*. The demagogic *caudillo* takes the old complaints and declares that he has solved them by a quasi-messianic summoning of the greatness of the people.

The demagogic *caudillo* represents a curious combination of regressiveness and advancement. He is of both worlds, old and new. He is regressive in that he builds firmly upon ingrained authoritarianism and creates a gigantic monument to personal leadership; he is a symbol of advancement in that he has realistically appraised a modern industrial society, wooed and won mass support, and undertaken a social mission in keeping with the twentieth-century's demands.

The prototype of this type of executive was, as mentioned, Juan Perón. Vargas of the 1930's merits some consideration but his claim to real legitimation was rather poorly founded until his return in 1950. Perón was popularly elected in 1946 and again in 1952 and it is clear that he would probably have been elected on both occasions even without the intimidations practiced by an enthusiastic party following. He was raised to heroic stature and from this eminence he clearly operated beyond the intentions of the constitution. It would not be correct to label Perón as the product solely of Latin American caesarism, or as the *duce* of a totalitarian system, or even as a military dictator. He was each of these in some measure but principally he represents a new departure—a leader with the characteristics of a constitutional president who, however, soared out of the constitutional cage into a personal venture so high as to allow for no safe return.

At the moment, there is no demagogic *caudillo* in any of the Latin American republics. If one were to explore potentialities and engage the risk of speculation, there appears only one real possible candidacy and there are many reasons why it might not develop. This possibility is Fidel Castro of Cuba. Cuba fits the pattern fairly well in terms of socioeconomic pressures reflected in voluble mass sentiments. It lacks the major ranking that could justify pretensions to Latin American leadership, but this could be outweighed by the image of Castro as a revolutionary leader already possessed of heroic stature. Castro could ascend to dizzy heights of personalism, particularly if there were added some of the provocations that attended the rise of Perón in Argentina.

Military guardian

The setting for the military guardian is the republic of major or medium power in economic terms wherein an appreciable—if not substantial—political awareness has been generated. Usually the political scene has been sufficiently active to provide for a number of political parties. One of these parties may be the vehicle of considerable popular sentiment for reform; its strength is potentially great enough to make a bid for power and, indeed, it may have done so only to be thwarted by perhaps illegal methods. One of the sociological factors of this setting is invariably the lack of a large middle class actively seeking change. In such a sociological situation, the military has usually flourished as a political determinant. In the period since the end of World War II, excellent examples have been found in Colombia, Peru, and Venezuela.

Against this general background, there may be viewed the various thought-patterns of the military officer intent upon political power. Military guardians may arise in an endless variety of combinations of local political considerations, but there are two major justifications cited by intervening military leaders that demand particular attention: Order and Neutralism. Ordinarily, these are found in combination and are closely related. Order is, of course, a major preoccupation of the military profession everywhere. In Latin American republics, there occur many opportunities for using this as a justification, although often the intervention of the military goes well beyond the demands of the situation. One of the best examples of military guardianship established in the name of order was that of General Rojas Pinilla in Colombia in 1953. Colombia had for generations enjoyed comparatively orderly government without military intervention. The bitter struggle between the Liberals and the Conservatives broke out into widespread violence following the assassination of a Liberal leader, Gaitán, in 1948. This soon assumed the magnitude of civil war with apparently little chance of bringing the warring political leaders to settlement. Breaking a tradition of long standing, General Rojas Pinilla stepped in and took over power. There were other personal motivations involved, but essentially some movement toward order was necessary. Once in power, General Rojas Pinilla was motivated by power itself and carried intervention to a point not justified by the situation.

More common in the ranks of military guardianship is the complicated motivation that might be said to result in a defensive military guardian. In this maneuver, neutralism is cited in order to protect the national dignity, honor, and traditions from the excesses of the masses. Stated more baldly, this is a last stand against popular government that threatens the old order. A large popular party presses forward with the electoral power to sweep into office; the language of reform fills the air. The military guardian comes forward to "save" the republic from this mass "chaos." The best recent examples were in Peru and Venezuela where the *Apristas* and Democratic Action, respectively, had demonstrated enough power to win elections. Accordingly, General Odría in Peru and Colonel Pérez Jiménez in Venezuela intervened and suppressed the parties battering at the gates. Both leaders stated that it was time to save the masses from their own ignorance, or words similar in meaning. General Odría, indeed, stated this most colorfully when he announced that "party politics poisons the hearts of the people and sickens their minds." One is reminded of Thomas the Cynic in Ignazio Silone's *School for Dictators* who stated that in socially backward countries "the army constitutes the only barrier against the so-called 'anarchy' of the popular masses and the corruption of the politicians." This belief has been entertained by many Latin American military guardians. The stated aim is "neutralism" but the result is suppression of popular will. A special version of this sort of guardianship took place in Guatemala in 1954 when Castillo Armas swept into Guatemala to combat the impact of communism.

All military guardians are, of course, driven by some degree of personal yearning for power. The military-officer class in a typical Latin American republic is a considerable reservoir for political ambitions. A leader of this class may be given an opportunity sooner or later to cite one of the ancient justifications for military intervention and thus launch a political career at the head of the republic. The military guardian, in our time, stands ultimately at the mercy of the popular movement he wishes to delay. Both Odría and Pérez Jiménez have given way to constitutional presidents, although the circumstances of their withdrawal differ considerably; Odría presided over an election and Pérez Jiménez was ousted from office.

Paternalistic caudillo

In the paternalistic *caudillo* we find a type that was more widely evident in the nineteenth century before the onset of industrialism and associated effects. At the present time, it is narrowed down largely to the Central American and Caribbean areas, particularly the Dominican Republic and Nicaragua. Although a special case, Paraguay belongs in this category. A decade or two ago, the paternalistic *caudillo* flourished in most of the Central American republics in spectacular fashion. As the title of this type indicates, the system of government resembles a large hacienda with strong superimposition of the *patrón*.

The paternalistic *caudillo* is, indeed, a national *patrón*. He may in fact possess large holdings in property and control a number of basic industries. Nepotism is especially evident in such a system; the total holdings of the *caudillo's* family connection will be staggering. The paternalistic *caudillo* carries to an extreme a long-entertained notion in Latin American political life: the possession of political power is a concession and the concessionaire manages as large a return as possible (much of which may be quite legal, or "honest graft" as it is sometimes called in the United States). The republic is in great part a private preserve. The *caudillo* need not be overpoweringly oppressive, although he protects his system with tightly controlled military forces. He may be viewed by many as a great national father who takes care of his own, at least to the extent he feels is good for them. The *caudillo* usually openly indicates that he is exercising a tutelage over ignorant and childlike people who are not ready for the bewildering machinery of a free system. Some of the major examples of recent years have been the following: Anastasio Somoza who, until his assassination in 1956, ruled Nicaragua for approximately 20 years (and left his "plantation" in the hands of two sons); Rafael Trujillo of the Dominican Republic who has dominated that country for 29 years; and Tiburcio Carías Andino who dominated Honduras for 17 years until 1949. In Venezuela, the last of the large republics to support a paternalistic *caudillo*, Juan Vicente Gómez managed to rule for 27 years until his death in 1935.

There are two electoral features that characterize the administrations of paternalistic *caudillos*. The technique of *continuismo* is employed to excess in such circumstances—that is, the application of presidential domination to extend one's tenure beyond the intention of the constitution. The other feature has to do with alternation in office. A paternalistic *caudillo's* position is usually so secure that he can occasionally afford the luxury of allowing someone else a turn in the presidential office, perhaps a member of the family (as Héctor Trujillo, brother of Rafael).

Provisional executive arrangements

Since at any given time at least one republic has undergone a coup, or other interruption of the constitutional pattern, some brief mention should be made of a highly significant Latin-American executive organization, the provisional government. The most common institution is the junta, a council of varying number of revolutionaries, though usually not more than five. The junta's aim is to provide temporary leadership until the constitutional electoral process be reinstituted. It may be several years before the provisional government deems it proper to hold such an election. In the meantime, a constitutional assembly may be reworking the constitution which will serve as

the banner of "the new era." Another provisional arrangement is simply to continue the use of the presidential office, the president being appointed by the successful revolutionary leadership. Cuba is at the moment employing the latter arrangement with a puppet president and Fidel Castro, the leader of the revolutionary movement, assuming the office of prime minister.

Since it may be said that provisional government is in great measure government exercised in a constitutional void, it must be observed that from this position the leader of a coup may go in any of several directions. He may, of course, simply provide for the resumption of constitutional activity in a short time without unnecessarily influencing the process, as appears to have happened in Argentina preceding the election of President Frondizi. He may employ his position to create electoral triumph for himself in due time, as witness Batista in the Cuban election of 1954. He may simply ignore the electoral process and establish himself arbitrarily in a presidential term of office either by a "plebiscite" as did Castillo Armas in Guatemala following the coup of 1954 or by arranging an appointment by a handpicked constitutional assembly as demonstrated by Vargas on the occasion of the 1934 constitution.

Conclusions

Surveying the trends of recent decades, New-World authoritarianism has developed a pattern that warrants a number of observations. In the first place, the days of the paternalistic *caudillo* appear to be numbered. It is observable that popular dissent may be easily aroused even in very unlikely places in the Latin America of the mid-twentieth century. Educated Latin Americans find it more and more difficult to look the other way. Latin Americans are active in the United Nations and in the specialized organizations associated with it. They have, for example, felt compelled, in the spirit of the Declaration of Human Rights, to observe more closely their internal problems. It is significant that women's suffrage has swept practically all of Latin America. Other more exciting factors are at work, too. For example, at the moment there is considerable international recrimination raging in the intimacy of Caribbean life. The Castro triumph in Cuba has fired the imagination and the courage of disaffected citizens of such countries as the Dominican Republic and Nicaragua. An abortive attempt to emulate the Castro technique in the mountains of Nicaragua apparently failed. Trujillo of the Dominican Republic called for investigation by the Organization of American States of an alleged invasion force staged in Cuba with Castro's approval. Even if these events do not herald immediate success, the trend does not favor existing paternalistic *caudillos.*

Constitutional presidents are increasing, and it is likely that the next few years will see a solidification of these in many cases and a wavering between these and military guardians in other cases. The military guardian waits in the wings for his cue practically everywhere. But out of this there emerges the conviction that Latin America may be entering the final phase toward solving the equation between constitutions and social institutions.

The only real doubt is one of time, not of promise. Latin American constitutionalism is a revolutionary commitment that awaits fulfillment, not death.

6

Trends in Social Thought
in Twentieth-century Latin America

Harold E. Davis

In the twentieth century, increased contact with world affairs and intellectual life has brought Latin America more fully into the general stream of Western thought. Rapid population growth and economic development have also brought many changes in society, increasing the tempo of social change and producing such political movements as the Mexican Revolution, Uruguayan *Batllismo,* Peruvian *aprismo,* and similar revolutionary developments in other countries. A population increase averaging around two per cent annually, and a rise in per capita income more rapid than the average increase in the United States during the years 1869–1952, go far to explain the striking increase in intellectual activity which has occurred. An additional factor of no mean significance, however, has been the immigration of refugee scholars resulting from the

From Harold E. Davis, "Trends in Social Thought in Twentieth-century Latin America," *Journal of Inter-American Studies,* Vol. I, No. 1 (January 1959). Reprinted by permission.

Spanish Civil War and World War II.

With more than half of the century now behind us, it is possible to view twentieth-century changes in Latin America with some historical perspective. What we see is an intellectual renaissance much greater than has usually been realized. Indeed, it may well be described as an intellectual explosion —a veritable flood of writing of all sorts. In the realm of social thought one sees, of course, the continuation of older scientific positivism, influenced by the new trends in psychology, sociology, economics, and political philosophy. Twentieth-century revisions of Marxism, including Russian Communist philosophy, continue to guide the minds of many writers. Most notable, however, are certain new trends: existentialist relativism, both idealistic and naturalistic, the neothomistic accent upon universalism and upon social voluntarism, humanistic personalism, and relativistic empiricism. To these should be added certain influences of American origin which stemmed from the revolutionary movements mentioned and a particularly significant argument over the philosophy of history, with particular reference to America.

Persistence of Older Trends

Positivist social science

Comptian positivism and Spencerian evolutionary thought had animated most of the significant development in social science in the late nineteenth century. Their concept of a free secular society, in which increase of knowledge gradually brought the benefits of freedom and economic well-being, provided the guiding principles of the parties and leaders who brought political stability to many countries previously dominated by revolutionary regimes bred in petty personalist politics. In this connection it would be difficult to overemphasize the important contribution of positivist doctrines in Latin America. In the twentieth century these ideas continue to hold a place of prominence in the thought of Latin American scholars, and perhaps even more in the minds of political leaders trained in the schools of a previous generation. Social studies of all kinds multiply greatly in the twentieth century, and much of this increased scholarly activity is dominated by the social concepts of the earlier age. These ideas have been modified under certain contemporary influences, however, and present-day "scientific" social thought reflects all the doubts concerning rationalism, reason, progress, materialism, and the nature of scientific knowledge which have troubled the present generation everywhere.

The older Spencerian and Comptian doctrines continued to be taught quite generally in the universities, with modifications, of course, until World War II, and there is still much contemporary theory taught which may be termed positivist. As in the past, the dividing line between positivist social thought and evolutionary Marxism in the present century has often been thin, because of the similarity of their philosophical structure. It is so thin, in fact, that critics have often confused the two, intentionally or otherwise. The chief changes which may be seen in the sociological concepts of such twentieth-century "positivists" as Raúl Orgaz of Argentina, Carlos Vaz Ferreira of Uruguay, and Fernando Azevedo of Brazil stem in considerable measure from the psychologism of Gabriel Tarde and the syncretic sociology of Emile Durkheim. Tarde's concept of imitation has been widely accepted, while Durkheim's emphasis upon the religious roots of culture and upon social control through moral restraints imposed upon the individual by the group appears in much of the social theory taught in the schools. Among other ideas which have tended to reinforce positivist thought is the anthropological theory of Franz Boas, as it appears, for example in the Brazilian Gilberto Freyre. Quite generally in Brazil, and occasionally among such Spanish American philosophers as Enrique Molina of Chile, it is possible to see the pragmatism and pluralism of William James and John Dewey. In general, these new trends have tended to supplant the historical and evolutionary explanations of the past with an analysis concentrated more upon forces of the present.

Marxism

In various forms of revisionism, Marxism has continued to spread through the middle classes of the increasingly urban society of Latin America as well as in the ranks of the incipient labor movement. Despite its revolutionary associations, Marxism challenged few of the basic ideas of evolutionary positivism, except as it reduced social philosophies, along with religion, to the secondary role of ideologies reflecting economic interests. In the twentieth century, Marxism's basic concern with the labor movement led to an emphasis upon economic planning and industrialization not much different from that of positivism. But its continued emphasis on the class struggle distinguished it from positivist thought. Moreover, as twentieth-century positivism abandoned its historicism, another aspect of Marxism stood out more clearly. This was its emphasis upon a concept of historical process which was directed toward certain ends —a dialectic or historical argument which yielded meaning and hence could be the basis of firm social belief.

Socialist thought has achieved prominence in several of the basic political movements in twentieth-century Latin America: in the *Batllista* reforms in Uruguary, in the Mexican Revolution, in the *Aprista* movement in Peru, and in related movements in Bolivia, Venezuela, Cuba, Guatemala, and elsewhere. This has been a kind of *criollo* or American socialism. Yet in these movements Marxist ideas seem to have found more acceptance, or at least more avowed expression in economics, than in any recent political movement in the United States.

Generally speaking, socialism permeated the liberal and reforming social thought of the turn of the century in Latin America more than one would assume from the weakness of the socialist parties which maintained precarious existence in a few countries, or from the similar weakness of organized labor. Socialism was found largely among the intellectual middle class, in university circles, and among immigrant labor leaders, as in Argentina, Uruguay, Mexico, and Brazil. On the other hand, while Russian communism gained such notable intellectual converts in the 1920's as Carlos Mariátegui of Peru, it made small inroads into general intellectual life.

Although Socialist thought found expression in the Mexican Revolution and in the reforming philosophy of José Batlle in Uruguay, neither of these movements produced an outstanding spokesman of its theoretical basis, probably because they were basically nationalistic and pragmatic. Batlle and his brilliant disciple, the later president Baltazar Brum, are the best spokesmen of the Uruguay development, and the most obvious general aspect of their thought is its socialism. But although the political leadership and the legislative and constitutional improvisations of both were brilliant, neither did much more in respect to basic concepts than accept the quasi-socialist principles so widespread among liberal leaders of the early years of the century. The nationalist preoccupation appears even more clearly in Chile in the socialistic expressions of Pedro Aguirre Cerda, whose socialism seems to have been inspired or at least greatly affected by political opportunism. The agrarianism of the Mexican Revolution and the Peruvian *aprismo* of Carlos Mariátegui and Víctor Raúl Haya de la Torre, particularly *aprismo*, add the most distinctive note to socialist thought, linking *indigenismo* with a Marxist analysis of the social or labor movements. Alfredo Palacios, who represents an older generation in Argentina, typifies numerous spokesmen of the older, pre-Lenin, socialism who are still to be found.

Communist thought of the second quarter of the century appears in two quite distinct forms: the unimaginative, "party-line" writing and that of such spokesmen as Juan Marinello of Cuba, and the Brazilian Luis Carlos Prestes. Marinello and Prestes, though closely identified with Communist tendencies, have retained considerable independence of thought. For artists like Diego Rivera of Mexico and poets like Pablo Neruda of Chile, communism seems to have been chiefly an expression of protest.

New Directions

Spanish influences

As in the past, Latin American thought has oscillated between Americanizing and Europeanizing influences. The European influences come from various sources, but notably from Spanish writers, who once again assume a role suggestive of Spaniards of an earlier age. The literary and philosophical renaissance which, ironically, accompanied Spain's loss of the vestiges of her empire in the New World and the Far East became a major stimulus to Spanish intellectual influence in Spanish America. Once again Spain has produced great poets such as Juan Ramón Jiménez, historians like Rafael Altamira, and philosophers of world renown like Miguel Unamuno and José Ortega y Gassett.

Unamuno and Ortega have considerable influence in Latin America, much more in certain countries than in others. Ortega popularized existentialist views derived from Wilhelm Dilthey and other Germanic sources, while Unamuno brought from Sören Kierkegaard a dramatic emphasis on the tragic sense of life, the proof of God on the basis of this sense of tragedy and suffering, the quest for meaning in Spanish history, as well as a special emphasis on personalism in his philosophy. Unamuno's appeal to Spanish America was enhanced by his interest in Spanish American literature and history. Like Bergson, he believed there was a kind of historical thinking distinct from that of science. His philosophy made history a sequence of states of belief, thus equating history with faith and making freedom a product of belief. Ortega's

identification as the spiritual father of the Spanish Republic added to his influence upon the liberal thought of Spanish America, while his fundamental belief that an intellectual elite must guide the masses, whose inevitable growth tended to degrade everything, had a natural appeal in a class-conscious society. Rival ideological loyalties arising from the Spanish Civil War make it difficult to assess the influence of Ortega and Unamuno objectively, but it would seem to be great.

Among the Spanish influences also to be noted is that of the vague and diffuse Krausism, which was popularized in Spain through the teaching of Julián Sanze del Río and was passed on to Spanish America in the late nineteenth century. Karl Christian Krause (1781–1832) was a disciple of Hegel, but also showed some influence from the metaphysics of Kant. He evolved an idealist philosophy in which God was equated with conscience, man and the universe were merged in a kind of pantheism, while man and society were assumed to develop in the image of God. Thus, as society became more closely integrated, man became God. Effects of this religious humanism may be seen in many young Spanish American writers and political leaders of the early years of this century, giving a religious idealism to their social consciousness.

The introduction of Krausism into Mexico centered around the use of the philosophy textbook of the Belgian Krausist Tiberghien. Its Mexican advocate, Teléforo García, emphasized the ideals of "God, *patria,* and liberty" in attacks upon the "conservatism" of positivist social thought. These ideas animated the minds of many of the younger followers of Francisco Madero in the Revolution of 1910. In Argentina, this "spiritualist" philosophy had a profound influence upon the leader of the Radical party, President Hipólito Irigoyen. In Uruguay it helped to form the idealism initiated with the writings of José Enrique Rodó, while in Peru Alejandro Deústua acknowledged his debt to Krausism, especially for the idea that liberty is grace. "Spiritism," which has become popular in Brazil, is also a related phenomenon, although it seems to have other roots as well in the persistent Kantian influence in Brazil.

Spanish America, particularly, reacted to this Spanish renaissance with a revived optimism and confidence which often was associated with pan-hispanism and the literary Yankee-phobia of the early decades of this century, as in the writing of Rodó, Manuel Ugarte, and Rubén Darío. But the philosophical interest which it aroused stirred more profound inquiry as well.

Existentialist philosophies

The most significant new directions, however, are what may be termed existentialist in a broad sense. They have roots in the irrationalism, intuitionism, and "creative evolution" of Henri Bergson, but derive more particularly from the Danish Sören Kierkegaard (by way of Unamuno) and from such German writers as Wilhelm Dilthey, Edmund Husserl, and Martin Heidegger. These, and other authors who have been widely read, represent a wide span in thought, joined chiefly by their common acceptance of being or existence as reality. Many of the German philosophers, particularly, first became known in Latin America through the pages of Ortega's *Revista del Occidente,* and not a little of Ortega's influence rubbed off in the process of their introduction to Latin American readers.

Acceptance of existence as reality led these "existentialists" to reject the Cartesian dichotomy of matter and idea, subject and object. Questioning the positivist idea of gradual progress, they tended to reject deterministic and evolutionary views of history. Sometimes a general tendency which might be termed "relativist" has seemed to lead to increased scepticism and disillusion, but more frequently it has brought increased confidence in the possibility of decision-making in history. As will be noted later, a lively argument over philosophy of history is one of the outstanding characteristics of today.

Personalism and humanism

One of the twentieth-century trends, of which Antonio Caso and Samuel Ramos of Mexico furnish examples, is what may be termed personalist and humanist. It is personalist in that it seeks the freedom of the individual from social determinism and humanist in regarding man as more than animal, though less than God, and in making philosophy neither primarily theological nor rationalistic. This personalism has numerous roots, including Nietzsche and Miguel Unamuno. A Krausist influence may be seen, as well as ideas from Bergson and William James. Sometimes this thought tends toward the stoic idealism earlier expressed by Rodó, manifesting ties with Renan. Stressing individual freedom within the limits of the cultural tradition, this kind of thinking has often, but not always, tended toward conservativism in its social thought. In particular it has been critical of reform proposals emanating from the socialist labor movement. Frequently it has been supported by literary and political pan-hispanism. This philosophical trend readily suggests comparisons with such literary humanists in the United States as Norman Foerster and Irving Babbit, as well as with the "personalist" philosophers—Edgar S. Brightman and his disciples.

Neo-Thomism

When Jacques Maritain launched his attack on the secularism and "anti-Christian" tendencies of the Bergsonian philosophy of intuitionism and creative evolution in the early years of this century, his ideas made a great appeal in Catholic Latin America, partly because they seemed to be a clear response to the appeal to philosophers made by Pope Leo XIII in the Encyclical *Rerum Novarum*. But although Maritain found many followers in Latin America, their voices were not heard much until after the 1930's, when the Spanish Civil War had aroused political passions, stimulating an anti-Marxist Christian labor movement and a lay movement for social action within the Church.

Since that time a revival of religious commitment may be seen among political leaders and in political movements. Several philosophers have dedicated themselves to reinterpretation of the philosophy of Aquinas, attempting to do for the twentieth century, and its bewilderment over the nature of being and knowledge, what the latter did for the thirteenth. Like Aquinas, they are searching for universals within the new scientific knowledge in biology, psychology, and physics. Whether these neo-Thomists and neo-Aristotelians really restore God and theology to the heart of philosophy as they claim, or whether they merely create an illusion to that effect, their influence upon social thought has been great, if for no other reason than the emphasis they give to social voluntarism and their consistent opposition to Marxism. Insofar as they share Saint Thomas' preoccupation with the problem of being, they tend to find a common ground with existentialists. Many of them, accordingly, assert what is a kind of troubled Christian existentialism.

Representatives of the neo-Thomist trend in Brazil include Jackson de Figueiredo, whose education, strangely, began in a Protestant mission school, and Alceu Amoroso Lima (Tristan de Athaide) whose *O problema do trabalho* shows clearly the *Rerum Novarum* influence in its discussion of the social significance of labor. The philosopher Clarence Finlayson and the journalist-politician Eduardo Frei M. represent the tendency in Chile, while Nicolás Derisi of the Catholic School of Philosophy and Theology in San Miguel, Argentina, and the late Oswaldo Robles of the National University of Mexico are other gifted spokesmen, each displaying elements of originality.

Americanism

Scholarly and scientific study by Latin Americans of their society, people, and geography has increased notably in the decades since World War I. Archaeology has opened up new vistas in indigenous history, while anthropological studies have widened acquaintance with the traits of native cultures and with the processes of cultural change, particularly transculturation, which have affected the mestizo and Afro-American peoples. Most of this study is merely an extension of scientific activity within previously established principles (generally "scientific" or "positivist") and raises little or no question concerning its theoretical or philosophical premises. It is possible, however, to discern in it a general trend away from the older nineteenth-century positivist premises of racial and cultural determinism. A number of writers have gone further along the lines of anthropological and historical philosophy in an effort to find a theoretical basis. Among these a number have looked for elements which may be presumed to distinguish thought and art in America or to give to American history some meaning which is distinctly its own. The resulting trends in thought, based upon aspects of American experience or existence, sometimes lay claim to being American philosophies. Usually they are pluralistic, empirical, naturalistic, and one frequently discerns the influence of North American anthropological thought, particularly that of the Franz Boas school. Occasionally, however, this Americanist quest is couched in neoidealistic terms.

Indigenismo

Studies of the indigenous peoples have been a significant source of this element of Americanism. These studies have often received official support through UNESCO, the Inter-American Indianist Institute, and various national institutes and museums, as well as private support from North American foundations and universities. Scholars connected with the French *Societé des Americanistes* have also played a role. Emphasis upon *indigenismo* appears in the literature and programs of the Mexican Revolution, in Peruvian APRA, in the Guatemalan Revolution under José Arévalo, and elsewhere. In some respects it is a more profound reassertion of the concept sometimes expressed by independence leaders, that the cultural history of America is significantly continuous with that of the pre-Conquest civilizations. Such a theory makes of indigenous cultures and their influence much more than a sociopolitical problem. It introduces cultural value-concepts to condition the science which seeks to analyze and ameliorate these twentieth-century problems. It is also accompanied by a profound disquietude, not limited by any means to America, but which in this continent has prompted philosophical inquiry into the meaning of the

term American and the concept of man which has developed in America. This line of inquiry has provided additional historical depth to our understanding of the constant vacillation in American thought between Europeanizers and Americanizers, by revealing the extent to which this process had its origin in the very discovery and colonization of America.

The study of history shows this indigenous influence clearly in Mexico, where the basing of national history upon indigenous origins has had obvious social usefulness in the assimilation of the native peoples. The concept of the continuity of Indian history through the period of European domination has resulted in a distinctly new perspective in American history and, accordingly, has produced a number of efforts to establish the significant epochs or decisive historical moments from this standard point.

Afro-Americanism, like *indigenismo*, has directed attention to non-European cultural influences which also appear among the results of American experiences. But its effect upon social thought seems, on the whole, to have been less profound than that of *indigenismo*. The racism and geographic determinism of Da Cunha continued for many years to influence such writers as Arthur Ramos, and to inspire regional novels expressing such ideas in Brazil. A note more distinctive of the twentieth-century was struck by Gilberto Freyre in his *Casa grande e senzala*. Freyre portrays the Negro outlook from within a changing culture, with special emphasis upon the effects of slavery as distinct from those of race. As he presents it, the process seems to escape mechanical determinism, both that of culture and of geography. At the same time, it asserts a cultural regionalism which enables the author to see many attitudes and cultural values in the Brazilian areas of former plantation-slave economy which are similar to those in North America. In somewhat similar vein, Fernando Ortiz of Cuba, in his studies of sugar production and of Negro cultural influences, has pointed to cultural influences which may be considered American.

A different kind of American philosophy, taking the form of a *mystique* of the land, has developed in Indian and mestizo Bolivia, perhaps reflecting some influence from the indigenous worship of nature. There a group of writers, including Franz Tamayo, Roberto Prudencio, Humberto Plaza, and Fernando Díez de Medina, ascribe to the Bolivian landscape the source of a spirit which is communicated in some mystic way to the subconscious in man, thus giving form to American culture and American thought. An idea of the Cuban Fernando Ortiz is similar, though it avoids the mysticism. Ortiz has found in the spiral form of the hurricane a cultural symbol whose highest expression is the generalized deification of the plumed serpent.

Sometimes the pursuit of an American element or influence in culture has led to the quest for an American aesthetic, as in Ricardo Rojas's *Eurindia,* or Luis Alberto Sánchez's *Vida y pasión de la cultura en América.* Pedro Henríquez Ureña, in his *Historia de la cultura en la América hispánica,* has traced the development of what he conceives to be distinctively American in the literature of Hispanic America.

The idea of man in America

Felix Schwartzmann of Chile has propounded the existence of a distinct concept of man, or of the human, in America. This idea, which he finds based upon experiences peculiar to American existence, should, he believes, furnish the key to the interpretation of American cultural history, and the phases of its trajectory should determine the epochs of American historiography.

Philosophy of history

This pursuit of Americanism, as might well be expected, has given special significance and a distinctive direction to the lively argument over philosophy of history in recent years. An argument over history has always characterized the Latin American scene in some degree, for nineteenth-century Latin Americans, as Leopoldo Zea has so clearly pointed out, rejected their historical past during their independence movements, as they later rejected the doctrines of evolutionary historical and economic determinism developed in European thought. Even when they accepted the idea of a natural and inevitable progress, their nineteenth-century historians continued to write national history in terms of the revolutionary natural-rights rationalism, displaying an almost complete preoccupation with national political history.

This inherited American view that the history of American nations was the building of a new civilization upon the ruins of the old inevitably gave a somewhat different turn in Latin America to the contemporary disillusionment of the Occidental world concerning history based upon inevitable and evolutionary progress. The neo-Hegelianism of Benedetto Croce, Oswald Spengler's concept of the decline of civilization, the Christian ecumenicalism of Arnold Toynbee, Unamuno's tragic existentialist view that history is the source of personal and cultural values, and the neoidealist existentialism of German origin expressed in the Spanish speaking world by Ortega y Gassett—these philosophies of history have had great vogue and have not lacked spokesmen in twentieth-century Latin America. But the advent of historical disillusionment also happened to coincide with a period of revolutionary social and political change —the Mexican Revolution, *Batllismo* in Uruguay, *aprismo* in Peru, and similar movements which called for social philosophies of action. Particularly in the case of the literature of the Mexican Revolution and that of *aprismo* in Peru, it is possible to see a special significance for the discussion of the meaning and philosophy of history.

An extensive and often vindictive argument over the nature and philosophy of the Mexican Revolution was initiated in 1935 with the publication of José Vasconcelos' controversial and widely read autobiography. The rapid pace of agrarian and labor reform under the presidency of Lázaro Cárdenas was arousing increased resistance in certain quarters, while the Spanish Civil War sharpened the conflict over socialist measures in Mexico as elsewhere in Spanish America. This mounting feeling gave a special pungency to the charges exchanged between the partisans of Madero, Carranza, Obregón, and Cárdenas in the form of reminiscences and polemics. While the argument failed to eventuate in a definitive expression of a social philosophy of the revolution, it served the purpose of bringing the divergent views more clearly into focus and stimulated the interest in an interpretation of Mexican history which has since become so striking a characteristic of the Mexican intellectual scene.

As in the past, twentieth-century Latin Americans have seemed to reject the more pessimistic and fatalistic views of history, preferring to find in Ortega, Croce, or Unamuno a philosophy which permitted historical decision-making, assigned a significant role to leaders, and accepted the possibility of change by revolution. Thus the increased interest in history brought new defenders

of Bolívar, not only in Venezuela, but elsewhere as well. San Martín's glory was revived upon the centenary of his death, and even Agustín Iturbide assumed more importance in the history of Mexico. At the same time, the exploitation of history for political purposes by Mussolini and Hitler stimulated a tendency to magnify the historical importance of Latin American "strong men" such as Diego Portales of Chile, Justo José Urquiza of Argentina, Antonio Guzmán Blanco of Venezuela, and Porfirio Díaz of Mexico.

The history of revolutions, and their critical analysis, has interested Latin Americans since the days of national independence, beginning with José M. Mora's *Means of Preventing Revolutions*. Early in this century Enrique José Varona had criticized contemporary revolutions as sterile, predicting the day, however, in which the forces of socialism and caesarism would "come like hurricanes." Around the year 1930 three Argentines produced significant studies of revolution: Alfredo Poviña, Antonio Grompone, and Alfredo Colmo. Luis Alberto Sánchez of Peru has also sought the meaning and popular basis of revolutionary change in America in a book entitled *The People in the American Revolution*.

José Gaos, who found refuge from Franco Spain in Mexico, influenced the thinking of a group of younger scholars there who were interested in the philosophy of history. Among this group was Edmundo O'Gorman who, while retaining the Hegelian concept of America as a land without a history (note how he differs from the *indigenistas*), has found the central meaning of America in a concept of experience in applying natural laws to the creation of a better society. His examination of the nature of historical knowledge, à la Heidegger, leads him to the existentialist concept that historical knowledge is authentic only "when the reality examined is raised to the level of personal revelation."

Leopoldo Zea, another of this group, has distinguished himself especially for his studies of the history of thought in Mexico and Spanish America. His neo-Hegelian interpretation emphasizes the paradox that Latin American thought began with an outright repudiation of the authority of historical tradition—that of Europe—yet has always sought to create a history of its own within the Occidental tradition.

Víctor Raúl Haya de la Torre, the organizer and leader of the *Aprista* party in Peru for more than a quarter of a century, is a Marxist theoretician of originality. He retains the concept of history as a dialectical process. But in his famous essay on historical time-space he accepts a philosophy of general relativism and pluralism which leads him to accept the idea of many histories and thus to find an historical basis for an American socialism distinct from that of Europe. Although his approach is fundamentally different from that of Haya, Gilberto Freyre resembles him in his pluralistic approach to the history of cultures. Interpreting the psychology of a culture from within, he too arrives at a regional concept—of regions determined by American cultural experiences as well as by geographic factors. In passing, it may be noted that the article from *Voprosy Istorii*...calls Freyre a "vulgar sociologist...under the baneful influence of various North American subjectivist schools," but does not even mention Haya de la Torre.

General Characteristics

It should hardly be necessary to point out the danger of generalizing concerning twentieth-century Latin American thought when its most obvious aspects are its wide variety and its manifest vigor. In fact, this vigorous emphasis upon speculative and philosophical aspects of the study of society and culture may well be one of the reasons for the obvious lag in descriptive and analytical studies in some branches. Perhaps no Latin American writer quite achieves the stature of an Unamuno or an Ortega y Gassett, but a very considerable number begin to approximate the ability of these two outstanding philosophers. Hardly a country lacks at least one writer who focuses the attention of students of social developments upon the problems connected with their underlying philosophical assumptions.

A few generalizations may be ventured. The newly critical writers of Latin America have generally turned against the evolutionary-historical social science which was so prevalent at the end of the last century. Marxist concepts may be somewhat more generally held than in the United States, but hardly more than in western Europe. Cultural relativism and pluralism are also widespread, particularly in Brazil, but seemingly less, on the whole, than in North America. One may also notice a general Latin American trend toward philosophical idealism, as contrasted with the prevalent naturalism, empirical and pragmatic, of philosophers in the United States and Britain. At least this is true if the term idealism is made broad enough to include such trends as those represented in Unamuno and Ortega, as well as the Kantian and Spiritist trends in Brazil. Even some of the neo-Thomism may be included, for the latter is far from being consistently Aristotelian.

The preoccupation of Latin American thought with what is American deserves a special note. Too much reading between the lines is not needed in order to see that while, philosophically, this is an interest in America in the continental sense, it is Spanish (occasionally Portuguese) American first, and continental, secondarily. It tempts one to see in it a reflection of the relentless

Spanish American quest for closer cultural, economic, and political unity.

Neo-Thomist thought, and its corollary social voluntarism, are indeed notable in the Latin American scene, and this may partly explain why the discussion of the philosophy of history has been somewhat less pessimistic than in other parts of the Occident. Even more likely causes, however, are the prevalence of idealist tendencies and the persistent emphasis upon the quest for an American meaning in American history. Whatever the cause, the result seems to be a rather general Latin American insistence upon a view of history in which man has freedom to move toward higher social goals. Many writers, but not all, would find the basis for this view in some specifically American concept.

This brief sketch of social-thought trends in Latin America leaves several important areas untouched. Perhaps the most notable of these is that of juridical thought, both in its domestic and its international aspects. Even a brief examination of this branch of literature, all too little known to scholars outside Latin America, would require another essay of this length. The literature of literary and art criticism is another area of great importance which has scarcely been touched upon here.

Interest in the analysis of these and other contemporary trends is growing, however, as indicated by the writing of Leopoldo Zea, Samuel Ramos, and Francisco Larroyo, of Mexico, João Cruz Costa of Brazil, Guillermo Francovich of Bolivia, and others. A series of studies currently emanating from the Inter-American Institute of Geography and History is providing much better bases for evaluation. At the same time, the rapid development of social science gives rise to hope that these fruitful ideas may begin to find concrete expression in valuable research.

7

Conditions Favoring
the Rise of Communism in Latin America

Robert J. Alexander

...The social classes which have been particularly active in the Latin American social revolution have been the working class, both the white-collar and the manual workers, and the growing industrial (and to some degree commercial) middle class. It was their voices, their votes, their money, and their strong right arms which, upon occasion, broke the crust of the landholder-dominated, semifeudal Latin American society of the days before World War I.

The Latin American social revolution has had four basic components: nationalism, economic development, change in class relationships, and political democracy. The Communists have tried with greater or less success to use each and all of these factors in their propaganda and organization.

As nationalism has spread in the modern world, Latin America has caught the infection. Generally, the growing nationalism of Latin America has taken the form of a desire to be "free" from real or alleged subservience

From Robert J. Alexander, *Communism in Latin America* (New Brunswick, N.J.: Rutgers University Press, 1957). Reprinted by permission.

to certain of the great powers. This has often led to a feeling of unity among the Latin Americans themselves, and perhaps helps to explain why growing nationalism has not more often been turned against Latin American neighbors.

Latin American nationalism has been largely "anti-imperialism." During World War I and the post-World War I period, it centered on the struggle against United States interference in the internal affairs of the Latin American countries, against United States invasions of Nicaragua, Mexico, the Dominican Republic, Haiti, and other countries, and against evidences of Latin American subservience to the United States, such as the infamous Platt Amendment to the Cuban constitution.

With the Good Neighbor Policy, and the agreement by the United States to recognize the juridical equality of all of the American nations, the emphasis shifted from opposing overt intervention by the United States Government to resisting what many Latin Americans conceived to be the intervention by United States private business interests in the internal affairs of their nations.

There developed a widespread resentment toward foreign ownership of key elements in the Latin American economy. Expropriation of United States agricultural and petroleum interests in Mexico and of American petroleum interests in Bolivia before World War II, as well as repatriation of British and French investments in the public utilities and railroads of Argentina, Uruguay, and Brazil after World War II, were evidences of this feeling.

The two world wars and the great depression undoubtedly fed the fires of nationalism in Latin America. During World War II, in particular, the Latin Americans were actively courted by both sides. They also were impressed with the importance to the Allied war effort of their provision of key raw materials and supplies. The importance of their role was even more evident to the citizens of Brazil and Mexico, because of the participation of their forces in the victorious armies.

The wars and the depression particularly aroused economic nationalism. The Latin American countries, whose role in the world economy had been largely that of producers of agricultural and mineral raw materials, became painfully aware of the dangers of an economy based on one or two such products.

In both wars and the depression, the Latin American countries had difficulty both in selling their mineral and agricultural products and in obtaining the manufactured goods which they needed from the industrial nations of Europe and North America. Those experiences convinced most thinking Latin Americans that their nations must become more self-sufficient. They became eager to diversify their countries' economies, and in particular to develop manufacturing industries.

This drive for economic development has become an integral part of the Latin American social revolution. Since the early 1930's, it has become almost an article of faith. Few politicians in the region would dare openly to proclaim opposition to industrialization and economic diversification. Virtually all of the countries have provided protection for infant industries, either through old-fashioned tariffs or through more newfangled exchange control devices. Many of the countries have established development banks or corporations, which have brought the government into active participation in the process of economic development.

The net result of this growing economic diversification has been to strengthen the urban against the rural elements in the economic and political life of the Latin American nations. It has also hastened the demands for fundamental redistribution of power in the economies and politics of the Latin American nations.

This class realignment is the third fundamental feature of the Latin American social revolution. It has taken two principal forms: a demand for agrarian reform, and moves to strengthen the position of the urban worker by organizing him for his self-defense and writing legislation on his behalf.

With the exception of Mexico, agrarian reform has at first been urged and promulgated by city folk. However, it has been the means of involving the agricultural worker and tenant in the civic and economic life of his community and nation. It is likely that pressure will come, increasingly, from the agricultural worker himself for an extension of agrarian reform in such parts of the region as it has not yet encompassed.

The growth of the trade-union movement and of protective legislation has also been an integral part of the realignment of classes. It has been closely associated with the nationalist drive, since the first large conglomerations of wageworkers were usually those employed by foreign enterprises—railroads, public utilities, mines, factory farms, and manufacturing enterprises—and labor organization thus took on a patriotic coloration. Union organizations, strikes, and other movements aimed against foreign-owned enterprises were often able to enlist a general sympathy in the community which they probably never would have aroused had the firms involved been owned and operated by nationals.

Labor legislation and trade unionism have been surprisingly advanced for the type of economy which Latin America has possessed. By the end of World War II there was virtually no nation in Latin America which did not have its labor code—detailing the treatment of labor in factory legislation, social security, regulation of collective bargaining, and support and control of trade unions.

In virtually every nation the great majority of "organizable" workers— those on railroads, docks, and ships, in factories, in public utilities, even in many factory farms—are now in trade unions. These workers' organizations are still weak, being too dependent upon the good will of a political party or the state, but they have succeeded in arousing the working class to its possibilities and, in a more limited way, to its responsibilities.

The growth of strong middle and working classes has had profound effects on the social, economic, and political structure of Latin America. In Mexico and Chile power over the state passed from the landholding aristocracy to the urban middle and working masses— though in the latter case, the city folk had not dared even by the 1950's to attack the aristocracy in its rural strongholds and carry out an effective agrarian reform.

In other countries, too, political power changed hands. The Vargas Revolution of 1930, despite all the subsequent vagaries, effectively took control of the national government out of the hands of the rural landholders, though there, as in Chile, the new political forces did not dare attack the aristocracy on its own home ground. The Perón Revolution, whatever else it brought, ended once and for all the control of the rural landlords and cattle barons over the destinies of Argentina.

The 1952 revolution in Bolivia signalized the end of the feudal era in that country. Events since the death of Juan Vicente Gómez in 1936 have greatly undermined the position of the rural landholding element in Venezuela, though that unfortunate country had not by 1957 been able to throw off the century-old curse of military domination of political affairs.

In all the countries in which the shift in class power has begun, it is a continuing process, in most cases still far from completion. Even in Mexico, the revolution which began in 1910 was still 45 years later a living and evolving phenomenon.

In some countries the shift in class relations had not occurred by the early 1950's. In Peru it lagged behind, the alliance of the military with the traditional landowning and mercantile classes keeping a firm if uneasy grip on the nation. Central America was still largely controlled by large landowners and military men. The dictatorship of Generalissimo Rafael Leónidas Trujillo had converted the traditional system of the Dominican Republic into a personal monopoly of power and wealth.

The shift in class relationships was accompanied by a struggle for political democracy. This is the fourth element in the Latin American social revolution.

The desire on the part of the masses of the people of Latin America for greater participation in the affairs of their government, and for the fundamental freedoms associated with political democracy, was profound indeed. However, the great danger in the Latin American social revolution has been that it might be diverted from democratic channels, that democracy might be sacrificed to achieve the other objectives of the revolution. This certainly occurred in Argentina under Perón. The Communists, too, have constantly sought—though frequently using democratic slogans—to direct the revolution into courses which would result in the establishment of their own particular brand of totalitarianism.

The Communists have consistently attempted to use all the slogans of the Latin American social revolution for their own propaganda. They have striven especially hard to portray themselves as ardent nationalists of the particular countries in which they were operating.

The Communists have embraced "anti-imperialism" with a vengeance. During most of their history they have been violently opposed to the United States' economic, political, and social influence in Latin America. Only during the late 1930's and the second part of World War II, when their "anti-imperialist" propaganda was directed against Axis influence in Latin America, have they modified their "anti-*Yanqu-ism.*"

During the 1920's and early 1930's the Communists had some success in enlisting Latin Americans in their worldwide campaign against "imperialism." Many Latin American intellectuals, including Haya de la Torre, people who were later active in the Venezuelan Democratic Action Party, and other non-Communists, were among the delegates to the World Congress Against War and Imperialism of 1928. Many of them continued to be active in the League Against Imperialism founded at the 1928 meeting and in the several Anti-war and Anti-imperialist Congresses held in America.

Since World War II the Communist campaign against the United States in Latin America has been renewed with increased intensity. Campaigns "for peace" and "against *Yanqui* imperialism" became the principal pre-occupation of the Latin American Communists.

In spite of the Latin American Communists' attempt to portray themselves as true-blue nationalists, it has been too obvious, in many instances, that their basic orientation was Russian, not Chilean or Brazilian or Argentine. This was particularly true during World War II. In the beginning they adopted a violent "anti-imperialist" position, aimed against the Allies and against the United States, and in some instances even bordered on anti-Semitism, so violent were their sympathies for the Axis.

Then, with the entry of the Soviet Union into the war, the Communists of Latin America, as everywhere else, adopted an equally violent pro-war attitude. So extreme was their position of "support for the United Nations," that they used their influence in the labor movement throughout the continent to put a damper on virtually all attempts at strikes and other movements upon the part of the organized workers. Frequently, such movements were denounced by the Communists as being of Nazi inspiration or worse.

During the war, too, they were less cautious about hiding their association with the Soviet Union. They tried to use the widespread sympathy for the Soviet Union's bitter struggle against the Nazis to aid their own positions in their respective countries. This tended to rebound upon them in later years, when popular sympathy for the Soviet Union had to a very considerable degree turned into hostility.

The Communists also have attempted

to make use of the strong drive for economic development in the Latin American countries. This often fitted in very well with their opposition to the United States. They spread widely the idea that the United States was purposely trying to hold back the development of the Latin American countries. They were ardent advocates of the industrialization of Latin America and at the end of World War II went so far as virtually to advocate "calling off" the class struggle for a longer or shorter period of time, so as to form an alliance between the labor movements they controlled or influenced and the national employers' groups. At various times they toyed with the idea that the national employers were a "progressive" element in the economies of the various countries of Latin America, and sought to enlist their support in the campaign against United States influence in Latin America.

Of course, the Communists have attempted to take the leadership, when the opportunity presented itself, in upsetting traditional class relationships in Latin American countries. Their own doctrine has naturally made them seek a leading position in the trade-union movements, and in some countries, such as Peru and Guatemala, Brazil and Cuba, they have attempted to develop support on the basis of appeals to suppressed racial groups—Indians in the first two instances, Negroes in the latter two.

From the early days the Communists have included in their programs demands for agrarian reform and other fundamental shifts in class and social relations in the Latin American countries. Only in Mexico and Guatemala have they had any real opportunity to take part in carrying out such changes, and in the former case they played only a very minor role.

At various times the Communists have attempted to theorize concerning the class changes which have been going on in Latin America. Their theories have varied with changes in the party line. Usually, however, they have urged that a bourgeois revolution of "national liberation" was the next step in the development of these countries; this was their line in Guatemala after World War II. However, they have also talked about a revolution which would result in the establishment of a "popular democracy" on the pattern of the early postWorld War II regimes of eastern Europe. This has been the line in Brazil and was adopted in Guatemala in the last months of the Arbenz regime. During the "Third Period" of the late 1920's and early 1930's the Communists tended to skip over the interim stages and seek the immediate establishment of an avowedly Communist regime. This was their line in Cuba, for instance, right after the fall of the Machado dictatorship in 1933, when they had the slogan of "Build the Soviets!" and actually attempted in some areas to establish their own governments on a local scale.

Finally, the Communists have attempted to capitalize on the fourth factor in the Latin American social revolution and depict themselves as supporters of democracy. There is no doubt that they have been severely persecuted by various Latin American governments from time to time, and they have pictured campaigns in defense of their own group as crusades for the general principles of political democracy and civil liberties. They laid particular stress on this role as defenders of the cause of democracy during World War II.

The Communists have thus attempted to use the rising tide of the Latin American social revolution as a means of bringing themselves to power. They have tried to seize the control of the revolutionary currents, and to divert them in the Communist direction. The surprising thing is not that they have occasionally succeeded in doing so, but rather that, in spite of the very profound feeling of revolt and change which has swept Latin America since World War I, the Communists have made comparatively little progress.

One of the key reasons why the Communists have not been more successful is that there have been other movements, of native Latin American origin, which have been able to seize and keep the leadership of the revolution in various countries. It is a very obvious fact that in any country in which there is another strong mass movement, the Communists have fared badly. Thus, in Peru, the Communists have never succeeded in getting any really wide base of support, and what importance they have had has come from the backing they have received from successive dictatorships. This has been due to the fact that the *Aprista* movement gained and held the support of the great masses of the people, who might otherwise have been influenced by Communist ideas and organization.

In Venezuela, too, the rise of the Democratic Action party completely checked the progress of the Communists, and again the Communists' influence was largely something engendered by the dictators to act as a check on the influence of Democratic Action. In Cuba, the *Auténtico* movement had the same effect; in Costa Rica, the rise of the *Liberación Nacional* movement of José Figueres cut the very base out from under the Communists. In Puerto Rico the rise of the Popular Democratic party of Muñoz Marín has undoubtedly prevented the Communists from getting a significant following.

Even in Argentina this same phenomenon has been repeated. The appearance of the *Peronista* movement in the middle 1940's undoubtedly had the result of checking the growing influence which the Communists had been enjoying inside and outside of the labor movement for about half a decade before the Peronista Revolution of 1943.

Chile and Guatemala further illustrate the fact that the best check for the Communists in Latin America has always been a native social revolutionary movement. The Communists in those two countries have been able to get real rank-and-file support and to wield tremendous influence on all aspects of the countries' life because of the lack of any such rival movement. In Chile such a movement existed in the decade of the 1930's in the Socialist party. However, as a result of a variety of circumstances the Socialist party crumbled away, and the Communist party gained an opportunity of which it made full use. Consequently, Chile was by the late 1940's one of the few countries in which the Communists had been able to build up a really substantial group of followers, who looked upon them as the only true defenders of the working class and the social revolution.

In Guatemala, the case was somewhat different, but equally informative. There, no rival social movement existed. As the result of peculiar circumstances, no leader and no party appeared able firmly to support and push forward the social revolution, but equally firmly reject Stalinism and all its works. As a consequence, in Guatemala the Communists achieved a degree of power which they probably have not obtained in any other Latin American nation and were able to build up a sizable body of popular support in the cities and in the countryside.

Those Latin American governments opposed to the social revolution have not infrequently worked with the Communists, in order to undermine the indigenous social revolutionary movements. This has been notoriously true of Peru and Venezuela. In the former country the Communists worked successively with the Sánchez Cerro, Benavides, Prado, and Odría dictatorships. In the elections of 1939 and 1950 Communists were elected to the dictator-controlled congress on the official ticket of the dictator. The Dictator-President Prado backed the Communists' bid for control of the labor movement, and General Odría in the late 1940's and early 1950's gave considerable help to the Communists in the labor movement.

In Venezuela, too, the dictatorial regimes opposed to the revolution worked with the Communists. While the democratically controlled trade unions were virtually destroyed after 1948, Communist-dominated unions continued to function with but little interference. Large public meetings were held by Communist trade unions, and they were allowed to hold regularly scheduled conventions. The work of the dictatorship was to turn control of a large part of the Venezuelan trade-union movement over to the Communists.

Dictator Anastasio Somoza, of Nicaragua, and Dictator Generalissimo Rafael Leónidas Trujillo, of the Dominican Republic, both worked with the Communists during a short period in the middle 1940's, using them to bolster up their tottering dictatorships. In both of those countries the Communists got their first real chance as a result of this coquetting with the dictators.

The prevalence of dictatorial regimes in Latin America led to the development of a policy which may or may not have been consciously planned by the international Communist leaders responsible for the operations of the Communist parties in Latin America. The widespread use of this new tactic, which was adopted in the late 1940's and early 1950's, makes it appear to be a well-designed, centrally directed move.

The tactic consisted of having more than one Communist party in dictator-controlled countries. One party, usually the "official" one, engaged in more or less bitter opposition to the dictatorship; the other, "unofficial" but nonetheless, in actuality, just as official, supported the regime. This tactic was adopted in Argentina, Peru, Venezuela, and Cuba. In Mexico, more than one Communist party was used, but for reasons which seem to be quite distinct from those in the other countries mentioned.

In Argentina the Communist party had some difficulty making up its mind concerning what position to take in regard to Perón. At first, so long as World War II was on, they bitterly opposed Perón, coining the term *"Peronazi"* to describe his followers. However, after the war was over, and after Perón had been elected president of the Republic, they faltered. The official party adopted a position of "critical support"; while a dissident faction broke away to form the Movimiento Obrero Comunista, under the leadership of former Politburo member Rodolfo Puiggros, which placed itself frankly in the *Peronista* ranks. In subsequent years, in spite of certain twistings and turnings, the official Communist party tended to continue to regard itself as part of the opposition, while the *Movimiento Comunista* was accepted as a fullfledged member of the Perón camp and came to have considerable influence in the inner circles of the Perón regime. It tried both to influence Perón and his followers in the Communist direction and to build up organizational strength in the *Peronista* trade unions.

In Peru the coming to power of the Odría dictatorship in 1948 resulted in the splitting of that country's Communist party. The "official" group, led by Secretary General Jorge del Prado, was outlawed and went into opposition to the Odría regime. Another element, led by the party's principal trade-union figure, Juan P. Luna, allied itself with the Odría regime, formed a Workers Independent Electoral Committee, and won a senator and various deputies in the Odría congress.

In Venezuela the split in the Communist movement was older, dating from the middle 1940's, when the Communist party split over the question of relations with the Medina Angarita dictatorship. Two separate parties were formed, one usually called the Red Communists, the other, the Black Communists. With the Army *coup d'état* in November 1948, which ousted the Democratic Action government, the Black Communists adopted a policy of friendship toward the resultant military dictatorship and, as a result, were allowed to function quite openly, maintaining a significant hold on the country's trade-union movement. The Red Communists, on the other hand, adopted a position of strong opposition to the military dictatorship and sought to work with the Democratic Action party.

In Cuba the same tactic was used, but with a somewhat different twist as a result of General Batista's *coup d'état* in March 1952. After a short period of hesitation, the Communist party officially took a position of opposition to the dictatorship. However, a significant number of Communist trade-union leaders withdrew from the party and joined the "Labor Bloc" of Batista's own *Partido Acción Progresista*. The P.A.P. was weak in labor support and welcomed them with open arms. The "unofficial" Communists were able to make some progress in rebuilding the Communists' trade-union strength, which had been completely destroyed during the democratic administrations of Presidents Grau San Martín and Carlos Prío Socarrás.

The split in Mexico has been of a somewhat different nature. It originated in considerable part from the prima donna attitude of Vicente Lombardo Toledano. During the 1940's Lombardo Toledano became the kingpin in the Communists' trade-union activities in Latin America, but he refused to join the official Communist party of Mexico, with whom he had fought many bitter battles in past years. Instead, he organized his own *Partido Popular* in 1947, which did not apparently lessen his position vis-à-vis the top leaders of the international Communist movement.

There is no doubt that, in some cases, democratic governments have also given aid and comfort to the Communists and have helped them to gain positions of importance. During World War II this tendency was widely prevalent. The Communists at that time were more pro-United Nations than the United Nations themselves, and their weight was welcomed in the fight against nazism and fascism both inside and outside of Latin America. The Communists won more freedom of operation, and not infrequently actual aid, from the governments of Latin America during that period than during any other part of their history.

In particular cases, democratic leaders have worked with or used the Communists. This was true of President Lázaro Cárdenas of Mexico during the 1930's. He was in the midst of a severe struggle to carry forward agrarian reform and other aspects of his revolutionary program, and he welcomed any support he could get. The Communists were allowed to occupy important posts in the government-sponsored and oriented labor movement, the *Confederación de Trabajadores de Mexico*. During subsequent administrations the Communists lost most, if not all, of the ground they had gained during the Cárdenas period.

In Guatemala, too, the history of the late 1940's and early 1950's is one of the democratic government leaders working with and giving strong support to the Communists. Such instances have occurred, as well, in Chile under González Videla in 1946–1947; in Ecuador on various occasions; in Colombia during the late 1930's and early 1940's, in Costa Rica during the administrations of Presidents Calderón Guardia and Teodoro Picado, to mention but a few examples.

One other factor has played a certain part in whatever success the Communists have had in Latin America— sympathy for the Soviet Union. It was to a very considerable extent admiration of the Russian Revolution which led to the founding of the Latin American Communist parties. The Anarchists of Brazil were very sympathetic, and out of their ranks came the Brazilian Communist party; the Socialist parties of Uruguay and Chile went over as such to the Communist International, largely because they wanted to be ranged alongside the "first workers' republic."

In the early years picturing the successes of "building socialism" in the Soviet Union was a very important part of the propaganda of the Latin American Communist parties, and aroused a good deal of sympathy, perhaps more among the intellectuals than among the manual workers.

The great era of the Soviet appeal, however, was during World War II. At that time the sympathy of the workers and the middle class people of Latin America was overwhelmingly with the Allies, and there was very widespread admiration for the way in which the Red Army first stood off and then rolled back the armies of Hitler.

The Communists capitalized to the utmost upon this wartime sympathy for the Soviet Union. They became almost the principal spokesmen for the Russians—or at least seemed to be regarded as such by many in the Latin American countries. They urged closer relations with "our great ally," the Soviet Union, and various Latin American countries during this period recognized or rerecognized the Soviet Union. Relations were close between the new Russian embassies or legations and the Communist parties of the various countries. There was little or no attempt to hide the close relationship between the Communists of Latin America and those of the Soviet Union. On the contrary, every attempt was made to capitalize upon this relationship.

The tide of sympathy for the Soviet Union ebbed after the war, a feeling of hostility developed in many parts as a result of the intensification of the Cold War, and the close relation of the Communists with the Russians lost its appeal. They became less ostentatious about it, and it seems likely that distrust arising from this relationship was a considerable factor in alienating a large part of the Latin American working class in the postwar years. Local Latin American nationalisms were ruffled by the professed adherence of the Communists to the Soviet Union.

In the early 1950's the Communists used their Soviet connections in still another way. Although they never ceased to picture the beauties of life in the Soviet Union, they began to lay emphasis on a somewhat more practical aspect of the subject. Resentment was widespread in many Latin American countries against the great dependence of their economies on that of the United States. The Communists, of course, helped in any way they could to stir up this resentment. One of their most potent arguments was to picture trade with the Soviet Union, eastern Europe, and China as an answer to this excessive dependence on the United States.

The Chilean Communists were using this argument as early as 1946–1947, when the González Videla government recognized the Soviet Union, a Soviet Embassy was established, and rumors flew that González was willing to negotiate with the Russians concerning the export of the country's copper output— which at that time was still selling at a low price fixed by United States authorities.

Later this became a theme exploited throughout the hemisphere. The success of some of the countries of western Europe in negotiating limited trade treaties with the Soviet Union contributed to a widespread belief that such trade accords could be reached by Latin America. The negotiation of a treaty between Argentina and the Soviet Union in September 1953, for the exchange of about $150,000,000 worth of goods each way further contributed to the popularity of this idea.

The Communists, naturally, did their utmost to publicize the virtues of the Communist countries as trading partners. In Bolivia they suggested such trade as a possible solution to the pressing tin problem. In Guatemala they encouraged the government actually to undertake negotiations with the Communist countries. Various Latin American groups attended the Moscow Economic Conference in 1952, though no concrete results seem to have been achieved by them there, and some of the delegates, at least, returned without any great enthusiasm.

Such success as the Communists have had in Latin America has been due, then, to three principal factors: their ability to exploit the Latin American social revolution; help which they have received from various governments, dictatorial and democratic; and their more or less close connection with the Soviet Union.

On the other hand, their chief stumbling blocks in the area have undoubtedly been indigenous social revolutionary movements which have been able to capture the imagination of the people of the various countries and to lead these people down the road to social, economic, and political change without making them instruments of international Stalinism and the Soviet state; and the ability of the United States and other non-Communist countries to demonstrate to the Latin American peoples that they can offer Latin America more effective aid in achieving its goals of higher living standards, more equitable distribution of income, and political democracy than can the Communists.

8

Southern Dialectic

George I. Blanksten

The first recorded use of the word *justicialismo* was made by Perón in April of 1949. The occasion was memorable. A Congress of Philosophy, sponsored by the University of Cuyo, met at Mendoza. Some 200 philosophers representing 19 countries attended the affair. That in itself was not remarkable. What was remarkable was that one of the philosophers was President Perón himself! He presented a curious paper on a new philosophy which had been brewed at the *Casa Rosada*. His speech revealed him to be more familiar with nineteenth-century German philosophy than many observers had previously thought Perón to be. He talked facilely of the ideas of two Germans in particular—Georg Wilhelm Friedrich Hegel, and Karl Marx. Perón was critical of both. He said that Hegel's worship of the concept of the state was intellectually sterile, and that Marxism led to the "insectification of the individual." Perón would accept neither equipping human beings with six legs nor "immoral individualism." If

extreme collectivism was wrong, so was extreme individualism. What was needed was something between the two, a "Third Position." The "Third Position" was *justicialismo*. "What we have to search for," declared the philosopher Perón, "is the well-proportioned man."

Justicialismo as an idea was not very well developed when President Perón first spoke about it in April of 1949. Since then, however, *Peronista* thinkers and propagandists have devoted some energy to an attempt to fashion *justicialismo* into something which might achieve the status of a political theory. By the end of 1951, three books on the subject had appeared—*El Justicialismo*, by Raúl A. Mende, who was minister of technical affairs in President Perón's cabinet; Julio Claudio Otero's *Ensayo sobre Doctrina Justicialista;* and Luis C. A. Serrao's *Justicialismo*. They endeavored to make systematic statements of *justicialismo* as a political and social philosophy, and to divorce Perón's system from the ideological relationships it had maintained with naziism and fascism during World War II. In 1951, President Perón declared himself pleased with the progress made in the development of what he called justi-

From George I. Blanksten, *Perón's Argentina* (Chicago, Ill.: University of Chicago Press, 1953). Reprinted by permission.

cialist thought. "I believe that a new political force has been born in the country," he said, "with a new orientation, a new doctrine, and new virtues."

In 1950 and 1951, when the present writer was in Argentina, it was fashionable among anti-*Peronistas* to say that nobody knew what *justicialismo* was. Most of Perón's opponents refused to regard it as a serious sortie into the realm of poltical philosophy. What is *justicialismo?* Hear some anti-*Peronista* answers: "I am a very busy man. Do not disturb me with such nonsense." Or: *"Justicialismo* is that doctrine before, during, and after which nothing happens." Nevertheless, *Peronistas* have attempted seriously to create a justicialist doctrine, and that attempt deserves a hearing.

As cultivated since 1949, justicialist thought has acquired a curious inheritance from the ideas of Hegel and Marx. As the two nineteenth-century Germans had developed dialectical approaches, so *justicialismo* has its dialectic. As the Hegelian and Marxist systems were theories of conflict, so there is a justicialist conflict theory. Hegel and Marx, it will be remembered, held that society was given life and meaning by the fact that forces were in conflict within it. The more abstract Hegel called his opposed forces within society "thesis" and "antithesis"; Marx called them "classes." And the dialectics held that society moved or progressed only through continuing conflict between the opposed forces. Hegel and Marx believed that there were only two societal forces in conflict—Hegel gave both his forces abstract names; Marx called one of his classes "capital" and the other "labor."

While many points of difference existed between Hegelian and Marxist thought, the two were in agreement on the basic proposition that there were *only two* opposed forces involved in the struggle within the social organism, and this conflict was resolved by the achievement of a species of "Third Position" between the struggling elements. Thus Hegel believed that the "Third Position" between his opposed "thesis" and "antithesis" was a "synthesis" (his perfect "synthesis" was called the "State"); whereas Marx held that "socialism" was the "Third Position" between the mutually hostile forces of "capital" and "labor." On the other hand, *justicialismo* maintains that there are not two but rather *four* basically conflicting forces in society. These are "idealism," "materialism," "individualism," and "collectivism." Two propositions are central to the justicialist interpretation of the four forces. In the first place, each of them has a necessary and desirable role to play in society. Second, a constant conflict rages among the four.

According to *justicialismo,* what is the proper societal role of each of the four elements?

First, *idealism* is legitimate in so far as it leads man to his destiny, "the complete possession of happiness, which is God." It is true that much idealism may be found in *Peronista* pronouncements. President Perón has said that "I have always believed that every human action, to be noble, must be based on an ideal"; and that his "doctrine is a doctrine of moral purity. . . . If it were an evil doctrine, I should be the first to oppose it, but being, as it is, nothing but good, we should aim at making it known everywhere and teaching it to every man and woman." The late Eva Perón, too, spoke at some length of the position of idealism in *justicialismo.* "Humanity is living through tremendous days," she said. "A cold materialism ridicules gentleness; a solemn hostility attempts to separate men from the human simplicity that gives hearts warmth and feeling. Mixed ambitions have made man forget... the humble things which surround us, and man, who needs to love, has been converted into an indifferent being."

Second, *materialism* is necessary and proper in society to the extent that it provides man with the earthly necessities for the attainment of the goals of idealism. As one *Peronista* philosopher has put it, "man comes before the machine; the [Perón] revolution is not so much interested in the conservation and expansion of material wealth as such, but more in the preservation and perfection of the present and future human factor; in this sense the revolution is profoundly humanist and, as Perón himself has said in one of his speeches, involves a 'rise in the standard of living to a level compatible with the dignity of man and his general economic betterment, freeing man from economic slavery.' "

In the third place, *individualism* is legitimate in so far as it permits man to attain happiness through knowledge of himself as distinct from other people. In the justicialist view, "the individual is the first and most important element in society"; indeed, "that the individual should meekly accept his elimination as a sacrifice for the sake of the community, does not redound to the credit of the latter."

On the other hand, man, being a political animal, has need of society or the community, which is represented in *justicialismo* by the fourth force, *collectivism*. This justicialist element aids man to achieve happiness insofar as he has need of the community or the collectivity. And the legitimate function of collectivism, in *justicialismo*, is to preserve the community for the service of all men. "Man does not possess anything which belongs to the human community," a justicialist writer has said; and "when private interests are incompatible—or collide—with those of the community, then the authority of the

state is applied to intervene directly."

Thus, each of the four forces is held to have a legitimate and proper role in human affairs. But, like the Hegelian and Marxist systems, *justicialismo* is a theory of conflict. In justicialist dialectic, the four elements are continually in combat with each other, and mutual hostility is the theoretically natural and necessary relationship among them. Idealism is always at war with materialism, and individualism is never at peace with collectivism. From this theory of conflict emerges the justicialist notion of evil and of tyranny. Injustice, evil, and tyranny arise whenever any of the four elements is subdued and not permitted to exercise its proper and legitimate role in society. In justicialist theory, this unfortunate circumstance may occur in either of two types of situations: one of the four forces may triumph over the other three, destroying them; or any two of the four may ally against the other two and demolish them. In either circumstance, according to *justicialismo,* the result is evil and fraught with injustice and tyranny.

Consider the forms of tyranny. Suppose idealism were to destroy materialism, individualism, and collectivism. This is probably easier for the Latin American than the North American to imagine, for the Roman Catholic Church occupies a peculiar place in the Hispanic-American states. Clerical dictatorships have indeed arisen in the Western Hemisphere. South Americans need look no farther afield for their illustrations than to Ecuador, where the fabulous Gabriel García Moreno presided over a theocratic regime from 1859 to 1875. In this dictatorship, man was a citizen only insofar as he was a practicing Roman Catholic; individualism, materialism, and collectivism were smothered; and the name of the country was changed to the "Republic of the Sacred Heart." In the end, however, even idealism disintegrated, the tyrant García Moreno fell at the hands of an assassin, and man became demoralized and "tired of God."

In the justicialist view, tyranny is no more tolerable if it results from a victory of materialism over the other elements. Materialism—property, the machine, the instruments of the "foreign imperialists"—can, according to *justicialismo,* be as terrible a tyrant as any of the other forces. "One fine day, wise men, technicians, and teachers created the machine," said one justicialist writer, giving voice to a somewhat typically Latin-American antipathy for gadgets invented by foreigners. "The machine became a substitute for man. The machine was the instrument which permitted the organization of great commercial and industrial companies." These, in turn, deified property, another form of triumphant materialism at its worst. "*Justicialismo* affirms—in the 'Third Position'—that property cannot be an absolute right of anybody, and that it is necessary to abolish, not the right to private property, but the abuses of that right when improperly used."

So much for the tyrannical aspects of idealism and materialism. Individualism triumphant over the other forces can also bring despotism and injustice. In justicialist thought, anarchy is the rise of extreme individualism at the expense of the other three forces. *Peronistas* have little desire for individualism they regard as extreme. President Perón has said that "we must do away with the individualistic mentality." The reader need not be reminded at this point that individual liberty—a form of "extreme individualism," according to *justicialismo*—has little place in the "new Argentina," and that the constitution of 1949 stipulates, in approved justicialist fashion, that "the state does not recognize the liberty to undermine liberty." As interpreted

by President Perón, this provision means that "individual freedom cannot signify an unlimited right, not only because this right must be in harmony with all other rights, but because at no time must it be turned into a weapon to be used against the essence of freedom itself. Only the protection of an irresponsible, uncontrolled liberalism has made possible the successful propaganda of despotic regimes which have ended by implanting in a democratic type of nation systems of rightist or leftist tyranny." Political individualism is bad enough to the *Peronista;* also intolerable is economic individualism. In justicialist terms, this involves "the resolve of the individualist to defend at all costs what he considers his inalienable right to make or sell whatever he likes, when and how he likes, and to engage in whatever business or industry he might think proper." According to Perón, "individualism of this kind leads to a society of inhuman egoists who think only of getting rich, although to do so it may be necessary to reduce millions of their less fortunate brothers to a state of starvation, poverty, and desperation."

Collectivism triumphant over the other forces is likewise tyrannical in *justicialismo.* This is a point which the *Peronista* would probably have less difficulty in explaining to the North American than in elucidating on other aspects of the doctrine of Peronism. Spokesman for the "new Argentina" say that they reject Hegel and Marx because both constructed systems providing for extremes of collectivism. "According to Hegel the individual is submitted to a historical destiny through the state, to which he belongs," Perón has pointed out. "The Marxists, for their part, would convert the individuals into beings all of the same pattern, with no landscapes or blue sky, part of a tyrannized community behind an iron curtain. What is very evident in both cases is the annihilation of man as such." And *justicialismo* eschews traffic with this class of annihilation.

Thus, one type of tyranny results from domination and destruction of three of the forces by any one of them. *Justicialismo* holds, further, that there is a second form of tyranny. This occurs when any two of the forces form an alliance against the other two, and are able to destroy them. What masks does this class of tyranny wear?

Suppose that idealism and collectivism were to unite against materialism and individualism, achieving their destruction. This is the current justicialist definition of naziism and fascism, which Perón since 1945 has said are evil. His postwar condemnation of naziism and fascism—he calls them "collectivist idealism"—stems ostensibly from his sudden realization that they are similar to communism. In the view of the manufacturers of *justicialismo,* naziism, fascism, and communism are alike in that all three are collectivist: "The only difference is that naziism and fascism have an idealistic concept of the state." But, since 1945, that difference has not been enough to save them. Since the end of World War II, fascism and naziism have been bad. Perón has said so.

Again, consider an alliance of materialism and collectivism, resulting in the elimination of idealism and individualism. This is Perón's definition of communism. Justicialist writers have no love for it. In communism, they say, "man has arrived at the lowest point in his history. This will be his most bitter hour." *Peronistas* who know their doctrine say that they can imagine nothing worse than the destruction of idealism and individualism.

But what of a combination of materialism with individualism, to the exclusion of idealism and collectivism? This, according to Perón, is capitalism. And he does not like it. Capitalism, regarded within the justicialist framework as shorn of idealism and collectivism, is viewed by *Peronistas* as the "abuse of property." Perón calls capitalism "dehumanized capital." And North Americans may do well to note that Perón is a sworn enemy of capitalism as he understands it. Occasionally, when the United States is plunged into crisis, some North Americans complain that they had no forewarning of where the danger lay. They may do well to consider themselves forewarned by *justicialismo. Peronistas* have asserted that "capitalism must be the enemy of this [that is, the Perón] revolution," and that *justicialismo* "intends to abolish capitalism." Hear President Perón himself: "We think that if we are against capitalism we cannot preserve anything that is capitalist." He has said that "the political, social, and economic middleman must be eliminated," and that he "will not allow despotic capitalism to prevail in Argentina." Time was when Hitler and Mussolini told North Americans that their system was decadent. According to Perón, that system is decadent again. "Capitalism, glorious perhaps in the eighteenth century in its constructive stage, is arriving at its final stage," he has said. "New forms—as has been the custom of humanity throughout the ages—struggle and contend in the world to replace capitalism in its final stage."

Thus the high priests of *justicialismo* have identified seven brands of tyranny. Four of them arise from the triumph of any one of the basic forces over the other three, whether the resultant evil be theocracy, all-inclusive materialism, anarchy, or complete collectivism. And three brands of tyranny spring from a victorious alliance of two of the elements to the exclusion of the other two, whether the product of the combination be fascism, communism, or capitalism.[1]

Can these tyrannies be avoided? *Peronistas* claim they have found a formula. Each of the seven tyrannies, it is argued, is a form of extremism, and what is needed is an arrangement which prevents extremism. This arrangement, says Perón, is *justicialismo* or the "Third Position." Perhaps only a college professor would bother to point out that the "Third Position" is theoretically not "third," but rather eighth, in the sense that it is an alternative to the seven tyrannies. But—the dubious mathematics of *justicialismo* aside for the moment —what is the "Third Position"?

It is an arrangement which guarantees each of the four basic forces the opportunity to exercise its proper role in society, neutralizes the conflict among the four, and prevents any one —or two—of them from dominating the others. In a sense, *Justicialismo* or the "Third Position" is the "new Argentina's" version of Aristotle's "Golden Mean," insofar as that concept sought the avoidance of extremes. The *Peronista* who knows his doctrine defines it thus: *Justicialismo* is "that doctrine whose objective is the happiness of man in human society achieved through the harmony of materialistic, idealistic, individualistic, and collectivistic forces, each valued in a Christian way." Or thus: "It would be a concordant and balanced combination of the forces that represent the modern state, designed to avoid strife and the annihilation of one of these forces; endeavoring to conciliate them, to unite them, and to put them in parallel motion to be able to form...a common destiny with

benefit for the...forces and without injury to any one of them." *Justicialismo,* then, envisages a temperate social order compounded of "just the right amounts" of idealism, materialism, individualism, and collectivism.

How much of each is "just the right amount"? Or, to put the question another way, *where* is the "Third Position"? If *justicialismo* were to be charted on a four-cornered diagram, with each of the corners representing one of the four basic forces, would the "Third Position" lie in the center of the diagram? According to Perón, the answer to that question is "no." He has said that "the 'Third Position' is not in any way a position of neutrality." How, then, can it be located? Each of the four forces must be assigned a value. Insofar as justicialist writing has attempted to do this, the general tendency of *Peronistas* is to value idealism and individualism more highly than materialism and collectivism. It will be remembered that the four forces are assumed to be in continual conflict. The "Third Position," then, locates at the point of equilibrium among the four. Since idealism and individualism are assumed to be of greater value, that is, to have greater force, than the other two elements, the "Third Position" or point of equilibrium lies closer to idealism and individualism than to materialism and collectivism. As Raúl A. Mende, Perón's minister of technical affairs, has put it:

The equilibrium is arrived at when each force expends its maximum possible energy against the maximum possible energy of its opponent.

These maximum energies logically must maintain their proportional relationships to each other.

If Force A equals 1,000 and Force B equals 100, the point of equilibrium will be C; but this point will be closer to A in the proportion of 1,000 to 100. . . .

To give to each force...the possibility of its maximum expression compatible

---

[1] Justicialist thinkers have said nothing about a combination of individualism with idealism. An alliance of materialism with idealism, or of collectivism with individualism, is held to be impossible in the nature of the system.

with the maximum expression of its opponent...is *to establish justice, to give each force its rightful place...in* proportion to its value.[2]

One further point: equilibrium is held to be the soul of *justicialismo*. The "Third Position" is fluid and dynamic rather than static. "We are not sectarians, Peronism is not sectarian," President Perón has asserted. "Some say, in grave error, that it is a centrist party. A centrist party, like a rightist or leftist party, is sectarian, and we are totally antisectarian. For us there is nothing fixed and nothing to deny... We are anti-Communists because Communists are sectarians, and anticapitalists because capitalists are also sectarians. Our 'Third Position' is not a centrist position. It is an ideological which is in the center, on the right, or on the left according to specific circumstances."

As employed by the "new Argentina," *justicialismo* is called upon to justify *Peronista* policies operating on three levels. First, in the area of foreign policy, *justicialismo* is the announced rationale of Argentina's "Third Position" between the United States and the Soviet Union. It might be noted at this point, however, that the "Third Position," being anti-Communist and also anticapitalist, provides the ideological context within which Perón explains his anti-Soviet and also anti-"Yankee" foreign policy. Second, the "Third Position" is the official justification for the *Peronistas'* domestic economic policies.[3] Peronism maintains a domestic "Third Position" between the rich and the poor. The regime says it is opposed to the "Oligarchy" and is the champion of the economically underprivileged,

but neither of these groups has lost or profited in spectacular economic terms in the "new Argentina." In effect, *justicialismo* says in economic matters what Mr. Dooley once said of the North American President Theodore Roosevelt's antitrust program: "On the one hand, bust the trusts; on the other hand, not so fast." Third, *justicialismo* provides the ideational context for Perón's domestic political actions. Individual liberties are curtailed; federalism is reduced; political parties are restricted. But none of these, argues the "Third Position," is completely destroyed. All are saved from "extremism."

In the "new Argentina," justicialist doctrine comes completely equipped with a group of slogans which serve as battle cries or symbols behind which *Peronistas* rally. Consider some of the slogans of Peronism: "Dignification of Labor," "Elevation of social culture," "Humanization of Capital," "Faith in God," "Solidarity among Argentines." Many of these acquire their especial significance from the ideological framework of *justicialismo*.

President Perón has declared himself to be very proud of the "Third Position," the "new Argentina's" contribution to the world of political philosophy. "When I think that we have been the first to announce this solution to men, and when I demonstrate that we have been the first to realize it, I can do no less than affirm my faith in the high destiny which God has seen fit to assign to our country," he told the congress in May of 1950. "My soul is filled with emotion when I think that the day cannot be far off when all of humanity, seeking some star in the night, will fix its eyes on the flag of the Argentines."

Justicialismo and Practical Politics

In the sense that *justicialismo* is whatever Perón does, it is an ingenious ideological device. Perón gives and

2 Raúl A. Mende, *El Justicialismo* (Buenos Aires: ALEA, S.A., 1950), pp. 94–96.

3 In his *Argentina's Third Position and Other Systems Compared,* Leonard T. Richmond treats *justicialismo* only as an economic system.

Perón takes away, and the "Third Position" likewise does both. The reader has seen that *Peronista* policies are turned on and off, as situations may appear to demand; and *justicialismo* is a doctrine of "now you see it, now you don't," a philosophy of turning things on and turning them off. Perón is primarily a successful political opportunist, and the "Third Position" is a theory of opportunism.

Justicialismo is a doctrine of the balancing of forces; in essence, the Perón regime is in itself a balancing of forces. Many people who do not know anything else about politics know that it makes strange bedfellows. Perón, like anybody else in power, finds that his regime depends for its existence on composing hostilities among various groups, and the "Third Position" is his method of persuading them to sleep with each other. The interplay of forces that brought Perón to power in the first place and the dynamic exigencies of Argentine politics are themselves an equilibrium. Perón realizes that if he is to retain power, he must preserve a peaceful working relationship, a balance, among the competing forces which make political Argentina what it is.

What is *justicialismo?* It is more than a dubious political theory; it is a system of practical politics. *Justicialismo* is a juggler's act, a huge vaudeville performance. Perón is the clown, and Argentine special-interest groups are the balls he juggles. The clown has seven balls. They are called the "army," the "Church," the "Oligarchy," the "foreign imperialist," "labor," the "interior," and the *"porteños." Justicialismo* is a juggler's act: the performer must keep all seven balls in motion, and he must remain equidistant from all of them. It is, in a sense, a tragic performance if the observer harbors sympathy for the clown. The juggler must preserve his "Third Position": he dare not catch one of the balls and call it his own, for the others will fall on his head and destroy him. This is not a performance that can be terminated successfully, for it is a species of marathon. The clown cannot catch all of the balls and accept ovations for a game well played. There is only one way the performance can end: at least one of the seven balls will fall on the juggler's head. Yes, *justicialismo* is a vaudeville performance. It is not true that *justicialismo* is "that doctrine before, during, and after which nothing happens." Rather, it is that performance before which the seven balls had a systemized relationship to each other, during which they are kept in dizzy motion, and after which at least one of them falls on the clown. The act can end in no other way.

Justicialismo says that there are seven tyrannies. This is true. For the juggler has seven balls, and at least one of them will kill him.

Perón gives and Perón takes away. Peronism is fluid and dynamic. The justicialist technique in politics means that the regime makes a studied and systematic practice of avoiding prolonged political honeymoons with specific interest groups. The juggler's seven balls are the interest groups, and Perón cannot perform unless all of them are kept in motion. There is much talk of the "army," the "Church," the "Oligarchy," the "foreign imperialist," "labor," the "interior," and the *"porteños."* Perón needs all of them. But none of them really belongs to him, for his is of necessity a "Third Position."

Consider the interest groups. The army will probably fall on Perón's head one day, but the "new Argentina" is the army's Argentina. The military is a major bulwark of the regime, but the army is in a constant state of potential rebellion. Some of its officers hated

"Evita," and some hate the workers, the *descamisados*. In truth, the army and organized labor have little in common except the accident of the revolution. Perón dare not say his regime is the army's regime, for the other interest groups will rise against him; he dare not cling too long or too stubbornly to the others, for the army will destroy him. His is a "Third Position"; he can take no other.

Or perhaps it will be the Church that will destroy Perón. He needs the Church, but the government does not —cannot—belong to the clergy. Here, too, it is necessary to juggle. Again, consider the "Oligarchy." Perón needs the landowners and the capitalists, he cannot destroy them. Without the "Oligarchy" there is no "new Argentina," just as there was no old Argentina without the "Oligarchy." He dare not throw the "Oligarchy" away, yet he cannot call it his own. And what of the "foreign imperialist"? Let the Yankee explain it himself: "Where else can you get twelve per cent on your money?" Where is the "Third Position"? It is somewhere between more than twelve per cent ("extreme materialism") and no percentage at all ("extreme idealism"). "On the one hand, bust the trusts; on the other hand, not so fast." Mr. Dooley might well have been an Argentine.

And the workers, the *descamisados*? The juggler needs them, but they do not belong to him. And perhaps, as many Argentines predict, it may be labor that eventually destroys Perón. If it is indeed the seventh tyranny, communism ("materialistic collectivism") that terminates the performance, it will have been Perón who brought it. After all, no matter which one of the seven balls is dropped, it is the same juggler. And what of the *provincianos* and the *porteños*? They of the "interior" claim that Perón belongs to Buenos Aires; the *porteños* say, partly because Rosas represented the provinces of the "interior," that Perón reminds them of "Bloody Rosas."

Thus the seven balls. At least one will fall with lethal effect.

An intriguing question remains. Perón has said—and so it is the truth from headquarters—that *justicialismo* envisages a temperate social order compounded of "just the right amounts" of idealism, materialism, individualism, and collectivism. How much of each is "just the right amount"? Beyond assigning greater values to idealism and to individualism than to the other two forces, *Perón does not say how much of each ingredient is the proper amount.* There is no objective standard for this; there is no quantitative formula, no mathematics, in *justicialismo*. The "Third Position" is whatever Perón says it is; *justicialismo* is whatever he does; and he is a juggler. Justicialist theory is, basically, a philosophy of opportunism.

9

Aprismo :
Peru's Indigenous Political Theory

Harry Kantor

In the period between the two world wars the Peruvian social scene produced one of the distinctive currents of Latin American political thought. The *Alianza Popular Revolucionaria Americana,* more commonly known as *aprismo* or the *Aprista* movement, combined ideas about the unique character of Latin American society with the general ideas of democratic socialism to create a program advocating revolutionary changes in the organization of Peruvian society. The *Apristas* advocated the integration of the Indian population into the main stream of development, democratic government, opposition to imperialism, unification of the Latin American states, a planned economy, state ownership of certain enterprises, industrialization, agrarian reform, and education of the population. The *Aprista* leaders won the support of the majority of the Peruvian population for this program in three elections, 1931, 1936, and 1945, but dictatorship did not permit them

to gain control of the government. The *Aprista* ideology has its weaknesses, the most conspicuous its neglect of a method of achieving power, but it is an impressive attempt to create a political program suitable to Latin American conditions and capable of transforming Peru into a constitutional democracy.

The *Aprista* movement was begun in the early 1920's by a group of brilliant young students who were pushed into political activity by the refusal of the Peruvian ruling class to tolerate efforts at reform. Led by Víctor Raúl Haya de la Torre, Manuel Seoane, and Luis Alberto Sánchez, the students had organized in an attempt to reform the old University of San Marcos in Lima. When their efforts were successful, they turned their energies to teaching the poor in night schools, which they named *Universidades Popular González Prada* in honor of the scholar who had inspired them to turn their efforts toward the improvement of their country. Through education the students proposed to raise the economic and social level of the illiterate. The administration of President Augusto B. Leguía stifled this effort by closing the

From Harry Kantor, *"Aprismo:* Peru's Indigenous Political Theory," *South Atlantic Quarterly,* Vol. LIII, No. 1 (January 1954). Reprinted by permission. Copyright, Duke University Press.

schools and exiling and imprisoning many of the young student leaders. Thus a group of energetic and talented young men and women found themselves either in jail, where they had much time to think, or in exile, where they could gather fresh impressions. The actions of the Peruvian government seem to have convinced the students that political activity was essential to enable them to achieve their aims of educating the underprivileged.

Convinced of the need for political action, the young Peruvian exiles traveled during a period which taught them much about politics. They observed the Mexican revolutionary scene, the ferment of the early days of the Bolshevik revolution in Russia, the rise of fascism in Germany and Italy, the general strike in Britain, and other stimulating events. They lived in Argentina, Chile, Ecuador, Mexico, and other American countries and in Europe. Probably because they were an unusually gifted group, they used their time in exile to study the political and economic organization of the countries they visited. From their study of Peru and their observations abroad evolved the program of the *Aprista* movement.

The *Aprista* thinkers have made their chief contribution in suggestions concerning the future organization of Latin America. They visualize a reorganized continent with its Indian population assimilated. They see the continent industrialized and democratized. It would be a powerful, unified nation-state, playing an important role in world affairs and inhabited by a healthy, educated, and progressive people. The language used by the *Aprista* leaders in describing the Latin America of the future is at times bombastic and florid, but the picture they paint is an attractive one for all who believe in democracy, equality, and

progress. Although the specific proposals to implement the plans of the *Apristas* are sometimes utopian, the general conception is one of a better life for all Latin Americans.

The *Apristas* maintain that Latin America is different from Europe and the United States and must cease imitating their economic and political institutions. They argue that Latin America is the home of two clashing cultures, one derived from Europe and the other derived from its indigenous population. Although Europeans conquered the area and introduced their language, religion, and economic system, they were never able to exterminate or assimilate the Indians, millions of whom continue to live as their ancestors did. But a stable society is possible only where people are in agreement about the basic rules to be used in the conduct of affairs. The *Aprista* thinkers maintain that a stable society will be impossible in Latin America until the two clashing cultures are merged. They believe their program would amalgamate the Indian and Europeanized sections of the population and produce a new, integrated Indo-American culture containing elements from both. Whether or not the *Aprista* program would provide a solution, the *Apristas* are stressing a real problem.

The *Apristas* understand that while millions of Indians continue to live on a subsistence level, not incorporated into the life of the country, Peru and its neighbors will stagnate. They insist, therefore, that Peru's great need is to teach the Indians to modernize their methods of farming, change their dietary habits, and participate in the life of the country. This may be a difficult task, but the *Apristas* draw inspiration from the achievements of the pre-Columbian civilizations and argue that the descendants of the builders of

Chan-Chan, Cuzco, and Machu Pic-chu can recover the talents of their ancestors.

From a study of history and their concern with the role of the Indian the *Apristas* have developed a theory that each geographical area lives with-in a certain historic time which creates for each area its own historical space-time. Historical space-time is the totali-ty of all the factors which combine to affect the life of a social group in such a way that the total is greater than the sum of the parts. The point emphasized is that there is a certain "rhythm" or "spirit" or "collective consciousness" which each people de-velops as a result of all the influences to which it is exposed. This X quality, which the *Apristas* call historical space-time, impels a people to develop in a certain way despite the introduction of social institutions from another area. The *Apristas* propose, therefore, that Peruvian institutions and laws take ac-count of the character of the people and not continue to be copied from the United States or Europe.

Concern with the integration of the Indians into the main stream of Peru-vian life leads the *Apristas* to empha-size the idea that their movement must be more than a political party. They propose that their followers undergo a spiritual transformation, that they create the revolution within themselves. They understand that as long as the majority of the Peruvian people remain illiterate, addicted to the abuses of coca and alcohol, diseased, filthy, and backward in every way, the *Apristas* can never remake the country, no mat-ter how many programs they write. As a result, the *Apristas* advocate honesty, an attempt by each person to develop a sound mind in a sound body, and the need for each person to develop a social consciousness. The *Apristas* de-sire to make their movement an educa-tional force, a way of life which appeals to the people to make a personal trans-formation in order to be capable of transforming the economic and politi-cal organization of Peru.

This is probably the most novel facet of the *Aprista* ideology. Few other political movements have attempted similar activity. The *Aprista* ideas re-semble certain of Gandhi's: Gandhi taught the close connection between ends and means and the need for a personal transformation. *Aprista* lead-ers do the same and insist that a better Peru depends upon creating an im-proved people.

Their recognition of the close rela-tionship between ends and means leads the *Apristas* to conclude that power must be achieved without violence. Various governments of Peru have ac-cused the *Apristas* of being terrorists, of having assassinated many people, of having attempted armed revolt, but language justifying violence in politics is not found in the *Aprista* writings. There is no incitement to revolt, but rather a consistent advocating of peaceful achievement of power.

The *Apristas* favor democracy in all its aspects such as free elections, free-dom of organization, and freedom of speech. They have faith that their ideas will inevitably win out if given an opportunity to be presented. They oppose the ownership and control of important natural resources of Latin America by foreign interests. They combine this opposition to what they call imperialism with a recognition of Latin America's need of foreign capital. They propose that Peru pay her de-faulted foreign debt. Their thinking on this subject is apparently realistic: they understand that capital is an essen-tial requirement for developing the Latin American economy, and they see no other source of it than the highly industrialized countries of the world.

Therefore, they advocate that foreign capital be welcomed in Latin America, but insist it should be used for the welfare of the people.

The *Apristas* insist that the United States and Latin America should cooperate for mutual benefit. They allege United States dominance in past relations, but, instead of complete separation, they advocate cooperation as a policy for the future. The *Aprista* proposal that all American states share ownership of the Panama Canal is a reflection of their desire for inter-American cooperation. Joint ownership of the canal, they believe, would knit the twenty-one republics together, serve as a symbol of inter-American unity, and strengthen the defenses of the canal.

Because imperialism is powerful, the *Apristas* believe that Latin America can oppose its penetration successfully only by becoming strong itself. They suggest that the way for Latin America to become powerful is for the twenty republics to unite. They are convinced that Latin America is a unit, the home of what they call a "continental people." This assumption seems to contradict their claim that the area is populated by two different civilizations which should be integrated, but the *Apristas* see no contradiction. They argue that Latin Americans are a mixture of European and Indian ancestry combined with a small proportion of Negro and Asiatic immigrants. Although the exact racial composition varies among the republics, all contain people who are a mixture of these elements. All twenty republics face the problem of integrating their populations, and the *Apristas* argue that this would be facilitated if the boundary lines were abolished.

It may be said that the people of Argentina do not consider themselves the same as the Haitians or the Para-

guayans or the Bolivians, but the resemblance is present. A landowner in Peru resembles a landowner in Mexico or Argentina. A Peruvian Indian is not much different in his way of life from a Mexican or Bolivian. The differences among the people of the twenty republics are not great enough to justify classifying them as twenty different peoples. No one would say that the Panamanians are different from the Colombians because the exigency of United States policy created a new republic in 1903. As the *Apristas* point out, Spanish is spoken by a majority of the population in all the republics except Haiti and Brazil. The Catholic Church commands the support of the overwhelming proportion of the population, and there is a certain rhythm which runs throughout all Latin America which gives the area a unified aspect.

Whether or not the *Apristas* are correct in regarding all the people of Latin America as a "continental people," they are on sound ground when they advocate the political and economic unification of the area. It is becoming apparent that to be stable and prosperous in the twentieth century a nation should be large and populous. It is also clear that a large market is needed to provide the basis for any extensive industrialization. The example of the United States is a telling argument for the advantages of unification. It contains within its borders many different kinds of people, yet the population of the forty-eight states thinks of itself as American. The attempt to establish a United States of Western Europe, the cooperation of the British Commonwealth of Nations, and the weakness of the small countries at the present time all point to the conclusion that the era of large and powerful states is emerging. The *Apristas* forecast this need as far back as 1924 and have continued to urge the unification of Latin America ever since.

The *Apristas* advocate over-all planning of the economy. The *Aprista* leader, Haya de la Torre, pointed out to the author that if the economic development of Latin America were not planned, industrialization might lead to war among the various republics. He was particularly concerned about the efforts to create a steel industry in half a dozen of the republics. Steel, he said, means armaments, and since no one republic, with the possible exception of Brazil, can provide a large enough internal market for a steel industry, the various countries may turn to conquest to win a market. The *Apristas* recognize the magnitude of Latin America's problems.

Education, agrarian reform, industrialization, state ownership of certain industries, and the stimulation of the cooperative form of organization are the chief specific proposals the *Apristas* make for Peru. The most far-reaching results would probably come from an improvement of the educational system. Although it would be extremely difficult to accomplish, this would perhaps automatically produce many of the other reforms advocated by the *Apristas.*

Agrarian reform is advocated by many others in Latin America besides the *Apristas.* Its need is almost self-evident, because the *latifundia* system of landowning tends to prevent progress in any country. When a small group owns most of the land, it is usually inefficiently utilized and is generally devoted to market crops which bring a cash return. The production of crops for a world market is usually accompanied by a shortage of food within an agricultural country. This system tends to keep farm workers uneducated and living in poverty. The *Apristas* propose, therefore, to

break up the large estates and to promote the production of food crops at the expense of market crops. Agrarian reform is also recognized by the *Apristas* as a prerequisite for democratic government. They understand that as long as a small group owns most of the land the *status quo* will find powerful supporters.

The desire for industrialization is not original with the *Aprista* movement. Almost every political group in Latin America advocates industrialization, but the *Apristas* are different in that they insist industrialization must be planned. The *Apristas* propose a continental development where free trade among the twenty republics can provide a mass market with a tariff barrier around the area to protect industry in its developmental stage. They understand that industrialization is an essential prerequisite to raising the standard of living in Latin America.

The *Apristas* believe that certain enterprises are so important that a modern country cannot permit them to remain under private ownership and control. They advocate, therefore, state ownership of these industries. In this they reflect a general tendency apparent in Western countries, where governments have progressively taken over more and more activities. The *Apristas* do not advocate state ownership of all industry, but propose it only in certain basic fields.

Aprista advocacy of cooperation as a method of conducting economic activity has two different roots. Most democratic socialist parties advocate the development of cooperatives, and the *Apristas,* who consider themselves democratic socialists, do the same. They see also that the Indian's insistence upon clinging to his communal method of landowning, the *ayllu,* makes necessary a method of proceeding that will fit him. Hence the *Aprista* idea that the *ayllu* should be developed into a modern, cooperative system of land-owning. The Peruvian *ayllu* resembles the Mexican *ejido,* which is a survival of the Aztec system of land tenure. Many of the *Aprista* leaders lived in Mexico for varying periods and had an opportunity to observe the attempts of the Mexican government to create the new *ejidos,* a form of cooperative farming. It is possible that this contact stimulated the *Apristas* to propose a similar arrangement in Peru.

An important weakness in the *Aprista* theory is its failure to answer the question of how to achieve power. The *Aprista* leaders try to make their movement an educational force, and they believe that eventually they can educate so large a proportion of the population that power will come to them. They always insist that they want to get to power through an election. This would not seem to be a realistic approach to the problem of the road to power. Events until now have not justified the assumption that a dictatorship would eventually permit the *Apristas* to be voted into office. The *Apristas* were permitted to nominate a candidate for the presidency only once in the five elections held from 1930 to 1951, and that one time, in 1931, they were defeated by a fraudulent count.

The keys to power in Peru are control of the executive branch of the government and the armed forces. Both are usually controlled by the president of Peru. Although the *Apristas* have demanded an opportunity to compete for the presidency in a fair election for twenty years, they have never achieved it. The closest the *Apristas* ever came to power was in 1945, and then they were not permitted to run a member of the *Aprista* party for the presidency. When they supported José Bustamante y Rivero and elected him to the presidency in 1945, they evidently thought that six years of legal activity would allow them to win the election in 1951 without difficulty. When Bustamante became president, he refused to appoint *Apristas* ministers of the powerful executive departments. The *Apristas,* therefore, refused to participate in the first Bustamante cabinet, and the series of events began which led to the new dictatorship. A democratic election in which the *Apristas* could win the presidency was not held in 1951.

Even when elections are held in Peru, the majority of the population is disfranchised. Only about one in ten voted in the 1945 elections, which were the freest ever held in Peru. The *Apristas* have always appealed for support to the whole population including the disfranchised majority, but it remains to be explained how power can be achieved in a country where the majority is not permitted to vote. The *Aprista* writings never discuss the general strike as a road to power or the use of passive resistance, although Haya de la Torre applauded the use of the latter technique by the people of El Salvador. The *Aprista* movement will have to devote attention to this question in the future if it is to achieve power.

The *Aprista* ideas demonstrate that the movement is neither Communist nor Fascist, although it has been accused of being both, sometimes by the same government officials. True, certain ideas of the *Apristas* have been used in a demagogic manner by Communists and Fascists, but the *Aprista* combination of ideas differentiates the movement from the two varieties of totalitarianism.

Though the *Aprista* movement has never succeeded in winning the power to put its ideas into practice, the strength of these ideas is attested by the fact that more than twenty-five years of violent and continuous opposition from all defenders of the *status quo,* including the army and the government, have failed to stifle either the ideas or the organization built to propagate them. Nor has the movement been a complete failure. As Professor Samuel Guy Inman wrote in 1942, "Apra has already accomplished what should make all Peruvians proud of it. It has awakened young men in every American land to devote themselves to solving their countries' problems. It has brought a new appreciation of the importance of economic questions, of the place of the Indian, of the power of political organization, and the necessity of a clean life for those who would serve a noble cause." Perhaps it is this which inspires the *Apristas* to continue to repeat, *"Solo el Aprismo Salvará al Perú"* (Only *aprismo* will save Peru).

PART TWO

The Nature of Change

The permutations and configurations of change and reform are kaleidoscopic. Evolutionary and gradualist ones may in the long run prove the most effective, although outwardly unimpressive. Such forces as nationalism and the impact of the middle sectors need not have the destructive force of more violent manifestations, yet they can lead to an ultimate restructuring of the social and political order. The most extensive statement on the middle sectors is John J. Johnson's *Political Change in Latin America; The Emergence of the Middle Sectors* (Stanford, Calif.: Stanford University Press, 1958). The trend toward democratization is argued in a series of studies by Fitzgibbon, the most recent of which appears on page 113.

Violence itself takes many forms, as Kling and Stokes both amply testify. The latter pinpoints the varying forms of civilian and military violence and, although his conclusions are not universally accepted, he offers a strong demurrer to those who think that the employment of armed force is axiomatically uncomplicated and virtually self-operative. Interested students will find relevant discussions in "The Etiology of Revolutions in Latin America," *Western Political Quarterly,* IV, No. 2 (June 1951), 254–68, by the Argentine scholar Segundo V. Linares Quintana; and Russell H. Fitzgibbon's "Revolutions: Western Hemisphere," *South Atlantic Quarterly,* LV, No. 3 (July 1956), 263–79.

Only very recently has the awareness grown that the political problems of change, to a considerable extent, have become those of implementing necessary reforms of an economic and social content. Thus political scientists are expanding their horizons at the same time as members of other disciplines are providing research that laps over into the political sphere. The ambitious drive for development, the *élan* that propels the champions of progress and improvement, is reflected in many sectors of society. Competing theories of development and of economic progress have thrust themselves into the political arena, and matters of industrialization, fiscal measures, and social-welfare programs are joined by agrarian reform, crop diversification, and educational programs that alter the social order.

Among the more suggestive recent

studies deserving citation here are Charles W. Anderson's "Political and Development Policy in Central America," *Mid-West Journal of Political Science*, V, No. 4 (November 1961), 332–51; also Frank Brandenburg's "A Contribution to the Theory of Entrepreneurship and Economic Development: The Case of Mexico," *Inter-American Economic Affairs*, XVI, No. 3 (Winter 1962), 3–24. Among the more thoughtful remarks on policy-making aspects are those in the conclusion of Albert O. Hirschman's *Journeys Toward Progress: Studies of Economic Policy-making in Latin America* (New York: Twentieth Century Fund, 1963). Anthropological viewpoints are expressed in the highly recommended collective work entitled *Social Change in Latin America Today* (New York: Harper & Row, Publishers, 1960).

10

Nationalism in Latin America

Kalman H. Silvert

Strong nations and social progress are synonymous terms for modernist Latin Americans. Both youth's rebelliousness and maturity's revolutions carry the banners of national integrity, economic development, and social justice. The entire revolutionary package also includes such other standard components as the growth of industrial cities, the proliferation of science and secularism, and a drastic broadening of the base of political participation. In their very nature, contemporary revolutionary movements in Latin America are not only nationalistic, but also populist in emotional overtone and in the ideological planning of the functions of the state.

This "massification" of nationalism in Latin America, as well as in many other underdeveloped lands, forces us to an amendment of classical thinking about the manner in which nationalism, middle classes, capitalism, and democracy may link themselves. Because nationalism bears an inevitable relationship to the development of a complex class structure—including middle groups, of course—many Latin-American revolutions of the past have been easily labeled as merely transplanted repetitions of that most classical bourgeois uprising of them all, the French Revolution. New factors, however, are now operating to make of Latin America's present wrenchings an epic of special and particularly absorbing interest. Ideologies of violence, mass communications, and a highly complex and productive technology are combining to speed the rhythm of change and to stamp a new nature into the process of social development. True it is that certain necessary characteristics define modernization anywhere and at any time. Just as in the France of 1789 to 1848, development still involves at least a certain degree of impersonal loyalty to fellow citizens, a necessary minimum of empiricism and secularism, an extended array of occupations and, thus, a complicated class structure, and an extension of the range of political participation. But wherever fundamental change has firmly begun in Latin America, special ideological as well as merely administrative solutions are needed to govern the rapidity of the

From Kalman H. Silvert, "Nationalism in Latin America," *The Annals,* CCCXXXIV (March 1961). Reprinted by permission.

direct jump into mass organization forced by the new techniques and communications and translated into a political imperative by the revolution of expectations.

The Matter of Definition

The study of nationalism is a particularly useful strategy, not only for lacing the past to the present, but also for comparing certain families of current happenings. The concept explains at least one way of using the past to justify what we do today; it defines the new powers of old political units in such areas as Latin America; and it assists the social scientist toward prediction, because its presence implies certain necessary correlatives among the persons and institutions involved in what we have been loosely calling modernism and development. A greater definitional precision than has been customary is required for these purposes best to be served. But precisely because nationalism is one of the fundamental social values of the Western, developed world, its manifestations in such societies impregnate all levels of behavior and evoke many partial definitions as a substitute for the complex and pervasive whole.

Although definition is not the purpose of this article, we cannot proceed without converting nationalism from amorphous word to objective term. This duty is not so easily discharged.

Nationalism is so much with us, plays so large a role in shaping the setting of our daily lives, that it is often taken as a simple matter about which we know more or less as much as we need to know. In fact we do know a great deal about it, but what we do not know or have taken for granted without adequate evidence adds up to an impressive body of ignorance and uncertainty which is all the more dismaying because of the frequent failure to face up to the limitations of our knowledge. It is a far more complex and elusive matter than it is usually given credit for being. . . .

. . . there is no real agreement as to what a nation is. No one has succeeded in devising a definition which is watertight in the sense that without opening up a number of leaky "ifs" and "buts," it enumerates the constituent elements of the nations we know in such fashion as to distinguish them satisfactorily from other types of communities in which men have intensely lived their lives through the ages. . . .[1]

From the copious writings on nationalism, despite their seeming confusions and contradictions, a coherent series of statements can be abstracted to serve at least the purpose of establishing grand categories and dimensions. The following paragraphs offer a proposed set of subdivisions of the many senses in which the word nationalism is used, with suggestions for their significance within the Latin American context.

Nationalism as patriotism

Nationalism as patriotism refers to the love of country and national community, on the one hand, and, on the other hand, to the collection of symbols expressing this love. Glorification of the race, military pomp and ceremony on the occasion of national holidays, martial anthems, and homage to the symbolic baggage" of the nation are celebrated on many occasions in Latin America. These evocations of a national spirit were the custom of small upper groups imitating European practice long before Latin American governments could, in fact, even dream of claiming to represent nationally conscious peoples. The transfer of the feel-

1 Rupert Emerson, *From Empire to Nation: The Rise to Self-assertion of Asian and African Peoples* (Cambridge, Mass.: Harvard University Press, 1960), pp. 89–90.

ings of local and neighborhood, *barrio,* identification still remains totally unaccomplished in many rural and depressed urban areas. There is even an objective shortage of national symbols in most countries, despite the solemn ceremonials, not only because the process of social integration has been completed nowhere, but also because of a relative shortage of war heroes, great exploits, and glittering conquests, the raw material of national mythology. The best known of all attempts to evoke a glorious past to serve as anchor for a justification of the future are the various *indigenista* movements—and especially those of Mexico and Peru which seek to find in the romance of past Indian greatness hope for a national flowering.

Indirect demonstration of the incompleteness of nationalist movements in Latin America may be found in the large numbers of historians to be found everywhere busily searching for cultural roots, as contrasted with the relatively tiny number of studies seeking justification out of contemporary happenings. This problem of the search for symbols is common in underdeveloped areas, as the following statement by an African demonstrates by implication:

> For young and emergent nations there is no study as important as that of history; the reasons are clear enough. Our past is very much a part of our present and as we comprehend that past so will the problems of the present be illuminated. Most great and far-reaching movements have begun with a romantic appeal to the past. History is full of examples of nations and communities, who in the hour of their resurrection looked back to their ancestors, their culture, for guidance and inspiration.[2]

There can be no doubt that not resurrection but, rather, the creation of myth is the way of the historian in the new nationalism. But the need to think in these terms appears universal, as the German Romanticists demonstrated to a shuddersome extreme.

Nationalism as social value

Nationalism as a social value refers to the norm defining the loyalty due to fellow citizens and to the secular state as the ultimate arbiter of all conflicts of public interest.[3] This aspect of nationalism is the crucial one, for a broad loyalty to fellow citizens and a fitting set of functional institutions is the critical social factor permitting the organization of the high degree of specialization—and, hence, interdependence—together with industrial urbanization which we call economic development. This feeling is at the core of such a definition as the following:

> Nationalism is a state of mind, in which the supreme loyalty of the individual is felt to be due the nation-state. . . . Formerly, man's loyalty was due not to the nation-state, but to differing other forms of social authority, political organization, and ideological cohesion such as the tribe or clan, the city-state or the feudal lord, the dynastic state, the church or religious group. . . .[4]

Social psychologists and sociologists have frequently used such terms as

---

[2] K. Onwuka Diké, "African History and Self-government: 3," *West Africa,* No. 1882 (March 21, 1953), p. 251.

[3] Karl Deutsch, in his *Nationalism and Social Communication* (New York: John Wiley & Sons, Inc., 1953), employs the word "nationality" to refer essentially to the same concept which we have labelled "nationalism as social value." These terminological variations which inevitably occur should not be allowed to confuse the issue, which is essentially one of how to tame the concept by submitting it to operational definition and, thus, to the possibility of verification through research.

[4] Hans Kohn, *Nationalism: Its Meaning and History* (Princeton, N.J.: D. Van Nostrand Co., Inc., 1955), p. 9.

identification, national consciousness, consensus, and even legitimacy which can be somewhat equated with the value referred to here. The essential difference in the construction of the concept, however, is that the idea of nationalism is here defined as a social psychological concept with its particular institutional referent, the state, rather than as an attitude in itself without regard to the power factors which support it and through which it expresses itself. Consider the following statement from a recent volume concerning the Middle East, in which the term "empathy" is used to indicate essentially the same loyalty toward fellows which we hypothesize as being a part of the very definition of a nationally integrated society:

> ...empathy [is]...the inner mechanism which enables newly mobile persons to *operate efficiently* in a changing world. Empathy, to simplify the matter, is the capacity to see oneself in the other fellow's situation. This is the indispensable skill for people moving out of traditional settings. ...
> ...high empathic capacity is the predominant personal style only in modern society, which is distinctively industrial urban, literate, and *participant*. ...[5]

Empathy, then, as it is structured in patterns of loyalty toward fellow citizens, legitimated in terms of an apposite set of symbols, and enforced and mediated by the state, is the essential measure of whether any particular Latin American country is a nation-state in more than appearances. Although no Latin American society can be counted as mature in this sense, Uruguay, Argentina, Costa Rica, and Chile are

[5] Daniel Lerner, *The Passing of Traditional Society* (New York: The Free Press of Glencoe, Inc., 1958), pp. 49–50.

probably farthest along the road to national integration. In Costa Rica, the phenomenon of a landed peasantry, and, in the other countries, the striking urbanization, relatively advanced degree of industrialization, and absence of ethnic disparities, all contribute to an ease as well as a necessity of national cooperation. In Mexico, Colombia, Brazil, Venezuela, and Cuba, ruling groups and significantly large portions of a relatively well-developed middle group are in agreement about the desirability of effective nationhood, but there is still too much ethnic disparity, too great a divorce between city and country, too harsh divisions among social classes, and, in Colombia and Cuba, too much political turmoil to permit this consensus to universalize itself. In such lands as Peru, Bolivia, Guatemala, Ecuador, El Salvador, and Panama, the small national groups are moving with one or another degree of speed and one or another ideological commitment toward their version of nationalism, but the response is sluggish in a social body not yet prepared for a complex level of national identification. Slow rates of movement among all groups characterize Honduras, Paraguay, Nicaragua, the Dominican Republic, and Haiti.

The recent political experiences of Cuba and Bolivia should warn us that slipping from one to another category is not such a difficult procedure when a strong motor force is provided by the changing ideological commitments of elite groups. The social ratification of and later participation in these commitments, dependent as these actions are upon really fundamental change in the structure of society, demand outside help, patience, and knowledge if the process is to be accomplished with a minimum of pain and a maximum of simple human decency. In the long run, these changes will come anyway, of course.

Nationalism as ideology

Nationalism as ideology involves those explicit bodies of thought employing the symbols of nationality in order to promote actions intended at least partially to glorify the nation as a good in itself. The ideologies of nationalism are the most discussed of all the aspects of the subject, not only because of their visibility, but also because they touch on the delicate subjects of expropriation, racism, xenophobia, anti-imperialism, and political extremism. The possible range of ideologies in any given situation depends upon such other factors as the stage of development of the society concerned, the relationships among social classes, the condition of the international marketplace of ideologies, and the availability of given types of political leaders and party and interest-group structures. The ideologies of nationalism, varying widely in their content as a function of other conditions, may take some of the forms discussed below.

In the early stages of national development, when a small socioeconomic and intellectual elite usually holds power, ideology may be expected to be aristocratic in tone and hortatory, rather simplistically imitative of other examples and but dutifully exclusivistic. The cases of Honduras, Nicaragua, El Salvador, Paraguay, and Ecuador come immediately to mind. And despite *aprismo* in Peru and the Arévalo-Arbenz leftist period in Guatemala, these two countries have probably not emerged from this family of ideological occurrences.

When the nation is in swift process of change as the result of the full commitment of the leadership in combination with rapidly growing middle groups, with mobility pressures high and public problems gross and uncomplicated, nationalistic ideologies tend to be strongly exclusivistic, economically protectionist, romantic, and as universal in appeal as possible. Left and left-center politics are certain to exist; conservative politics are, of course, impossible. Bolivia, Venezuela, and Cuba clearly fit this category, as probably does Brazil.

Once a fairly high, fruitful, and unthreatened level of national integration has been achieved, ideological appeals can become more rational and flexible. The necessity for continued interdependence serves to promote continued communications among the now more complex social divisions. Chile, Argentina, Uruguay, Colombia, Mexico, and Costa Rica are varying distances from this level; the process has not as yet reached a stable culmination anywhere.

A state of arrested national integration at any one of the three stages given above can lead to ideological excess and politics of violence. Such extremist ideologies as the *justicialismo* of Perón may arise in answer to a situation of twisted growth in which important parts of the functionally national body social are deprived of institutional access to the seats of power and prestige. Another type of response may well be one of ideological emptiness, highly characteristic of Colombia, which vented its importance in a tragic letting of blood from 1948 to 1958; Chile, which has been in economic depression for the last six years; and Guatemala, which has not yet been able to find a new politics of development after the revolution of 1954.

The development of nationalism within a context of growing democracy would seem to be favored by a steady movement as unhindered by uncontrollable inhibitions as possible. And yet there appears a strong likelihood in Latin America that there are inherent cultural brakes to an even social development.

Other Development

Available statistics exist to demonstrate clearly that not all of Latin America is by any means an undifferentiated desert of the underdeveloped.[6] In addition, we have readily at hand completely conventional theory to point out to us what "should" be the relationship between socioeconomic development and nationalism. A standard line of reasoning runs as follows: in developing countries, new occupational groups arise to operate the new machinery;[7] a change in occupational structure leading to higher productivity must be supported by extended educational systems and a greater penetration of the communications apparatus; new measures of prestige and political power thus develop which, together with the economic shifts, produce a changed class structure; this new social-class system containing "middle groups" demands values of social cohesion different from, let us say, feudal norms, so that continuity and predictability may be built into the more complex and interrelated society. In its political

expression, this new value is nationalism, as we have said. In order, then, to be able crudely to infer what likely degree of nationalism we may find in the Latin American republics, we might employ statistics concerning occupational stratification, industrialization, urbanization, the production of consumers' goods, and so on.

We should not be deceived by the appearance of rigor which the use of statistics in this case might seem to afford. A recent attempt to relate economic indices to democracy in Latin America demonstrates clearly how difficult it is to go beyond a simple two-way split of the countries by the use of such data.[8] Employing historical analysis, this study first divides all the Latin American countries into two camps: one, democracies and unstable dictatorships and, two, stable dictatorships. In the former are Argentina, Brazil, Chile, Colombia, Costa Rica, Mexico, and Uruguay, and in the latter are all the rest. A consistent tendency naturally appears for the democracies and unstable dictatorships to enjoy higher per capita incomes, higher educational levels and the like than the others. Even though the averages hold up well enough to demonstrate the undeniable trend, the range of the figures allows for such an overlap as to create many marginal cases not at all adequately handled by this method of demonstration. For example, the spread of annual per capita income for the more democratic is from 112 to 346 dollars, while the less democratic roam from 40 to

6 United Nations Economic Commission for Latin American publications are usually easily available. Especially appropriate to the subject of this article is *Estudio sobre la mano de obra an América Latina,* Séptimo período de sesiones, May 15, 1957, which unfortunately, is still in mimeographed form.

7 I do not mean to imply that a changed occupational structure is the necessary starting point. On the contrary, in many Latin American cases I should argue that a greater initial impulse has come from the importation of ideologies and aspirations by a cosmopolitan elite, implying a primary shift in the political structure only later felt in the economic institution.

8 Seymour Martin Lipset, *Political Man* (Garden City, N.Y.: Doubleday & Company, Inc., 1960), Chap. 2 and particularly pp. 51–54. This attempt to correlate democracy with economic development is not alien to our own purpose, of course, for democracy itself correlates positively with nationalism in the sense that the latter is a necessary but insufficient condition for the former, at least as democracy has developed in the West.

331 dollars. The literacy range for the former is from 48 per cent to 87 per cent and for the latter from 11 per cent to 76 per cent. Not only do all the figures demonstrate this great overlap, but even in one most significant case, enrollment in primary schools, the less democratic come off seemingly more advantageously than their more libertarian brethren.

Figures concerning occupations, which should be very indicative for our purposes, leave us with the same problems of grossness. Let us assume that all persons except those at the lower levels in primary occupations form a potential universe of modern persons because of their incomes and the fact that they are engaged in urban occupations. This assumption is crude and open to much objection, especially at the lower levels of urban service occupations, but it must be remembered that we are speaking of an immediately potential universe only. By the use of this device, the Latin American

nations rank themselves as shown in Table 1.[9]

The most obvious difficulty with this chart as an indicator of development is the relatively low positions of Brazil and Mexico. The figures are averages, of course, which means that the large peasant populations of those two countries depress their rankings. If the statistics treated of only the non-Indian population in Mexico and of the southeastern part of Brazil, then the developed parts of both countries would take the high positions which they do, in reality, occupy. If we make these corrections and aid our interpretation with other figures, then the dividing line appears to fall between Colombia and Ecuador, and our common sense remains unviolated. What we learn with some objectivity is that the countries of the top half of the list—Argentina, Chile, Venezuela, Cuba, Costa Rica, Colombia, Mexico, and Brazil, but not in that order—have a greater capacity and social need for national coordination than the others. What we do not explain is why Bolivia has committed itself to a nationalist-populist solution while Paraguay has not, or why Mexico has had a gaudily revolutionary past while Brazil has been content so far with softer solutions.

Such statistics are still so rudimentary for our purposes as to gain significance only through such other research as historical analysis, case studies of power distribution, attitude testing, and care-

TABLE 1 Persons Engaged in Secondary and Tertiary Occupations plus High Occupational Categories in Primary Occupations in Latin America—1950

Ranking	Country	Percentage
1	Argentina	80.9
2	Chile	71.1
3	Venezuela	62.6
4	Cuba	(59.4)
5	Costa Rica	53.6
6	Colombia	53.4
7	Ecuador	48.9
8	Paraguay	47.1
9	Panama	46.5
10	Brazil	39.5
11	Mexico	39.3
12	Guatemala	39.1
13	El Salvador	37.4
14	Nicaragua	(31.6)
15	Bolivia	27.4
16	Honduras	16.9
17	Haiti	15.4

9 These figures have been taken from Gino Germani, "La estructura socio-ocupacional de América Latina según el censo de las Américas," which is in preparation. The censuses of 1950 are the ultimate source of the data, with the exception of the Mexican figures which are extrapolations of 1940 statistics. Figures not strictly comparable with the others are in parentheses, and insufficient data concerning Peru, Uruguay, and the Dominican Republic made their inclusion impossible.

ful assessment of ideological currents. Let us briefly look elsewhere for an at least interim understanding.

Special Nature

No other economically retarded part of the world has for so long been so intimately tied to Europe by language, religion, custom, and ethos. That the silver cord is connected with Iberia rather than with Scandinavia or the United Kingdom is, of course, a fundamental working concept of all persons connected with Latin American affairs. We must ineluctably consider this relationship once again in the case of Latin America's national revolutions, for by such measures as technological advance, access to world intellectual currents, and intensity of commercial traffic with the United States and Western Europe, certain portions of Latin America might have been reasonably expected by now to have arrived at a reasonably stable national existence. Instead, we find Argentina still pimpled by barracks revolts and other stigmata of classbound politics, Chile unable to digest her postwar industrialization, Uruguay wandering in an ideological desert, and even Mexico in an unexpected stasis with respect to full integration of lower class and Indian groups. As for such truly economically retarded countries as Paraguay, Honduras, and Nicaragua, all rates of movement are remarkably slow for this part of the century. The fitful nature of change, the long periods of quiescence, the recurrent fascination with solutions of force, even in the most advanced countries, need more explanation than we can give them here.

A kind of social psychoanalysis is an intuitive and often employed stratagem of explanation. We are told that Latin Americans are individualists, romanticists, that they bear the mark of a feminine ethos, that they have never recuperated from the imprint left by the *hidalgo,* that the *conquistadors* who sired the generations are unwilling to dirty their hands. However true these explanations may be, the easily ascertainable fact of the matter is that everywhere the development of impersonalism, science, empiricism, and pragmatism has lagged. But, at the same time, great cities have arisen with astounding speed; impressive factories sell their products through television; and admirable personal sacrifices have been made in the name of man's dignity and freedom. In a modern world, these currents are contradictory, for science and technology must be mutually supportive; and, in a democratic world, these currents are contradictory, for individualism and nationalism must also be mutually supportive if the strength of national organization is not to flow to totalitarian solutions. The firm decision to build these relationships has not yet been generally made in Latin America. The great cities, thirsty hopes for higher standards of living, and brave aspirations for political freedom cannot be supported in the presence of landless peasants, Byzantine aristocrats, feckless intellectuals, and ravenous merchants.

The peculiarity of nationalism in Latin America is that nowhere, even in the most advanced countries, has there been an irrevocable and hard decision to renounce the advantages of traditionalism and an oversimplified universalism—a renunciation which is in itself the price of social development. The Latin American is taught to jump from loyalty to family and small group to transcendental identifications. He does not recognize the functionalism of an intermediate level of loyalty to impersonal community, and so he makes difficult the establishment of the only processes which can supply the material things for which he is clamoring so loudly. Like it or not, there is a metaphysical price to be paid for modernism.

Intensive economic assistance, technical advice, and educational interchange can help to reduce the difficulty of the adjustment to a sane national integration, but they are no guarantee of libertarian results. Style, ideology, and ethos can convert the new economic and social power thus created into monopolistic, repressive, and fraudulently humanistic molds. If one's experience in Latin America is based on Mexico, he will probably be optimistic; if on Argentina, then he may well be pessimistic. In any case, however, the recognition must be clear that the growing national power of the Latin American states is not yet securely devoted to democratic principles and that at least one major reason for this irresolution is that the nation-state has not yet been accepted merely as a social device or artifact, but is still seen either as a vicious and un-Christian evocation of original sin or as a pristine god to be worshipped for itself alone.

11

The Political Role
of the Latin American Middle Sectors

John J. Johnson

In Latin America, one of the major developments thus far in this century has been the rise to political prominence of the urban middle sectors in Argentina, Brazil, Chile, Mexico, Uruguay, and Venezuela.[1] These six republics comprise over two-thirds of the total area and population and produce over three-fourths of the gross product of the twenty Latin American nations. One of the major questions to be answered, perhaps in this decade, is whether or not the middle sectors can maintain their political positions in a milieu made increasingly complex by

newly aroused, rural working groups and by the intensification of the contest between democracy, communism, Castroism or *Fidelismo,* and neutralism.

Social Groups

Nineteenth-century Latin America had a traditional middle sector of intellectuals, artists, government bureaucrats, Catholic priests, and junior officers of the armed forces. These were aligned politically with the elites and served as a buffer separating the favored few from the popular masses. The modern decision-making middle groups are essentially the product of a transformation that began in the more advanced republics of Latin America between 1885 and 1915. In the three decades prior to World War I, farm hands and skilled laborers—mainly from southern Europe, investment capital—almost entirely from western Europe and the United States, and technicians and managers—primarily from Great Britain and the United States, poured into Latin America, especially into Argentina, Brazil, Mexico, Uruguay, and Chile. They played a leading role in the technological

From John J. Johnson, "The Political Role of the Latin American Middle Sectors," *The Annals,* CCCXXXIV (March 1961). Reprinted by permission.

[1] The terms middle sectors, middle groups, middle segments, and middle components are used in this paper rather than middle classes and middle strata, because the latter terms have come to possess essentially economic connotations in western Europe and Anglo-America. In Latin America, it has only been in recent years that income and wealth have successfully vied with learning, prejudices, conduct, way of life, and aesthetic and religious sentiments as social determinants. The terms employed herein, it is hoped, will convey the idea of middleness without paralleling any fixed criteria of middleness employed in areas outside Latin America.

awakening of the republics and in driving them headlong on the road to semi-capitalistic industrialism. Sleepy old cities became booming metropolises as administrative centers and as nexuses tying together agricultural and mineral-producing hinterlands to overseas markets. The newly activated urban centers, with their ever-growing cultural, social, economic, and bureaucratic requirements, provided a favorable climate in which the middle sectors flourished. Today the middle groups probably constitute 35 per cent of the total population of Argentina, 30 per cent in Chile and Uruguay, 15 per cent in Brazil and Mexico, and 12 per cent in Venezuela.

Prior to World War I, "middleness" was determined almost wholly by learning and family background, and members of the middle groups were mentally much closer to the elites than they were to the working classes. After the war, the republics gave added emphasis to their material needs. This development had the effect of giving added status to the technicians, managers, and owners of modern commercial and manufacturing establishments. Thus, they acquired middle-sector standing. Meanwhile, the traditional middle groups expanded in response to the demands of education, the press, and, especially, the proliferation of posts in national, state, and municipal governments. The effect of these developments was to make the new middle groups considerably more "popular" in their origins and thinking than were the traditional middle elements.

The middle groups, in this century, have never formed a compact social layer. Their members have not had a common background of experience as there has been much movement in and about them. Some are middle sector because of their learning, others because of their wealth. Property owners are associated with persons who have never possessed property and have little prospect of ever operating their own businesses. Some take their status for granted and know where they are headed and what they want when they get there. Others are unsettled and are undergoing tensions inherent in passing from one socioeconomic group to another. Those belonging to the more settled elements ordinarily have been members so long that they have only a paternalistic interest in and a theoretical understanding of the working elements. Those who only recently have achieved middle-sector status know the lower levels of society because they have risen from them. Their feelings for those groups are likely to be highly personalized and may be highly negative.

Alliance with Labor

Diverse backgrounds have prevented the middle sectors from becoming politically monolithic. Representatives of all ideologies can be found in their ranks. This has not prevented them from gaining political pre-eminence in a major part of the Latin American area. The politically ambitious elements within the middle groups since World War I—and before then in Uruguay—have created working arrangements with industrial laboring groups who began to éxpand and become articulate shortly after 1918. It was, in fact, the emergence of the urban working groups, militant, economically depressed, and unable to provide leadership from their own ranks, that offered the middle sectors an alternative to their century-long political partnership with the elite.

The various elements of the middle sectors historically have had three significant common characteristics which they have shared to a large extent with the politically conscious working groups.

First, both have been overwhelmingly urban. Only Costa Rica and Argentina contain important rural middle groups, and, in Argentina, the ownership of machinery rather than land is the primary status determinant. Second, both have been, in the vast majority of cases, subject to wage-worker contracts and have drawn salaries. Third, both have lacked the capabilities to take independent political action at the national level and, consequently, have been tempted to seek support wherever they can find it. Starting from this commonalty, the political leaders from the dominant segments of the middle sectors supplied at least five issues which have had lasting appeal to large numbers within their own general social categories as well as among the industrial workers. These issues related to the role of public education, industrialization, nationalism, state interventionism, and political parties in each country.

The public education issue has provided a many-edged sword for the middle sector political leadership. Public education has been looked upon as meaning mass education, and it has always been assumed in modern Latin America that national progress and viable representative government are dependent upon an informed public. The anticlericals, whose numbers are decreasing, have seen the public school as another blow to the prestige and influence of the Catholic Church, which, for some four centuries prior to 1900, was almost the exclusive source of tutors for Latin American youths. Business men support public education—scientific rather than humanistic education—because they expect it to afford them more skilled and efficient employees. And the laborers look to the public schools to provide their offspring with opportunities they themselves did not enjoy. Thousands of public schools have been constructed.

Tens of thousands of teachers have been trained. Still, about 50 per cent of the total population of Latin America over six years of age remains illiterate, and the number of illiterates is much greater than in the 1920's. There are more children in Catholic schools today than at any time in Latin American history. Efficient skilled laborers, foremen, and clerical help are still in short supply. A vast majority of middle-sector parents, including those who are politicians, when they can afford it, send their children to private schools. This constitutes, in a very real sense, an admission that public education has failed to meet its projected standards.

Industrial policy

Industrialization became an obsession with the middle-sector politicians. Originally, industry meant to them light industry devoted to the production of consumer goods and semidurables, and it was promoted, in part, to help distinguish the new groups from the old, free-trade, land-oriented ruling elite. Today, industry means automobile factories and integrated iron and steel plants. The need for industrialization is accepted as a self-evident truth by all significant middle sector and urban labor components. Important and highly necessary steps have been taken in the industrial area, but numerous problems remain. Capital continues to flow into industry, often at the expense of other sectors of the economy. Industry has not resolved the problem of providing employment for those entering the labor pool, now at an estimated rate of 500,000 a year.

Nationalism

Before the middle sectors achieved political prominence after World War I, there had been only scattered appeals to nationalism. They were highly abstract appeals directed to the intellectuals. They were defensive appeals. Sometimes they stressed the protection of national boundaries, mainly against the imagined threats of the United States, and often they stressed national cultural values. In the face of the threatened collapse of France, to whom the Latin Americans looked for cultural guidance, and the emergence of "materialistic" United States, replacing Great Britain as the economic capital of the world, the new political leaders portrayed the old leaders as the tools of the foreigner, and they brought nationalism to the masses in its concrete and politically charged form. Its economic aspects were stressed more, its juridical and cultural aspects less. It sometimes served to keep out immigrants who might compete with nationals for jobs. It sometimes regulated the foreign investor to the advantage of national capitalists and workers. It sometimes protected natural resources, as, for example, petroleum in Brazil, from supposed foreign exploitation. And, at times, it has assumed a xenophobic character or an assertive posture, as, for example, when its proponents have pressed claims for control over coastal waters and submerged lands. Nationalism is currently riding a rising crest of popularity and is considered by the middle-sector leadership to be a major political ideology. It has made several of the Latin American republics more concerned with their internal problems and less responsive to their international obligations.

National economy

The middle-sector leadership early linked itself to the doctrine of state interventionism to rise to great political heights as the doctrine gained popularity. The politicians promised to make the state directly responsible for social welfare and the expansion of the economic sector. Once in power, they wrote the states' social obligations into the national constitutions. Before World War II, several of the governments had assumed primary responsibility for the protection of various distressed elements and, in fulfillment of the state social function, had taken over the direction of the labor movement. Thus, the laborer was encouraged, if not actually coerced, to equate his own welfare with that of the party in power. Particularly since World War II, middle sector governments have freely intervened in the industrial sphere. They have based their actions essentially upon three socio-economic tenets: (1) Industry cannot survive without protection from outside competition; (2) Since the accrual of domestic private capital is slow, the state, with its ability to raise funds through taxation and by loans from abroad, must intercede in order to maintain the highest possible rate of industrial development at the same time that it reduces the share of private foreign capital in the economy; and (3) Solicitude for the working groups requires that the state exercise some control over prices of necessities. The contest between state capitalism and private capitalism has not been definitively decided. State capitalism has long been predominant in Uruguay. Private capitalism has remained strong elsewhere, except in the Mexican agriculture system and even there it is staging a strong comeback. Since 1958 it has been the national policy of Argentina to promote private capital at the expense of state capitalism.

National political focus

The middle-sector leaders have fought with considerable success to substitute the organized political party for the family as the focus of political thinking. Their success probably has been due less to their political acumen than to the fact that political parties simply are better adapted to the contemporary social, economic, and cultural environment of the modern states. The family as a political entity had meaning when the electorate was limited to a small percentage of the total population. Today the political base is being broadened rapidly, and the mass voter comes from those social sectors where the family as a social unit has been the least strong. The political capabilities of the family probably have never been as effective in the cities as in the countryside: in 1925 Latin America was approximately 33 per cent urban; today it is approximately 45 per cent urban. Increased mobility has encouraged the younger generation to make associations outside the home. Women have achieved a high degree of emancipation and increasingly are able to reach rational political decisions independently of the male members of the household. Large and impersonal businesses and governments have reduced the role of the family head as a job finder, and, consequently, the sense of dependence on or obligation to him tends to weaken as the children approach voting age. The total effect has been for the post-World War I generations to transfer their allegiances to political parties, which they feel provide a common ground for those who have similar objectives based on educational and occupational interests and on social relationships outside the home.

Political Moderation

The middle sectors have been on the political stage for a half century since they first rose to power in Uruguay. With perspective it is possible to discern some of their basic long-range tendencies, to estimate their present political status, and to anticipate some of the political problems they will con-

front in the foreseeable future. We know, for example, that the responsibility of public office almost invariably has had a sobering effect upon them. In seeking office, they have often attacked private property, but, in power, they generally have systematically protected domestic property. They have also reserved an important segment of commerce and industry for individual initiative. They have ameliorated the age-old clerical issue. At no time since the liberation movement—1810–1825— have church-state relations, as a whole, been better than at the moment. The middle groups have stood and are standing, at times almost alone, as a barrier between the worker and completely irresponsible left-wing and right-wing organizations, although it is not to be believed that they do not have extremists in their own ranks. They have often objected to the Latin American policies of the United States, and their objections are becoming louder and more frequent. But they have, with few exceptions, supported the Western powers against the Soviet bloc and have opposed any suggestion that hemispheric matters be debated in the United Nations. In brief, they have learned the art of compromise while balancing a mass of political antagonisms.

The middle groups have, thus, become stabilizers and harmonizers. They have learned the danger of dealing in absolute postulates, and their political experiences have given them a positive psychology, as opposed to the negative one so often exhibited by opposition groups.

Political Status Today

Because the middle-sector leaders have not always stayed ahead of the fires they have lighted, their political position at the present must be rated as only fair. They won the most recent national elections held in Mexico, Argentina, and Venezuela, but lost them to the right in Uruguay and Chile and to the center-right in Brazil. In Uruguay, the Nationalist party in 1958 replaced the *Colorado* party, which had controlled the government for 93 years, largely because of the country's failure to maintain exports at a sufficiently high level and to cope with a serious inflation. In Chile, the voters in 1958 turned to conservative businessman Jorge Alessandri, who promised to keep a firm hand on the economic area in an effort to slow down the persistent inflation that had devalued the Chilean peso from 33 to the United States dollar in 1945 to a high of over 1,100 to the dollar. In 1960 Brazilian voters elected to the presidency the conservative-supported but politically unpredictable Janio Quadros, whose campaign symbol was a broom with which he promised to sweep out corruption. But, as is permitted in Brazil, the voters crossed party lines and chose as vice-president the incumbent, who had associated himself with Vargas as long as that popular dictator was alive, and who subsequently sought to inherit the Vargas mantle. There is every reason to believe that recently inaugurated President Quadros will pursue essentially the same social and economic policies as did his predecessor, Juscelino Kubitschek, whose administration was successful beyond the expectations of all but the most optimistic.

Each of these defeats resulted basically from a voter discontent with the management of national affairs, rather than from a disapproval of the middle sectors' basic human welfare and economic objectives or international policies. But, now that it has appeared, opposition may become fashionable, and, if it does, there certainly is no reason to believe that it will remain a monopoly of those to the right of the middle sectors. Ironically, the opposition of the future will feed upon many of the developments and dogmas that the middle groups politicized.

Extension of suffrage

In the countries where they have been predominant, the middle sectors have been highly successful in expanding the political base. Thus, in Mexico, between 1940 and 1958, the number of voters increased over 300 per cent. In Brazil, 1,500,000 cast ballots in 1930, 9,000,000 in 1955, and approximately 12,000,000 in 1960. This achievement, if it may be so considered, was reached by enfranchising women, reducing literacy requirements, lowering the voting age, and removing property qualifications.

But the popularizing of the suffrage may, in the near future, place strains upon alliances between the middle sector and labor. When the middle-sector leadership first approached the workers, the factory employees were capable of exercising political influence far out of proportion to their number. They were militant; they could be organized on short notice, and, more often than other workers, could meet then existing literacy requirements. As long as the electorate remained relatively narrow and the income of the industrial laborers relatively low, politicians could buy their vote without placing an undue hardship upon the national economies. But the conditions have changed. Formerly, factory workers were few in number and each earned a few cents a day. A ten per cent wage increase could mean a lot to the individual worker while being felt hardly at all by the community as a whole. Today, the number of industrial workers is vastly larger, and their wages are in. dollars rather than in cents. A ten per cent pay raise can have a national impact. Also, the expansion of the electorate to include a much larger percentage of the nonindustrial labor force has required the politicians to measure the industrial worker's share of the national income less in political terms and more in terms of his productive capacity, which has not increased outstandingly in the recent past.

Possible realignment

A not inconceivable outcome of this situation is that the middle-sector leadership may be induced to depend less on the industrial workers and more on the nonorganized urban labor sector and the farm labor element, whose depressed conditions can be improved at relatively small cost compared with that of the organized urban industrial worker. In other words, at present, many more votes can be won in the agricultural sector than can be gained in the industrial sector at the same price to the over-all economy. This would suggest that, in the near future, land reform, social reforms in rural areas, and improvement of conditions for farm workers may well be increasingly used as appeals by the middle-sector leadership. It also suggests that organized urban labor may well be left in the hands of extremist groups. There are, of course, many other possibilities, but the one above is given for purposes of indicating the extent of the political ferment in the area and its possible consequences.

The alliances between the middle sectors and industrial labor are also being altered by developments that have taken place in the ownership of industrial and commercial enterprises. When the alliances were created, a large share of industry in each country was controlled by foreign investors who did not have direct representation in government. They were made to bear directly a large portion of the original financial burdens of increased wages

and other benefits awarded the workers in return for their political backing. Under such circumstances, the middle sector politician could offer himself as a friend of the workers and as a watchdog against possible abuses from foreigners. The trend since the late 1930's, when Mexico nationalized its railroads and petroleum industry, has been for commerce and industry to become domestically controlled through either state or private ownership. As a result, the nation itself or its investing public has been called upon to carry an augmented share of the cost of gain to industrial labor. In view of this, private domestic capital increasingly has insisted that the public good really requires a concern with expanded production rather than an equalitarian distribution of income. Business men are using their legal rights and economic power to dissuade politicians who would disregard realities in currying the favor of workers. They demand that the state alert the working man to the fact that he cannot expect the same friendly consideration when he fights local interests as when he served as the protagonist against foreign rapacity. Their campaign partly explains why the position of the industrial work has not improved significantly in the more highly developed countries of Latin America during the past decade.

The middle sectors can no longer claim an option on sponsorship of nationalism. When they first gave that ideology national stature, it was rejected by the old ruling elite, which was then the only element that contested with the middle sectors politically. But nationalism is currently embraced by all articulate elements, some of whom hold it more ardently than do the politically dominant elements of the middle sectors. In Brazil, the armed forces have become the depository of nationalism, while, according to Vice-President João

Goulart, the workers there claim the authority to exercise the function of the vanguard in the nationalistic struggle in which the Brazilian people are involved. In Chile, the Communists have seized the nationalist label and are running with it. In Argentina, the extreme right, including some senior armed forces officers, vies with the Communists as the champion of nationalism. In Venezuela, both the Communists and the *Fidelistas* are forcing the Betancourt government to be more nationalistic than the president would prefer or conditions would dictate. Under these circumstances it is inevitable that the middle-sector elements must periodically cast off the cloak of nationalism in which they enshrouded themselves and seek to moderate the issue, a role which will not be politically popular over the short range.

Military alignment

The armed forces have held a unique position as far as the middle-sector political leadership is concerned. When the middle sectors were still politically untried and the anarchosyndicalist-oriented labor organizations preached the end of both the military and private property, the officers of the armed forces remained faithful to the traditional ruling element. But, when the middle sectors began to supplant the old political aristocracies and to demonstrate their basically centrist position and their worker following accepted more moderate doctrines, the military officers, who were overwhelmingly of middle-sector backgrounds, ceased their traditional elitist associations and extended their support to the middle sectors. This relationship persists in all of the countries dominated by the middle sector. But there are indications that it is weakening. During the 1930's, and particularly since World War II, there has been a tendency to dip into

the lower middle groups and the working groups for officer material. As this has occurred, the military's appreciation of the working man's problems and his political capabilities has grown. Today there is good reason to believe that the military establishments would accept constitutionally elected labor governments. There is, furthermore, a growing body of evidence which suggests that military officers in certain of the republics, such as Venezuela, might be reluctant to shoot down enough compatriots to stem a serious attempt on the part of either Communists or *Fidelistas* to take over the government by force. This is not idle speculation. There are many in Venezuela and elsewhere in Latin America who believe that the next series of military uprisings will come when Communist or *Fidelista* inspiration prompts noncommissioned officers to turn on their superiors.

Other forces

Communism and *Fidelismo,* both of which are in highly dynamic and aggressive stages of their development, probably offer the greatest threat to the favorable political position of the middle sectors in the foreseeable future. Although the Communists were already operating in Latin America when the middle sectors bid for political recognition, their appearance was premature, and the middle sectors could, prior to World War II, generally ignore them. Since the war, with Latin America in ferment and the military and scientific prestige of the Soviet Union at an all-time high, the Communists have pushed their advantage relentlessly. Their anti-United States attack wins them the support of nationalists. They direct their demagogic campaign to the still unsophisticated groups to whom the middle sectors were instrumental in giving political articulation. Because they do not operate the governments, the Communists can attack without responsibility. They can exploit the failure to improve the working man's position during the past decade and the middle sector's sometimes paternalistic attitude toward the labor movement. The *Fidelistas,* whose objectives early in 1961 were indistinguishable from those of the Communists, have the advantage of being indigenous. They appeal to certain elements, especially among the students, who have been reluctant to accept communism because of its international overtones, but whose hatred for the United States often rivals that of Castro himself.

The popularity of communism and *Fidelismo* are near their all-time highs. A considerable share of Communist and *Fidelista* support comes from middle-sector intellectuals and bureaucrats, who, under past regimes, had no prospect of gaining great wealth or great power. The Cuban revolt showed them that a determined group of such people can take over a government and achieve power, at least the power to make what they regard as vital decisions about the direction and pace of social and economic change.

As this article goes to press, Venezuela, with huge foreign investments in its natural resources and a shocking inequality in the distribution of its wealth and income, seems acutely susceptible to the blandishments of both communism and *Fidelismo.* Next to Venezuela,

the situation is probably most precarious in Ecuador, where all that stands between the extreme left and a takeover of the coastal area of that country is the nation's armed forces, who, as late as June 1959, suppressed riots in Guayaquil only after shooting down hundreds of Ecuadorean citizens. The armed forces of Latin America will not have the capability or the willingness to hold off the masses indefinitely. It thus becomes incumbent on the middle sectors to offer the popular elements some attractive substitutes for their present unsatisfactory and slowly changing state. On the basis of their over-all record, the middle sectors are capable of providing aggressive and imaginative leadership. But, if they do not move ahead more rapidly and with greater originality in the 1960's than they did in the 1950's, they will fail. The stakes will be large in the present decade. The political and economic alternatives will be more numerous than at any time in world history. If the middle sectors, who represent more than any other group in Latin America those values that the United States professes to cherish, are to remain politically strong, they will need help on a much larger scale than responsible elements among them previously have dared to advocate. They will also need greater freedom than they hitherto have enjoyed if they are to work out their problems in their own way.

12

Measurement of Latin American Political Change

Russell H. Fitzgibbon
Kenneth F. Johnson

Social scientists are finding an increasingly useful and stimulating tool in the application of statistical techniques to their problems. As in the employment of any new tool, both the utility and the limitations of this one must be learned. It seems beyond reasonable doubt, however, that quantification of data in the social sciences will become a more widely used and rewarding procedure as time goes on.

Prudence dictates that stress be laid on its limitations. The enthusiasm with which a new tool—toy, some would say —is adopted should not blind the user to dangers which may be implicit in its overuse. One cannot squeeze more juice from an orange than the orange contains, no matter how modern the squeezer. Care must be exercised, too, lest the bitter essence of the rind become mixed with the nourishing juice of the fruit itself.

From Russell H. Fitzgibbon and Kenneth F. Johnson, "Measurement of Latin American Political Change," *American Political Science Review,* Vol. LV, No. 3 (September 1961). Reprinted by permission.

I

The present analysis is an attempt, in not too complex a fashion, to make use of such techniques to organize and validate data which might otherwise permit only the broadest sort of generalizations by way of conclusion, conclusions unsatisfactory roughly in proportion to their breadth. The senior author of this article has for more than a decade and a half been interested in the problem of objective measurement of certain aspects of political change in Latin America with particular respect to the sum total of phenomena falling under the rubric of "democracy." On four occasions, 1945, 1950, 1955, and 1960, he conducted a survey among groups of specialists on Latin America to elicit evaluations which then, with the help of such statistical procedures as seemed useful, were summarized and analyzed. In the study of the most recent survey, undertaken on a more comprehensive basis than earlier ones, he was joined in the analysis and presentation of findings by the junior author, whose contribution has been such as to justify coauthorship. Results of these surveys have previously been published[1] with a degree of response which indicates keen and widespread interest in the approach and methods. The present paper embodies an attempt to make a purely statistical analysis of the consensus of judgments by forty specialists; other sorts of analyses are possible and it is hoped can subsequently be made.

The objective of the successive surveys was to determine, with as much certainty as the necessarily subjective approaches by individuals to their respective evaluations would permit, trends of democratic or undemocratic change in the several Latin American states and the correlations and interrelationships among contributory factors. It was premised, as the preceding sentence suggests, on the assumption that democracy is a complex process, shaped and conditioned by many and diverse factors. It cannot be equated simply with, say, free exercise of the ballot. In ultimate analysis, of course, democracy can be said in large degree to be merely a state of mind; but to approach the appraisal on such a basis involves one in a subtle interplay of intellectual, spiritual, and other factors which scarcely lend themselves to any sort of precise expression, if indeed, they are wholly identifiable in the first place.

Another problem inherent in this brash undertaking is simply that of definition of terms to begin with. We shall not now attempt that, but rather simply point out that a definition of democracy which might be widely acceptable, perhaps even unconsciously,

in, say, Great Britain, Switzerland, Belgium, and the United States might not find such acceptance or even recognition in states of Latin America.[2] It is an oversimplification, but suggestive, to say that much public opinion in the first group of states mentioned above is inclined to regard the problem as one of political democracy, although the approach in much of Latin America is likely instead to emphasize social democracy. We know too little about the whole amorphous and involved problem to propose as more than a highly tentative hypothesis, that a shift to emphasis on the political aspects is a result of longer experience with self-government; the very complexity of the matter immediately suggests caution in making deductions.

II

It seemed necessary first to specify criteria which had an apparent relationship to the sum total of democratic attainment in a given country, with especial reference to states of Latin America. Some of these criteria were social, some economic, some cultural, some political in nature. Fifteen criteria, listed below, finally suggested themselves as having an important relation-

---

[1] By the senior author, "Measurement of Latin American Political Phenomena: A Statistical Experiment," *American Political Science Review*, XLV, No. 3 (1951), 517–23; "How Democratic Is Latin America?" *Inter-American Economic Affairs*, IX, No. 4 (Spring 1956), 65–77; "A Statistical Evaluation of Latin American Democracy," *Western Political Quarterly*, IX, No. 4 (1956), 607–19.

[2] Gabriel A. Almond has warned against the error of applying the norms of mature Western societies to developing nations characterized by preindustrial societies. The basic methodological danger of this mixture of Western rational systems with traditional routines is that the researcher may find himself treating the underdeveloped societies as pathologies. The present writers have kept this admonition in mind. In instructing the respondents as to judgmental components for evaluating the fifteen basic criteria, a conscious effort was made to apply norms which reasonable men in preindustrial societies would regard as valid. Cf. Gabriel A. Almond "Comparative Political Systems," *Journal of Politics*, XVIII, No. 3 (1956), 391–409, *passim*.

ship, direct or indirect, to the determination of where States X in Latin America stood on a scale of political change relevant to democracy. They were:

1. An educational level sufficient to give the political processes some substance and vitality.

2. A fairly adequate standard of living.

3. A sense of internal unity and national cohesion.

4. Belief by the people in their individual political dignity and maturity.

5. Absence of foreign domination.

6. Freedom of the press, speech, assembly, radio, and so forth.

7. Free and competitive elections—honestly counted votes.

8. Freedom of party organization; genuine and effective party opposition in the legislature; legislative scrutiny of the executive branch.

9. An independent judiciary—respect for its decisions.

10. Public awareness of accountability for the collection and expenditure of public funds.

11. Intelligent attitude toward social legislation—the vitality of such legislation as applied.

12. Civilian supremacy over the military.

13. Reasonable freedom of political life from the impact of ecclesiastical controls.

14. Attitude toward and development of technical, scientific, and honest governmental administration.

15. Intelligent and sympathetic administration of whatever local self-government prevails.

The order of arrangement above is what appeared to be a logically contributory and developing order and not one which indicates the relative importance of the respective criteria. Obviously such a criterion as freedom of elections is more significant than some of the others in determination of ultimate results. Hence, it seemed desirable to weight the different criteria to indicate that degree of importance. Of those listed above, items 1, 2, 3, 4, 5, 9, 10, 11, 14, and 15 were weighted one; items 6, 8, and 12, one and one-half; item 7 (which appeared the most important of all), two; and item 13 (now partially of historical importance only), one-half. Respondents in the surveys were asked to rank the various states by the letters $A, B, C, D,$ and $E,$ indicating in general an individual judgment of excellent, good, average, poor, or insignificant (virtually no) democratic achievement, respectively, on the particular criterion. A rating of A was evaluated at 5 points, one of B at 4 points, and so on, to 1 point for E. The variation in ratings given to one country by a single respondent (taking into account the different weightings of the several criteria) could therefore range from 17 to 85 points.

Brief explanatory material regarding the criteria and the method of ranking was sent the respondents and in addition an evaluation form on which each person was asked to express 300 judgments—his evaluation for each of 15 criteria applied to each of 20 states. In addition, in the 1960 survey, each respondent was asked, in a self-rating, to indicate his degree of familiarity, whether "considerable," "moderate," or "little," with each state and each criterion. The evaluation sheets used were in the form of a 15-by-20 matrix, 15 components of democratic practice listed to correspond to rows of cells for recording evaluations, and 20 states listed to correspond with the same cells in columns. The evaluation sheet also included an additional row and column of cells for indication of the respondents' "familiarity level" with the states and the criteria, respectively. This aspect of the analysis cannot be considered in detail at this time but it can be summarized by saying that the self-confident evaluations ("considerable familiarity") of the states did not usually differ significantly from the non-self-confident judgments ("little familiarity").

Although no sacrosanct quality is claimed for the phrasing of the criteria used, it seemed desirable to keep them identical in successive surveys in order to assure greater comparability of results. Each respondent was asked to view the scene in each state as of "recent months," though no specific time span was prescribed. It was also suggested that average conditions within a given country should be considered, though the difficulty of doing that for one as large and complex as, say, Brazil is immediately apparent. Given the somewhat exacting conditions laid down, the respondents certainly participated in the survey "above and beyond the call of duty" and the authors are deeply grateful for their collaboration.

Replies were received in the early months of 1960; time since then has been spent in various sorts of analyses of the data, in part of which an advanced type of electronic computer was used.

A necessary first step in the analysis was the compilation of original or "raw" scores for the various states, determined simply by totalling the points for evaluations of the several criteria, taking into account their different weighting. "Raw" scores for the various states as shown in the four surveys are given in Table 1.

Use of the "raw" scores is open to serious statistical objection, however, because of the natural (and perhaps unconscious) optimism of this respondent and the pessimism of that. That is, one person will be inclined to view the Latin American states through rose-tinted glasses, another through lenses

TABLE 1   Raw Scores by Country

	1945		1950		1955		1960	
	Points	*Rank*	*Points*	*Rank*	*Points*a	*Rank*	*Points*b	*Rank*
Argentina	628	5	536	8	499½	8	704½	4
Bolivia	308	18	334	17	374½	15	439	16
Brazil	481½	11	605	5	633	5	648½	7
Chile	712½	3	732½	2	713	3	741½	3
Colombia	683½	4	597½	6	507	6	651½	6
Costa Rica	730	2	702½	3	746	2	768	2
Cuba	590½	6	659	4	504	7	452	15
Domin. Rep.	301	19	320½	19	307	19	315	18
Ecuador	379½	14	474	9	487	10	556½	10
El Salvador	411½	13	424	14	461½	11	508½	12
Guatemala	416	12	472½	10	393½	14	483½	13
Haiti	330½	16	329	18	367	17	309½	19
Honduras	328	17	379	15	418½	12	452½	14
Mexico	545½	7	569½	7	639½	4	664	5
Nicaragua	345½	15	354	16	329½	18	370½	17
Panama	528	8	471	11	498	9	519½	11
Paraguay	289	20	293½	20	291½	20	284	20
Peru	494	10	428	13	369½	16	562½	9
Uruguay	772	1	788½	1	820	1	785	1
Venezuela	504	9	451	12	397	13	611½	8

a Initial "raw" score divided by two and rounded to next low one-half point if necessary.
b Initial "raw" score divided by two and rounded to next low one-half point if necessary.

TABLE 2   Adjusted Scores by Country

	1945			1950			1955			1960		
	Points	*Rank*	*Per Cent*	*Points*	*Rank*	*Per Cent*	*Points*	*Rank*	*Per Cent*	*Points*	*Rank*	*Per Cent*
Argentina	634	5	63.9	542	8	53.3	513[a]	7[a]	47.8[a]	652	4	78.0
Bolivia	315	18	19.2	335	17	23.4	384	15	29.5	406	16	39.2
Brazil	495	11	44.4	612	5	63.4	651	5	67.4	600	7	69.2
Chile	745	3	79.4	740	2	81.9	735	3	79.3	688	3	83.7
Colombia	718	4	75.6	602	6	62.0	524	6	49.4	602	6	70.1
Costa Rica	765	2	82.2	713	3	78.0	773	2	84.7	713	2	90.8
Cuba	619	6	61.8	667	4	71.4	513[a]	7[a]	47.8[a]	422	14	41.7
Domin. Rep.	310	19	18.5	318	19	20.9	312	19	19.3	290	18	20.9
Ecuador	387	14	29.3	479	9	44.2	498	10	45.7	514	10	56.2
El Salvador	417	13	33.5	422	14	36.0	469	11	41.6	468	12	49.0
Guatemala	426	12	34.7	478	10	44.1	398	14	31.5	445	13	45.3
Haiti	336	16	22.1	331	18	22.8	375	17	28.2	283	19	19.7
Honduras	331	17	21.4	378	15	29.6	426	12	35.5	414	15	40.4
Mexico	562	7	53.8	570	7	57.4	657	4	68.2	613	5	71.9
Nicaragua	349	15	23.9	351	16	25.7	336	18	22.7	341	17	28.9
Panama	537	8	50.3	468	11	42.6	505	9	46.7	478	11	50.6
Paraguay	304	20	17.6	293	20	17.3	297	20	17.1	261	20	16.3
Peru	505	10	45.8	425	13	36.4	378	16	28.7	518	9	56.9
Uruguay	804	1	87.7	804	1	91.2	850	1	95.6	767	1	96.2
Venezuela	518	9	47.6	448	12	39.7	404	13	32.3	564	8	64.1

[a] Tie.

befogged with various smudges of prejudice. Then, too, the ranges of scoring varied widely for the respondents.[3] Inasmuch as the ranges rather neatly straddled 1,000 points it seemed expedient and helpful to adjust or "normalize" the scoring of the various respondents by allotting each of them 1,000 points for all countries and recalculating individual state scores correspondingly. This was done by calculating reciprocals of the total scores given by each respondent to all states on all criteria and then determining the adjusted score to be given each state by multiplying the reciprocal by the "raw" score for each state. This statistical adjustment meant, of course, a change in the total for each state but not a change in relative ranking. Adjusted scores, omitting fractions

[3] Minimum and maximum scores given by a single respondent in the four surveys were: 1945, 750 and 1,229½ (a range of 479½); 1950, 798 and 1,184 (a range of 386); 1955, 741½ and 1,186 (a range of 444½); and 1960, 911½ and 1,334½ (a range of 423).

(which are statistically insignificant) are shown in Table 2; a graphic indication of the progressive changes is shown in Figure 1. Later aspects of the analysis are all based on adjusted scores.

Table 2, in addition to giving the adjusted point-score for each state in the first column of each year's tabulation, shows in the second column for each year the rank order of the state in that year's survey. Ranks are somewhat delusive, however, in that two states with immediately adjoining rank positions (that is, 4th and 5th places or 17th and 18th places) may be close together or relatively far apart in terms of points. It is desirable, then, to determine percentage positions and shifts for the several states. It would not be feasible to do this on the basis of a perfect or even an optimum "democratic measurement"; but it can be done by assigning to the lowest possible score a percentage of zero, and to the highest possible a percentage of 100. If "raw" scores were to be used, the variation—in a 10-respondent survey—would be between

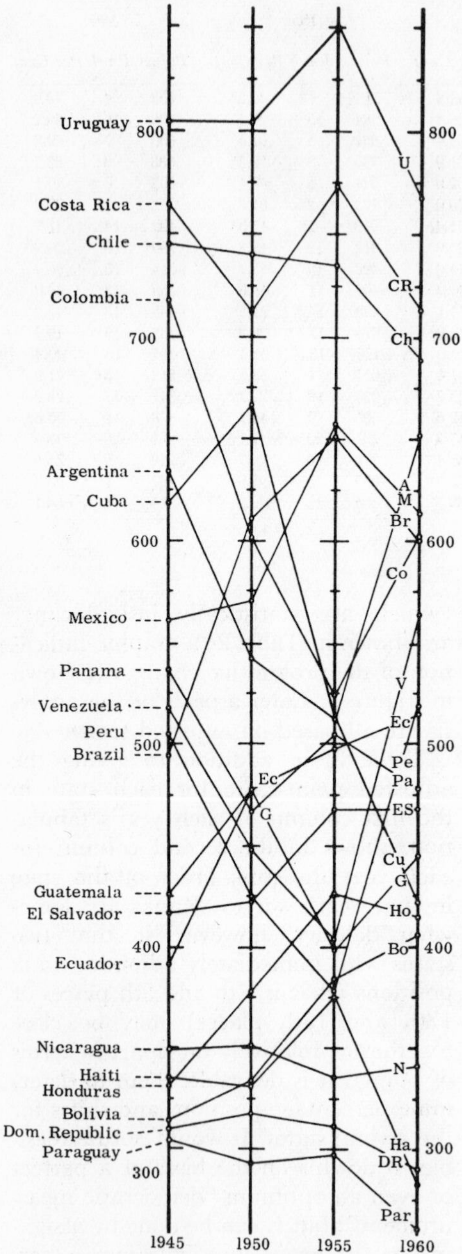

FIGURE 1 Movement in Adjusted Scores
by Countries, 1945–1960

170 and 850 points; that is, if a given state were rated *E* on all criteria by all 10 respondents it would receive a total of 170 points, while if another state were rated *A* in similar fashion its total would be 850 points. Using adjusted scores, however, it was necessary similarly to adjust the minima and maxima employed for determining percentages.[4] On this basis percentage achievement in the various years surveyed could be determined, and the results are shown in the third column of each year's tabulations in Table 2. Percentage positions are more revealing than rank positions in that they show up what would otherwise be occasionally concealed by "bunching."[5]

Table 3 gives certain summary information extracted from Table 2. The first 3 columns show percentage changes by states from, respectively, 1945 to 1950, 1950 to 1955, and 1955 to 1960; the 4th column cumulates these and shows the net percentage change from 1945 to 1960. The 5th column indicates the maximum point fluctuation by states over the 15-year period, and the last column shows the net point change over that period.

In the broadest terms, a tentative conclusion might be reached that Latin America has gained somewhat in recent years in total democratic achievement. This may be determined by totaling

---

[4] *Adjusted* minima and maxima for the successive surveys were: 1945, 178 and 892; 1950, 173 and 865; 1955, 176 and 881; 1960, 158 and 792.

[5] An apparent anomaly will be noted in the case of six states (Bolivia, Brazil, El Salvador, Honduras, Mexico, and Panama) whose rank positions declined between 1955 and 1960 although their percentages improved. This is explained by the considerably higher total scores assigned by respondents in 1960 over those given in 1955. This same apparent contradiction occurred, but less frequently, in the changes between 1945 and 1950 and between 1950 and 1955.

TABLE 3 Percentage and Point Changes by Country, 1945–1960

	1945–50 Per Cent Change	1950–55 Per Cent Change	1955–60 Per Cent Change	1945–60 Per Cent Change	Maximum Point Shift	1945–60 Net Point Shift
Argentina	− 10.6	− 5.5	+ 30.2	+ 14.1	139	+ 18
Bolivia	+ 4.2	+ 6.1	+ 9.7	+ 20.0	91	+ 91
Brazil	+ 19.0	+ 4.0	+ 1.8	+ 24.8	156	+ 105
Chile	+ 2.5	− 2.6	+ 4.4	+ 4.3	57	− 57
Colombia	− 13.6	− 12.6	+ 20.7	− 5.5	194	− 116
Costa Rica	− 4.2	+ 6.7	+ 6.1	+ 8.6	60	− 52
Cuba	+ 9.6	− 23.6	− 6.1	− 20.1	245	− 197
Domin. Rep.	+ 2.4	− 1.6	+ 1.6	+ 2.4	28	− 20
Ecuador	+ 14.9	+ 1.5	+ 10.5	+ 26.9	127	+ 127
El Salvador	+ 2.5	+ 5.6	+ 7.4	+ 15.5	52	+ 51
Guatemala	+ 9.4	− 12.6	+ 13.8	+ 10.6	80	+ 19
Haiti	+ .7	+ 5.4	− 8.5	− 2.4	92	− 53
Honduras	+ 8.2	+ 5.9	+ 4.9	+ 19.0	95	+ 83
Mexico	+ 3.6	+ 10.8	+ 3.7	+ 18.1	95	+ 51
Nicaragua	+ 1.8	− 3.0	+ 6.2	+ 5.0	15	− 8
Panama	− 7.7	+ 4.1	+ 3.9	+ .3	69	− 59
Paraguay	− .3	− .2	− .8	− 1.3	43	− 43
Peru	− 9.4	− 7.7	+ 28.2	+ 11.1	140	+ 13
Uruguay	+ 3.5	+ 4.4	+ .6	+ 8.5	83	− 37
Venezuela	− 7.9	− 7.4	+ 31.8	+ 16.5	160	+ 46

"raw" scores of the four surveys, dividing the totals for 1955 and 1960 by 2 and 4, respectively, because of the larger number of respondents. The resulting totals are: 1945, 9,763½; 1950, 9,943; 1955, 9,760; 1960, 10,827½. The considerable jump in 1960 may well be a reflection of the impression caused by the fall of various Latin American dictatorships in the late 1950's. Greater comparability and hence more validity might be gained by using only the totals of those 7 respondents who participated in all 4 surveys. On this more limited basis the respective totals were: 1945, 6,452½; 1950, 6,995; 1955, 6,338; 1960, 7,132. In the shift from 1955 to 1960, the most marked of any of the 3 quinquennia available for comparison, the 7 "veterans" are an even 3 per cent more liberal than the total of the 40 respondents.

The monopoly of certain states on relative positions among the Latin American group in terms of democratic achievement is illustrated in part by Table 2. It can be further demonstrated by determining the respective number of ratings of excellent, good, average, poor, and insignificant given the several states in total. Each state in the 4 surveys received a total of 1,200 ratings (the 4 were, chronologically, 150, 150, 300, and 600). If State X had received from every respondent in each survey a rating of A it then would have had 1,200 A's and no other ratings of any kind. The actual distribution of ratings is indicated in Table 4.

Similarly, 1,200 opportunities were offered in the 4 surveys for complete concentration of evaluations or a partial or complete spread among the respondents. That is, all respondents could evaluate criterion X for State Y as good, for example; or, on the other hand, their evaluations could wholly or partially cover the gamut from A to E,

TABLE 4   Distribution of Ratings by Country

	Excellent	Good	Average	Poor	Insignificant
Argentina	342	465	214	91	88
Bolivia	29	127	318	452	274
Brazil	213	464	420	86	17
Chile	494	526	162	17	1
Colombia	205	458	417	94	26
Costa Rica	563	511	120	6	0
Cuba	127	336	383	220	134
Domin. Rep.	31	100	234	301	534
Ecuador	55	256	509	303	77
El Salvador	49	216	500	347	88
Guatemala	40	145	476	435	104
Haiti	14	72	226	453	435
Honduras	38	97	427	470	168
Mexico	248	511	339	77	25
Nicaragua	19	75	326	579	301
Panama	76	264	507	284	69
Paraguay	8	45	155	463	529
Peru	64	208	511	306	111
Uruguay	799	360	37	4	0
Venezuela	111	310	480	196	103

that is, excellent to insignificant. Since the number of respondents increased in the 3rd and 4th surveys chance would make it more likely that disagreement or spread rather than agreement or concentration would prevail; but curiously, of the 7 instances (out of 1,200) when complete agreement was registered 5 occurred in 1955, with 20 respondents participating. In that year all 20 judged that attainment in freedom of party organization in the Dominican Republic was insignificant and that Uruguay's achievement in freedom of expression, freedom of elections, significance of party organization, and civilian supremacy should be regarded as excellent. In 1950 all 10 respondents had agreed that civilian supremacy over the military was good in Cuba and that the Dominican Republic's progress toward free elections was insignificant. No instances of complete agreement occurred among the respondents in 1945 or in 1960.

Among the 1,200 ratings in the 4 surveys, 133 instances—more than half of them in 1960—showed the respondents evaluating particular criteria for given states all the way from excellent to insignificant; even specialists may disagree. A complete spread in evaluations was commonest with regard to Panama, where in 14 instances the respondents registered clear across the spectrum from excellent to insignificant, and Cuba, El Salvador, and Honduras, where all gradations of judgment were represented in 12 instances. The degree of spread or concentration of evaluations is shown in Table 5. In it Column 1 indicates the instances, by states, in which all respondents agreed on a single evaluation, whatever it was. Column 2 shows the number of times in which all respondents concentrated their judgments on two evaluations, even though these might not be contiguous evaluations, that is, excellent and good, good and average, and so on. Columns

TABLE 5   Concentration and Spread in Evaluations by Country

	1	2	3	4	5
Argentina		11	21	22	6
Bolivia		6	25	22	7
Brazil		6	30	21	3
Chile		15	35	9	1
Colombia		10	25	20	5
Costa Rica		20	37	3	
Cuba	1	8	19	20	12
Domin. Rep.	2	12	19	17	10
Ecuador		1	23	28	8
El Salvador			11	37	12
Guatemala		3	26	20	11
Haiti		9	27	19	5
Honduras			23	25	12
Mexico		3	24	24	9
Nicaragua		3	25	27	5
Panama			15	31	14
Paraguay		9	37	10	4
Peru		4	24	29	3
Uruguay	4	35	17	4	
Venezuela		1	19	34	6

3 and 4 indicate the numbers of cases in which the spread was proportionately greater, and Column 5 shows the number of instances in which the spread was complete, that is, representing all evaluations from excellent to insignificant.

Among the several criteria, it appeared that the respondents found it easiest to disagree on the status of internal unity and the absence of foreign domination. In the former case there were 20 instances of disagreement "across the board"; in the latter, 21. An extreme illustration of divergence of views was presented by opinions on Cuba's freedom from foreign domination in 1960; for 10 respondents its situation in that respect was excellent, for 10 it was good, for 10 it was average, for 6 it was poor, and for 4 its freedom from foreign domination was insignificant. Table 6 indicates, by criteria, the concentration or spread of judgments in similar fashion to Table 5.

III

The data are subject to analysis also from the point of view of the criteria used. In such an analysis it may be possible to determine tentatively, for one thing, the nature of the shifts taking place in the various components of democracy in Latin America. Totals of points in each survey for each criterion, the corresponding rank achieved by

TABLE 6   Concentration and Spread in Evaluations by Criteria

	1	2	3	4	5
Educational level		19	44	17	
Standard of living		20	42	18	
Internal unity		5	20	34	21
Political maturity		16	27	30	7
Lack of foreign domination		5	23	31	21
Freedom of speech, etc.	1	16	30	25	8
Free elections	2	17	27	27	7
Free party organization	2	9	34	26	9
Judicial independence		6	34	33	7
Government funds		5	24	40	11
Social legislation		8	46	23	3
Civilian supremacy	2	15	28	25	10
Lack of ecclesiastical control		6	29	29	19
Government administration		6	32	37	5
Local government		3	41	28	8

TABLE 7 Changes in Evaluations by Criteria, 1945–1960

	1945		1950			1955			1960			
	Points	Rank	Points	Rank	Change in Points 1945–50	Points[a]	Rank	Change in Points 1950–55	Points[b]	Rank	Change in Points 1955–60	1945–60
Educational level	521	15	586	6	+ 65	562	8	− 24	590	13	+ 28	+ 69
Standard of living	525	13	563	11	+ 38	559	9	− 4	571	15	+ 12	+ 46
Internal unity	623	4	639	3	+ 16	627	3	− 12	666	4	+ 39	+ 43
Political maturity	561	8	576	8	+ 15	582	6	+ 6	617	10	+ 35	+ 56
Lack of foreign domination	659	2	669	2	+ 10	686	2	+ 17	724	2	+ 38	+ 65
Freedom of speech, etc.	650	3	609	5	− 41	605	5	− 4	689	3	+ 84	+ 39
Free elections	552	9	538	15	− 14	541	12	+ 3	659	5	+ 118	+ 107
Free party organization	546	10	548	14	+ 2	533	14	− 15	630	7	+ 97	+ 84
Judicial independence	574	5	581	7	+ 7	547	10	− 34	620	9	+ 73	+ 46
Government funds	523	14	552	12	+ 29	544	11	− 8	602	12	+ 58	+ 79
Social legislation	562	7	622	4	+ 60	609	4	− 13	629	8	+ 20	+ 67
Civilian supremacy	567	6	568	10	+ 1	521	15	− 47	632	6	+ 111	+ 65
Lack of ecclesiastical control	732	1	717	1	− 15	722	1	+ 5	739	1	+ 17	+ 7
Government administration	539	12	569	9	+ 30	565	7	− 4	612	11	+ 47	+ 73
Local government	542	11	551	13	+ 9	540	13	− 11	583	14	+ 43	+ 41

a Initial score divided by two and rounded to next lower whole point if necessary.
b Initial score divided by four and rounded to nearest or next lower whole point if necessary.

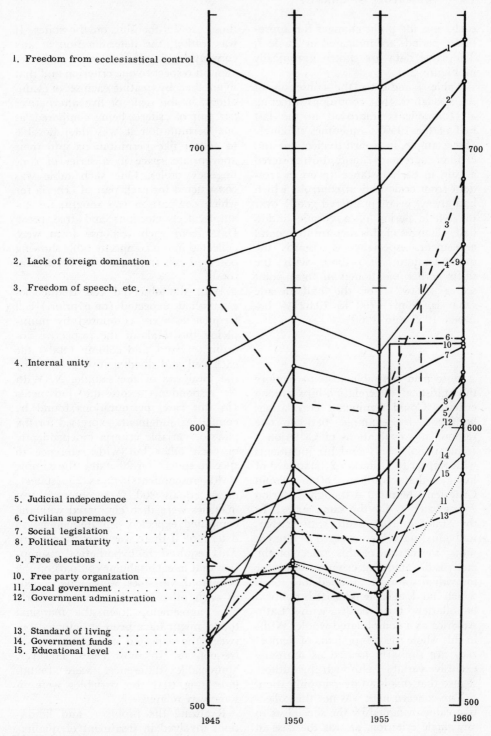

1. Freedom from ecclesiastical control

2. Lack of foreign domination . . . . . .

3. Freedom of speech, etc . . . .

4. Internal unity . . . .

5. Judicial independence . . . .
6. Civilian supremacy . . . .
7. Social legislation . . . .
8. Political maturity . . . .
9. Free elections . . . .
10. Free party organization . . . . . .
11. Local government . . . .
12. Government administration . . . . .

13. Standard of living . . . .
14. Government funds . . . .
15. Educational level . . . .

700

700

600

600

500

500

1945   1950   1955   1960

FIGURE 2 Movement in Evaluations by Criteria, 1945–1960

each, and the point changes for appropriate periods are indicated in Table 7. The same data are shown graphically in Figure 2.

Table 7 indicates the consensus of the specialists, that conditions affecting all components improved in the last half of the 1950's, sometimes strikingly (for example, in regard to elections and civilian supremacy), and also registered a gain in each instance (even in freedom from ecclesiastical controls, which had always been considered good) over the whole period of a decade and a half. Changes of this sort are in general agreement, especially as regards the quinquennium 1955–1960, with the shifts earlier mentioned in total point scores ("raw") for the half decade (that is, from 9,760 to 10,827½ between 1955 and 1960).

IV

It seemed desirable also to explore the statistical interrelationships among criteria. Could significant correlations be found, for example, between one respondent's evaluations of Criterion 1 (educational level) and his judgments with respect to Criterion 2 (standard of living)—that is, how often would Criterion 1 be rated A though Criterion 2 was rated C for the same states? In the state analysis dealt with earlier, individual states were treated as discrete units; the nature of this aspect of the analysis dictated that criteria ratings for individual states be grouped into totals which no longer emphasized political boundaries but dealt with Latin America as a consolidated whole. Within this whole the components of democracy are similarly treated as mutually exclusive variables although the authors realize that this is an oversimplification.

The concern here was not the collective values assigned by the specialists to any single criterion, as was the case in those aspects focusing on the states. It was, rather, the determination of any correlations between relative achievement in respect to one criterion and that in another. By treating each set of evaluations, in the scale of five alternatives per pair of criteria being compared, as one permutation it was then possible to collect like permutations into their appropriate space in a series of contingency tables. One such table was constructed for each pair of criteria for which comparison was sought, for example, free elections and free press. Data from each response form were collected into a composite table showing observed cell frequencies and marginal totals.

With the observed cell frequencies established, expected (or a priori) cell frequencies were computed by multiplying the totals of the respective coordinates (row and column totals) for each cell and dividing this product by the total size of the sample, N. With 40 respondents expressing judgments (in this case, permutations found by comparing judgments expressed for the pairs of variable criteria independently of each other but with reference to specific states) on 20 states, the sample is 40 (respondents) times 20 (states), or N equals 800. The observed frequencies were then compared with the computed expected cell frequencies to determine if there was close agreement. This required the hypothetical assumption that in each tabular comparison the compared variables were independent of each other. If this were so, fairly close agreement, given the marginal totals, might have been anticipated between the expected and observed cell frequencies. In most cases, however, appreciable differences were found, indicating that the variables were in some way related.

Realizing the problems and limitations involved in treatment of qualitative variables in quantitative terms, it was decided to test the pilot study contingency tables by the chi-square formula:[6]

$$X^2 = \sum \frac{(oij - eij)^2}{eij}$$

Inasmuch as large values of chi-square indicate significant discrepancies between observed and expected cell frequencies the relationship between variables in this analysis can be accepted as significant if the sample value of chi-square exceeds a certain critical value, .05 (accepting that as the level of significance). Correspondingly, a small value of chi-square is taken to imply that the discrepancies between two sets of frequencies, in terms of cell content, are to be attributed to chance. It can be argued that extremely small values of chi-square indicate that the whole analysis is null, that is, that the evaluations probably had not been conducted in an objective manner. As the values in this analysis are generally large, this is not a problem here.

It might also be urged that extremely large values of chi-square imply that variables are being compared which, on the basis of consideration of the substantive area involved, are obviously related. This may be a fair criticism, but the authors of the present study emphasize that its focus is neither the methodology per se nor an attempt to quantify the obvious. Rather, it is an endeavor to view the substantive area of Latin American democratic components and their changes, using the methodology that has been described simply to put intuitive assumptions on a more precise and scientific basis.

Use of the chi-square formula tests assumptions as to whether the relationship between two qualitative variables is or is not meaningful. It does not, however, tell which variable is a function of another, that is, a dependent variable. To develop a more accurate measure of the degree of correlation between variables an additional step was taken. The coefficient of contingency correlation was determined, to help define the measure of mutual dependency displayed by the variables of the contingency tables. The coefficient is defined mathematically by the formula:[7]

$$C = \sqrt{\frac{X^2}{X^2 + n}}$$

The fact that the relationship between criteria (variables) is meaningful was first indicated by the diagonal progressions of observed cell frequencies in contingency tables. That this relationship is statistically significant has been underscored by use of the chi-square formula. The formulation of a coefficient of contingency correlation further verifies intuitive assumptions.

Three of the 15 criteria were selected as key variables to be statistically compared, with the aid of an electronic computer, with all other criteria. These were items 2, 7, and 12, respectively, the standard of living, freedom of elections, and the degree of civilian supremacy over the military. Results of the comparisons are shown in Table 8.

Comparing the standard of living with all other criteria variables exhibited a range of chi-square values with limits of 1,116 and 158. At the upper limit was the value produced by comparing the standard of living with the educational level. The lower limit was the result of contrasting the standard of living with ecclesiastical freedom. In both cases, intuitive assumptions about

---

6 In the X^2 formula oij represents the observed cell frequencies of the various contingency tables and eij the expected or theoretic cell frequencies.

7 N represents the total number of cases, i.e., 800.

TABLE 8 Correlations among Evaluations of Selected Criteria

	Standard of Living		Free Elections		Civilian Supremacy	
	X^2	C	X^2	C	X^2	C
Educational level	1116.563	.76327	486.792	.61506	354.207	.55397
Standard of living			338.692	.54538	208.427	.45463
Internal unity	410.279	.58223	369.361	.56202	341.652	.54705
Political maturity	585.817	.65017	747.083	.69491	609.329	.65754
Lack of foreign domination	231.177	.47348	315.884	.53205	239.337	.47987
Freedom of press, etc.	326.933	.53862	1328.490	.79003	804.038	.70800
Free elections	338.692	.54538			918.761	.73113
Party organization	328.278	.53940	1234.761	.77900	778.881	.70236
Judiciary	351.861	.55269	1055.157	.75417	713.785	.68668
Government funds	382.503	.56874	762.526	.69858	558.450	.65101
Social legislation	530.661	.63150	537.295	.63386	506.552	.62266
Civilian supremacy	208.427	.45463	918.761	.73113		
Ecclesiastical freedom	158.578	.40673	224.431	.46806	313.417	.53056
Government administration	481.821	.61310	621.626	.66126	510.669	.62420
Local government	357.406	.55594	618.745	.66063	484.212	.61428

the criteria as analytical categories were confirmed.

When freedom of elections, the second key variable, was compared with all others, chi-square value limits of 1,328 and 224 were obtained. The upper limit indicated a strong relationship between this and freedom of the press, certainly no unexpected finding. The lower limit pointed to a not-so-strong relationship between free elections and freedom from ecclesiastical domination.

Similar results were obtained from comparisons between civilian supremacy and all other variables. The upper limit of 918 was produced by contrasting this variable with freedom of elections and the lower limit, 208, resulted from comparing the third key variable with the standard of living. This latter finding, namely that the standard of living and civilian supremacy were not substantially related variables, may suggest the need for further inquiry into both the substantive area and the methodology itself. Informed judgment might suggest to some that a substantially stronger correlation ought to have appeared

here, and its apparent absence points up the need for more intensive inquiry.

These findings notwithstanding, it must be emphasized again that the size of the scores obtained in the chi-square analysis is no absolute basis for judgment. Rather, the scores act as a guide as to further inquiry. The scores themselves are not nearly so important as the reason for their occurrence. If intuitive "hunches" about the analytical categories can be confirmed statistically, there is every reason to suggest their continued use. If the statistical procedures tend to contradict well-based intuition then an additional analysis into latent structures and operative subvariables may remove the contradiction or reveal errors in method.

Before considering deductions or findings it may be well to acknowledge certain potential methodological problems. It might be argued that a basic blunder has been committed by treatment of the criteria as discrete, cardinally defined variables, when clearly, in actuality, they are not such, or at least not entirely such. Yet, in an effort to expand the statistical utility of such an analysis, they have been so treated and, in fact, instructions to the respondents prescribed that the criteria be rated in accordance with certain factors of relevance which implied a mutually exclusive and cardinal definition. But the statistical refinements were used merely to lend confirmation to intuitive assumptions based on intensive and long-continued field study and observation. Many analyses which involve quantitative treatments of qualitative variables are apt to be suspected of a primitive reduction of human events to numbers. The present analysis is only in part an attempt to subject democratic components and trends to statistical testing and measurement. The tabular score composites of the panel of specialists may in themselves be claimed to be an adequate measurement of democratic conditions. A major value in the use of the chi-square formula is its test of the adequacy of the criteria used as conceptual categories of analysis.

Additionally, the method employed here would seem to invite further and expanded use of the panel-analysis technique. Panel analyses have usually been devices for focusing attention upon population segments with a view to inquiry into the social processes in which the given segments (panels) were involved, for example, studies of change and processes of opinion and attitude formation. Such studies have sought to examine sociopolitical subprocesses by intensive inquiries addressed to participants. The present effort has involved instead a panel of spectators of, not participants in, a process—spectators who, by virtue of their continued observation may be thought to be knowledgeable interpreters of the process of political change that is taking place in the complex world of Latin America. Statistical manipulations apart, the fact that the panel of specialists is in pronounced agreement as to the evolution

of democratic trends in Latin America is noteworthy.

V

What sorts of substantive—not procedural—conclusions does the series of surveys seem to justify? These, it must be emphasized, are, and will doubtless continue to be, tentative. But, on the basis of the statistical analyses conducted, they have an impressive weight of consensus about the evidence behind them, a weight reenforced by the individual and collective expertise of the respondents.

Three of the states, Uruguay, Costa Rica, and Chile, regularly have occupied the first three rank positions for the past fifteen years—Uruguay uniformly in first place. A significant percentage gap has usually prevailed between the lowest of the three and the next highest ranked state. These three states may justifiably be segregated, then, as a top group which thus far has monopolized a premium position in terms of democratic achievement. That such a monopoly may not be permanent is perhaps indicated by the fact that the adjusted point score obtained by Colombia in 1945 exceeded that of the third-ranked state in 1950 and those of the second- and third-ranked states in 1960.

Turning to the bottom of the ladder, five states, Paraguay, the Dominican Republic, Haiti, Nicaragua, and Bolivia, have regularly occupied rank positions among the lowest six in the four surveys, with Paraguay consistently holding lowest rank. Bolivia's continued place in this unenviable low group seems uncertain in view of its consistent and relatively striking gain over a period of fifteen years both in terms of point and percentage ranking. In three of the four surveys Honduras occupied the other position among the lowest six.

It, too, however, like Bolivia, has shown a considerable improvement in respect both to points and percentages.

It is among a middle dozen, excluding a top three and a bottom five states, that the greatest and most interesting changes occur. These twelve are Argentina, Brazil, Colombia, Cuba, Ecuador, El Salvador, Guatemala, Honduras, Mexico, Panama, Peru, and Venezuela. Changes in them are, of course (as with all the states, for that matter), to be set against the backdrop of specific political change in the respective states during the decade and a half covered by the surveys. Substantial net percentage gains during the fifteen years were recorded by Brazil, Ecuador, Honduras, and Mexico; and a striking net loss by Cuba because of the combined impact of Batista and Castro. Average maximum point fluctuations (see Table 3) were substantially larger for this group than for either the top three or the bottom five; in the case of Cuba the pendulum swung through the fantastically wide arc of 245 points. The greatest net gainers (Brazil and Ecuador) and the greatest net losers (Colombia and Cuba) are also in this group. It is in this intermediate group, then, that the greatest flux appears; it is there that in the foreseeable future we may probably expect the most change, either upward or downward.

Turning to conclusions to be drawn from scrutinizing the data involving the criteria, the consensus is striking that conditions with regard to all criteria improved during the quinquennium 1955–1960 and also during the total period covered by the four surveys. The impact on democratic attainment registered by the relative absence of ecclesiastical controls continued uniformly to be regarded as the most positive (or least negative) factor conditioning democratic achievement; by the same token, it reflected the lowest net gain

during the decade and a half. It can similarly be concluded that foreign political domination of Latin American states—the controversial Cuban case apart—is not now significant: uniformly during the four surveys that criterion was given the second most favorable rating. Conditions surrounding free expression and internal unity have also been regarded favorably.

On the other hand, the educational level, the handling of governmental funds, the status of governmental administration, and conditions of local government have regularly been considered as leaving much to be desired. The toppling in the late 1950's of dictatorial regimes, so often supported by military props (beginning with that of Perón in 1955, *after* the 1955 survey was made) is reflected by the spectacular change in the consensus regarding civilian supremacy over the military: that criterion was put in last place in 1955 but in 6th in 1960, for a gain of 111 points. A roughly parallel improvement, for obviously related reasons, was shown in the consensus on freedom of elections a gain of 7 rank places and 118 points.

Freedom of elections, in the context described in the directive distributed to the respondents at the beginning of the surveys, is doubtless the most directly contributory of the fifteen criteria devised for the mensuration. Its close relationship to the other criteria is strikingly confirmed by the tabular material obtained from use of the chi-square and the coefficient of contingency correlation formulas. This is also true of the two other criteria thus tested: one, an essentially economic component of democracy (the standard of living) and the other a political or quasi-political component (civilian-military balance).

Democracy and political change in Latin America (or anywhere else, for that matter) are far more fluid and subtle phenomena than can be described and delimited simply by statistical data and techniques. But, the authors believe, the use of such tools gives a means of refining and confirming subjective and intuitive conclusions which must otherwise by their very subjectivity and intuitiveness remain partially unsatisfactory. The political scientist can probably, with profit, make more use of such tools.

13

Toward a Theory of Power
and Political Instability in Latin America

Merle Kling

I

Political instability in Latin America is distinguished by three characteristics: (1) It is chronic; (2) It frequently is accompanied by limited violence; (3) It produces no basic shifts in economic, social, or political policies.

Political instability in a Latin American country cannot be evaluated as a temporary deviation in a pattern of peaceful rotation in office. In many Latin American republics, despite prescriptions of written constitutions, an abrupt change of governmental personnel through violence is a regular and recurrent phenomenon. [According to William S. Stokes] in Honduras, "from 1824 to 1950, a period of 126 years, the executive office changed hands 116 times." [George I. Blanksten has stated,] "During the 9-year interval ending in 1940, Ecuador had no less than 14 presidents, [and had] 4 of them during the single month which ended on September 17, 1947. Instability is likewise

From Merle Kling, "Toward a Theory of Power and Political Instability in Latin America," *Western Political Quarterly,* Vol. IX, No. 1 (March 1956). Reprinted by permission.

dramatized on the cabinet level: 27 different ministers occupying 8 cabinet posts between May 29, 1944, and August 23, 1947. Twelve foreign ministers attempted to administer Ecuadorean foreign policy in the 2-month period between August and October 1933." And the observations of a member of a United Nations mission to Bolivia in 1951 [Albert Lepawsky] would not be inapplicable in substance to many Latin American states: "In the past 10 years, Bolivia has had 9 major revolutions. None of its presidents has served out his constitutional term of office during the last 25 years. There have been 18 Ministers of Labor in 4 years; 8 Ministers of Finance in 18 months."

Reflecting the persistence of political instability since World War II, governing personnel, including presidents, have been displaced by "irregular" methods on at least the following occasions:

October 1945. Venezuela
October 1945. Brazil
January 1946. Haiti
July 1946. Bolivia
January 1947. Paraguay
May 1947. Nicaragua
August 1947. Ecuador

September 1947. Ecuador
March 1948. Costa Rica
June 1948. Paraguay
October 1948. Peru
November 1948. Venezuela
December 1948. El Salvador
January 1949. Paraguay
November 1949. Panama
May 1950. Haiti
June 1950. Peru
May 1951. Bolivia
May 1951. Panama
March 1952. Cuba
April 1952. Bolivia
December 1952. Venezuela
June 1953. Colombia
May 1954. Paraguay
July 1954. Guatemala
August 1954. Brazil
December 1954. Honduras
January 1955. Panama
September 1955. Argentina
November 1955. Argentina
November 1955. Brazil

Occupancy of key governmental positions, consequently, has been secured at least thirty-one times in disregard of formal procedures since World War II. Nor does the above list take into account the numerous "unsuccessful" plots, suppressed uprisings, arrests, deportations, declarations of state of siege, boycotts, riots, and fraudulent "elections" which have punctuated Latin American politics in the last decade. And the list, of course, does not include references to political irregularities in nonsovereign areas such as British Guiana.

Revolts, uprisings and *coups d'état*, moreover, constitute incomplete evidence of the range of political instability in Latin America. For obscured by data of these kinds is the presence of "concealed" instability. The protracted tenure of a Vargas in Brazil (1930–1945), of an Ubico in Guatemala (1930–1944), the single candidate (*candidato único*) "elections" of Paraguay, Honduras, the Dominican Republic, Nicaragua, and Colombia; the

abortive "elections" of 1952 in Venezuela are not to be construed, of course, as symptomatic of political stability. For these also constitute instances in which governmental authority has been retained by the exercise of force in disregard of formal requirements. *Continuismo,* prolonged office-holding by a strong *caudillo,* in its essence represents the reverse side of the shield of political instability. *Continuismo* signifies not the absence of political instability, but the effective suppression of potential and incipient rebellions by competing *caudillos. Continuismo,* in fact, may be regarded as perpetuation in office by means of a series of successful *anticipatory* revolts.

Unlike cabinet instability in France, political instability in the Latin American states is neither sanctioned by the written constitution nor dictated by the rigidity of domestic party alignments. Latin American instability, in contrast with the French version, occurs in an environment of amorphous political parties and involves the limited employment of violence. It is not the withdrawal of votes by a doctrinaire bloc of deputies which precipitates the collapse of a Latin American regime; rather, it is the personal military following of an opportunistic *caudillo* which impresses a Latin American president with the timeliness of seeking asylum in a foreign embassy. The pervasiveness of violence justifies the conclusion of William S. Stokes: "Violence seems to be institutionalized in the organization, maintenance, and changing of governments in Latin America."[1]

Although violence provides a continuing strand in the fabric of Latin Ameri-

1 William S. Stokes, "Violence as a Power Factor in Latin American Politics," *Western Political Quarterly,* V, No. 3 (September 1952). See the following article (chapter 14).

can politics, revolution, in the sense of a fundamental transformation of society, "is [according to Stokes] rare in Latin America, and even mass participation in violence is only occasionally found." A leader may be assassinated or exiled, a new junta may assume the posts of political authority, but control of the economic bases of power is not shifted and the hierarchy of social classes is not affected; in short, there is no restructuring of society. The label "palace revolution," as defined by Lasswell and Kaplan, can be appropriately applied to the pattern of political change in Latin America; for political instability in Latin America, like a palace revolution, involves "a change in governors contrary to the political formula but retaining it." Again violence in Latin America, in conformity with the characteristics of a palace revolution, produces [in Stokes' words] a "change in government without corresponding changes in governmental policy." General Gustavo Rojas Pinilla may be a party to a successful revolt in Colombia, and General Zenón Noriega may be a party to an unsuccessful revolt in Peru; but the basic economic, social, and political policies of Colombia and Peru are not altered by either the successful or the unsuccessful general. Violence is virtually always present; fundamental change is virtually always absent.

II

"In the general course of human nature," wrote Alexander Hamilton in *The Federalist* (No. 79), "a power over a man's subsistence amounts to a power over his will." And research in Latin American studies suggests that the distinguishing characteristics of the Latin American economy, despite the influence exerted by the Church and other institutions, are of primary importance in determining conditions for the retention and transfer of power.

Traditionally, ownership of land has been regarded as a major economic base for the exercise of power in Latin America. Despite the continued dependence today of more than two-thirds of the Latin American population on agriculture as a chief source of income, the system of land tenure operates to prevent the widespread diffusion of economic power. Concentration of land ownership in the hands of a tiny minority—whether symbolized by the *latifundio,* hacienda, *estancia, fazenda,* or *finca*—represents the prevailing, as well as historic, agrarian pattern of Latin America. "In many countries in Latin America," concludes a recent analysis by the United Nations Department of Economic Affairs, "the main feature of the agrarian structure is the high degree of inequality in land ownership."[2]

Although they can be introduced only with qualifications as to reliability, statistical estimates offer striking evidence of the narrow agrarian base of power. In Chile, whereas 43.4 per cent of all land holdings are under 5 hectares, they account for only 0.5 per cent of the farm area; large holdings (1,000 hectares and over), on the other hand, constitute only 1.4 per cent of all holdings, but they incorporate 68.2 per cent of the farm area. Acknowledging that "the agrarian structure of Chile is characterized in the main by an abundance of very small holdings and a large concentration of large estates in the hands of a small number of proprietors," the government of Chile, in reply to a United Nations questionnaire, emphasized the difficulty of modifying the pattern of land ownership.

Owing to the economic and political structure of the country, land reform in Chile is difficult to carry out. Land-

2 United Nations, Department of Economic Affairs, *Progress in Land Reform* (New York: United Nations, 1954), p. 37.

holders who would be affected by any action of an economic, political, administrative, legal, or social nature will vigorously oppose its implementation, and their political and economic influence is very powerful.[3]

In Brazil, 1.5 per cent of all land holdings account for 48.4 per cent of the farm area. According to the 1950 census of Bolivia, 4.5 per cent of the rural landowners possess 70 per cent of the private landed property. In the province of Pichincha in Ecuador, 1.5 per cent of all holdings incorporate 65.3 per cent of the farm area, and the government reports that "Ecuador has not developed a policy of land reform." In Cuba, 1.4 per cent of all holdings comprise 47 per cent of the farm area. Even in Mexico, where the government claims that about 23 per cent of the total area in holdings was distributed to *éjido* farmers between 1916 and 1940, in lands not under the *éjido* system 0.8 per cent of all holdings constitute 79.5 per cent of the farm area. And patterns of highly concentrated land ownership persist in Argentina, Peru, and Venezuela.

This monopolization of agrarian wealth injects an element of rigidity into the power relations of Latin American groups; for the effect of the land tenure system is to establish relatively fixed economic boundaries between the landowners and the peon, since "the relationships growing out of the large estates have matured into deep inflexibility."[4] Indeed, the authors of a very carefully documented study of Latin America have concluded: "Monopolization of land has been and still is both the source and the technique of political power in Latin America."[5]

Yet it is possible to exaggerate the independence, the freedom from restraint, of the landowner in Latin American society. Viewed solely in terms of domestic Latin American patterns of land tenure, the landowner appears almost to personify the classical definition of sovereignty. He seems to possess virtually absolute power. But an analysis of the nature of agricultural production reveals important inhibitions on the discretionary power of the landowner, and he fails to qualify as an economic sovereign. For as a producer of crops peculiarly dependent on foreign markets, in an agrarian economy characterized by monoculture, the landowner finds his economic base of independence subject to severe limitations. When 50 per cent to 60 per cent of Brazilian exports consists of coffee, when normally 80 per cent of the total value of exports of El Salvador consists of coffee, when "coffee cultivation . . . contributes more than 70 per cent of total exports and is the basic cash crop on which nearly everything else depends" in Guatemala (according to a Mission sponsored by the International Bank for Reconstruction and Development), when coffee represents 73.2 per cent of the value of all exports in Colombia for 1953, when coffee is the predominant export of the Central American Republics (representing 56.4 per cent of all exports in 1953)—when the Western Hemisphere produces about 85 per cent of the world's exportable coffee and the United States consumes 65 per cent to 75 per cent of all the coffee shipped— the domestic proprietors of coffee plantations cannot be immune to the pressures (regardless of the indirection, diplomacy, and circumspection with which they may be exerted) that emanate from their principal export market. When over half of the total value of

3 Department of Economic Affairs, *Progress in Land Reform*, p. 37.

4 Simon G. Hanson, *Economic Development in Latin America* (Washington: Inter-American Affairs Press, 1951), p. 67.

5 George Soule, David Efron, and Norman T. Ness, *Latin America in the Future World* (New York: Holt, Rinehart & Winston, Inc., 1945), p. 63.

exports of the Dominican Republic and about three-fourths of the total value of Cuban exports consist of sugar, the domestic owner of sugar plantations cannot be indifferent to the influence of international markets. "Sugar," reported an Economic and Technical Mission organized by the International Bank for Reconstruction and Development, "is not only Cuba's principal source of livelihood. It dominates the economy—and the outlook of the people—in various ways. Sugar plays an even greater part in the exports of Cuba today than it did in the past." Hence the fundamentally colonial and monocultural nature of the Latin American economies, as evidenced by the role of coffee and sugar exports, constricts the economic base even of the apparently omnipotent landowner.

The main characteristics of the ownership of mineral wealth and the conduct of the mining industries in Latin America further accentuate the colonial nature of the economies and add to the obstacles in the path of discovering native, local command over decisive economic elements of power. Foreign ownership of mineral resources and foreign utilization of mineral products imply that an important economic base of power in Latin America is not indigenously controlled. Thus over 90 per cent of Chilean copper is regularly produced by United States-owned enterprises; of 351,000 tons of copper mined in 1953, in excess of 325,000 tons were produced by large mining companies financed by United States capital. The United States-owned Cerro de Pasco Corporation of Peru accounts for about two-thirds of the Peruvian copper output. In the case of Bolivia, despite the nationalization of the principal tin mines, the virtually complete reliance on exports of the mining industry as a source of indispensable foreign exchange perpetuates a political climate which is subject to foreign pressures. For "the products of the mining industry account for some 98 per cent of the country's total exports. And tin concentrates account for some 75 per cent of the total mineral exports." Consequently, "the financial position of Bolivia is always peculiarly sensitive to —is indeed dangerously dependent upon—fluctuations of price and demand in the world markets for nonferrous metals."[6] Control of petroleum production in Latin America resides almost exclusively in the hands of foreign-owned corporations. A United States company produces more than 70 per cent of Peru's crude petroleum; in Venezuela, which accounts for almost 80 per cent of the crude petroleum output of Latin America, a subsidiary of a United States company ranks as the largest oil company in the country.

Venezuela and its oil industry perhaps may be cited as a case study in the predominant role of foreign capital with respect to the control of the mineral bases of power in Latin America. Petroleum, which is exploited almost exclusively by foreign-owned companies, operating under government concession, occupies a crucial position in Venezuelan exports. In one fashion or another, more than 60 per cent of the revenue of the treasury in Venezuela is contributed by the oil companies; during the budget year 1949–1950, about one-third of the total budget receipts consisted of petroleum *royalties* alone. Unlike other mineral industries, moreover, petroleum has continued to attract new capital investment from the United States. Since 74 per cent of United States private direct-investment in the period following World War II (1947–1949) was channeled to the petroleum industry, a

6 Harold Osborne, *Bolivia: A Land Divided* (London: Oxford University Press, 1954), p. 107.

considerable share has been invested in Venezuela as a country with exploitable petroleum resources. Clearly the foreign-owned oil companies constitute factors which cannot be ignored in the power structure of Venezuela. But a precise description of the manner in which power is exercised by the petroleum industry cannot be documented. It would be valuable, for purposes of a study of power, to have accessible a public record of the specific reactions of the oil companies to the seizure of governmental authority by a revolutionary junta led by Rómulo Betancourt in 1945. It would be valuable, for purposes of a study of power, to have available an accurate record of the policies and decisions of the oil companies insofar as they affected the deposition of President Rómulo Gallegos and his supporters, including Betancourt, in 1948. But details of this type are unavailable not only to academic investigators of power in Latin America; they elude public detection and identification in most systems of power. The obscure nature of certain details, however, cannot serve to justify the rejection of an inference that a correlation exists between the economic dominance of the oil companies and the pattern of political behavior in Venezuela. While the exact techniques of the exercise of power are not easily demonstrated, obviously a substantial economic base of power in Venezuela is controlled by economic institutions beyond the geographical boundaries of the country. The control of mineral wealth, consequently, with the framework of colonial economies, introduces an external element of restraint on the exercise of power by domestic forces and movements within Latin America.

Industrialization would appear to represent a significant challenge to the economic forces of colonialism in Latin America. Undoubtedly a successful program of industrialization could alter radically the distribution of power in the Latin American area. Tangible fragments of evidence, in fact, suggest that the present level of industrialization has stimulated modifications in the established patterns of economic power. Consumer goods industries, particularly textiles, have expanded rapidly. Reflecting the influence of domestic manufacturing interests, Latin American governments have been anxious to maintain protective-tariff policies. With industrialization, labor organizations have evolved and have made it possible for new leaders, drawing upon fresh sources of support, to compete for the possession of power. The well-publicized role of Lombardo Toledano in Mexican politics, the prolix constitutional and statutory provisions for social security, the turbulent strikes in some of the Latin American states, the ostentatious, if demagogic, manifestations of solicitude for labor on the part of Juan Domingo Perón, testify to the enhanced prestige of labor and labor unions in a society experiencing the initial tensions and strains of industrialization in the twentieth century.

But the position of manufacturing as an economic base of power in Latin America can be overstated. Hitherto a level of industrialization has not been achieved which would make possible the displacement of the conventional economic bases of power. By United States standards, the Latin American consumer continues to absorb only a small amount of manufactured goods. The Latin American countries continue to be dependent on imports for many items utilized in manufacturing, as well as for much of their machinery, transportation facilities, and factory equipment. And "the most significant economic trend in 1953," according to the Secretariat of the Economic Commission for Latin America, "was, without doubt, the clear indication of a slackening in the rate of industrialization. . . . As a consequence, the industrial share of the gross product in 1953 was only 25.6 per cent, no greater than in 1945." The fact, moreover, that the industrial labor force, compared with total manpower, has not increased since 1950 constitutes evidence of a "fundamental decline in industrialization" in Latin America.[7] A decline of 21 per cent in total Latin American imports of capital goods in 1953, in relation to 1952, also emphasizes the limited potentialities of industrialization in the immediate future.

Notwithstanding the somewhat spectacular construction of the Volta Redonda steel plant in Brazil and the opening of the earthquake-proof Huachipato steel works in Chile, heavy industries remain in an embryonic stage of evolution. By 1954, for example, Brazilian industry produced only 1,100,000 tons of steel ingots annually, and total Chilean production of steel ingots in 1954 amounted to 320,000 tons. "Such industrialization as exists," Gordon concludes with ample evidence, "is either an undernourished image of the Great Society or else a highly specialized form, such as in mining, which exists by grace of foreign ownership and foreign markets."[8]

From the point of view of locating the economic sites of power, the current program of industrialization in Latin America presents an apparent paradox. The desire for industrialization evidently originates with leaders who seek to transfer economic bases of power from foreign to domestic jurisdiction; and the economic nationalism which normally has accompanied the drive

for industrialization would seem to substantiate this assumption. But the financial techniques utilized have not hastened the transfer of power, based on control of industry, to native groups in Latin America. For, lacking huge reservoirs of local capital to finance heavy industry, unwilling (and perhaps unable) to compel modifications in the investment practices of landowners, the Latin Americans, in their attempt to move toward the goal of industrialization, once again have sought foreign capital. Prominent among the suppliers of new capital to Latin America has been the Export-Import Bank of Washington. Every sovereign state in Latin America except Guatemala has received funds from this bank. By 1954, the Export-Import Bank, which supplied more than half of the investment capital required by the Volta Redonda and Huachipato steel plants, had authorized credits of $2,152,023,000 to the Latin American countries. In addition, half of the states in the Latin American region have received loans from the International Bank for Reconstruction and Development. By 1954 this specialized agency of the United Nations had authorized loans of $426,-000,000 to Latin American countries. Since voting power in the International Bank for Reconstruction and Development is based on the proportion of capital subscribed by each member, the United States speaks with a dominant voice in the affairs of the Bank.

Potentially, then, industrialization may prove of large consequence in creating new economic bases of power in Latin America. At some future date, it may modify drastically the position of the conventional economic bases of power. But industrialization on such a scale as yet has failed to materialize. Promise, hope, and aspiration must be distinguished from performance and accomplishment. Accordingly, at the present time, industrialization in Latin

---

[7] United Nations, Department of Economic Affairs, *Economic Survey of Latin America, 1953* (New York, 1954), pp. 10–11.

[8] Wendell C. Gordon, *The Economy of Latin America* (New York: Columbia University Press, 1950), p. 20.

America, realistically appraised, is taking place within the context and environment which in its economic content remains basically colonial.

III

An analysis of the distinguishing characteristics of the economic bases of power in Latin America suggests that the conventional economic sources of power constitute relatively static elements of power. Since ownership of land or mines does not pass readily from the hands of one group to another, control of conventional bases of power cannot be secured by the ambitious mestizo, mulatto, or Indian without a major social upheaval. The system of land tenure dooms to frustration ambitious individuals in search of a new agrarian base of power. Foreign exploitation of mineral resources effectively blocks the possibilities of shifts in the possession of mineral bases of power. And at its current pace of development, industrialization has failed to expand into a broad, substantial base of power.

But while the conventional economic bases of power, landownership and control of mineral resources, represent essentially economic constants in the contemporary equation of power in Latin America, government and the army—often indistinguishable in Latin American society—represent notable variables. For in Latin America, government does not merely constitute the stakes of a struggle among rival economic interests; in Latin America, government itself is a unique base of economic power which, unlike the conventional economic bases of power, is subject to fluctuations in possession. Whereas direct profits from oil fields or copper mines may not be within the grasp of the Latin American, the legal sovereignty of the Latin American states demands that the governmental personnel who serve as intermediaries between the foreign-owned company and the domestic concession shall be of native origin. Thus the discrepancy between the political independence and the economic colonialism of the Latin American states permits government, in the power system of Latin America, to occupy an unusual position as a shifting base of economic power. With the number of lucrative governmental and army posts necessarily limited, the competition understandably is keen. As political office provides a uniquely dynamic opportunity to acquire an economic base of power, however, sufficiently large segments of the population are prepared to take the ultimate risk, the risk of life, in a revolt, in a *coup d'état*, to perpetuate a characteristic feature of Latin American politics—chronic political instability. In the distinctive power structure of Latin America, government serves as a special transformer through which pass the currents of economic ambition.

The pattern of political instability, significantly, has not evolved as a challenge to the conventional economic bases of power, for irregular shifts in control of government take place without disturbing the established economic bases of power. Although widespread industrialization, accompanied by an intensification of economic nationalism, could alter the existing pattern of power, although an extensive program of land reform could not help but affect the distribution of power, seizure of government by a new *caudillo*, on the contrary, does not provoke profound social and economic repercussions in Latin America. Thus chronic political instability serves as an avenue of socio-economic mobility, but it does not pose a genuine danger to the control of the conventional economic bases of power. When a "revolutionary" junta replaced Federico Chaves as President of Paraguay in May 1954 with Tómas Romero Pereira and subsequently, in July, arranged for the election of General Alfredo Stroessner without opposition, the pattern was a familiar one: the cast of political characters was shuffled, and the colonial economy of Paraguay remained intact. Indeed, such events can be evaluated adequately only in terms of the French aphorism, *"Plus ça change, plus c'ést la même chose."*

The interpretation of power and political instability in Latin America developed by this study may be summarized in a series of generalized propositions. A decisive correlation exists between the control of the economic bases of power and the real exercise of political power in Latin America. Control of the conventional economic bases of power remains relatively static. Because of the colonial nature of the Latin American economies, an exceptional economic premium attaches to control of the apparatus of government as a dynamic base of power. Whereas the conventional bases of power effectively restrict mobility in economic status, control of government provides an unusually dynamic route to wealth and power. Thus the contrast between the stable character of the conventional economic bases of power and the shifting, unconventional position of government provokes intense and violent competition for control of government as a means of acquiring and expanding a base of wealth and power. In the vocabulary of mathematics, *chronic political instability is a function of the contradiction between the realities of a colonial economy and the poltical requirements of legal sovereignty among the Latin American states.*

IV

Significant implications for both public policy and research appear inherent in the interpretation of Latin American politics here formulated. In the field of public policy, this interpretation implies that it is not possible for the United States to have powerful allies in Latin America so long as present economic patterns persist. Contemporary economic patterns of colonialism are conductive to the maintenance of reliable *diplomatic* allies for the United States in Latin America; and the *diplomatic* reliability of the Latin American states is faithfully registered, on many issues, in the voting records of the General Assembly of the United Nations. But the same economic conditions which ensure diplomatic reliability weaken the *power* position of the Latin American states. For, as Hans Morgenthau recognizes in the second (and not the first) edition of his *Politics Among Nations,* the quality of government itself is a factor of power in international politics. Hence economic colonialism promotes political instability, which detracts from the power of reliable diplomatic allies of the United States; but, while the achievement of political stability would augment the power of the Latin American states, the elimination of a status of economic colonialism may diminish the diplomatic reliability of their governments! And the dilemma thus brought to the surface by the interpretation of Latin American politics offered in this study has never been publicly acknowledged by the United States Department of State.

For research, the implications of this interpretation of Latin American politics are rather obvious. If political studies of the Latin American area are to rest on more than superficial foundations, they can rest neither on formal analyses of constitutions nor on the diplomatic exchanges between the United States and various Latin American countries. Nor, in the light of this interpretation, can a study nourish the illusion that it has penetrated to the realities of Latin American politics when it has applied the label "dictator" to a particular holder of governmental office in Latin America. The Latin American *caudillo,* according to the implications of the interpretation presented here, operates within a narrowly circumscribed range of power, since he may not tamper with the traditional economic bases of power. Serious attempts to analyze the nature of politics in Latin America, therefore, must seek to identify the ambits of political maneuverability within which power may be exercised by those who occupy posts of governmental authority in sovereign states with colonial economies. The successful conclusion of such attempts should result in a new awareness of the limitations on the nature of the power actually exercised by presidents and junta members in the politically unstable environment of Latin America.

14

Violence as a Power Factor
in Latin American Politics

William S. Stokes

Introduction

Violence seems to be institutionalized in the organization, maintenance, and changing of governments in Latin America. The methodology of force is found in advanced and in backward countries, in Indian, mestizo, and white republics, in the large states and in the small ones, in urban and in rural areas, in agricultural and in industrial organization, in the beginning of the twentieth century, in the present period, and in the early, middle, and late nineteenth century—in a word, wherever and whenever Hispanic culture is to be found in the Western Hemisphere. The governments of the following states were changed by force in the recent past: Argentina, June 1943; Haiti, January 1946; Bolivia, July 1946 and April 1952; Nicaragua, May 1947; Ecuador, August 1947; Costa Rica, March 1948; Paraguay, June 1948; Peru, October 1948; Venezuela, November 1948; Panama, November

From William S. Stokes, "Violence as a Power Factor in Latin American Politics," *Western Political Quarterly*, Vol. V, No. 3 (September 1952). Reprinted by permission.

1948; El Salvador, December 1948; and Cuba, March 1952.

Force is a unifying factor in Latin American political culture, yet the fact of geographical and ethnic differences and of varying rates of social and economic development leads to the logical inference that the mobilization of violence for political purposes is not likely to revolve around one simple formula. This is, however, exactly what is done when the general term "revolution" is employed to describe all use of force in Latin American politics. Violence is, instead, a highly developed technique for obtaining power. Direct action procedures include *machetismo, cuartelazo, golpe de estado,* and revolution. The monopolization of the power factors of the state by a single political leader, a group, or a class sometimes renders unnecessary the direct employment of violence, and in such cases the methods of *imposición, candidato único, continuismo* and election (in the Anglo-American sense) may be selected. These are, of course, outwardly peaceful methods of obtaining and maintaining power, but they rest upon a foundation of force. . . .

Machetismo

Machetismo is a crude, primitive method of mobilizing violence primarily in local, rural politics but occasionally in national, urban areas as well. The term emanates from the word "machete," the general utility knife employed widely throughout Latin America. In an extractive, agricultural economy guaranteeing little more than subsistence to the majority of the people, poverty is seldom or ever so great as to deny the rural resident his machete. It is a major implement in the construction of habitation, the production of foodstuffs, and in the establishment of political power. To survive, the rural inhabitant must develop proficiency in its use, and the process of becoming expert begins as a child. Whoever can command the authority represented by the machete in rural areas possesses political power of an important nature and automatically constitutes a factor to be reckoned with in the affairs of government.

If it could be demonstrated that no political leader has exercised sufficient discipline over the rural masses to employ their collective strength in direct action, then it might be possible to argue that *machetismo* no longer characterizes Latin American rural politics. However, leadership of a highly personal nature can readily be observed in Latin America. The matters that vitally concern the rural resident include distribution of government patronage, rights to water holes and grazing areas, military service to the central government, road-building in lieu of payment of taxes, and adjudication of social disputes. In many instances, the leader who exercises authority and issues judgments on such issues is the *alcalde, jefe de operaciones militares, comandante de armas,* or official in the church hierarchy. But on the other hand the political leader might very well possess no official position at all. That his power exists there is no denying; his authority is so well known that almost anyone in the area of his jurisdiction can identify him as *el que manda* (the one who commands). This kind of absolutist personal leadership is local, rural *caudillismo.*

Many writers, Latin Americans included, have associated *caudillismo* with the violent struggle for leadership among the generals in the early independence period, and hence terms such as the "Age of the *Caudillos,*" and "Men on Horseback" are common in historical literature. It is correct to define *caudillismo* as a principle of personal leadership in politics, but it cannot be restricted to any one age or period in Latin American history. Indeed, its origins are to be traced in part at least to the feudal institutions of Spain and Portugal and to the nature of government in the colonial period. *Caudillismo* as personal authority, as a substitute for direction and control by institutional means, such as law, is to be found in all periods of Latin American development, including the present. Nor is it accurate to think of the *caudillo* solely as a man on horseback, for he may be a civilian, such as Carlos Antonio López of Paraguay, García Moreno of Ecuador, Estrada Cabrera of Guatemala, and Fulgencio Batista of Cuba (who although a sergeant in the army did not even learn to ride a horse until after he had first achieved power!).

The determinants of leadership in Latin American politics have never been investigated with sufficient objectivity and scholarship to permit definitive generalizations. How are personal qualities, education and professional training, religious and other social beliefs, location in a rural or urban area, and affiliation with organizations and institutions related to the development of leadership? We do not know. In my own field experience I have known *caudillos* who fitted various physical and psychological patterns. The *caudillo* exists, however, and exercises an almost omnipotent personal authority in his designated area, an authority his people will respect without question to the point of enforcement on the field of battle. He is in his own person law, constitution, party, flag, and political principle.

Although Latin American rural communities are frequently isolated by poor communication facilities, the local *caudillos* are thrown into contact from time to time (to divide the spoils of government, for example), and occasionally, in activities such as drinking, card playing, carousing, and brawling a man so stands out that the others automatically accept his authority and extend to him their loyalty. When this occurs for an area as large as a province or a department, institutional means for resolving major issues of public controversy have been created which frequently may be entirely disassociated from the formal structure of government. The sectional *caudillos* are usually the group from which "available" presidential candidates are to be found. When a sectional leader commands the loyalty of all other major *caudillos* in the country, then a *jefe máximo* (or *caudillo supremo*) is recognized, and if he wants the presidency he will have it; he assuredly will determine who *will* have it. This procedure for the establishment of executive power is one that is essentially based upon violence, because any leader at any time may challenge the hierarchy of power, with immediate local, sectional, or national conflict resulting. Indeed, case studies

of *machetismo* can be discovered somewhere in Latin America at all times, although most frequently in the local areas.

Widespread evidence of *machetismo* at the national level can still be observed among backward and advanced countries alike from time to time. Thus, for about half of the year 1947 Paraguay was in what news dispatches termed "civil war," and ever since April 1948, Colombia has been in a state of violence that includes geographically almost the entire country. When no one *caudillo* can peacefully subjugate existing opposition, when one or more challenges claim to "supreme power," *machetismo* becomes a costly and time-consuming methodology for establishing authority. Among seventy nationwide examples of *machetismo* in Colombia in the nineteenth century, one conflict alone took approximately 80,000 lives, and the struggle which covered the years 1899 to 1903 took about 100,000 lives. . . .

Cuartelazo

Cuartelazo (sometimes called *sargentada* or *golpe de cuartel*), a more highly developed, complex method of organizing and changing governments than *machetismo*, has its focus in the barracks *(cuartel)*. Its classic pattern is the treason of a single barracks; the *pronunciamiento, manifiesto,* or *grito;* the march on centers of communication, sites of military supplies, the exchequer, government headquarters, and ultimately the capital itself; the announcement to the populace that the government has changed hands; and finally the appointment of a patriotic junta to guide the country in the interim period. Even the most cursory examination of illustrative *cuartelazos* reveals that it is a mistake to think of the technique as involving massive, overpowering military force repressing the legitimate desires of the people. To be successful the *cuartelazo* requires consummate skill in the selection of leadership, the drafting of a program, the equating of the power factors, the technical problems of logistics, and the drafting of at least a temporary series of policies to meet the most pressing problems of government when power is obtained. He who would play barracks politics must know his fellow officers and men well indeed to suggest that they follow his leadership in a calculated plan of treason. Betrayal by a single officer or soldier means at least ignominious failure in the venture and possibly death by firing squad.

The *cuartelazo's* success depends upon capturing the support of other centers of military power as well as that of public opinion. This is a problem which effectively deters all but the most well-prepared politician. Many Latin American armies, particularly those in the South American area, have been trained by German technicians, whereas the navies have been trained or inspired by the British. In the century of air power, the plane must be considered, and as a competing unit with the older vested interests in the area of defense, it can constitute a delicate source to be placated. Even assuming that a barracks has been captured and that it is able to obtain sufficient support from other segments of the armed forces to justify some optimism for success, what about the civilian *caudillos* in both the rural and urban areas? As has already been demonstrated, they also command power in politics, including from time to time the authority to plunge an entire country into civil war. Thus, it usually develops that the successful *cuartelazo* involves substantial support from the sectional leaders, the leading university and professional men, and the leaders of several of the principal political parties in the country. . . .

Golpe de Estado

The *golpe de estado,* frequently called the *coup d'état,* and sometimes referred to as *golpe militar,* with the noun *derrocamiento* being occasionally employed along with the descriptive phrase *desplazar del poder,* is the fastest, the most difficult to plan and implement successfully (short of genuine revolution), and potentially the most dangerous of the forceful methods of establishing and changing governments in Latin America. The *golpe* is a direct assault on power—almost always personal in Latin American countries—which means the immobilization of the president either through assassination or detention. The possibilities of success are obviously enhanced if the president's cabinet, high-ranking members of the armed forces, and the head of the police system can be seized when the assault on the president is consummated. The *golpe de estado* is distinguished from the *cuartelazo* by the fact that professional military experience is less needed, and by the procedure of attack which bypasses the *cuartel* entirely. Whereas considerable military skill is required to capture the loyalty of troops and lead them successfully against a major *cuartel,* even a civilian with literary, professional, or scholarly training can, assuming ingress to the *casa presidencial,* blow out the president's brains and proclaim a change in governments. The *golpe,* then, is a forceful method of organizing and changing governments which definitely permits, even encourages, civilian participation.

Inherent in the technique is ecstatic

excitement for leaders and masses alike, for the *golpe* guarantees that a "bad" *caudillo* can be replaced by a "good" one, that "justice" can be substituted for "injustice," *immediately,* without the time-consuming and demoralizing limitation of such institutional restraints as law or constitutions. To the predilection toward extremism in politics in Latin America is added the factor of extreme speed and flexibility. The leader can ascertain easily and quickly the extent to which public opinion has been conditioned to the kind of change in administrations he is attempting. Politically, his status might well be nothing one moment, everything the next; his *golpe* might be rejected upon its announcement and he, himself, put to flight or captured and subject to penalties that might include death.

Yet the *golpe* is not spontaneous combustion in the field of organizing and changing governments. As with the *cuartelazo,* mastery of the elements of politics within the environmental framework of each Latin American country is required by the successful politician (some of whom have participated in many *golpes* during a lifetime). The first step in the process is almost invariably the organization of the cadre of leaders and subleaders. To cement loyalty and guarantee incentive, the *jefe supremo* of the proposed *golpe* is likely to appoint his key personnel in advance. Sometimes there is no need to carry on any propaganda whatever prior to the assault; public opinion might be favorably disposed toward a change by the ineptitude of the incumbent. If this is not the case, however, then media of communication are required to attack the government, more frequently than not (unfortunately for the research scholar who faces the task of separating objective evidence from falsification), through lies, slander, and license. As insurance

against failure, the *caudillo* should have an airplane, an automobile, or other means of locomotion ready for immediate departure. Recognition by the United States and other major powers is no longer a primary determinant, if it ever was, for the existence of a government, yet it is undeniably true that immediate recognition of a new regime might have a positive effect on public opinion in the Latin American country concerned. The leaders, therefore, endeavor to plant competent diplomats in the several capitals to negotiate speedy recognition. Timing is of the utmost importance, and although circumstances vary from country to country, Sundays and holidays, when the official offices are closed and the president probably is separated from his major supporters, are to be preferred. Colonel Kurt Conrad Arnade, former military advisor to the Government of Bolivia, described a well-timed *golpe*:

> I once received an invitation to attend a party at the house of a high government official. On entering the house I discovered that the junta had originated the invitation, and, after assembling the entire government in one reception room, locked the doors and assumed power.[1]

The recent political history of Bolivia provides excellent case studies of the *golpe de estado.* Eight different men occupied the presidency from 1930 to 1943. One resigned under pressure, one committed suicide or was murdered, two transmitted power peacefully, and the others were forcibly ejected. The most dramatic and the most completely analyzed *golpe* in recent years took place on July 21, 1946, in connection with the government of President Gualberto Villarroel who obtained

---

[1] Kurt Conrad Arnade, "The Technique of the *Coup d'Etat* in Latin America," *United Nations World,* Vol. IV, No. 2. (February 1950), 24–25.

power by *cuartelazo* on December 20, 1943, possibly with official aid from the Argentine government. It was so well planned and executed that when the junta's assassins cornered President Villarroel in his own offices and shot him, then thew him, still alive, from the second-story window where a mob seized the body and hanged it from a lamp post, the belief was common in the United States, despite very convincing evidence to the contrary, that this was a popular movement. . . .

Revolution

The history of Latin America from independence to the present time is a history of violent struggles of "ins" versus "outs," but it is not a history of revolutionary movements designed to remold the institutional bases of Latin American life. By "revolution" I mean ". . . fundamental change in the nature of the state, the functions of government, the principles of economic production and distribution, the relationship of the social classes, particularly as regards the control of government— in a word, a significant breaking with the past." Revolution so defined is rare in Latin America, and even mass participation in violence is only occasionally found. It is an obvious and inescapable fact that revolution is too big and too difficult a power mechanism to employ in Latin America with any frequency. Problems of leadership, ideology, policy, planning, logistics, and timing are all maximized in genuine revolution.

Profound institutional transformations have taken place in Uruguay since the first decade of the twentieth century, but such changes have not occurred in an atmosphere of revolution, despite the ferocious violence of the nineteenth century. The Liberal revolution in Central America which

began in the 1870's dramatically established in theory the doctrines of the liberal-democratic state and attempted some institutional changes, such as relations between Church and state. But the revolution lacked sustained vitality and continuity, and its effect was shadow rather than substance. Systematic research might well reveal that revolutions have been under way in various Latin American countries in recent times, such as in Brazil from 1930 to 1945, in Argentina since 1943, and in the Dominican Republic from the 1930's to the present. The Cuban revolution assuredly deserves study. But I would also argue that the only clearcut illustration of revolution in Latin America since independence is the Mexican revolution, which began in 1910–1911 and which continues to exist as the dominant characteristic of Mexican economic, political, and social life today. Despite the difficulties of mobilizing violence in revolution, of all the forceful methods of organizing power in Latin America, it is probably the most democratic. Revolution is the only method which invites mass participation and renders imperative the formation of decisions on basic issues of public policy by virtually all members of the state.

Imposición

Imposición is a nominally peaceful method of organizing power in which the dominant political element in the state hand-picks a candidate and then rigs the election to guarantee victory. Its major principle is the presupposition of success for the privileged candidate. That being the case, the opposition must never become convinced that an *imposición* is operating because then there logically is no further premium in maintaining peace and force is likely to result. The conditions under which *imposición* enjoys maximum possibilities for development include: (1) the existence of a *caudillo* of such stature, power, and personal popularity that no opposition dares stand against him; (2) a government firmly in power; (3) the principal parties or major elements of political strength in the country in agreement on the same candidate for supreme power. Even under the most favorable conditions, however, *imposición* is exceedingly difficult to exploit, and only the most mature, prepared, and experienced individuals or groups have been able to utilize it successfully.

A firmly established, confident government can, of course, openly announce support for a particular candidate and successfully carry through a campaign. On the other hand, such a course invites the opposition to unite and opens the way to charges of official unfairness which might result in undesirable violence. The typical *imposición* usually begins, therefore, with an official announcement from the highest sources in the state that the government is neutral and will guarantee free, fair elections. These protestations of impartiality and fairness are repeated continually throughout the campaign through all the media of communication. The president frequently will issue an impressive order to all government personnel calling attention to the principles of representative democracy and outlining specifically the provisions of the electoral law relating to proper conduct by government employees.

The government is likely to encourage a large number of candidates to offer their names in the election. The politically ambitious *caudillo* can reason thus: if the election is really fair, perhaps the vagaries of public opinion will favor his candidacy; if an *imposición* is under way perhaps he is the chosen candidate of those who are manipulating power. All during the campaign the perpetrators of the *imposición* carefully select and sharpen for effective use the methods required to insure success, whether they be control over the nominating machinery, registration fraud, appointment of key personnel at the polls, intervention in the *escrutinio* (official check of balloting), or cruder techniques involving purchase of votes or employment of violence through party workers, the police, or the armed forces....

Candidato Único

Candidato único, or an election in which there is but one candidate running, occurs occasionally when a *caudillo* develops who is so overwhelming in stature that no other political figure dares oppose him. An excellent illustration is General Manuel Odría of Peru who obtained power by *cuartelazo* in October 1948, then developed his position so strongly that he was able to run for the presidency on July 2, 1950, without opposition. It is true that General Ernesto Montagne offered his name as an opposition candidate, but the National Electoral Board refused to accept it, and the General wisely did not persist in his presidential aspirations. President Felipe Molas López of Paraguay achieved power in a *candidato único* election of April 17, 1949. When so employed, however, it becomes an open, blunt repudiation of representative democracy and opens the administration to attack at home and abroad. More frequently the astute *jefe supremo* of the country will select *imposición* as a more subtle, mature method of realizing his objectives. For an outstanding *caudillo* it is a relatively simple matter to persuade a respectable, distinguished man to run against him, with the understanding that the dummy candidate will receive enough votes to make the campaign appear authentic and to maintain his honor.

Candidato único is used much more frequently when one major party is unified, the other hopelessly fragmented. When victory for the latter seems utterly impossible it commonly will refuse to campaign, and will count its strength by the number of people who stay away from the polls. Utilizing Colombia as a case study, the following men won the presidency in *candidato único* elections in recent years: Dr. Miguel Abadía Méndez, a Conservative, in 1926; Dr. Alfonso López, a Liberal, in 1934; Dr. Eduardo Santos, a Liberal, in 1938; and Laureano Gómez, a Conservative, in 1949. In instances in which it appears that neither of two *caudillos* will give way *candidato único* may be resorted to in order to preserve the peace by awarding the presidency to a third man.

Continuismo

Continuismo is a peaceful, constitutional methodology for maintaining a chief executive in power beyond the legal term of his office. From time to time a *caudillo* will discover at the termination of his tenure that no one wishes to challenge him. He might even be approached by representatives of major power groupings in the country with the appeal that he continue in office. If the constitution prohibits re-election, then *continuismo* must be embraced. This usually involves amending the constitution, drafting a new document (in which the major change will be a section providing for temporary abrogation of the no-re-election article), enactment of legislative statute, plebiscite, or judicial interpretation. Russell H. Fitzgibbon's important study of *continuismo* in Central America and the Caribbean presents in detail some of these techniques. But *continuismo*, like the other forceful and peaceful techniques for organizing political power, was in use before the period covered by the Fizgibbon study, and it applies not only to the small countries in the Caribbean and Middle American area but to the larger countries of South America as well. The new Argentine constitution of 1949, for example, eliminated the no-re-election clause of the document of 1853 in order to permit General Juan Domingo Perón a second term of office.

Elections

Finally, the electoral method of organizing power has been employed at least once in all of the Latin American countries. It is my hypothesis, however, that elections in the Anglo-American sense for the determination of executive leadership are resorted to mainly in Latin America when more satisfactory methods have for one reason or another proved inadequate. Election under such circumstances is not likely to produce a strong, popular leader, but the technique may provide time for reassembling and again bringing into play the more fundamental bases for determining political power.

If the assumption of force in Latin American politics possesses validity, the question quite fairly can be raised: Why have elections at all? The reasons include the following: (1) The need for the friendship and financial assistance of the United States dictates at least superficial respect for the idiosyncrasies of that country in the field of organizing and changing governments. (2) Elections have a public-opinion role to perform for the government. Through the media of communication the government can help to strengthen the conviction that it has chosen the right candidate. (3) Elections are also useful to the opposition which can employ the campaigns to build up moral justification for revolt. (4) There is the belief that the electoral technique of the liberal-democratic state should be developed as the most satisfactory procedure for organizing and changing governments.

Concluding Implications

The thesis of violence in the organization, maintenance, and changing of governments in Latin America is susceptible of considerable demonstration through ample objective evidence. As democracy is assumed to be imperative to American foreign policy in the Western Hemisphere, and as it is evident that violence tends to characterize politics in the Latin American countries, it is only logical that a strong effort should be made by the Department of State of the United States to eliminate violence. Two main approaches stand out for consideration. One is associated with the name of the late Laurence Duggan, who argued that we could never further the development of democracy in Latin America by supporting the landed oligarchs or the reactionary army and church groups. Instead, he insisted, we should extend our aid and assistance to the labor unions, which, if they achieved a position of power in Latin American politics, would strive for democracy. What Mr. Duggan did not make clear was that the major unions, during the time he was advocating his policy, were dominated by militant Communists. If they were to achieve power it seems reasonably clear that they would offer modest support indeed for such principles of the liberal-democratic state as individualism, the basic freedoms, and parliamentary organization. It is fair, however, to agree with Duggan that failure to support the labor unions in all probability would mean retention in some countries and development in

others of clerico-military authoritarianism, almost as much opposed to democracy as is communism.

The other approach, one that seems to be widely accepted, is that political instability in Latin America finds its origins in economic distress among the masses. The concomitant argument is that if the Latin American countries are assisted in raising their living standards, democratic procedures will in some way result. The fact that violence has a long history even in the most advanced Latin American countries, such as Argentina, negates for me so simple an explanation. Furthermore, it is instructive for us to observe that right-wing authoritarianism as exemplified by Perón's *justicialismo,* and left-wing authoritarianism, as exemplified by the Mexican Revolution or *aprismo,* also call for higher material standards of living for the masses.

My own research has led me to the conviction that the problem of violence is much more basic and a good deal more complicated than either of these approaches would suggest. There is much evidence which leads one to believe that there is no one simple cause for violence, which, if removed or corrected, would produce stable, democratic politics in the Anglo-American conception. It seems more defensible to me to argue, first, that Hispanic culture tends everywhere in Latin America to dominate in the power sense; second, that the institutions of Hispanic culture such as the family, church, army, educational institutions, and economic systems, are essentially authoritarian in nature, hence, conditioning the individual to more frequent acceptance of processes of dictatorship, including violence, than processes of political democracy.

The Hispanic family, characterized by stratified inequality of rights, duties, and responsibilities based upon differentiations of age, sex, and other factors;

the Church, hierarchical, authoritarian, and absolutist in both organization and dogma; the educational system, with its theories of exclusion which reduce the extent of educational services to a few, its segregation of the sexes, particularly in the primary and secondary fields, its discouragement of women in higher education, and its widespread retention of scholasticism in method; the exaggerated importance and influence of the army in social and political life; and an economic organization which discourages individual initiative, imagination, and enterprise, and which seeks solutions through collectivism—all these are data in support of the generalization that the individual is constantly conditioned to authoritarianism. If the hypothesis here presented is valid, then it is possible to say that Point Four and the program of the United Nations in respect to Latin America, both of which assume that modification of one aspect of Latin American culture—the economic—will produce attitudes conducive to the development of democracy, are doomed to confusion and disillusionment.

Indeed, the eradication of force and violence takes on monumental proportions, for it implies fundamental reorganization of large parts of an entire way of life. Effective exploitation of those few aspects of Hispanic culture which tend toward the development of political democracy, and modification or elimination of the many that do not, presuppose almost unlimited time, power, and material resources, which are denied to any one state, such as the United States, or collection of states, such as the United Nations or the Organization of American States.

In this connection the question might well be raised as to whether the employment of violence in organizing political power in Latin America necessarily negates the principles of representative democracy. Or, to put the issue in another way, to what extent have governments established by force lacked majority support? Is it possible that Latin American political culture has developed procedures for measuring and representing opinion different from but as valid as the techniques of election, initiative, referendum, and plebiscite of the Anglo-American and western European states? This is a subject on which firm judgments already exist, but I submit that it is an area of research which might profit through comprehensive elaboration. Systematic analysis of the pathology of violence in Latin American countries is a necessary introduction to mature and meaningful speculation on the meaning of the phenomenon in terms of both comparative government and international relations. The definition of terms and the survey of selected case studies found in this paper point to the obvious conclusion that other facets of the broad, fundamental problem of the nature of power in Latin American politics require research. The most important of such areas include: (1) the development of techniques for determining accurately where power is to be found in such areas as the appointment of personnel, the formulation of policy, the administration of the functions of the state, and the adjudication of competing interests; (2) an analysis of the nature of power and its classification and application to given circumstances, including the extent to which it is personal; the extent to which it is institutional, associated with the family, church, army, or economic organization; and the extent to which it is structural and found in federal, unitary, executive, legislative, or judicial forms; and (3) an evaluation of the pattern of power from the standpoint of its relationship to forms and philosophies of government.

15

The Aspiration for Economic Development

George I. Blanksten

Much of Latin America may be included among what have been dubbed the underdeveloped areas of the world. In general, these are recognized by three distinguishing characteristics. In the first place, industrialization is either nonexistent or in its earliest stages in the underdeveloped areas. Second, the standards of living there, frequently expressed in terms of gross national product per capita, are relatively low. Finally—and perhaps most significantly—these areas are theaters of remarkably rapid change.

Obviously, there is a wide range of difference among the twenty countries of Latin America, and even within some of them, with respect to these characteristics. Indeed, it is as inaccurate to regard all of Latin America as one huge uniformly underdeveloped area as it is to indulge in many another gross generalization about the economies or the politics or the cultures of the region. The countries of the area range from those with extremely under-

From George Blanksten, "The Aspiration for Economic Development," *The Annals,* Vol. CCCXXXIV (March 1961). Reprinted by permission.

developed economies—such as Haiti and Bolivia—through typically underdeveloped situations—such as Costa Rica and Guatemala—to fairly well-developed economies—such as those of Argentina and Uruguay.

Underdeveloped areas are, essentially, changing or growing areas. Economic development, the basic change process, is not a vague or general umbrella covering all varieties of economic change. Rather, this process is the more sharply defined phenomenon of technological innovation resulting in greater efficiency on the part of the productive arts. A more effective technology draws a higher level of production—that is, a greater gross national product per capita—from the same initial input into an economy. Despite the great attention devoted since the end of World War II to the underdeveloped areas, it should not be assumed that economic development is a recent or new phenomenon in Latin America or, for that matter, in any part of the world. "One of the enduring questions about man is his inventiveness," an anthropologist has pointed out. "We know that man invents; we know that primitive man invents. ..."

TABLE 1 Economic Development in Latin America[a]
(Rank order of countries based on
gross national product per capita)

Rank	Country	Gross National Product Per Capita (in U. S. dollars)
1	Argentina	$ 688
2	Venezuela	457
3	Cuba	454
4	Uruguay	382
5	Panama	382
6	Chile	335
7	Brazil	278
8	Colombia	231
9	Costa Rica	203
10	Mexico	199
11	Dominican Republic	189
12	Guatemala	182
13	Nicaragua	168
14	El Salvador	167
15	Paraguay	166
16	Honduras	134
17	Peru	118
18	Bolivia	109
19	Ecuador	93
20	Haiti	62
For comparison	United States	2,200

[a] See Harold E. Davis, ed., *Government and Politics in Latin America* (New York: The Ronald Press Company, 1958), pp. 50–93, especially 60–71; and Gabriel A. Almond and James S. Coleman, eds., *The Politics of the Developing Areas* (Princeton, N.J.: Princeton University Press, 1960), pp. 455–531.

It would appear that the process of economic development not only dates from the earliest phases of human society, but also alters the life circumstances of all communities, be they traditional or modern, underdeveloped or westernized.

Given this enduring universality, both in time and place, of technological change, it is worth asking why social scientists—particularly economists and political scientists—in the United States have developed a particularly strong interest in economic growth in the underdeveloped areas at this juncture in history. Two answers suggest themselves. The first has to do with the relationship of this problem to the foreign policy concerns of the United States. Although it is often denied—and, in some contexts, quite properly denied—that scholars' research interests are oriented toward questions in public policy, a strong correlation between the two is evident in much of the current thinking and writing about the underdeveloped areas. Since World War II, the foreign policy problems of the United States have come increasingly to embrace the underdeveloped areas. Latin America was chronologically the first of these to demand North American attention as a matter of public policy. During the past fifteen years, more than a score of new nations have achieved independence in the Middle East, Southeast Asia, and sub-Saharan Africa. All of these present problems in foreign policy. Scholarly interest in the underdeveloped areas—ranging from the simplest healthy curiosity about the new nations among them to more sophisticated theoretical questions —must inevitably follow.

Beyond matters of public policy, it seems likely that a second influence attracts economists, political scientists, and other social scientists to the underdeveloped areas at this juncture in the intellectual history of the academic disciplines involved. In general, these scholars see the underdeveloped areas as centers of change. Various terms— not only economic development, but also westernization, political modernization, and political development— have recently been coined to identify the change process or components of it. What is economic development?

What is westernization? What is political modernization? What is political development? Can it be that the relevant social sciences are involved, here and now in the twentieth century, in a species of revival of evolutionary theory?

Evolutionary Approach

Twentieth-century evolutionary theory, if that is indeed what we are up to, might well take its predecessor as a point of departure. This evolutionary thinking held that whatever came next exhibited three essential characteristics —it passed through an identifiable and prescribed set of steps and stages, it was more complex than that which preceded it, and it was to be assigned a higher value than that accorded its predecessor. Do we mean to say of Latin American and other underdeveloped areas that, as they experience economic growth, it is necessary that their economies pass through a common ordering of steps and stages, that each is more complex or less primitive than what went before, and that the aspiration for economic development is essentially the assignment of a higher value to the later than to the earlier stages?

Let us consider these three propositions. While economists are as yet far from agreement on the issue of whether an economy passes through a common set of steps or stages during the course of economic development, this case is being argued. Prominent among the proponents of a steps-and-stages formulation of economic development is W. W. Rostow, who holds that a society passes through at least five stages during the course of its economic growth. These are the traditional stage, the period of preconditions, the take-off, the stage of sustained growth, and the

period of the mature economy[1]. Of these, the first three stages are applicable to the underdeveloped areas, with the situations of preconditions and take-off especially relevant to much of Latin America.

Traditional stage

In the traditional stage—to be found in contemporary Latin America almost exclusively in the indigenous communities in countries like Ecuador, Peru, and Guatemala, where these communities' economies are essentially, unintegrated with the national systems—the economy, albeit dynamic, changes slowly. In such Guatemalan Indian communities, a recent study has shown, "the classic form is still the ideal, and that which is believed. . . . The large bulk of the Indian population remain[s] relatively passive."[2] But, as the developmental process carries the economy to the precondition stage—as in much of contemporary Latin America—there emerges a situation in which the leading elements of the system are still traditional, but the invasion of westernizing or modernizing influences has been great

---

[1] W. W. Rostow's leading writings on the stages of economic growth are *The Process of Economic Growth* (London: Oxford University Press, 1953); "Trends in the Allocation of Resources in Secular Growth," in Léon H. Dupriez, ed., *Economic Progress* (Louvain: Institut de Recherches Economiques et Sociales, 1955); "The Relation between Political and Economic Development" (Cambridge, Mass., unpublished manuscript, 1956); "The Stages of Economic Growth," *The Economic History Review,* second series, XII, No. 1 (August 1959), 1–16; and *The Stages of Economic Growth* (New York: Cambridge University Press, 1960).

[2] Raymond L. Scheele, "Santo Domingo Xenacoj: 1944–51," in Richard N. Adams, ed., *Political Changes in Guatemalan Indian Communities* (New Orleans, La.: Tulane University Middle American Research Institute, 1957), pp. 38–39.

enough to increase the rate of speed of change. In Latin America, the economies of Haiti, Ecuador, and Paraguay—to mention but a few illustrations — are representative of this situation. In this stage, the first pains of development come to be felt, and resistances to it frequently become manifest. Noting that in precondition economies "some Latin American leaders don't want technological change," one observer [Stokes] has pointed out that "those people with the maximum status, dignity, power, and influence in Latin American society have not seen fit to spend their time and money in studying science, technology, and administration for adaptation to their own cultures."

Take-off

The take-off, following the precondition stage, is of peculiar potential importance in the analysis of economies like those of Brazil and Mexico. This is the stage in which change appears to be most rapid and spectacular. Indeed, with the coming of take-off, change appears to be irresistible. It is frequently thought of as the chief characteristic and the main preoccupation of the society. Puerto Rican Governor Luis Muñoz Marín is said to have declared that in such situations the per capita national income is a figure of such widespread interest that it is known by virtually all literate persons in the society. Rostow has defined this stage as "the interval during which the rate of investment increases in such a way that the real output *per capita* rises and this initial increase carries with it radical changes in production techniques and the disposition of income flows which perpetuate the new scale of investment and perpetuate thereby the rising trend in *per capita* output." Whether this

current Rostow formulation eventually stands or falls, it seems likely that there is indeed a phase, largely economic in character, of decisive transformation during the course of the developmental process and that this is a time of more rapid and spectacular change than is characteristic of other stages of growth. It is significant that the governing elites of take-off are usually committed to the support of continued rapid transformation. The devotion to enduring rapid change of Mexico's governing Party of Revolutionary Institutions (PRI) is a case in point.

With respect to the second element of evolutionary thought—the proposition that what comes next is more complex or less primitive than was what went before—it seems clear that this is generally accepted as an integral component of our contemporary thinking about technological innovation and economic development. Impressive evidence can be amassed in support of the proposition that the history of technological change has been, among other things, a history of progression from simple to increasingly complex gadgetry. This appears to be true also of the structure of society, which takes on more complicated forms as economic development progresses. "By virtue of the patterning demanded by a particular technological development," it has been pointed out, "people come to have different occupations and roles, to have different amounts of wealth, and different amounts of economic and political power."[3] A recent study of political change in Mexico, Argentina, Uruguay, Chile, and Brazil indicates that the social and political structures of those countries have

---

3 H. J. Eysenck, *The Psychology of Politics* (New York: Frederick A. Praeger, Inc., 1955), p. 15.

become increasingly complex as economic development has occurred.

Values

And, finally, what of the value question? Is the aspiration for economic development essentially the assignment of a higher value to the later than to the earlier stages of the change process? This matter stands on two legs. In the first instance, the formulation of economic development as technological change carries with it a built-in neutralization of the value question. Ostensibly, a more efficient technology merely provides an easier way to achieve an objective or to realize a value than had previously been the case; it does this and nothing more. The value had already been held, or else the new technology would not have been adopted. It has been pointed out:

> In the realm of technology, innovations are most apt to be acceptable, because of the peculiar character that technology has as distinct from, say, family organization or religion. . . . Technology is a goal-directed aspect of culture. . . . The direct impact of technological results can usually be seen in terms of explicit, commonly held goals in the society. . . . The chances for technological innovation to prove itself are relatively good.[4]

In this sense, the aspiration for economic development, or the assignment of a positive value to the adoption of a more efficient means to an already accepted end, is a species of prerequisite for economic growth. Typically, however, that development, as it proceeds, induces a number of unforeseen and undesired social and even economic dislocations. In this second instance,

the changes are likely to be resented and opposed. In some cases, as in Argentina during the presidency of General Juan Domingo Perón, the publicists of resentment may even possess sufficient insight to point the finger of recrimination at technology. "One fine day, wise men, technicians, and teachers created the machine," a *Peronista* writer complained. "The machine became a substitute for man" and placed him under the tyranny of "dehumanized capital" and the "abuse of property."[5] In the process of economic development, such painful afterthoughts come typically as the uncomfortable morning-after hangover following the initial acceptance of the values of technological innovation.

In its contemporary drive toward economic development, Latin America thus presents a twofold spectacle. In the first place, the American nations are providing increasing numbers of theaters of rapid economic and political change, about which policy decisions must be made. Second—and curiously—Latin America, together with other underdeveloped areas of the world, raises for social scientists the question of whether evolutionary theory is indeed dead.

Economics and Politics

Latin America was chronologically the first area whose underdeveloped economies demanded the attention of the United States as a matter of public policy. In May of 1939, the Washington government embarked upon programs of technical cooperation with the other American republics. Since then, technical cooperation—also known as tech-

---

4 Walter Goldschmidt, *Man's Way* (Cleveland, Ohio: World Publishing Company, 1959), p. 113.

5 George I. Blanksten, *Perón's Argentina* (Chicago: University of Chicago Press, 1953), pp. 286, 289.

nical assistance and Point Four—has come to be a central feature of the policies of the United States toward, initially, Latin America and, later, other underdeveloped areas of the world as well. Technical cooperation, from its beginning, has been thought of as an attempt to encourage and to accelerate technological innovation in developing economies. The Congress of the United States has defined technical cooperation programs as "programs for the international interchange of technical knowledge and skills designed to contribute primarily to the balanced and integrated development of the economic resources and productive capacities of economically underdeveloped areas."[6] The bulk of the technical cooperation programs in which the United States has participated in Latin America have been in the fields of agriculture, education, health and sanitation, industrial productivity, and public administration.

From its inception in 1939, United States technical cooperation with the other American republics has proceeded on the assumption that technological innovation would not only raise standards of living and encourage economic development in the participating countries, but also somehow contribute to political changes there. The first part of this assumption stands on more reliably demonstrated ground than the latter. The political consequences or expression of economic development are not at all clear, although a faith—at this stage in our knowledge it is primarily that—that such implications are involved has underlain not only the bilateral programs of the United States but also the multilateral technical assistance endeavors in Latin America of

the United Nations and of the Organization of American States (OAS).

Wartime objectives

Formulation of the political consequences of economic development through technical cooperation has had a curious, and perhaps instructive, history. From the inception of the programs in 1939 until the end of World War II six years later, technical cooperation was conceived of essentially as a war measure, the assumption being that the political consequences of economic development in Latin America would transform the countries of the area into stronger and more reliable wartime allies of the United States. The first renewal of technical assistance to Latin America was undertaken "in order to render closer and more effective the relationship between the American Republics."[7] The third meeting of American Foreign Ministers, held at Rio de Janeiro, Brazil, in January of 1942, immediately after the formal spread of World War II to the Western Hemisphere, took place in an atmosphere of hectic mobilization for war. Among other measures adopted by this Rio conference was Resolution XXX, institutionalizing an inter-American framework for technical cooperation. The text of the resolution cited two reasons for this step—the preservation under wartime conditions of the vital and strategic products of the hemisphere, and contribution to "reconstruction of the world order."

The concept during World War II of the economic development of Latin America through technical cooperation as a war measure, an additional instrument for military victory over the Axis, clearly emerges from the writings of the United States personnel who helped

---

[6] *Public Law 665* (Mutual Security Act of 1954), 83rd Congress, Title III, Section 302.

[7] *Public Law 355,* 76th Congress, 1939.

to launch the cooperative projects in the field. "A considerable proportion of these cooperative activities," wrote Lieutenant-Colonel Edward A. Westphal, the first United States chief of field party in Peru, "were aimed at facilitating the extraction or the production of raw materials needed to further war effort." And, added a pioneer in technical cooperation in Brazil, "a large number of employees did not interpret the development of SESP as something more fundamental than a wartime activity. Many who left at the end of the war did not have faith that their own contributions would be more lasting than those of a purely military nature."[8]

Postwar development

In the years since the end of World War II, the United States has not only continued its participation in bilateral programs of technical cooperation, but has also entered into multilateral programs in the United Nations and the OAS. Moreover, technical assistance has been broadened to include, in addition to Latin America, many other underdeveloped regions of the world. Curiosity about the noneconomic, especially political, implications of economic development persists. While the question of the political concomitants of economic development is as yet far from answered completely, it is possible to say more about this in the 1960's than could be said twenty years ago. Some, but by no means all, of the political changes accompanying economic growth may be identified today

---

[8] Serviço Especial de Saúde Pública, *Notas Diplomáticas e Contratos entre o Brasil e os Estados Unidos da América de 1942 a 1952 para Desenvolvimiento de um Programa Cooperativo Bilateral de Saúde* (Rio de Janeiro: Serviço Especial de Saúde Publica, 1953), pp. 11, 58–59.

in terms other than the strengthening of wartime allies.

For example, it seems likely, as economic development takes place in an underdeveloped economy in Latin America, that increased divisions of labor among economic groups are accompanied by growing divisions of labor—or differentiations of functions—among noneconomic entities as well. Both militarism and the changing political roles of the Roman Catholic Church appear to illustrate this change process in Latin America. In the more underdeveloped countries of the area, the armies perform a wide range of unspecialized and undifferentiated functions, including the administration of elections, the use of military bands to bring music and culture to outlying areas, political socialization and citizenship training of conscripts, often the active management of political and governmental affairs, and—last and probably least—the defense of the community against foreign enemies. There is some evidence that, as economic development progresses, the function of the military becomes increasingly specific and differentiated until it reaches the point at which it is limited virtually exclusively to the specialized military task of defending the community. Similarly, it can be said that in the more underdeveloped parts of Latin America the Church is a landowner, operator of the public education system, the manager of political parties like the Conservatives of Ecuador and Colombia, and a performer of a religious function. With the march of the developmental process, it is likely that the last of these functions will tend to become the exclusive, specialized, and differentiated role of the Church.

Additional concomitants of economic development appear to be linked to stages in economic growth. In the precondition stage, or something like it, nationalist movements tend to stiffen in futile resistance against the change process. It is, of course, one of the earliest propositions of elite analysis that governing groups resist change likely to displace them from their ruling positions. Latin American politics abound with instances of the desperate opposition of landowing aristocracies to change. In Ecuador, for example, the traditional landed gentry of the mountainous Sierra region has long viewed trends toward commercialization of the economy as a grave peril. An interesting study of political change in Guatemala has indicated that the *Ladino* elite "felt threatened" by the change process. "The psychological impact was obviously one of great threat, insecurity, and, perhaps most of all, insult to the 'dignity of the individual.' "[9] It is a curious characteristic of precondition systems that desperate attempts to preserve disappearing orders often create violent nationalisms.

Political aspects

Finally, the take-off—or whatever the eventual formulation of the decisive transformation comes to be—appears to be accompanied by two political phenomena. The first of these has to do with the nature of the political party systems. Countries in this stage tend to have what have been called dominant nondictatorial or democratic one-party systems. These resemble one-party systems in that the dominant groups are not seriously challenged by rival political parties, but they differ from dictatorial systems in that other political parties may and do exist legally in addition to the dominant organizations.

9 Ruben E. Reina, "Chinautla: 1944–53," in Adams, *Political Changes in Guatemalan Indian Communities*, p. 35.

The PRI, Mexico's governing political party, presides over such a democratic one-party system. The unchallenged political force in a country experiencing rapid change, the PRI is well worth examining.

The second political characteristic of take-off appears to be the commitment of governing elites to change. Everywhere the dominant parties through which these elites function politically are oriented toward economic development and other forms of change. The clear—sometimes passionate—devotion of these ruling elites to change is inescapable. The conventional conception of a ruling elite struggling to preserve the *status quo* for fear that change might spell disaster—however applicable to precondition societies— seems curiously irrelevant to the attitudes and commitments of the governing groups in those countries where the decisive transformation is under way. This is abundantly illustrated by the predispositions of the dominant groups in Mexico and Puerto Rico. And in an interesting study of the attitudes of Jamaican elites, Bell has found that over sixty per cent of those who believed that their careers would be affected by change expected to benefit from it! The spectacle of dominant groups dedicated to change is as widespread among underdeveloped communities as it is peculiar to them.

The Road Ahead

Gross and easy generalization about Latin America is to be avoided. This is as true of its levels of, and aspirations for, economic development as of other questions about the area. It was pointed out at the outset of this article that the countries of the area range from those with extremely underdeveloped economies through average or typical situations to fairly well-developed economies.

As there are differences in levels of economic development, so, too, are there divergences in attitudes toward and aspirations for further growth. It should not be denied that there are sectors of Latin American society in which the change process is opposed and feared. Traditional elites may feel that economic growth threatens them with displacement from their ruling positions. Indigenous societies, struggling against detribalization and other manifestations of the passing of the old order, may see —and see correctly—in economic development the destruction of an honored way of life. And some may feel cheated of the promised benefits of growth, fruits which in some cases come to be misinterpreted or denied. Those who complain bitterly of "the progress we have suffered" are not to be treated in jest.

But theirs is a losing struggle. The course of development, and the weight of aspiration, are against them. The revolution of rising expectations every day draws great numbers of deserters from the cause of resistance to change. The governing elites of take-off are enmeshed in a curious, and sometimes dizzying, upward spiral. Newly emerging industrializing and enterpreneurial groups—the middle sectors prominent in commercialization and developing industry—have been bitten by the bug. And wars against evolution are never easy.

Moving at different rates of speed in different parts of the area, economic development is clearly afoot in Latin America. The foreign policy implications of this are many for the United States. It is crude and one-sided to see the process simply as the manufacturer of stronger political allies should the hemisphere again become engulfed in a general war. Many—and perhaps the most significant—of the political implications of the economic development of the area are more subtle than that. Some point to more specialized functions of political institutions, some to changing political parties and party systems, and some to basic alterations in the commitments of governing elites. Many political questions springing from economic development remain unanswered. It is perhaps significant that among them is the matter of the implications of the change process for the further democratization of Latin American political patterns and processes. It would indeed be gratifying to be in a position to make a solid— especially an affirmative—pronouncement on the relationship between the economic development of the area and the strengthening of democracy there. However, the current state of our knowledge does not yet offer definitive insight into this crucial question.[10]

---

[10] See Seymour M. Lipset, "Some Social Requisites of Democracy: Economic Development and Political Legitimacy," *American Political Science Review*, LIII, No. 1, (March 1959), 69–195.

16

Ideologies of Economic Development
in Latin America

Albert O. Hirschman

Why is there so much wretchedness, so much poverty in this fabulous land...? Ah, says one—it is the priests' fault; another blames it on the military; still others on the Indian; on the foreigner; on democracy; on dictatorship; on bookishness; on ignorance; or finally on divine punishment.

—Daniel Cosío Villegas,
Extremos de América, Tezontle,
Mexico City, 1949, p. 105

This paper attempts to review the principal ideas on the character of Latin America's development problems which have been and are being put forward by Latin American writers and social scientists.[1] Such an undertaking, if at all successful, will be more than a contribution to the history of ideas. We need not go all the way with Keynes' dictum that "the world is ruled

by little else" than by the ideas, both the right and the wrong ones, of economists and political philosophers to recognize the importance of these ideas for the shaping of reality. Yet the subject is strangely neglected. We are far better informed about changes in the balance of payments, terms of trade, capital formation, and so on of foreign countries than about the climate of opinion, the alignment of contending economic theories on policy issues, or about the emergence of new reform proposals. When we are called upon to advise a Latin American country on economic policy it is only natural that, hard pressed, we should first of all attempt to get at the "facts," a difficult enough undertaking. But frequently our advice will be futile unless we have also gained *an understanding of the understanding* Latin Americans have of their own reality.

A better knowledge of Latin American economic ideas seems particularly important at this time. Rapid political and social changes in the area lead to the sudden appearance of new leaders. Without much experience in the handling of public affairs and with a strong desire quickly to solve their country's

From Albert O. Hirschman, ed., *Latin American Issues; Essays and Comments* (New York: The Twentieth Century Fund, 1961). Reprinted by permission.

[1] The term "ideology" (of economic development) is used here, without derogatory connotation, to designate any moderately consistent body of beliefs, ideas, or propositions, tested or untested, that aims at explaining Latin America's economic backwardness and at indicating its cure.

problems, they are apt to reach out for the ready-made policy prescriptions of various ideologies. . . .

The Present Scene
and the Commanding Position of ECLA

The historical background which has been all too briefly sketched in the preceding pages serves to bring out the considerable change which has occurred in the discussion of Latin American economic problems during the last ten years: While economic ideas have previously had to be gleaned from political writings or from general essays on Latin American society, we now possess a voluminous literature dealing exclusively with Latin America's economic problems. By all odds, the central body of this literature is represented by the writings of the United Nations Economic Commission for Latin America (ECLA).

ECLA was organized in 1948 as a regional commission of the United Nations with its seat in Santiago, Chile. Its members are the twenty Latin American countries, the United States, and the three European countries with possessions in the Western Hemisphere—Great Britain, France, and the Netherlands. While its membership is thus wider than that of the Organization of American States with its twenty-one Western Hemisphere governments, it has, in reality, become much more a strictly Latin American affair than the OAS; unlike the latter, it has been able to avoid an undue dispersion of its activities and has largely achieved its objective of being considered as the recognized spokesman for Latin America's economic development.

The arresting feature of ECLA is that it possesses attributes not frequently encountered in large international organizations: a cohesive personality which evokes loyalty from the staff, and a set of distinctive beliefs, principles, and attitudes, in brief an ideology, which is highly influential among Latin American intellectuals and policy-makers. To a considerable degree, this achievement is due to ECLA's director, Dr. Raúl Prebisch, who, in 1949, while not yet heading the organization (he was appointed Executive Secretary in 1950), wrote that veritable ECLA manifesto, *The Economic Development of Latin America and Its Principal Problems* (United Nations, 1950).

Before the principal thesis of this brochure is examined, it is useful to point out briefly that ECLA's twelve-year history can be divided into approximately three phases, in accordance with changes in the central locus of its interests and activities. During the first period—to about 1953—the ideology was forged, elaborated, and tested with the help of such basic data on the Latin American economies as were being assembled; during the second period, intensive studies of individual Latin American countries were undertaken with the aim of "programming" their future economic development; and since about 1958, the principal interest of the organization has shifted to the intensive study and promotion of Latin American economic integration or cooperation, principally through the formation of a Latin American common market. It should be noted that the new interests of the organization have not superseded the old ones, but have rather resulted in an extension of its field of action.

The elaboration of the ECLA doctrine

In Latin America, reality is undermining the outdated schema of the international division of labor. . . . Under that schema, the specific task that fell to Latin America, as part of the periphery of the world economic system, was that of producing food and raw materials for the great industrial countries. There was no place within it for the industrialization of the new countries. It is, nevertheless, being forced upon them by events. Two world wars in a single generation and a great economic crisis between them have shown the Latin American countries their opportunities, clearly pointing the way to industrial activity.[2]

These opening sentences of Prebisch's brochure convey its militant flavor and mark their author as another great figure in the series of outstanding political economists who have preached protection, industrialization, and "catching-up" to their respective countries. In describing the plight of the "periphery" and the need for a policy of deliberate industrialization, Prebisch and ECLA[3] created and adapted a series of arguments and tools of analysis. It would be highly instructive to trace in detail the evolution of the ECLA doctrine and to relate it to Latin American political writings such as those of Haya and to Western economic theory. All that can be done here is to give a synopsis of the essential ingredients of the doctrine.

The basic emphasis is on the *asymmetry* in the relations between the "center" and the "periphery," and it is this asymmetry that traditional theory is accused of having overlooked.

2 United Nations Economic Commission for Latin America, *The Economic Development of Latin America and Its Principal Problems* (New York: United Nations, 1950).

3 In the following I am drawing also on ECLA's *Economic Survey of Latin America, 1949,* United Nations, 1950, Part One of which (pages 1–88) contains an elaboration of the Prebisch essay. A further development of the doctrine is in *Theoretical and Practical Problems of Economic Growth,* United Nations, E/CN 12/221, 1951. A recent reformulation is in Prebisch, "Commercial Policy in the Underdeveloped Countries," *American Economic Review,* XLIX, No. 2 (May 1959), 251–73.

1. In the first place, the *gains from trade* are not equally divided between the center and the periphery; the terms of trade are constantly moving against the primary producing countries. The empirical basis for this statement was a 1949 United Nations study of Britain's terms of trade between 1876 and 1946; an explanation of the phenomenon was sought in the alleged tendency of productivity advances to lead to wage and other factor price increases (and, therefore, constant commodity prices) in the "center," but, largely because of disguised unemployment, to commodity price declines in the periphery. This so-called Prebisch-Singer thesis about the unequal distribution of productivity gains between the industrial and underdeveloped countries and the secular tendency towards a worsening of the latter's terms of trade has been hotly contested and the empirical data which the theory invoked were certainly insufficient to support so broad a generalization. Nevertheless, international price developments of recent years have given fresh support to the Prebisch-Singer views. In any event, what is important for our purposes is that ECLA found a fairly persuasive way of propounding a modern, sophisticated version of the old idea that trade can be a vehicle for exploitation rather than a means of increasing welfare all-round.

2. Subsequent ECLA publications have made less of the unequal division of productivity gains and have rather directed attention to another asymmetry: that between the income elasticity of demand for imports of the center compared to that of the periphery. The former was seen as continually declining, largely because of Engels' Law,[4] whereas the latter was believed to be

4 Engels' Law states that percentage expenditure on food is on the average a decreasing function of income.

potentially extremely large because of the high import content of new investments and because of the demonstration effect. Thus, as income rises in the center, the percentage expenditure on imports from the periphery declines. As income rises in the periphery, however, the percentage of income that goes for imports from the center increases. This discrepancy is held to cause a recurrent tendency toward balance-of-payments difficulties and, therefore, once more toward a deterioration of the terms of trade for Latin America, at least in the absence of substantial capital imports.

3. Protection plays a different role in developed and underdeveloped countries. In the developed center it interferes with the optimal allocation of resources; but in the periphery, because of disguised unemployment in agriculture and a natural increase in population that cannot be absorbed there, protection of industry is required from the very point of view of resource allocation: Within rather wide limits any increase in industrial output is a net addition to the total product. This argument, which has been presented in theoretically precise form by Arthur Lewis, goes considerably beyond the infant industry case for protection.

4. A corollary on which ECLA has frequently insisted is that in the periphery the impact of import restrictions is different from that in the center. In the latter, such restrictions will lead to a shrinkage of total trade, whereas in the periphery they will merely lead to a redirection of total imports, since (a) exports are what they are—the periphery exerts a negligible influence by its own purchases in the center on what the center will buy abroad; and (b) given the high and eternally unsatisfied demand for imports, the holding-back of some imports will only lead to their substitution by some others.

The preceding propositions share two characteristics. In the first place, they supply an answer to the fundamental question about the reason for Latin America's backwardness: It lies with the international trading system with which Latin America has become involved, and with the misleading free trade doctrines insofar as they have been applied. Second, they all point to the need for public policies designed to correct the faults of that international system through deliberate intervention: The need is for the promotion of industrialization through systematic interference with the balance of payments, that is, through protection and import controls. Moreover, since exports cannot be relied on to provide the Latin American economies with the "engine for growth," it is necessary actively to plan and accelerate the process of import substitution, since otherwise continued economic development will run into a rigid foreign-exchange barrier.

These tenets have remained deeply ingrained in all the important ECLA pronouncements. Logically enough, ECLA conceived its mission as a dual one: to alert the Latin American countries to the precariousness of their position, and to appeal for outside help to an area which was being buffeted and victimized by forces beyond its control. These preoccupations are reflected in ECLA's annual surveys, which consistently point to the dark spots in the economic picture. Even though many Latin American countries achieved considerable economic progress during the first postwar period, the successive annual reports frequently read as though things were tolerable enough until a few months ago, but have *now* started to take a definite turn for the worse. In this fashion, Latin America's situation was dramatized with the aim of stimulating both national and international action. In the latter respect,

ECLA documents stressed the inadequacy and unreliability of foreign capital inflow, criticized certain of the lending policies of international institutions such as the World Bank, and proposed additional international financial facilities and agencies. In 1954 a special committee appointed by the Secretariat proposed an annual foreign aid and investment target for Latin America of one billion dollars for at least ten years.

The programming technique

While ECLA was in these various fashions acquiring a distinct and militant personality, the organization felt that it had to undertake something practical if it were to acquire a more direct influence. For this purpose, ECLA chose to interest individual Latin American governments in the detailed programming of economic development and to lend them a helping hand in this unfamiliar task. This work marks the second major phase of ECLA activity. As with the first, it also has its basic document, namely, the brochure *An Introduction to the Technique of Programming,* which was presented at the fifth session at Rio in 1953; a revised version was printed in 1955.

This brochure represents an attempt to provide guidance in the drawing up of medium- and long-term aggregate and sectoral projections of economic growth on the basis of empirical knowledge and various theories that were then being rapidly accumulated by economists concerned with development problems: the projection of domestic demand in accordance with consumer budget studies; the projection of the capacity to import on the basis of an estimate of foreign markets; estimates of savings and capital-output ratios; and the application of various investment criteria and of input-output analysis. In conjunction with the setting of a certain growth target, say a two per cent annual increase in per capita income, these techniques, if combined with adequate statistical information (admittedly a large "if"), can be made to trace out in detail the path which the economy appears likely to follow.

The brochure is at pains to point out that the technique does not imply anything with respect to the extent of "rigid state control of the economy." It does imply, however, that without state action to call forth the correct amount of investment and to direct it into the proper channels, the Latin American economies would make numerous wrong decisions; they would choose too much consumption and too little investment, too much export promotion and too little import substitution, too much investment in secondary industry and not enough in basic power and transportation facilities, too much capital-intensive technology, and so on.

The "technique" has been applied by ECLA to a number of countries: Brazil, Colombia, Bolivia, Argentina, Panama, and Peru. In the process, ECLA has learned much about the real conditions and problems of these countries and has contributed to the economic education of those in the countries who collaborated with the ECLA team; but in terms of actually influencing national economic development policies, this activity has been less rewarding.

At first, ECLA's studies were acquiesced in rather than actively promoted by the national governments; under these conditions and since the development programs drawn up by even the most highly placed official bodies have frequently remained "on paper," it is not surprising that this very fate has befallen most of the ECLA-sponsored programs. In the most recent country studies, those of Panama and Peru, local governmental agencies have cooperated more intimately with the ECLA teams, and ECLA is now also extending some direct technical assistance to governmental planning agencies, as recently in Colombia, Bolivia, and Cuba. But the fundamental problem which faced ECLA in this phase of its effort was not so much that of cooperation with the governmental agencies in charge of development planning, but the question whether development planning of the kind pursued by ECLA was felt to be a compelling need by the principal policy-making officials. ECLA itself expressed some doubts on the subject in a study on Bolivia:

> Programming is not entirely the task of experts in the central organizations; it also requires the collaboration of public and private technical and economic offices. . . . without energetic support of the highest policy circles. . . it is difficult for the programming authorities to carry out their work. This is not only a question of status. In Bolivia, as well as in other countries, the National Commission for Coordination and Planning or its equivalent is placed at the highest level, but it still cannot be said to have received wholehearted official support. What is chiefly required is the "will to plan" on the part of the supreme political authorities. . . . Certain factors appear to have militated against this spirit.[5]

Thus, the "programming" activity of ECLA was not without its frustrations, and it is probably being pursued at the present time with a somewhat diminished ardor, the more so since a new and powerful interest has arisen for ECLA: the Latin American Common Market.

The Latin American Common Market

As early as in his 1949 "manifesto," Prebisch pointed out that one limita-

tion to industrial growth was "the present division of market, with its consequent inefficiency" and that this obstacle "could be overcome by the combined efforts" of the Latin American countries (p. 47). In the early fifties ECLA compiled a study of inter-Latin American trade, and its Mexico branch was entrusted with technical assistance for the economic integration program which was being undertaken by the five Central American republics. The fairly satisfactory experience with this program was one of the elements that in 1958 rather suddenly moved the Common Market into the forefront of ECLA's activities. Other factors were: perhaps, as already mentioned, some feeling of frustration over what was being achieved with "programming"; certainly the establishment of the European Economic Community, with the example it provided and the threat it posed for some of Latin America's export products; and the fact that even in some of the bigger countries industrialization was reaching a stage at which a fairly large number of industries could best be established if they could count, at least initially, on some export markets.

In making the case for closer economic integration in Latin America, ECLA relied on some of its earlier analyses. According to its projections, so it argued, Latin American exports could not possibly expand as fast in the next fifteen years as would be required to maintain the present ratio of imports to national income; and the only way, therefore, in which economic progress could be maintained would be by intensifying the import substitution process. Given the industries which have to be developed, primarily in capital goods, such an expansion can only be achieved if industrialization is no longer pursued and "duplicated" within twenty "watertight compartments."

---

5 "The Economic Development of Bolivia," *Economic Bulletin for Latin America*, October 1957, p. 44.

In ECLA's thinking the Common Market is thus primarily required to avert a disastrous slowdown in Latin America's economic growth rather than as a means to improve economic efficiency, organization, and policy; among the possible arguments in favor of the Common Market, little attention is given to the advantages of continent-wide competition for some of Latin America's young, yet already run-down or poorly run industries, or of the check which economic integration might constitute for unwise national economic policies.

The ECLA proposals and their influence on the emergence of the Montevideo treaty for a Latin American Common Market are described in some detail elsewhere in this volume.

The direction of ECLA influence

The foregoing summary makes it clear that ECLA, while it has transferred the principal center of its activity from one area to another as it ran into difficulties or decreasing returns, has maintained the identity of its personality throughout these shifts.

The "ECLA doctrine" has essentially consisted in assuming a critical and militant attitude toward the industrial "center" on behalf of the underdeveloped "periphery" and in calling upon the governments of the latter to undertake new responsibilities in the promotion of economic development. In doing so ECLA gave expression and direction to feelings that are diffuse among important intellectual and middle-class circles in Latin America: first, to various resentments against the United States and in particular to the suspicion of exploitation; and, second, to the idea that the cure for society's ills lies in empowering the state to deal with them. But while ECLA has mirrored these basic emotions, it has also controlled them, and has progressively turned them to increasingly constructive tasks, such as the detailed study of national economic structures and inter-Latin American economic cooperation.

To perceive the specific direction in which ECLA has exercised its influence, it is useful to realize which are the areas where ECLA has not brought a particularly intensive effort to bear. Thus, while the need for import substitution has been a constant theme, the possibilities of promoting new or traditional exports have not received similar emphasis. Industries which are to be established or substantially expanded, such as iron and steel, or pulp and paper, have been intensively studied, but the efficiency of industries which already exist has received scant attention, except for an excellent but isolated early report on the productivity of the textile industry in four Latin American countries. Problems such as those of agrarian reform and social security (not to speak of excessive military expenditures) have been shunned, partly because ECLA could not afford to prod and antagonize its members in these highly sensitive areas; partly, perhaps, because they were felt to be in the area of competence of other international agencies: the Food and Agriculture Organization and United Nations headquarters for agrarian reform and the International Labor Office and the Organization of American States for social security.

In discussing the problem of inflation, ECLA has stressed various "structural" factors responsible for inflationary pressures, and has been skeptical of the "orthodox" remedies of fiscal-monetary retrenchments and realistic exchange adjustments advocated by the International Monetary Fund. With respect to the analysis of the growth process in general, ECLA is rather firmly committed to the notion that development depends primarily on the generation of an adequate supply of capital, domestic and foreign. In this connection, the International Bank has on occasion been criticized for inadequate lending and overrestrictive criteria. But ECLA has not only been a claimant for new resources; it has also attempted to instruct Latin American governments and planning agencies in the best use of whatever funds they have at their disposal; the programming technique has been communicated through seminars held in all major Latin American countries to a large number of economic policy-making officials.

ECLA has undoubtedly advocated the assumption of larger economic responsibilities on the part of the national states, and eventually, perhaps, on the part of regional authorities in a variety of fields. But the principal task of government is, in ECLA's view, to give long-range direction to economic development by means of detailed plans which must be carefully laid and observed. Formulated in this way, ECLA's design has a utopian ring for societies where simple ministerial changes frequently mean total reversals of policies and where the policy-makers themselves take pride in being unpredictable. But it is this very situation that permits us better to understand ECLA's intent. Its programming activities can perhaps be interpreted as an attempt to "reform" certain inveterate traits such as the propensity to improvise, the lack of foresight, the failure ever to see the handwriting on the wall. ECLA's detailed projections where all economic sectors are made to mesh harmoniously are in a sense the twentieth-century equivalent of Latin America's nineteenth-century constitutions—and are as far removed from the real world. They are a protest, both pathetic and subtle, against a reality where politicians relying on brilliant or disastrous improvisations hold

sway, where decisions are taken under multiple pressures rather than in advance of a crisis and emergency situations, and where conflicts are resolved on the basis of personal considerations after the contending parties have revealed their strength in more-or-less open battle rather than in accordance with objective principles and scientific criteria.

Some years ago, an impressive amount of evidence was marshaled to show that the movement and style of the Bolsheviks was born out of a protest against, and a determined negation of, the Russian character and "soul" that had been popularized by the great Russian novelists of the nineteenth century. Similarly the style that ECLA would like to implant in Latin America is perhaps born from the desire to stamp out those traditional traits which are felt to be hindrances and handicaps on the road to economic progress. Here ECLA rejoins essentially those earlier analysts of Latin American backwardness who had concluded that the Latin American character has to be thoroughly remolded before anything useful can be achieved. ECLA never says so; on the contrary, as we have seen, it has devised new arguments in support of the idea that the "periphery's" difficulties are to be blamed on the "center"—but these difficulties being taken for granted, ECLA's prescriptions are nevertheless implicitly premised on a revolutionary overhauling of the basic realities of economic policy-making in the continent.

ECLA's Critics

ECLA's voice is, no doubt, the one that is heard loudest today in the debate on Latin America's economic problems, and there is little doubt that its views are representative of a large section of the new middle class. But it would be a mistake to think that its doctrines are unquestioningly accepted by all influential economic circles in Latin America. The opposition comes essentially from two different sectors: in the first place, from those who are highly skeptical of the ability of the state in Latin America to operate competently in the field of economic policy and planning; and, second, from those who simply dissent in various other ways from ECLA's diagnosis and emphasis.

Distrust of the state's capabilities

For many Latin Americans, the state has so thoroughly demonstrated its total ineptness in the discharge of economic functions that the idea of entrusting it with some sort of general staff functions in the direction of the national economy seems utterly ludicrous to them. Their "ideological vision" is similar to that of Adam Smith, who, as Schumpeter said, felt nothing but "disgust...at the inefficiency of the English bureaucracy and at the corruption of the politicians."[6] This kind of feeling is far more widespread in Latin America than might be supposed from a perusal of current Latin American economic writings.

It has been said, and perhaps with good reason, that the private entrepreneur does not command nearly as much prestige in underdeveloped countries where he merely "imitates" as he once enjoyed in the pioneer industrial countries where he truly innovated. But that does not mean that correspondingly more prestige is held by the state. Long experience with official corruption and incompetence has led to an attitude of distrust and contempt toward the state and a bureaucracy which has no civil-service tradition and where all major as well as most minor appoint-

ments are political. Frequently the state is compared to the organized bandits of the backlands exacting their tribute and leading a purely parasitic existence. The idea that economic development takes place in spite of, rather than because of, state action is well expressed in the Brazilian saying "Our country grows by night when the politicians sleep." Even those who are anxious to have the state carry out important new functions and tasks for economic development show occasionally an awareness of the considerable difficulties of such an undertaking, difficulties arising from the bureaucratic, parasitic, and "clientelistic" traditions of what is known in Brazil as the *"Cartorial* (paper-shuffling or Notarial) State." The violent desire to put an end to the *"Cartorial* State" and to start afresh in an atmosphere dedicated to economic and social progress and uncontaminated by old-time *clientelismo* goes far toward explaining the move of Brazil's capital from Rio to Brasília.

The lengthy period of civil war and virtual anarchy punctuated by military dictatorship through which most of Latin America passed in the nineteenth century was ill-suited to create in the Latin American mind a very respectful picture of the state. During that period, a particularly confusing stretch of Colombia's history is known as the time of the *"patria boba,"* the "stupid fatherland"; and *"hacer patria,"* "to make (or build) the fatherland," denotes there typically the activity not of agents of the state but of farmers who are settling virgin territories or of engineers and entrepreneurs building new plants and factories. In all countries many tales are current about the utter incompetence of the state as an entrepreneur; some draw the conclusion that "better planning" is needed, but others are convinced that state-run enterprises are necessarily stillborn.

---

6 Joseph Schumpeter, "Science and Ideology," *American Economic Review,* XXXIX, No. 1 (March 1949), 353.

These diffuse feelings of skepticism about the state's entrepreneurial and planning abilities found, of course, particularly vigorous spokesmen in the nineteenth century. Thus, most of Alberdi's economic essays lead up to the moral that "there is no better or safer way to impoverish a country than to entrust its government with the task to enrich it."

The depression of the thirties and the rise of Soviet power have made it impossible for the contemporary observer to be quite so trenchant, but Latin American experiences of recent years with their widespread and often misguided interventionism have nevertheless permitted some strong critics to appear on the scene, the best known of whom is perhaps Professor Eugenio Gudin of Brazil. In a discussion of the ECLA programming technique, after enumerating all the factors of uncertainty (particularly irrational governmental policies) to which economic life in Latin America is subject, Gudin writes:

Considering all these factors...to pretend to frame quantitative estimates of demand, supplies, savings, investments, sounds like discussing the sex of the angels in the midst of a serious battle.... What the governments of these countries can do for their economic development is not programming: it is simply *not to disturb or prevent it* by indulging in such evils as political warfare, demagogy, inflation, hostility...to foreign capital, unbalanced or excessive protection to industry and/or agriculture, etc. If these evils can be avoided, then economic development is almost automatic; if they cannot, then economic development is doomed.[7]

We are almost back here to Adam Smith, who said: "Little else is requisite

[7] Eugenio Gudin, Discussion Paper presented at the Rio roundtable of the International Association, 1957.

to carry a state to the highest degree of opulence from the lowest barbarism, but peace, easy taxes, and a tolerable administration of justice." However, in the positive part of his paper and in other writings, Professor Gudin has principally stressed the importance of agriculture (where foreign techniques cannot simply be copied), of the export sector (where underdeveloped countries are under compulsion to turn out a quality product), and of education (because of the cessation of large-scale immigration Latin America must devote more resources to education than did the United States at a corresponding stage of its history).

Sentiments similar to those of Gudin are also expressed in a recent "primer" on Colombian economic problems, written by one of Colombia's most progressive industrialists:

In the Latin American countries there exists an important school which maintains that economic progress must necessarily be directed by the state. ...What foundation is there for such a statement? None.

...The public should not accept blindly development plans. It must recall that bureaucracy is always interested in elaborating such plans, since they give it economic power and advantages. ...

The paperwork imposed by public agencies is one of the biggest obstacles to production in Latin America...the state complicates the life of the citizens and it doesn't care if it makes them lose their time. It behaves with an unshakable indifference, like an occupation army in a defeated country.

In Colombia the state has invested huge sums to build low-cost houses, but has accomplished nothing in spite of the money that has been spent. The reason of this failure is that the state is a very poor manager. This goes for every state and particularly the Colombian one. Now, of all economic activities the one most difficult to manage and where opportunities for thievery are greatest is that of construction. As was to be expected, the building of low-cost houses by the state has resulted in a huge destruction of national wealth.[8]

Seldom does one find these ideas expressed so openly and candidly; their most vocal advocates are businessmen ordinarily not given to putting their opinions on paper. Nevertheless, it is useful to realize the strength of these feelings of distrust toward the state's actions and capabilities; periodically they gain the upper hand in one or the other of the Latin American countries, and we find ourselves surprised to deal with a minister of finance whose enthusiasm for the dismantling of all controls and whose aversion to public investment in industry and to development planning seem a bit hysterical and old-fashioned to us!

Policy versus projections

Apart from the groups which are out of sympathy with ECLA simply because its view implies what they deem to be an excessive degree of governmental intervention in the economy, there are those who oppose or criticize ECLA because they disagree with parts of the ECLA analysis and with some of its policy implications. Perhaps the most outspoken of this group of ECLA's critics is the Brazilian economist, Roberto de Oliveira Campos, who, as director of the Brazilian National Bank

---

[8] Hernán Echavarría Olózaga, *El sentido común en la economía colombiana* (Bogotá: Imprenta Nacional, 1958), pp. 176–77, 230, 301. It should be noted that Echavarría started his career as an economist with an exposition of Keynesian ideas. He played a prominent part in the overthrow of the Rojas Pinilla regime and was Minister of Communications in the first Lleras Cabinet. Recently he has been a strong advocate of stiffer land taxation as a means to improved land utilization and distribution.

for Economic Development from 1955 to 1959, frequently came into close contact with ECLA. The following account of Campos' views is based on several of his papers, primarily on a memorandum he prepared for the Seventh Session of ECLA at La Paz in 1957. In this memorandum Campos does not criticize ECLA directly, but his emphasis is markedly different.

Campos pays the compliment to Prebisch that he has been a "creator of enthusiasms and a destroyer of illusions, tasks which are not always easy to reconcile." Evidently, he believes that Prebisch has been more successful in the former role than in the latter, for he devotes most of his paper to an analysis of the illusions which the Latin American countries still have to overcome: (1) the illusion that inflation can be used, except for brief and intermittent periods, as an instrument to increase capital formation; (2) the illusion that merely by substituting state for private management (for example, in public utilities) new economic resources are being created; (3) the illusion that social progress and redistribution of income can be legislated regardless and ahead of output and productivity gains; and (4) finally he speaks of a "mechanistic" illusion which consists in giving undue priority to industrial development in comparison with agriculture, and to physical capital in comparison with investment in education and technical skills.

In listing and commenting on these illusions, Campos probably intended to prod ECLA into giving more attention to influencing the *current* economic policies of Latin American governments. In general, his principal point of difference with ECLA appears to consist in the position that many more economic variables are subject to change through *policy* than ECLA's projections would lead one to believe. In analyzing shortages in power and transportation, he focuses less on inadequate capital formation and faulty programming than on more proximate factors such as utility and railway rate-fixing policies. If export receipts are inadequate he does not proclaim an inevitable tendency toward low price and income elasticities of demand for Brazil's export products, but suggests to his own country the adoption of a realistic exchange rate and to Brazil's customers a reduction in their revenue duties and excise taxes.

Campos thus is concerned with present and pressing dangers, and appears to look at problems in a pragmatic or, to use Lindblom's term, "incrementalist" way. Several other Latin American economists could be similarly characterized. For the time being, they are clearly an exception on the emotion-ridden Latin American scene. But the exception is significant for it appears among those who have been wrestling with the real problems faced by economies in the process of rapid growth. . . .

Concluding Remarks

The search of Latin Americans for the cause of their continent's economic backwardness has focused successively on a number of possible explanations: on the supposedly intrinsic defects of the Latin American character, on imperialist exploitation and on being subjected to false economic doctrines, on the lack of purposeful action by the state or alternatively on excessive and arbitrary state intervention, on the deadening rigidity of the social and economic structure inherited from the Spanish Conquest, or on a combination of several of these factors. Every one of these explanations then leads naturally and logically to the espousal of certain policies and positions over a wide range of social and economic issues;

in other words, each determines a "system," is part of an ideology.

With increasing frequency, we are told these days that in the West ideology is dead, that "the old passions are exhausted,"[9] that we no longer are in the "disposition to approach policy as though great ideological issues were to be decided."[10] We are no longer ready to become partisans of systems, spoiling for a fight with our opponent over the minutest issue; rather, we are now picturing ourselves as reasonable, sophisticated "incrementalists" bored with yesterday's ideological bouts.

If this is so, then we are seriously out of phase with the mood prevailing in Latin America. For, there, ideologies are in their accustomed roles, holding men in their grip, pushing them into actions that have important effects, both positive and negative, on economic growth.

Part of the mutual difficulties between Latin America and the United States may derive from this disparity. Given our present distaste for ideology, we are unwilling to grant that certain convictions which may seem naive to us can be held with the utmost sincerity and intensity. We are unable to understand that certain propositions which we feel have long turned into half-truths are essential ingredients of the intellectual atmosphere elsewhere. In general, we are annoyed by the doctrinaires of Right and Left, and a few traces of such annoyance may well be found in this paper.

Latin Americans, on the other hand, frequently misinterpret our actions. They look for the "system" behind our policies and impute to us rigid princi-

---

9 Daniel Bell, *The End of Ideology* (New York: The Free Press of Glencoe, Inc., 1960).

10 C. E. Lindblom, "Policy Analysis," *American Economic Review*, III, No. 2 (June 1958), 301.

ples which we have long decisively qualified or given up.

Mutual awareness of the disparity in intellectual climate should be helpful in mitigating such misunderstanding and frictions. This paper, incomplete and exploratory as it is, also has attempted to show that the ideologies which hold sway in Latin America frequently have considerable originality, are usually less rigid than may at first appear, and are themselves in a continuing process of adaptation to the fast changing reality. The scene we have surveyed is varied and vigorous; it is part of the vitality which today characterizes the Latin American economy and society.

17

The Land Reform Issue in Latin America

Thomas F. Carroll

There is no doubt...that sweeping changes in Latin American land-tenure systems are inevitable. Only one question remains to be answered. How will these changes come? By bloody revolution or by long-range democratic planning?

—Chester Bowles
New York Times Magazine,
November 22, 1959

The land reform issue, which only a few years ago was under a sort of taboo in Latin America, has rapidly moved to occupy a key position among the policy problems of the region. The Cuban land reform, introduced in 1959 as one of the main props of the revolution, has dramatized both the necessity for overhauling existing land-tenure systems and the ideological and power struggle inherent in such changes. Nowadays, land-reform problems are vigorously debated throughout Latin

From Thomas F. Carroll, "The Land Reform Issue in Latin America," in Albert O. Hirschman, ed., *Latin American Issues; Essays and Comments* (New York: The Twentieth Century Fund, 1961). Reprinted by permission.

America and there is a proliferation of projects and proposals in almost every country. While the issue is extremely complex and has many political aspects, the principal interest of economists has centered on the relationship between land reform and development. The purpose of this essay is more modest: it is to sketch with broad strokes the agrarian situation that calls for changes, to review some of the recent attempts at reforms or those currently in progress, and in the light of past experience to advance some ideas on how continued pressure for land reforms is likely to affect policy-making in Latin American countries.

Amidst all of its inherent complexity, the core of the land-reform problem is relatively simple and can be stated in straightforward terms: The existing pattern of land tenure (that is, ownership and control over land resources) is such that it corresponds neither to the aspirations of the rural population nor to the requirements of rapid technological progress. What this usually means in action is redistribution of landed rights in favor of the cultivator, and greater social control over land resources.[1] Such changes are now being advocated both by politicians wishing to capitalize on growing popular sentiment and by intellectuals interested in modernization of their countries' institutions. Economic developers are becoming increasingly aware of the key role of agriculture in Latin American economic growth and there is a tendency to look more closely at the land-tenure system as a major factor in the stagnation of the farm sector. What gives the land-reform issue its peculiar fascination, however, is the income-redistribution aspect. Land reform, if it is seriously done, implies a drastic rearrangement of property rights, income, and social status. In some ways, therefore, every reform is revolutionary.

Agrarian Structure

In looking at the agrarian structure

---

[1] The concept of land reform is itself a controversial and semantically intriguing topic. Its narrowest and traditional meaning confines it to land distribution. A broader view includes in it other related changes in agricultural institutions, such as credit, taxation, rents, cooperatives, etc. The widest interpretation makes land reform practically synonymous with all agricultural improvement measures—better seeds, price policies, irrigation, research, mechanization, etc. The writer is of the opinion that land tenure is the central problem in land reform and agrees with the view put forward by Doreen Warriner, in her brilliant series of lectures at Cairo (*Land Reform and Economic Development,* National Bank of Egypt, 1955), that we should "not confuse the definition of a concept with the conception of a policy. To use the term land reform in this wide sense [i.e., a change in all agrarian institutions] confuses the real issues. The redistribution of property in land is a very difficult change to carry through, far more difficult and controversial than the other measures, and we cannot really put it on the same level as other institutional improvements. The order of magnitude is too different, and we take the edge off it if we ignore this fact."

in Latin America what is most striking is the great concentration of ownership in relatively few large units, and the vast number of very small units at the other end of the scale. While it is difficult to generalize for so large and varied a region, the tenure systems have much in common in most countries. Broadly speaking, the main features of the agrarian structure are: (1) the importance of *latifundios,* or very large farms; (2) the large number of *minifundios,* or very small farms; (3) the special situation of the *comunidades,* or communal holdings; and (4) the peculiar form of farm labor known as the *colono* system. A knowledge of the principal features of each system and the main problems it represents is essential in order to understand what is supposed to be "reformed."

The latifundio

Let us first consider the large farms and their importance. As practically all the statistics are in terms of management units (*explotaciones*) rather than ownership units (*propiedades*), the degree of concentration is usually even greater than the data indicate. A few figures will illustrate this concentration.[2] In Guatemala 516 farms (0.15 per cent of all farms) represent 41 per cent of the agricultural land. In Ecuador 705 units (0.17 per cent) include 37 per cent of the farm land. In Venezuela 74 per cent of the farm acreage, comprising 6,800 units (1.69 per cent of all farms), is in holdings of over 1,000 hectares. Half the farm land in Brazil is in the hands of 1.6 per cent of the owners. In Nicaragua 362 owners have control over fully one-third of the

---

[2] Most of the quantitative information in this paper is based on the extensive mimeographed Spanish documentation prepared for FAO's Second Latin American Seminar on Land Problems, held in Montevideo, Uruguay, in November–December 1959.

agricultural acreage. The most extreme concentration could be observed in Bolivia prior to the land reform; there 92 per cent of the land was in fewer than 5,500 units, representing 6.4 per cent of all farms.

These figures, based mostly on census data, are of course not exact, yet they give a good indication of the magnitude of land concentration. If it were possible to calculate cultivated or cultivable land by farm sizes, the index of concentration would diminish, as many of the large units include mountain, desert, or swampland of doubtful value. On the other hand, it is generally acknowledged that for historic reasons the *latifundios* include the best land in most of the countries, a fact which from the standpoint of quality tends greatly to increase the land monopoly. Census counts, moreover, are usually short in the small-farm category, so that the *minifundios,* worked frequently by squatters and migrant cultivators, are underestimated. Therefore, the true percentage position of the large units is likely to be even greater.

A rapid summation of the available data yields the figures shown in Table 1 for Latin America as a whole. Roughly 90 per cent of the land belongs to 10 per cent of the owners. This degree of concentration is far greater than that in any other world region of comparable size.

Much has been written about the historic origins of the *latifundio* system. Basically, it reflects the organization of society in Spain and Portugal at the time of colonization, and the superimposition of this pattern on native cultures through large land grants. The *latifundio* pattern has two main variants: the hacienda type of extensively cultivated estates, and the intensively worked plantations. They give rise to quite different problems and call for different measures of reform.

TABLE 1   Estimated Percentage Distribution of Land Holdings in Latin America, around 1950

Size of Farms (hectares)	Per Cent of Farms	Per Cent of Land Area
0—20	72.6	3.7
20—100	18.0	8.4
100—1,000	7.9	23.0
Over 1,000	1.5	64.9
Total	100.0	100.0

Source: Based on the very helpful regional summary provided by Oscar Delgado in his *Estructura y reforma agraria en Latinoamerica,* prepared for the Sociedad Económica de Amigos del País, Bogotá, 1960 (mimeographed).

The hacienda is typically a livestock-cereal operation, with very low capital investment and labor applied per unit of land area. Ownership is often of the absentee type and labor is provided by the *colono* system or one of its variants. While there are notable exceptions, the hacienda system is a paragon of inefficiency both on the firm level and nationally. Output per man and per land unit is low. The plantation, on the other hand, generally shows a high capitalization combined with stricter labor organization and controls. As a result, output per land unit is generally high, and farm efficiency is above average. However, both systems embody monopoly elements, both result in extreme maldistribution of income, and in social conditions which have often been described as deplorable. The plantation problem is complicated by some foreign ownership and management, especially in the Caribbean area. But perhaps the worst feature of land concentration is the resulting concentration of power which in innumerable ways infuses the whole structure of society. It is against this concentration of power that most of the fury of popular land reforms has been directed. It is the destruction of *latifundismo* rather than other more positive goals, such as "family farming" or better land use, that provides the emotional and political mainspring of future reforms.

The minifundio

Now let us look at the other end of the scale. The great majority of the farms are small, often so small that at the present levels of technology these *minifundios* cannot give the farm family an acceptable minimum level of living. In Guatemala 97 per cent of all farms are in units of less than 20 hectares. The corresponding figures for both Peru and Ecuador is 90 per cent, for the Dominican Republic it is 95 per cent, for Venezuela 88 per cent and for the private sector of the Mexican farm economy 88 per cent. In Colombia some 325,000 farms average one-half hectare, and a further half a million farms average 2½ hectares.

The gravity of the *minifundio* situation is increased by fragmentation, by illegal occupancy (squatting), and by shifting cultivation. In many areas (especially in the Andean mountains) these small holdings have become subdivided as a result of population pressure into tiny plots, often only a few feet wide. Métraux reports, for example, that in the Conima region on the eastern shore of Lake Titicaca there is not a single holding that is not broken up into fifteen or twenty plots. Many of the smallest units are operated by squatters on either public or private land who hold no title and whose farming operations both from the point of view of security and use of resources are extremely unsatisfactory. Finally, there is the problem of migrant or shifting small-scale agriculture, practiced in vast areas of usually forested land in the tropical belt, mostly accompanied by burning and other wasteful methods. The vast majority of *minifundios* represent a hand-to-mouth type of farming and are outside the market economy.

The origin of the *minifundios* also goes back to colonial times, when land grants were "bestowed on the lower order, the conquering armies or upon civilians of humble rank."[3] Some of the more recent ones are homesteads conferred upon or sold to colonists who settled in frontier regions. Some are the result of simple occupancy, which may or may not have been confirmed legally. The extraordinarily rapid growth of population in recent decades has aggravated the *minifundio* problem both through further subdivision by inheritance and through spontaneous migration into new areas. The owners or occupants of small plots of land are beset by many problems. Many are at the margin of the market economy and represent neither a producing force of farm commodities nor an effective demand for industrial products. They generally lack not only land but other inputs necessary to raise productivity. Their plots are frequently exhausted and eroding. Institutional services, schools, roads, and hospitals are conspicuously lacking in *minifundio* areas. The peasants are at the mercy of unscrupulous tradesmen, money lenders, lawyers, and petty officials.

It should be emphasized that the *minifundio-latifundio* patterns are not independent, but are often closely interrelated. Large estates are surrounded by many small *ranchos, chacras, huertas, hijuelas* or *sitios*, drawing seasonal labor from them and in many ways contributing to the maintenance of the system. The *latifundios* exercise an influence far beyond their own boundaries, and they are frequently a limiting force on regional development. More impor-

---

[3] See article by George McBride on "Land Tenure—Latin America," *Encyclopedia of the Social Sciences,* 1950 edition, IX, 118–27.

tantly, perhaps, the system acts as a barrier to social mobility, participating citizenship, and the emergence of a broad base for upgrading the quality of human effort, which is a prerequisite for dynamic development.

The comunidad

The third major type of land holding in Latin America is the *comunidad*, far older in origin than the hacienda or the plantation. The Incas, Mayas, and Aztecs all held land in collective fashion, and the survival of the system is today localized in areas of native Indian populations, mostly in the Andean areas. The number of Indians living on the plateaus and in the valleys of the Andean chain between northern Argentina and Ecuador has been estimated as between five and six million. The Indian *comunidad*, while being slowly eroded away, is a remarkably durable institution. Its base is the aggregation of extended families, who together have claim over a specific land area. The territory of the community is deemed nontransferable, but the proprietary rights of the several families are recognized and every individual is free to dispose of his land within the group. In modern times many communities have *de facto* subdivided and individualized their land holdings, but in most there is a periodic reallocation of land among members. Much of the work is performed collectively on an exchange basis. Sociologists and anthropologists have given considerable attention to the Indian *comunidades* and have viewed them as heirs to the Inca *ayllus*.

A throwback to the *comunidades* is the Mexican *ejido*, product of the revolutionary land reform. Half the farmers in Mexico today are *ejidatarios*. Although the *ejido* system is much more closely connected with the social and economic mainstream of the country

than are the geographically and culturally isolated *comunidades* of Peru, Bolivia, or Ecuador, it suffers from very much the same economic ills. These communal arrangements, while embodying the seeds of cooperative economics, are excessively rigid and inhibit developmental forces. Members of the Andean communities are not able to obtain credit. There are no incentives for talented or ambitious individuals, and the system is not conducive to the emergence of effective leaders or group action in behalf of greater productivity. Capital investment by individuals is not encouraged. Thus the system in its present form represents a stagnant type of agriculture. Its main justification is on sociological grounds. For that part of the agricultural population which cannot be absorbed by the commercial farming sector or by urban occupations it offers perhaps a more secure and satisfactory way of life than that of the *colonos* or *peones*.

There has been considerable speculation about the possibilities of transforming the *comunidades* into modern cooperatives or true collectives, but apart from a few isolated cases, this has never been attempted on any meaningful scale. Several of the most recent land-reform proposals (notably in Peru and Ecuador) contemplate such a transformation. While the obstacles are formidable the basic idea is intellectually attractive and challenging. Why wait until small independent owners can be organized into cooperatives, when the basic cultural framework may permit skipping such an intermediate stage? Yet it seems a long way from the communal *fiestas* to the bookkeeping system of a modern cooperative.

The colono system

The last major feature of the Latin American tenure system worth recording here is the pattern of agricultural labor. In a region where the majority of farm people are not owners of land, the systems of farm labor have a decisive influence on productivity and levels of living. In spite of its importance, this is a greatly neglected field. The available information on farm labor, and its multiple combination with sharecropping and tenancy, is conspicuously deficient.

In general, only a small fraction of workers in the countries are paid on a cash basis. Most have the status of tenant laborers, a typical arrangement that assumes many names and variants throughout Latin America. This is known as the *colono* system, in which the worker is paid in the temporary or traditional usufruct of a parcel of land and certain other privileges. In return, the *colono* must serve a specified number of days on the estate and fulfill other customary obligations, such as making available members of his family for certain tasks in the field or in the owner's household. This system is often combined with sharecropping or with tenancy on a cash-rent basis. Most of the resident labor force on the hacienda is made up of *colonos*. They have different names in different countries: *yanaconas* in Peru, *inquilinos* in Chile, *huasipungos* in Ecuador, or *conuqueros* in Venezuela. Basically, all these represent similar arrangements.

The *colono* pattern is regarded as inefficient and as a poor base for economic development. The duality of the structure with its quasi-security aspects is not conducive to production incentives for the *colonos,* thus compounding the debilitating effects of landlord absenteeism.

In countries that have introduced land reforms the *colonos* were the first and most important beneficiaries of the programs. In Bolivia, for instance, the major immediate effect of the reform was to confirm the possession of the tenant workers who have been occupying and working small plots on the haciendas.

In contrast with other world areas, tenancy in its pure form does not loom large in the agrarian structure of Latin America. Important exceptions are Argentina and Uruguay. In Argentina, commercial tenancy is numerically more important than owner operation. In Uruguay, about one-third of the land in farms is managed by tenants. In the rest of the countries the degree of tenancy is relatively low. Contracts are generally of very short duration, and are verbal more often than not. Few of the norms of equitable and forward-looking tenancy arrangements are observed.

This review of the agrarian structure, brief and sketchy though it is, clearly shows the inadequacy of tenure institutions throughout the region. Units of production are either too large or too small, ownership and occupancy are often precarious, the communities are tradition-bound and inflexible, farm labor conditions are not many steps removed from serfdom, land as a resource does not freely exchange hands but is hoarded and unavailable to the small cultivator. There is no "tenure ladder" in the sense that a landless person could gradually work his way into the ownership class. Owners and nonowners of land are frequently separated by strict racial and cultural class barriers. The system reinforces the *status quo* and confers power upon those with inherited position and wealth. Farm investment is low, demand for consumer goods restricted, and large segments of the population are held at the margin of the economic mainstream in the countries. Political democracy and social mobility are greatly circumscribed. For brevity and simplicity the picture described is based only on land-tenure conditions. If one were to superimpose the effects of the other institutional factors—which in addition to what may be called "access to land" include access to capital and access to markets, the tax structure, education, local government, and other related aspects—the situation would appear even darker. . . .[4]

Concluding Comment

The foregoing does not pretend to cover all aspects of the complex problems of land-tenure reform. Notably, policies introduced to benefit small farmers in the field of farm credit, marketing, price supports, and social services have not been discussed, although many people refer to them collectively as "land reforms." It is the conviction of the writer that these and similar measures represent the focus not of land reform but of agricultural development, and that they are most effective where a healthy land-tenure situation exists.

To put it in another way, land-tenure improvement and agricultural development must go hand in hand. Past investments without land reforms have shown that the benefits are not shared by the large masses of farmers but go to a few big landowners and to those who monopolize the markets in farm products. Land reform without

---

[4] Agriculture is lagging behind other sectors in Latin America. In spite of good advances in some areas and with respect to some products, its overall growth barely keeps pace with population. During the decade 1950–1960 population increased at an average rate of 2.5 per cent per year, while the rate of growth for agricultural production was 3 per cent per year.

Of course, not all the ills of Latin American agriculture can be ascribed to land-tenure conditions. Many other factors are also at work. But the land systems are undoubtedly among the fundamental causes of the slow rate of growth in agriculture.

supporting measures of development—which has been the pattern so far—produces poor economic results and undue delays in raising levels of living. But on the basis of "first things first," more equitable tenure relations rate the highest priority and are a prerequisite for other types of action.

Vast land reserves are still available in Latin America for development and settlement. While the amount and accessibility of this reserve varies greatly from country to country and its quality is largely unknown, it can be said that Latin America is one of the few remaining world regions where an "agricultural frontier" still exists. Most of the frontier is in the tropical belt and the lands involved are state property.

There is a tendency to think of these new lands as the main solution for the region's land problems. Frequently it is asked: As the governments are the biggest landowners, why all the fuss about privately owned lands? True, these reserves offer opportunities to relieve the pressure in many areas, especially in the Andean, highlands where the population density is most acute. However, the public land reserves offer neither a quick enough nor a full enough solution to the present tenure problems. Experience of all countries that have settlement programs has shown that it is difficult to move large numbers of people into new areas, and that such an operation is extremely costly. Agricultural economists have repeatedly pointed out that in terms of potential production increases, the already established areas offer a much greater, more immediate, and less expensive possibility. Social overhead facilities are already available in these areas which are close to the population and market centers.

This does not mean that land settlement in new zones cannot be an important factor in the agricultural development of Latin America. As a matter of fact, these new areas offer great opportunities, not only for new production, but also for the establishment of a healthier type of tenure, less encumbered by the traditional forms. Yet the colonization of far-off lands is too often used as a diversionary tactic by those who are opposed to land reforms. Settlement on public land is, of course, politically inoffensive. But even if the present rate of colonization were to be doubled or tripled, it is not likely to take the steam off the unrest and agitation in crowded areas. The bulk of the tenure problems must be resolved and the needed additional production opportunities can be found in the already settled areas.

With respect to land reform proper, the goals of tenure policy and the new institutions which would promote the frequently announced aim of economic development are only dimly visualized. The emphasis is on tearing down the old structure (principally the *latifundio* complex). Frequently there is no exploration of alternative models, beyond a vague concern with "family farming," an essentially north European and North American concept. It is doubtful, however, if the North American model in its fully commercial form is realistic for Latin America in more than a portion of the area. The medium-sized market-oriented farms in Latin American countries almost never operate with family labor alone. Even small units frequently have a *patrón* who manages and some *colonos* or *peones* who do the work.

There is little exploration of possible cooperative or communal types of tenure (the *ejido* was a very special Mexican solution). While the preoccupation with breaking up the existing system (and with it the bonds of a paternalistic and rigid class structure) may be far from wrong, there is real

danger of aggravating the *minifundio* problem in the process.

Perhaps the Puerto Rican experience with what is known as the proportional-profits farms may be relevant. This arrangement is carried out under the island's Land Law of 1941. Sugarcane areas expropriated in excess of the constitutional limitation of 500 acres (applying to corporations) are operated by the Puerto Rico Land Authority, a public corporation, and farmed by unionized workers. These workers receive, in addition to their wages, part of the profits, distributed in proportion to the work done during the year. This arrangement seems to have maintained productive efficiency and is one way to distribute rights in land without excessive subdivision of the land itself. There are many possible variants of such an arrangement. The search for viable alternative tenure systems that strike an appropriate balance between social equity and productive efficiency is perhaps the most important and urgent task of land-reform experts.

The preoccupation with "legalism" and with legislative details is striking. Land-reform laws are invariably long, complicated, and detailed. This makes their implementation very difficult. Only a fraction of the laws have actually been carried out (Bolivia is a prime example). In addition, the many detailed provisions are not only hard to implement, but are equally hard to change if they prove unworkable. The tendency to complicated laws resulted frequently in a veritable jungle of previous legislation which must be cleared away. Most of the legislative detail has of course very little meaning when it comes down to the peasants. In Bolivia, for instance, few of the illiterate Indians understand the land-reform law, even though it has been translated into their native languages.

A key issue, and perhaps the most controversial one, is the expropriation procedure. With the exception of oil-rich Venezuela, no major land reform provides for acquisition of land at going market values. The exact conditions of compensation are dictated by the current conception of social justice and the relative power position of the various groups involved. Where inflation has accompanied reforms, the real value of compensation has been greatly reduced. The reforms could be placed on a self-financing basis if the landlords accepted compensation of a magnitude which was within the repayment capacity of the average beneficiary, but none of the land reforms thus far carried out has been self-financing in this sense. The basic dilemma of expropriation is how to minimize the injustices inherent in a land-distribution program, which by definition goes against present market forces and pretends to change the prevailing distribution of wealth. Given overwhelming political power, a government such as Cuba seems to have no difficulty in nationalizing property. But where power is more delicately balanced, the problem of how much to pay for land and on what terms becomes more crucial.

One word about implementation. With land traditionally the basis of power, political and economic, there is an almost irresistible tendency to let personal favoritism, political influence, and outright bribery intrude upon the land-granting process. The land settlement programs of most countries, on however modest a scale, have been traditionally important means for the rewarding of political favors by the ruling party. Thus land frequently does not get to the people who need it most and who are legally entitled to it. This is a further reason to justify a more drastic approach in which the peasants themselves can take an active role. Unfortunately, the framers of even revolutionary land programs seldom appreciate the necessity to make the cultivators participate actively in the land-reform process. There is a tendency to manage the whole program from the top. This not only dissipates the potential contribution of the peasants to community development and self-help projects but causes great delays and frequent hardships in the distribution process itself.

It is the conclusion of this paper that, as a consequence of economic and social pressures, the central focus of land reforms in Latin America has been and will continue to be a substantial redistribution of rights in land in favor of the masses of cultivating farmers, and a corresponding shift in power and income-producing capacity. Developmental measures, such as credit, education, and market assistance, must accompany tenure reforms *but are not substitutes for them.* The bulk of the reforms will take place in the already cultivated areas and will involve thorny problems of expropriation. Land-settlement programs on public land and such indirect measures as land taxation can be an important complement to land-tenure reforms but cannot replace them.

What are the chances for "peaceful, democratically planned reforms"? The available evidence is not encouraging. In fact, on the basis of past experience alone, an outlook of pessimism is warranted. With the possible exception of Venezuela, policy tends to polarize on one side in a "do nothing" attitude and on the other in a radical, revolutionary stance. The former group may tinker with some land settlement or tax reforms, and is likely to appoint commissions to "study the problem." It may even pass some laws—which, however, are likely to remain on the books. With this group, in general, the hope is that the problems will go away. Where, on the other hand, land reforms have been imbedded in violent revolutions, there is either a nearly complete neglect of the technical and development aspects (as in Bolivia) or a tendency toward political excesses (as in Cuba) which not only involve a very high social cost but may eventually cancel out the possible benefits and may even (as in Guatemala) lead to a reversal of the whole process.

Yet the picture is not without hope. An important outside factor is the future attitude and aid policy of the United States. The Act of Bogotá represents a significant new line of thinking in this respect. For the first time, an important policy document speaks of the need for "land-tenure legislation and facilities with a view to ensuring a wider and more equitable distribution of the ownership of the land."[5] It is possible that the resources

to be devoted to land reform under the new Special Fund for Social Development and other technical assistance will provide exceptional opportunities to support new and effective programs.

Moreover, the spectacle of Cuba dispossessing not only the wealthy upper classes but also the middle-income groups has profoundly affected the attitude of many of the ruling elements in the rest of Latin America. Meanwhile the *campesinos* have in a number of places made their voice heard, either through the ballot box (as in Chile in the last election) or, more commonly, through agitation, occupancy of haciendas and general rural unrest (Colombia, Peru).

This conjunction of events may eventually lead to meaningful land reform over wide areas of Latin America.

---

[5] *Act of Bogotá* (Measures for Social Improvement and Economic Development with the Framework of Operation Pan America), in Document OEA/Ser. G/IV C-i-487, Council of the Organization of American States, November 26, 1960, p. 6.

PART THREE

The Agents of Change

The study of groups by North American political scientists goes back many years and includes work by such men as Arthur F. Bentley and Peter Odegard. Interest in this kind of analysis gradually expanded to include the field of comparative government and, more recently, Latin America. To some extent this movement has been accidental, and there has been little effort to construct a formalized theory applicable to Latin American groups. In addition to the excellent general statement of Blanksten, however, Latin Americanists have found their interest turning toward segments of the polity that can properly be regarded as groups. Thus, the informal, associational groups are the parties, student movements, and labor, whereas those more properly regarded as institutional are the military and the Church.

None of these has received exhaustive attention, although parties and the military have attracted some. In the former case, Fitzgibbon's admonition that "a generation of graduate students should study Latin American parties" seems not to have been highly productive. Gibes at the personalistic and factional nature of many parties do not conceal the fact that in many cases they are becoming the most important agents of significant change. Neither labor nor the student unions have received equal scrutiny, although the developments in several countries have been significant. A notable study of students in politics is Frank Bonilla's "The Student Federation of Chile: 50 Years of Political Action," *Journal of Inter-American Studies*, II, No. 3 (July 1960), 311–35. A country study of labor is John D. Martz's "The Growth and Democratization of the Venezuelan Labor Movement," *Inter-American Economic Affairs*, Vol. LIII, No. 1 (Autumn 1963).

The changing role of the military holds primordial importance in contemporary ·Latin America and is contributing to the nature of political change through its gradual acceptance of a new set of duties and responsibilities. McAlister and Wyckoff discuss the question thoroughly, although the best extended discussions to date are Edwin Lieuwen's *Arms and Politics in Latin America* (New York: Frederick A. Praeger, Inc., 1959) and John J. Johnson's *The Military and Society in Latin America* (Stanford, Calif.: Stanford University Press, 1964).

18

Political Groups in Latin America

George I. Blanksten

I feel it necessary to begin with an attempt to define the term "political group" as used in this paper: it is a system of patterned or regular interaction among a number of individuals. The interaction is sufficiently patterned to permit the system to be viewed as a unit, and the action of the unit is directed toward some phase of the operation of government. Every political group has an interest. This is simply the central and continuing type of activity that gives the group its property as a system or a unit. Interest, then, is consistent with the observed pattern of interaction, and not contrary to it. "The interest and the group are the same phenomenon observed from slightly different positions, and an 'interest group' is a tautological expression. The interest is not a thing that exists apart from the activity or that controls activity."[1]

Let me add a few points regarding the relationship between the political group and its member individuals. If the group be regarded as the pattern of interaction among its members, then it follows that the group has an existence apart from that of the individuals associated with it. So a political group may have a history or a career of its own, distinguishable from those of the individuals participating in the interaction. Further, at any given time a single individual may take part in more groups than one; a person with such "overlapping memberships" may pursue different and, in some cases, contradictory interests. Finally, the size of a group is not material here. No issue is raised by queries as to how large or small a political group may be. It is defined by the pattern of interaction, and not by the number of individuals contributing to it.

From "Political Groups in Latin America," by George I. Blanksten, *American Political Science Review,* Vol. LIII, No. 1 (March 1959). Reprinted by permission.
[1] Charles B. Hagan, "The Group in a Political Science," in Roland A. Young, ed., *Approaches to the Study of Politics* (Evanston: Northwestern University Press, 1958), pp. 38–51, particularly pp. 44–46.

I

Two propositions about political groups should be obvious. First, the number of such groups functioning in a given political system is likely to be quite large. Second, a wide variety of types of groups exists, suggesting the feasibility of some system of classification. Several bases for classification are, of course, possible; let me advance one scheme here. Political groups may be regarded as (1) institutional, (2) associational, and (3) nonassociational. Each of these categories, as used in the context of research in Latin American politics, calls for some discussion.

1. *Institutional* groups are formally constituted agencies, or segments of them, with established roles in a political system, roles usually recognized and generally accepted. It is useful to distinguish between two broad types of such institutional groups. One is the species which is formally and ostensibly assigned authoritative political functions—such as rule-making, rule-application, and rule-adjudication—and which performs them. In other words, formally established government is itself composed of a number of groups whose role it is to carry out political functions, and so some political groups can be studied in the examination of formal agencies of government. If to nothing else, American political scientists have been conventionally trained to direct their attention to such structures. Let me therefore pass by this category, pausing only to remark that, while we are still with the old familiar subject matter of conventional political science—the formal structures of government—the group emphasis does imply a difference in the *manner* in which these agencies are studied. I plan to return to this proposition at a later point.

The second type of institutional political group needs to be examined more closely. This is the group which, while associated with a formal institution, performs a political function differing markedly from the established or ostensible role of the institution. The study of political groups of this type in Latin America is of high importance and deserves priority among political inquiries in the area. Let me mention a few such institutional groups of this type in Latin America—not an exhaustive list, but rather a relatively small sample illustrative of one type of political organization to which the attention of research scholars is urgently invited.

The Roman Catholic Church is one of the major political groups of this sort in Latin America. Historically, Church and state were united in the Spanish tradition. This was true throughout the colonial period; indeed, the movement for separation of Church and state is, in a sense, a relatively recent development in the area. In most of the countries, the Church pursues political objectives, and in some of them its functions resemble those of a political party. Some Latin American political parties are essentially Church parties, as for example the Conservative parties of Colombia and Ecuador. Consider this statement by the Conservative party of Ecuador of its *political* program: "Man is essentially a religious being and religion, consequently, is a natural phenomenon. . . . The end of man is God, whom he should serve and adore in order to enjoy after death the beatified possession of divinity. . . . The purpose of the state is to facilitate religious action so that its subjects will not lack the necessities of the spirit and will be able to obtain in the next life the happiness which can never be achieved in this." The power of the Church as a political group varies, of course, from country to country. It is perhaps strongest in Ecuador and weakest in Mexico, but there is no Latin American state in which the Church is not to be counted as a major political group. It has, of course, been studied from several points of view, but published assessments of it in this capacity are rare.

Similarly, there are very few studies of the armed forces, particularly the armies, of Latin America as political groups. This is a curious indictment of political scientists interested in the area, since militarism has long been recognized as a fundamental characteristic of Latin American politics. "The last step in a military career is the presidency of the republic" is a well-known and frequently practiced precept in the area. Rather than the defense of the community, the basic functions of the Latin American military lie in domestic politics. Everywhere high-ranking army officers are important politicians; everywhere the military influence provides a species of backdrop for politics. Generally this is more true of the armies than of the other armed services, although in a few of the countries—notably Argentina and Paraguay—the navies also operate as significant political groups. Political studies of the Latin American armed services are sorely needed. Topics especially requiring investigation include the process of political clique-formation among military and naval officers, and the relationship between militarism and the class system. Certain military ranks—for example, major and lieutenant-colonel—appear to be of peculiarly critical political significance.

Few studies, again, have been made of bureaucracy in Latin America, and consequently little can be said of the roles of public workers as political groups. In some of the countries government work, like other types of occupations, is organized on the basis of part-time jobs. Moreover, few of the republics have developed effective merit systems of civil service, and a spoils system is generally characteristic of the area. These considerations suggest patterns of action differing from those to be found in western Europe or the United States. Latin American government workers no doubt may be regarded as political groups. However, the current state of research on this problem does not permit evaluation at this time of their full significance.

2. Let me now turn to the *associational,* or second major category, of political groups. These are consciously organized associations which lie outside the formal structure of government and which nevertheless include the performance of political functions among their stated objectives. Generally speaking, associational groups carry out less authoritative functions than the institutional organizations. That is to say, this second category tends to concentrate its activity on such matters as political recruitment, interest articulation, interest aggregation, and—in some cases—political communication, rather than on more authoritative political functions such as rule-making, rule-application, and rule-adjudication.

Two chief types of associational groups may be distinguished. The differences are roughly similar to those, familiar to students of politics in the United States, between political parties and pressure groups. However, the distinction sought here is not quite the same as that. In the United States and in many of the countries of western Europe, "political parties tend to be free of ideological rigidity, and are aggregative, that is, seek to form the largest possible interest group coalitions by offering acceptable choices of political personnel and public policy." On the other hand, pressure groups in those same so-called "Western" systems "articulate political demands in the society, seek support for these demands among other groups by advocacy and bargaining, and attempt to transform these demands into authoritative public policy by influencing the choice of political personnel, and the various processes of public policy-making and enforcement."[2] In many Latin American countries, particularly in those with the more underdeveloped economies—and, no doubt, in most of the so-called "non-Western" political systems—the dividing line does not fall in quite the same place. Political parties tend to be more nonaggregative than aggregative, and some of the functions of the other associational groups include activities usually restricted to political parties in the United States and in some of the western European systems.

Despite the fact that political parties have long been included among the accepted concerns of political scientists, it remains a curious circumstance that very little research has been done on these organizations in Latin America. Indeed, only one political party in the area has been the object of a full-blown monographic study. "The field is one which needs a vast amount of spade work of a primary sort and on top of that additional synthesis in order to put the raw materials in proper arrangement and perspective," Russell H. Fitzgibbon has said. "I commend the field of Latin American political parties to a whole generation of prospective graduate students in political science." [See Fitzgibbon's article, "The Party Potpourri in Latin America," on page 203.]

Not only the party systems, but also the parties themselves, are of various types in Latin America. Let me once again, therefore, undertake the task of classification. Although the existing literature of political science contains a number of fairly elaborate attempts at categorization, nothing more complicated is necessary for the present pur-

pose than a simple dichotomy separating one-party systems from competitive party systems. Both types are to be found in Latin America.

The one-party system, of course, is the situation in which a single political party holds an effective monopoly of public power and controls access to government office. In some one-party systems, this may be provided for by law, other political parties being considered illegal or subversive; in another type of one-party system, other parties may exist legally but—for reasons largely unrelated to legal questions or government coercion—find themselves unable to challenge effectively the dominant party's hold on the system.

Thus conceived, two varieties of dominant parties hold power in the one-party systems of Latin America. One may be dubbed the "dictatorial" party. Where it exists, an official attempt is made to obscure the distinction between the party in power and the government of the country, and so to render opposition to the party virtually synonymous with treason against the state. By definition, then, the party in power being the only legal party, any others are not merely in opposition but in rebellion, open or covert. The best current Latin American illustration of this type of party is to be found in the Dominican Republic. Such a system has also operated in Venezuela. Paraguay's arrangement is a borderline case—other parties than the *Colorado* are theoretically legal, but the price of participating in them is often imprisonment or exile.

The other type of group holding power in a one-party system may be designated as the "dominant nondictatorial" party. In this case, one party holds a monopoly of political power in the sense that it is victorious in virtually all elections, but other parties are legal and do exist. This is somewhat similar to the stereotype—but I beg you not

---

2 Gabriel A. Almond, "A Comparative Study of Interest Groups and the Political Process," *American Political Science Review*, Vol. LII, No. 1 (March 1958).

to hold me responsible for its validity—of the "Solid South" or of northern rural areas in the United States. The leading Latin American case is in Mexico, where the Party of Revolutionary Institutions (PRI) is without a serious rival. Other Mexican parties exist legally, but they exercise virtually no authority in government. Uruguay's system may also be included here, if we agree with Fitzgibbon that it cannot be regarded as a two-party affair. Further, it has been noted that the situation in Paraguay's case is borderline—if one Paraguayan foot is in the "dictatorial" party camp, the other is with the "dominant nondictatorial" party.

Competitive party systems exist where two or more parties, none of them a dominant or "official" organization, contend among themselves. In general, there are two classes of competitive systems, multiparty and two-party arrangements.

A multiparty system contains three or more major political parties, normally making it impossible for any one of them to command a majority of the seats in a representative assembly. Politics in these systems frequently operates through coalitions or blocs involving two or more parties, and these understandings are designed to produce working majorities. Latin America's best illustration of a multiparty system is to be found in Chile, where there are at least six major political parties, none of which controls a legislative majority. Multiparty arrangements also exist in Argentina, Bolivia, Brazil, Costa Rica, Cuba, Guatemala, Panama, and Peru.

Two-party systems contain two major political parties sufficiently matched in strength to permit their alternation in power. "Third" or "minor" parties are legal in these systems, but are rarely serious rivals at the polls of the two major parties. Thus conceived, two-party systems are rare in Latin America;

indeed, they are rare outside the English-speaking world. The best Latin American illustration is to be found in Colombia, where the Conservative and Liberal parties, roughly evenly matched, have historically alternated in power. Uruguay also has two major political parties—the *Colorados* and the *Blancos* —but there is some question as to whether this is a clear case of a two-party system. Fitzgibbon, for example, believes that, since the *Colorados* have been victorious in almost all national elections, it cannot be said that Uruguay's is a true two-party arrangement.

Most of the major parties in the competitive systems of Latin America are what might be called traditional political parties. In general, they have two major characteristics. First, the issues which concern them have historically troubled Latin Americans as long-range political problems of their respective countries. Primarily, these issues have been the questions of land tenure and the temporal role of the Roman Catholic Church. Second, the traditional parties draw their membership, in terms of the class systems of Latin America, primarily from the upper classes; the other classes—often involving majorities of national populations—virtually are excluded from direct participation in these parties. The traditional parties may be roughly branded as conservative or liberal. Conservative parties generally defend the interests of the large landowners and advocate an expanded temporal role for the Church, sometimes including union of Church and state. Conservative parties have been in power in most of the countries of Latin America during most of the years of their respective national histories. Representative conservative parties include the Conservative party of Argentina, the Conservatives of Colombia, the Conservative party of Ecuador, the *Blanco* party of Uruguay, and COPEI of Venezuela. Liberal parties, on the other hand, have generally advocated some kind of land reform, separation of Church and state, and a general reduction in the temporal influence of the Church. Representative liberal parties are the Radical party of Argentina, the Radicals of Chile, the Liberals of Colombia, the Radical-Liberal party of Ecuador, and the *Colorados* of Uruguay.

The parties which participate in the competitive systems of Latin America may be classed as pragmatic, ideological, and particularistic. Pragmatic parties are those which make no major ideological or philosophical demands upon their membership. Such parties are far more interested in commanding the votes than the minds of their followers, who may enter or leave the pragmatic groups without benefit of the trauma of ideological, philosophical, or religious conversion on such occasions.

Pragmatic parties may be broadly or narrowly based, depending on how large a sector of the politically articulate population the group appeals to. Perhaps Latin America's best illustrations of the broad-based pragmatic party are the Argentine Radical party (UCR) and the Chilean Radical party. The UCR has endeavored with some success to appeal for the electoral support of organized labor, commercial and industrial interests, associations of university students, and professional and intellectual organizations. Indeed, under the leadership of Arturo Frondizi in the presidential election of 1958, the UCR, which had bitterly fought the Perón dictatorship (1946–1955), successfully campaigned for the votes of those who had formerly supported Perón! In Chile, the Radical party has joined together university students, labor organizations, teachers' associations, and the smaller commercial and industrial interests.

Narrow-based pragmatic parties are more numerous in the area. In general, these are of two types—personalistic and *ad hoc* parties. Personalistic parties are an outgrowth of *personalismo,* a long-standing ingredient of Latin American politics. *Personalismo* may be defined as the tendency to follow or oppose a political leader on personality rather than ideological grounds, through personal, individual, and family motivations rather than because of an impersonal political idea or program. This historic attribute of the politics of the area has been noted by many students of Latin America. Pierson and Gil, for example, point to "the high value placed on the individual and personal leadership," promoting "a disposition to vote for the man rather than the party or the platform."[3] Another student has said: "From earliest days the Latin Americans...have always been more interested in their public men than in their public policies. They have tended to follow colorful leaders, to the subordination of issues. ...A picturesque demagogue is virtually assured a large following."[4]

Latin Americans like to say—and this exaggerates the situation—that "Every 'ism' is a somebody-ism." Personalist parties are "Somebody-ist" groups organized in support of the political ambitions of strong personal leaders. Paraguay has its *Franquista* party, composed of the followers of General Rafael Franco; Brazil had a *Querimista* party; Ecuador a *Velasquista* organization, made up of the followers of Dr. José María Velasco Ibarra; and Uruguay a *Batllista* "faction," founded by the nineteenth-century statesman, José Batlle y Ordóñez. There is some evi-

---

3 William Whatley Pierson and Federico Guillermo Gil, *Governments of Latin America* (New York: McGraw-Hill Book Company, 1957), p. 31.

4 Austin F. Macdonald, *Latin American Politics and Government* (2nd ed.; New York: The Crowell-Collier Publishing Co., 1954), p. 2.

dence that personalist parties are currently declining in number and influence in Latin America.

Finally, there are *ad hoc* parties. These are fluid organizations created for the purpose of achieving short-range political objectives and disappearing when these ends have been accomplished or defeated. These parties are particularly important in the politics of Bolivia, Ecuador, and Paraguay. "In these times," a Bolivian wrote in 1942, "nothing is simpler than to found a political party. To form a political party only three people and one object are necessary: a president, a vice-president, a secretary, and a rubber stamp. The party can get along even without the vice-president and the secretary. . . . There have been cases in which the existence of only the rubber stamp has been sufficient."[5] Parties of this type are especially important in times of political instability and so-called revolution, times not infrequent in a number of the countries of Latin America.

Ideological parties are also to be counted among the actors in the competitive party systems of the area. Communist parties, for example, exist throughout the Americas. The most important Communist organizations are in Argentina; Bolivia, where the party has long been known as the Leftist Revolutionary party (PIR); Brazil; Chile; Cuba; Guatemala; and Mexico, where the group is called the Popular party. Although the Mexican party system is not a competitive one, the Mexican Communists are nevertheless worth mentioning here. Despite indications that the party is small and weak from the standpoint of its influence upon domestic politics in Mexico, the Com-

munist organization in that country does perform a noteworthy international function in serving as a point of liaison, and as an informational clearinghouse, between European Communists and those of Central America and the Caribbean islands. Meetings of the Communist leaders of the smaller countries of Middle America are occasionally held in Mexico.

Socialist parties also exist in virtually all of the countries of Latin America. The membership of these parties is generally dominated by middle-class intellectuals with a strong interest in Marxism. Despite their avowed interest in the problems of the working classes, the Socialists of Latin America have, in fact, developed little genuine influence with the masses. In country after country, the Socialists "have become increasingly doctrinaire, academic, and intellectualized."[6] Ray Josephs once remarked that "the Socialist weakness lies in addiction to theory and philosophy and what we might call their lack of practical, sound common sense." It need hardly be added that Socialists have never been in power for any appreciable length of time in any country of Latin America.

A number of Church-oriented parties are to be found in the area, and these too may be regarded as largely ideological parties. The best current illustrations are the Conservative parties of Colombia and Ecuador. Heavily Catholic in doctrinal orientation, Church parties have participated in most of the competitive systems of Latin America during the past century. Not since the regime of Gabriel García Moreno in Ecuador (1859–1875) has a Church group been the dominant party in a one-party system. In that case, religious

5 Luis Terán Gómez, *Los Partidos Políticos y su Acción Democrática* (La Paz: Editorial La Paz, 1942), pp. 60–61.

6 Russell H. Fitzgibbon, "The Party Potpourri in Latin America," *Western Political Quarterly*, X, No. 1 (March 1957), 13.

intolerance was revived, only practicing Catholics were permitted to be citizens of the country—then called the "Republic of the Sacred Heart"—and government was heavily authoritarian in character.

Nationalist groups also may be counted among the ideological parties of Latin America. The typical Latin American nationalist party is narrow-based, addressing a concerted appeal to a small sector of the society in which it operates. Indeed, it is not unusual to find a given country in the area with two or more small nationalist parties functioning in rivalry relationships with each other. While anticlerical nationalists are not unheard of—one such group once effectively employed "We are Ecuadorans, not Romans!" as its slogan —the nationalist parties more frequently embrace the Church, demand religious intolerance, oppose secularization, and attempt to eradicate foreign influence in their countries. Often such parties are active centers of anti-Semitism. In recent times the most important nationalist parties of Latin America—all of them narrow-based rather than comprehensive—have operated in Argentina, Bolivia, Paraguay, and Venezuela.

The area also has its share of Fascist parties. For many of these, "Fascist-like" or "quasi-Fascist" would probably be better designations since they generally combine selected elements of Fascist ideology with enough indigenous Latin American ingredients to render the organizations difficult to equate with European Fascist parties. During World War II, most of them pressed pro-Axis foreign-policy objectives in Latin America. Representative parties of this type are the *Peronista* party of Argentina, the Nationalist Revolutionary Movement (MNR) of Bolivia, the Integralist party of Brazil, the *Nacista* party of Chile, and the National Sinarquist Union of Mexico.

Also occupying a significant place on the roster of the area's ideological parties are the agrarian-populistic group. In Latin America, these have come to be called *Aprista* parties. They have two distinguishing characteristics. First, they seek far-reaching social and economic change, usually including radical land reform and the integration of the lower classes into the political process. Indeed, there is a greater percentage of lower-class adherents in the membership of *Aprista* groups than in any other type of Latin American party. Second, *aprismo* is indigenous to the area. Such international connections as the movement has—and they are not many—are entirely within Latin America. The chief prototype of this class of political party is the celebrated *Aprista* party or APRA of Peru. Other *Aprista* parties include *Acción Democrática* of Venezuela, the *Auténtico* party of Cuba, the National Liberation party of Costa Rica, and, in a sense, Mexico's PRI.

Particularistic parties have on occasion appeared in the competitive systems of Latin America, although there is no clear illustration of the type operating in the area today. Such organizations, concerned in a separatist fashion with selected ethnic groups or regions and including some form of secession among statements of political objectives, have from time to time filled major roles in the Americas. Indeed, this is one of the reasons why what were once only eight Spanish colonies are now as many as eighteen independent states. In the historic past, particularist parties have been led by such personalities as General José Antonio Páez, who directed the secession of Venezuela from Gran Colombia; General Juan José Flores, who presided over the separation of Ecuador from the same entity; and Dr. Amador, prominent in the detachment of the isthmus of Panama from Colombia. Particularistic parties were also active in the reduction of the former Central American Confederation to its present five separate heirs. So far as the contemporary scene is concerned, although no major particularistic parties are functioning in the area, there are significant evidences of the presence of some of the ingredients of which such groups may be fashioned. In Brazil, for example, the two states of São Paulo and Minas Gerais, which had stubbornly opposed the regimes of President Getulio Vargas (1930–1945; 1951–1954), have fallen into a political collaboration against other sections of the country which approximates particularism. Again, in the countries where regionalism is a major political force—such as Peru, Ecuador, and Bolivia—there is a tendency for political parties to become regionally based. The record of the past and the current scene combine to suggest that it might not be unreasonable to expect the reappearance of such organizations in the area from time to time in the future.

I attempted earlier to distinguish between two chief types of associational political groups, offering parties as the first of them. I turn now to the second type, roughly resembling what are called pressure groups in the United States. In Latin America these organizations perform some of the functions usually restricted in the "North American" system to political parties. Without presenting an exhaustive list I shall mention a number of them to illustrate their functions in the political systems of Latin America.

Associations of landowners, in one form or another, exist in all countries of the area. In view of the significant role of the land in the economy of Latin America and the predominance of feudal-like systems of land tenure, these groups are of high importance.

In Argentina, for example, fewer than 2,000 families' landholdings constitute a combined area greater than England, Belgium, and the Netherlands put together; and statistics produced by some of the American republics indicate that approximately three-fourths of their respective land surfaces are owned by about two per cent of their respective populations. Landowning groups wield political as well as economic power. The best-known landowners' association in the area is the Argentine Jockey Club; similar organizations operate in most of the other states.

Foreign companies function as political groups in some of the countries. In northern Latin America—particularly in the Caribbean area—United States corporations are prominent among these groups. Excellent illustrations can be found in the United Fruit Company as it operates in a number of the states of Central America, and in the influence of a number of oil companies in Venezuelan politics. In southern South America—Argentina, Uruguay, Paraguay, and Chile—British firms function in a similar fashion.

Labor organizations, though still small, are of growing importance as Latin American groups. The role of these organizations is expanding as industrialization begins to take hold in the area. From the standpoint of their functions as political groups, the most important labor organizations in the area are Argentina's CGT, Chile's CTCH, Cuba's CTC, and Mexico's CTM. Organized labor in Latin America is, in general, quite politically articulate, and its support has long been sought by Socialist parties.

Student associations are vigorously active groups in all of the countries involved. Hear this account of student life in the area: "The...university, traditionally, is a miniature battleground of national politics. Students strike, riot, and stage political demonstrations on the slightest provocation."[7] Politics "becomes a passion that invades and confuses everything. I myself remember many postponed examinations; many study hours disturbed; countless meetings, discussions, strikes—a whole year lost in them—elections that ended with gunfire. . . ."[8] As political groups, student associations are far more significant in Latin America than in the United States.

Professional associations should also be counted among the active groups of the area. Lawyers' associations are perhaps the oldest of these. With the growing economic development of Latin America, associations of engineers, still small, are of rising importance. Business groups are also small in the area. However, these may be expected to grow in significance as industrialization and economic development continue.

Veterans' associations, important in the United States, are of little significance as Latin American political groups, except in Bolivia and Paraguay. In both countries, organizations of veterans of the Chaco War (1928–1935) have become major pressure groups. In Bolivia, such a group served as the nucleus for the MNR party. In the absence of systematic studies, however, any explanatory statement at this point can be little more than conjecture. My guess—and it is only that— is that in most of Latin America such influence as veterans' groups might have had has been more than engulfed by the groups representing the armed services. International wars producing veterans are, after all, rare in contem-

porary Latin America; on the other hand, militarism and the military are ever-present.

3. Finally, some discussion of the *nonassociational* category of political groups is in order. These are not formally or consciously organized. Indeed, they may be regarded more as latent or potential than as currently functioning political groups, for the nonassociational variety is far less structured than the institutional and associational types. In Latin America, nonassociational interests tend to coalesce around such symbols as class, status, ethnic groups, kinship and lineage, and regionalism.

The class systems are fairly rigid in most of the countries of the area. Classes, of course, are not formally or consciously organized groups; yet significant political interests arise from them. With some variations from country to country in Latin America, the typical class system is composed of three levels. The highest class is usually referred to as the creoles or "whites"; the middle group is known as the mestizos or, in some countries, *cholos;* and, in the countries with large Indian populations, these have constituted the lowest class. Scholars who have examined these classes in Latin America have devoted more attention to the creoles, and to the Indians, than they have to the mestizos or *cholos.*

The highest class—creoles or "whites" —are the most politically articulate of the three, and in most of the countries of the area their interests—the preservation of the systems of land tenure, the control of the Church and of the high military ranks, and the maintenance of a European rather than an indigenous cultural orientation—are the best-protected and espoused. Where commercialization and industrialization have taken hold, new interests are created, primarily among the "whites." In some of the countries, this has a

[7] Ysabel F. Rennie, *The Argentine Republic* (New York: The Macmillan Company, 1945), p. 212.

[8] Luis Guillermo Piazza, "There'll Always Be a Córdoba," *Americas,* January 1950, p. 27.

divisive effect upon "white" interests, for land ownership is sometimes held to be threatened by commercialization and industrialization. Conscious of themselves as the ruling group in most of the countries of the area, the "whites" share an interest in the avoidance of true revolution and, in general, oppose political reforms believed to imperil their dominant position.

Less is known about the mestizo or *cholo*. A detribalized Indian but not yet a "white," the mestizo accounts for over thirty per cent of the populations of some of the countries. He is not politically articulate, and rarely organizes. He is interested in working his way into the "white" group, and usually, in severing his ties with the Indians. The mestizo is frequently employed as an artisan or a tradesman. In some of the countries of the area, the mestizo is an important source of the labor supply. As a class, the mestizos no doubt have interests. But given the paucity of available data, little more can be said here regarding their nonassociational interests without risking the hazards of a major excursion into the realm of speculation.

About the Indian, entire libraries have been written. Indian communities and villages are tightly organized, and the Indians feel strong loyalties to them, but the Indian class as a whole is not organized in any of the Latin American countries. In general, the Indians resist incursion upon their way of life by the "whites." They desire, as they frequently put it, to be left alone. They seek decentralized, loosely organized, or inefficiently administered government, so that the number of "white" government officials entering their communities bearing rules and regulations from the national capital will be held to a minimum. Having normally a deep love for their villages and communities, they strongly resist resettlement programs involving relocation of the lower classes. Typically, the Indian does not own much, if any, land. Many writers have argued that in Latin America the Indian problem is basically a land problem, and have urged land-reform programs which would deliver holdings to Indian ownership. The Indians, however, have rarely expressed this sentiment themselves, and have been slow to respond to land-redistribution programs. Being quite inarticulate politically, they rarely communicate their desires to the "white" officials of the governments which rule them.

Interests also arise from the concept of status, especially within the "white" groups. In colonial times the upper class was acrimoniously divided within itself, with the creoles—persons born in the colonies—pitted against the *peninsulares*—born in Europe—who enjoyed higher status. Indeed, this intraclass struggle was one of the factors giving alignment to some of the fighting during the wars of independence. Since then, the *peninsulares* have dropped from the Latin American class structure, but the concept of the "old families" or "good families" remains. These— when they can establish themselves as such—enjoy considerable prestige within the ruling class. Although the "whites" are at least as racially mixed as any other group in Latin American society, the "old families" are constantly engaged in heraldic research designed to demonstrate their unmixed Spanish descent. To be accepted as an "old" or "good" family is to be the aristocracy of the aristocracy. Families which have achieved this enviable position have a strong interest in preserving those elements of the system—particularly the older patterns of land tenure—that lend security to the prestige system, and in making it difficult for "new" families to become "old" and share the higher status.

Again, in view of the paucity of research on the mestizo or *cholo* group, little can be said here of the prestige patterns within that class. In general, however, the mestizos strive to become "whites."

Status is at least as important among the Indians as it is among the "whites." A significant difference, however, should be noted. Whereas those who acquire high prestige among the "whites" enjoy it on a national—and, in some cases, international—basis, status among the Indians has meaning only on a local village or community level. As in the case of the "whites," status among the Indians rests on ascriptive more than achievement considerations. Village elders, and their relatives, enjoy prestige, as do witch doctors and medicine men. To hold high status in the Indian community is to exercise some power—frequently of government—within it, and those who have this prestige are interested in preserving it and preventing its adulteration through too-easy access of other Indians to the status positions.

Nonassociational interests also arise among some ethnic groups in Latin America. For example, Negroes—numerous in the Caribbean island republics and in some parts of Brazil—have developed strong interests though they emerge on an unorganized basis. So, too, have a number of the European immigrant groups, notably the Italians, Germans, Spaniards, and Jews. The European immigrant groups are normally more articulate than many of the indigenous groups, particularly the Indians and mestizos, and generally have developed interests, usually directed toward the preservation of their social and economic positions in society.

Patterns of kinships and lineage also produce systems of nonassociational interest in Latin America. This is especially true among the "whites" and Indians; the mestizos again, for the time being at least, stand as an unknown quantity. Among the "whites," reference has already been made to the "old" or "good" families. High values are assigned to belonging to them, or if that is impossible, to being somehow related or connected to them. The extensive use made of, and the exaggerated importance given to, the famous letters of introduction among the "whites" have frequently reached the proportions of a joke. A letter of introduction from a well-known member of an established "good family" is, in many of the countries, indispensable to the candidate seeking employment or some other favor from government. "The municipal department had become a perfect teeming house of *recomendados*—persons for whom jobs had been found whether jobs were to be had or not," an observer has said of local politics among the "whites." "In the old days of the Deliberative Council, it used to be a standing joke that business offices could be wallpapered with the letters of introduction given to job applicants."[9] Although this particular reference is to local government, the practice is general.

Three generalizations can safely be made regarding the role of kinship and lineage among the Indians of Latin America. First, as a determiner of interest, it is even more basic in this class than among the "whites." Next, in many Indian groups, kinship and lineage are more centrally and directly related to politics and government than is true of the upper classes. Finally, in contrast to the situation among the "whites," this is important among the Indians on the local—village and community—level to the almost total exclusion of other levels of politics. Unfortunately, these are virtually the only generalizations on the subject that can

---

[9] Ray Josephs, *Argentine Diary* (New York: Random House, 1944), p. 26.

be made with assurance. Practices in this field vary widely among the indigenous peoples of the area, for two major reasons. First, it is in many senses unrealistic to lump all of the Indian groups together and treat them as a unit. These people have differing cultures, languages, and social, economic, and political systems. Second, the extent to which "white" practices have penetrated Indian systems varies considerably, not only from country to country but also within many of the countries. Kinship and lineage functioned as a major determinant of political station and interest in the overwhelming majority of the indigenous Indian systems of Latin America. In some areas, where these systems have been relatively little interfered with by the "whites," this is still true. Indeed, instances exist in which Indian systems of village government continue to function undisturbed despite the fact that the "whites" have promulgated written constitutions providing for very different patterns of local government. But there are cases—often in other regions of the same countries—where acculturation has taken the form of Indian responses to "white" influences which have fundamentally altered, or even obliterated, the indigenous practices. A number of monographic studies of such cases in specific Indian communities have been published. Short of reporting these detailed findings, there is little alternative to stressing the importance of kinship and lineage and emphasizing that, as a rule, Indian groups are markedly less politically articulate than the upper class. Thus, this type of interest, while often more crucial in the lower classes, typically receives far less of a hearing when emanating from the Indians than from the "whites."

Nonassociational interests also arise on regional bases. Regionalism is characteristically a major feature of the pattern of Latin American politics. It stems not only from the role of regional loyalties in Spanish culture, but also from the historic difficulty of transportation and communication across the mountains and through the jungles of Latin America. Living in a species of isolation from each other, the regions of Latin America have developed their own sets of interests. In Peru and Ecuador, for example, the regions known in each country as the "Coast" (located west of the Andes Mountains) are receptive to secularization and commercialization, fostering commercial and industrial interests; whereas, in both countries, the "Sierra" (lying between the eastern and western cordilleras of the Andes), less secularized, cultivates the interests of the landowners and the Church. In both countries, the sometimes bitter conflict of interests between these regions is a major element of the national political patterns. In Argentina, to cite another illustration, the interests of the landowners and the Church in the "interior" have historically been pitted against those of the secularized and far more commercialized metropolitan region of Greater Buenos Aires. A second major aspect of the regional base of nonassociational interests arises from the process of urbanization. A number of the Latin American countries have had to cope with the problem of la cabeza de Goliat (Goliath's head): a giant metropolitan center (usually the capital city) rests on the dwarflike body of the rest of the country. In some cases, as much as half the national population lives in the one large city. The secular, commercial, and sometimes industrial interests of the metropolis are in chronic conflict with those of the religious and quasi-feudal "interior." In Latin America, the major illustrations of this pattern are to be found in Argentina, Cuba, and Uruguay.

II

My concluding task is to attempt to show that this sort of group analysis has some merit and may stimulate some productive new departures for political scientists interested in the field of comparative politics. Let me first enter two disclaimers: novelty is no guarantee of merit, and an interest in political groups is not new among American political scientists. Nevertheless, previous expressions of that interest have not, in general, included two elements significant here. One of these is the application of group analysis to foreign political systems, and the other is its use in comparative studies. Notwithstanding the regrettable tendency within our profession to regard "foreign governments," "comparative government," and "comparative politics" as synonymous terms, the study of political groups in foreign systems and in comparative analysis are two separate and distinct matters. Let me, then, turn my attention to the first of them. The bulk of the work—particularly the earlier work—done by "North American" political scientists in Latin America has generally involved, in one way or another, the description of formal structure of governments. It has often taken the form of translating the written constitutions of the various countries and abstracting or summarizing these legal provisions. This type of research has its uses, for some familiarity with constitutional forms is, if not necessary, at least helpful, in the analysis of other political problems. But while there are always new Latin American constitutions to be translated and summarized—and I will even concede that there is room, in the off years when no new constitutions are promulgated in

the area, for the improvement of the translations and summaries of the older texts—this type of activity reaches the point of diminishing returns. Indeed, I will argue that we long ago arrived there.

It is, in short, necessary to work with more than the formal structures in Latin America. Again, this is not a new point. For some years Latin Americanists have been looking to nonconstitutional materials. Seduced by the anthropologists, many of us have experimented with cultural approaches. We have become enamored of political styles arising from alien cultures. We have examined the class systems and made much of the "whites" while we neglected the mestizos in order to carry the torch for the downtrodden Indians, until it took a Moisés Sáenz to tell us that "in order to be fair to the Indian, it is not necessary to stick feathers in our hair or wield a war club."

There are considerable advantages in examining political groups in Latin America as alternative nonconstitutional materials. Beginning with the most unstructured considerations, I might start by pointing out that this is a major area of our ignorance in Latin American politics. We know virtually nothing about the area's political groups, and there is some virtue in our beginning to acquire that knowledge for its own sake.

On a little more structured level, it can also be said that research on political groups would help us to understand problems which have long concerned us in Latin American politics. Take the Argentine case as an example. I choose Argentina because it has long been regarded as one of the more important of the countries of the area and because much research has been done there; more articles and books have been published by "North American" scholars about that country than about most other Latin American states. On June 4, 1943, the Argentine government was overthrown in one of the area's most significant so-called "revolutions" of recent times. Who or what was directly responsible for the revolution? A political group: a clique of army officers known as GOU or "colonels' clique." What was the GOU? Where did it come from? How did it operate? Nothing in all our research—none of the product of our long-standing interest in Argentina, nothing in all our scholarly articles and books—could suggest answers to such questions. So far as the existing political science was concerned, the Perón revolution came from nowhere.

If we agree that the Perón coup was one of the more significant political developments of our time in one of the most important countries in the area, how did it happen that the GOU took the area specialists by surprise? How does it happen that we have let militarism and the process of military clique-formation, one of the more basic characteristics of Latin American politics, go unstudied? Why is our ignorance so inclusive that it covers not only the military but most of the other political groups in Latin America? If it is argued that this is an unfair challenge, that as political scientists we have been trained to examine institutions rather than the amorphous entities embraced by the unfamiliar jargon of associational and nonassociational groups, I reply that the GOU was an institutional group, part and parcel of the formal structure of government, and nothing so exotic as associational or nonassociational.

How many more translations and summaries of Argentina's Constitution of 1853, as remarkable as that celebrated document may be, can we afford to make before we undertake the analysis of the political groups of that and other Latin American countries? Or, to put the question in another way, which route to the mainsprings of the area's politics is more fruitful for the scholar —to wait for GOU after mysterious GOU to ambush him, or to seize the initiative in seeking out these groups, tracking them even to associational and nonassociational sources? No doubt this has policy implications as well, but they are not my concern at the moment. My point has been the relatively simple one that the study of political groups in Latin America would not only close considerable gaps in our knowledge of the area but also improve significantly our understanding of its politics.

This is among the less structured of the merits of the study of groups. To move to the arena of comparative analysis is to enter a more sophisticated level. Before taking that step, let me reiterate the high importance of the distinction between comparative politics and the study of foreign governments. In comparative analysis, as I understand it, an attempt is made, through precise study of two or more objects, to isolate and identify their similarities and differences. The techniques of comparative study may be, of course, of varying degrees of complexity. I have heard it claimed for some of the more complex modes of comparative analysis that through them similarities and differences may be not only isolated and identified but also explained. I am not myself convinced that the comparative method alone can do the explanatory job. Isolation, definition, and identification of properties can be handled in this way, but the task of explanation seems to require that the comparative method, where used, be assisted or supplemented by additional modes of analysis.

One of the constantly recurring problems in the comparative study of politics is the circumstance that in this field we generally deal with the so-called "macro" materials—that is, with large units or universes such as entire countries or political systems. In doing this, so far as precision is concerned, we are at a decided disadvantage in comparison with the scholar engaged in a "micro" analysis of a small unit which lends itself more readily to precise study. No doubt, this is one reason why much of what is called "comparative government" consists of roughly parallel descriptions of two or more "macro" systems, without benefit of comparative analysis. It is not easy—and some may think it impossible—to handle two or more national systems in a fashion permitting them to be compared precisely. Countries, cultures, even systems of government, appear in many ways to be unique as large universes. Argentines behave differently from Cubans; even the task of comparing the Mexican congress with the Chilean national legislature presents formidable pitfalls.

One solution to this "macro" problem might involve a conceptualization permitting the abstracting of precisely defined components common to two or more large universes, components which could then be subjected to comparative analysis with some promise of precision. Political groups are among the forms such components might take. So it might be claimed for the introduction of political groups into comparative analysis that it has the advantage of furnishing a method of abstraction rendering political systems more precisely comparable, thereby making comparative analysis more manageable. Indeed, it could be argued that this method creates the possibility of comparative studies of large units which would be intrinsically incomparable in the absence of some such abstractive device.

Another potentially significant contribution of the group emphasis to comparative politics lies in the examination of structures in terms of their political functions. Structural-functional analysis holds some promise of advancing comparative studies. Consider a relatively simple variation of it. If we were to devise a list of the functions performed in all political systems, such as political recruitment, communication, interest-articulation, interest-aggregation, rule-making, rule-application, and rule-adjudication, the group focus might serve to locate the structures performing each of these functions in the systems being compared. These structures, which are groups, might then be analyzed for their political functions.

Suppose, for example, a comparative analysis of the political systems of Chile, Mexico, and Paraguay. The national legislatures of these three countries are given similar names—"Congress" in Chile and Mexico, and "Chamber of Representatives" in Paraguay—by the constitutions, which contain a few additional similar stipulations about the legislatures. But the bases for comparative analysis end here. If, on the other hand, we seek the groups which perform the political functions common to the three systems, we might well be on more significant ground. For example, I suspect that much of the rule-making function is indeed performed in the congress in Chile, but in the PRI, the dominant nondictatorial party in Mexico, and by a military clique within the Asunción garrison in Paraguay. If that is so, a comparative analysis of the Chilean Congress, the Mexican PRI, and the Paraguayan military should give us a far more significant result, and a deeper insight into the three political systems, than a comparison of the three national legislatures. Thus, the second branch of my case for the use of political groups in comparative analysis is the argument that it would not only give us greater precision but would also permit us to direct that accuracy to more important propositions about the actual functioning of political systems.

Further, the group emphasis may be expected to make a major contribution in a field of rapidly growing concern in comparative politics, the problems of underdeveloped areas. "Underdevelopment" or "underdevelopedness" has been chiefly an economic concept related primarily to technology. The proposition central to this concept can be demonstrated in comparing two models of economic systems, one "advanced" or "developed," and the other underdeveloped. In the "advanced" model, a given input into the productive process (capital, raw materials, man-hours of labor, and so on) is subjected to a given technology, from which a measurable production emerges. In the underdeveloped model, the same input may go into the productive process, but is subjected to a less efficient technology, and so results in a measurably lower level of production characterized by low standards of living. Owing largely to technological problems affecting the state of their productive arts, the underdeveloped areas present us with a challenge.

These underdeveloped areas, of course, include much of Latin America. A major key to the problem lies in technological change, to raise the levels of production, and so the standards of living, in the underdeveloped areas. A number of public programs based on this solution are currently in operation. A modest sector of the foreign-aid programs of the United States —variously known from administration to administration as technical assistance, "Point Four," and technical cooperation—has as its objective the stimulation of technological change in the underdeveloped areas. The technical assistance programs of the United Nations are similarly conceived. All of the Latin American countries participate in the foreign-aid programs of the United States; some of these countries are also involved in United Nations technical assistance. Partly on account of these programs, technological change and economic development should be counted among the more significant movements afoot in contemporary Latin America. In some of the countries—witness Brazil and Mexico—the rapidity of this change is little short of spectacular.

Thus far the economist has done the work for us. But the political scientist interested in Latin America—or any other underdeveloped area—cannot much longer neglect the major analytical task awaiting him there. It is widely assumed that there is some interplay between levels of economic development, on the one hand, and political systems on the other. It is believed that the politics of, say, Bolivia, Haiti, and Paraguay are integrally tied to their underdeveloped economies, and that, as these change, so must their political systems. Again we have policy implications: many of the foreign-aid programs of both the United States and the United Nations are based on the assumption that political change goes hand in hand with economic development, but others, in the name of prudence, take recipient institutions as they find them.

Yet all this is still in the realm of belief, of assumption, and even of faith. Apart from the rival slogans of private enterprise and socialism, we have not even the beginnings of a theory of the relations between economic levels and political systems. When the political scientist undertakes, as he must, the search for this theory, he will no doubt have recourse to comparative analysis. I do not claim foreknowledge of the direction this theory will take, but I think it reasonable to expect that again we will be dealing with political groups. I say this because I see one road to the remarriage of economics and politics for this purpose through the theory of interests. Economic development, technological change, and trends toward industrialization imply changes in employment patterns; these alter the distribution of interests. Interest theory is closely allied to group theory; indeed, they may be the same. I suggested early in this paper that every political group has an interest, which could be regarded as the central or continuing type of activity giving the group its property as a system or unit. If such a formulation comes to underlie our understanding of the relationship between economic development and political change, the comparative analysis of groups might then unlock new doors not only to Latin American but also to other underdeveloped areas which, after all, embrace most of the people of the world.

These other areas bring me to the fourth element in my case for the comparative analysis of political groups, the problem of interarea comparison. Specialists on an area like Latin America are in some danger of becoming the victims of inertia and other forces restricting them to that area alone. It is a danger because it is a form of imprisonment. We should not devote our careers to learning more about Latin America for the sole purpose of learning more about Latin America. Science seeks to generalize, and the more we can apply to other areas what we learn in Latin America, the greater the likely contribution to comparative politics and to political science as a whole.

Substantial obstacles make the practice of this preachment difficult. It is not easy to learn new languages or to develop, in working with the nuances of strange cultures, the skills that we

have cultivated, and at some sacrifice, in Latin America. Yet sooner or later we should be prepared to do this. As political scientists in the confines of a single area, we do serious harm to ourselves as well as to our discipline. Actually, there are grounds for optimism on this score. In the last few years, scholars working in other foreign areas have made noteworthy progress toward interarea comparison. But its difficulties are hard and real. This is another point at which we might make substantial strides through the comparative analysis of political groups. The formula here may be similar to what I have suggested above with respect to the "macro" problem of comparing large universes. In principle I see no serious methodological difference between applying this as between two or more countries in the same area, and as between two or more systems in different areas. If it is feasible to compare the Chilean Congress, the Mexican PRI, and the Paraguayan military, the theoretical task is not substantially different in comparing, say, the *Apristas* with *Mau-Mau* or the GOU with the Young Turks. My point is not merely that this can be done, but rather that, sooner or later, it must be done.

Further, we should realize that while in loosening our areal shackles in order to work in the underdeveloped areas at large we enter a wider field, this bigger, better, more comfortable, and more significant realm is still an intellectual prison. We will not be fully free until we can compare *all* political systems, inside and outside of the underdeveloped areas. It is in this light that we should view the recent work of the SSRC's Committee on Comparative Politics, which has proposed the curious dichotomy distinguishing "Western" from "non-Western" political systems. We can quarrel with this terminology—for my own part, I am not happy with it, particularly as it applies to Latin America—but to concentrate our attention on the terms is to miss the larger point. Some political systems are significantly more urbanized, secularized, commercialized, integrated, and receptive to technological change than others, and we should be able to compare these extremes, whether we call them "Western" and "non-Western" or something else. Essentially, this would bring us back to the examination of political structures in terms of their functions. Where these political functions are performed in a "Western" (that is, secularized, integrated, and so on) fashion in one system and in a "non-Western" (that is, traditional, unintegrated, and so on) manner in another, we can study these systems by examining structures (for example, political groups) exercizing the functions. Once again, then, we find ourselves with the comparative analysis of political groups.

A final problem remains. This is the question of the extent to which comparative analysis in necessary to the development of general theory. There are those who argue that the comparative method can be—some even say ought to be—bypassed in the development of general theory. But to the extent that comparative analysis has a role to play in the achievement of this objective, we have the final component of my case for the comparative study of political groups. Two aspects of it need mention. First, this would give added point to our re-examination of the work of Bentley, Truman, and Latham. If comparative analysis of political groups is necessary to arrive at a general theory of groups, this is one element that has been missing from the existing literature on the study of groups and the basic justification for dusting off a book published in 1908

to say something new about it. In the second place, if comparative study is necessary to arrive at a general theory of politics, the comparative analysis of political groups carries still deeper significance. In the current stage in the development of political science it has become increasingly clear that the field of comparative government or comparative politics is not paying its own way in the discipline. If the field is to hold its own, it must contribute to political science as a whole; that is, comparative study must take part in the search for a general theory of politics. This is the fundamental element in the case—it may well be that, in the long run, this is the *entire* case—for the comparative analysis of political groups.

This may seem too ambitious an argument for the study of political groups in Latin America. Let me say in conclusion, however, that basically I have made only three claims in its defense. The first is that it would close important gaps in our knowledge of Latin America and thereby lead us to greater understanding of the mainsprings of its politics. In the second place, it would give a sharper edge to comparative political analysis, and so contribute to an improvement of the quality of research in the field of comparative politics by encouraging more meaningful comparisons of the Latin American systems with each other, and with "Western" and "non-Western" systems in other areas. Finally, the types of inquiry I have suggested here would stimulate a more significant contribution from the field of comparative politics to political science as a discipline. If this is indeed too ambitious a case, I hope to learn of a formula whereby the student of foreign politics may shrink from this ambition and at the same time enjoy a respectable role as a useful political scientist.

19

The Party Potpourri in Latin America

Russell H. Fitzgibbon

Students of comparative politics have usually had a blind spot with regard to Latin American parties. Even a well-known and highly perceptive and penetrating work by the eminent French scholar Duverger tends to dismiss Latin American parties with casual and impliedly derogatory references. But these associations have much in common with those found in countries whose parties we more commonly put on the dissecting table. If these organizations in the other American republics were given a collective voice they might paraphrase one of Shakespeare's famous characters and ask: "Hath not a Latin American party eyes...hands, organs, dimensions, senses, affections, passions? Fed with the same food, hurt with the same weapons, subject to the same diseases, healed by the same means, warmed and cooled by the same winter and summer as another party is? If you prick us, do we not bleed? If you tickle us, do we not laugh? If you poison us, do we not die? And if you wrong us, shall we not revenge? If we are like you in the rest, we will resemble you in that. ...The villainy you teach us we will execute; and it shall go hard but we will better the instruction. ..."

With especial reference to Latin America, how shall party systems, in terms of gross morphology, be initially classified? The traditional method, as with other areas, has been to say that one or another country has a multi-party, a biparty, or a single-party system. Ranney and Kendall[1] have suggested that such a scheme is oversimple and have proposed that an improvement would be to adopt a five-way division, making use of the traditional labels and adding a "modified one-party" and a "totalitarian one-party" system. The proposed modification is obviously useful and it certainly has applicability to the Latin American scene. It should be stressed, however, that a score of countries through more than a century of independent history have shown such an infinitude of variations in party pattern that even an expanded five-category analysis can by no means fit

From Russell H. Fitzgibbon, "The Party Potpourri in Latin America," *Western Political Quarterly*, Vol. X, No. 1 (March 1957). Reprinted by permission.

[1] Austin W. Ranney and W. Kendall, "The American Party Systems," *American Political Science Review*, XLVIII, No. 1 (March 1954), 477–85.

all situations. In part, it is more in order to look at the party system horizontally rather than vertically, that is, not to try to determine whether this or that country has a party system which falls neatly into one or another of five types but rather to seek to find out how far down the socioeconomic scale of consciousness party organization and activity have descended; in other words, to what extent parties have "grass roots" in a given country. . . .

If most Latin American parties very largely lacked the organizational characteristics of those in the United States or Britain, they certainly far surpassed them in the role played by the individual leader. This was the omnipresent and often glamorous *caudillo*. The word cannot well be translated into English —it loses so much of overtone and color in the process. It is true that the *caudillo* had some elements of the party boss in Jersey City or Chicago or Kansas City or Memphis, but he was and is significantly different from a Hague or a Kelly or a Pendergast or a Crump. The latter breed usually avoided the limelight and frequently operated deviously; the *caudillo* as often gloried in every lumen of calcium glare he could command. He was a man on horseback, a man whose gaudy uniform had to be ample to accommodate all the medals, ribbons, and braid which he either devised for himself or exchanged prodigally with his fellow *caudillos*. The *caudillo's* European cousin, the dictator, says Neumann, "is responsible to no man but to God and the nation (who are conveniently removed from any direct interference), and in his very irresponsibility he is revered by the emotional, rootless, and amorphous masses seeking mystery, devotion, and the miraculous."

The party was largely incidental in the power structure erected by the *caudillo*. So completely did he dominate it that it often took its popular designation from his name, family or Christian: thus we have the *Peronistas* (in this case a legal as well as a popular name), the *Monttvaristas, Arnulfistas,* and many others. Even in a country where party stability probably exceeds that of any other in Latin America—Uruguay —the major parties, or at least the leading wings of them, are known as *Batllistas* and *Herreristas* as commonly as they are called *Colorados* and *Blancos*. We have very little in United States experience which can provide a counterpart for the Latin American *caudillo*. Possibly the closest example would be Huey Long, who for a number of years operated as the erratic, publicity-seeking, strong-willed, egocentric owner of the Democratic party in Louisiana. But the Democratic party in Louisiana did not disintegrate with Long's removal from the scene and in that way it differed from many *caudillo*-dominated parties in Latin America. In this latter aspect our best example, and indeed one of only a few illustrations, would be found in the relationship of Theodore Roosevelt to the short-lived Progressive party which followed him on his brief crusade to Armageddon with something of the fanatic fervor of a *caudillo's* party in Latin America. . . .

Can we find a useful and valid typology of Latin American parties— not party systems? I suggest that it might be found, in one direction, in terms of whether a party's ideology is prominent and probably primary in the party's operation or whether, on the other hand, the philosophical basis of the party's organization is only incidental or at least secondary. In the first category would come all Communist and Fascist parties, most Catholic and Christian Democratic parties, many Socialist parties, and several labor parties. This seems to be designating strange bedfellows, but at least all the above-mentioned groups—even Luis Carlos Prestes' Brazilian Communists and Plinio Salgado's Brazilian *Integralistas*—have in common the possession of and emphasis on a quasi-ideological foundation which they sometimes pursue with almost religious fervor. "Today the term party," says Duverger, "includes veritable churches with their clergy, their faithful, their belief, their orthodoxy, their intolerance."[2]

Now, obviously, these ideology-based parties in Latin America have important differences among them. The differences are not only those of rightness or leftness but also, at least as exemplified by the Communist parties, those of control. The key to the frequently greater success of Latin America's Communist parties over their Marxian cousins, the Socialist organizations, is to be found in the international and more rigid control exercised over the former. The various Socialist parties are domestically controlled even if they share a common imported ideology. This internal control has inevitably resulted in a certain divergence of orientation and a greater ineffectiveness in political action. It has also meant that as among the several Latin American Socialist parties little more than a sentimental entente exists or can exist. The same sort of control is evident among the neo-Socialist *Aprista*-type parties such as the prototype, the *Aprista* party itself in Peru, *Acción Democrática* in Venezuela, the *Auténtico* party in Cuba, the National Liberation party in Costa Rica, and one or two others, with the almost inevitable result that the same kind of entente and nothing more exists among them

[2] Maurice Duverger, *Political Parties*, translated by the Norths (London: Methuen & Co. Ltd., 1954).

internationally. Since the various Fascist parties have operated within vertical and highly nationalistic segments of the political spectrum it was even more their fate to be controlled domestically and to have no intercommunication, much less a unified superior control. Even in the heyday of fascism in the 1930's no faint Latin American resemblance of a Berlin-Rome-Tokyo axis emerged on the party scene, even though some one suggested years ago in inspired phrase that the Brazilian Green Shirts, the Mexican Gold Shirts, and their counterparts in one or two other Latin American countries were all parts of the Textile International. In the case of the Catholic or Catholic-oriented parties, such as *Unión Cívica* in Uruguay or COPEI in Venezuela or, to a lesser degree, *Acción Nacional* in Mexico, the situation is subtly different. Certainly the intellectual and philosophical entente is present, and probably in addition a certain amount of common direction (dictation would be too strong a word) under the banner of the effectively organized and omnipresent Catholic Church, sometimes exercised through the channel of Catholic Action groups. The neo-Catholic Christian Democratic parties are too recent arrivals in Latin America to enable us to draw conclusions about them.

Ideology-based parties operate under certain inherent disadvantages in Latin America. They may develop capable leaders, such as communism's Luis Carlos Prestes of Brazil or Manuel Mora of Costa Rica. They may develop respected leaders, such as socialism's Alfredo Palacios of Argentina or Emilio Frugoni of Uruguay. But, so lacking in integration, cohesion, and maturity is the socioeconomic structure of most Latin American countries, that these parties are faced with the inevitable disadvantage of being unable to enforce effective internal discipline; only the Communist parties provide a possible and partial exception and even they have been faced by schisms and dissensions, as the existence of Trotskyist parties in Mexico, Argentina, Chile, Bolivia, and other countries' footnotes.

Another difficulty faced by many of these parties is that they so often become so deeply involved in the implications of their ideologies that they fail to respond to the exigencies of practical politics. Latins, in Latin America and elsewhere, are said to be fond of playing with ideas but this fondness, at least in Latin America, is often not accompanied by a corresponding intellectual discipline and toughness which would enable the ideas to be properly assorted and evaluated. Hence, the ideology-based parties have in some instances tended to lose touch with reality and progress, such concrete realities as the growth of industrialization, changing patterns of land tenure, and so on. Latin American Socialist parties provide a good case in point. Being originally Marxian, their orientation should be toward the working classes. But in country after country they have become increasingly doctrinaire, academic, and intellectualized. They have developed undeniably articulate leaders and their newspapers have had highly stimulating editorial pages, but Latin American Socialist parties have had relatively little genuine influence over the masses; they have allowed that role to be pre-empted by such organizations as the Communist parties and the *Peronista* party in Argentina. Jorge Gaitán, the later-to-be-murdered Colombian political leader, put it neatly when he said, in almost the only English phrase he used in an evening of conversation with me in 1944, that the Colombian Socialist party lacked "political sex appeal." "The Socialist weakness," wrote Ray Josephs about the Argentine party (but it could describe other Latin American Socialist parties as well), "lies in addiction to theory and philosophy and what we might call their lack of practical, sound common sense."

Fascist parties in anything like a pure form have of course declined in Latin America with the worldwide regression of fascism itself. One needs to distinguish between Fascist and what might be called quasi-Fascist parties in the area. The former *Integralistas* in Brazil, the National Socialist (*Nacista*) party in Chile, and one or two others were of a nature that would justify us in calling them pure Fascist parties. Certain other groups—the *Peronista* party in Argentina, the *Sinarquistas* in Mexico, the *Movimiento Nacional Revolucionario* or MNR in Bolivia, for example—displayed certain of the characteristics of Fascist parties but sometimes not such more than incidentally so. The *Sinarquista* group has only a part of the time since its establishment in 1937 deigned to operate through conventional party channels and its Fascist trappings have been intermingled with a considerable coloration resulting from the impact of Catholic philosophy upon it; it is hence almost *sui generis* among Latin American parties of political organizations. The other two groups mentioned above, however—the *Peronistas* and the MNR —could more properly be called nationalist rather than quasi-Fascist parties. They, and a few others which can be put in the same category, have attempted to make themselves the conscious custodians of the explosive nationalism which is so prevalent a characteristic of virtually every Latin American country. This role has not so immersed them in a theoretic concern, however, that they have lost sight of the main objective of seizing and continuing to control power. The *Peronista* party was and the MNR is an eminently practical party. The former, incidentally, provided the only example, so far as I know, of a Latin American party which has created a full-fledged distaff counterpart; the *Peronista* Feminist party, under the astute organizing ability and leadership of the president's lady, his former mistress, became a temporarily effective political instrument. The *Peronista* party was also unique in having gone further than any other in Latin American history in consciously developing a dialectic seeking to undergird it philosophically.

The proliferation of ideology-based parties, whether Communist or Fascist, nationalist or Catholic, Socialist or *Aprista,* is an inevitable result of the expansion and diversification of the social and economic interests and issues in the several countries. When the body social was clothed in unchanging agricultural garments the political issues were simple and few: chiefly those of Church-state relations and of the degree of governmental and political centralization which should exist.

The role of Latin American armies in relation to ideology-based parties is interesting and significant but deserves far more study than has been given it. Traditionally the army's participation in politics was crude and simple. More recently various Latin American military establishments have allied themselves in whole or in part with nationalistic, labor, or *Aprista*-type parties or political movements. The former "military sector" of the government party in Mexico was a case in point. Other examples would be found in the Argentine army's dalliance with the *Peronista* party and the Venezuelan army's uneasy flirtation with *Acción Democrática* from 1945 to 1948. Parties (usually Fascist or semi-Fascist) have occasionally developed their own militias, a sort of "Brown-Shirt auxiliary." Illustra-

tions would be the Mexican *Sinarquistas,* the Brazilian *Integralistas,* and the Chilean National Socialists. The *Peronista* party was tending in such a direction before its master's downfall.

The traditional[3] parties, or their descendants, have usually failed to keep or gain much ideological distinctiveness. It is doubtless not true to say that no more valid philosophical differences exist between Liberals and Conservatives in Colombia, among Radicals, Liberals, and Conservatives in Chile, or between *Colorados* and *Blancos* in Uruguay than do between Republicans and Democrats in the United States, but those traditional and major parties, like their opposite numbers in this country, are primarily interested in getting and keeping power rather than in consistently promoting a philosophical position.

Some of the major parties which retain a vestige of ideological coloration have suffered the fate of being pushed progressively to the right by the rise of newer and more leftist parties. This has been true of Chile's and Argentina's "Radical" parties (both of which are now moderate) and Chile's "Liberal" party (now conservative). It is less true of Uruguay's *Colorados* and Mexico's PRI because the massive position occupied by each in its own party landscape defies easy displacement.

---

[3] The use of this adjective is intended to suggest more a party of conventional non-ideological appearance than one of long life. Major parties which have survived for more than, say, a generation are relatively few. They would include: Argentina's Radical and National Democratic (Conservative) parties; Chile's Radical, Liberal, and Conservative; Colombia's Liberal and Conservative; Ecuador's Conservative and Radical Liberal; Honduras' Nationalist; Nicaragua's Conservative and Liberal (sometimes with modified names); and Uruguay's *Colorado* and *Blanco*. This list would be far exceeded in size by a catalog of the ephemeral parties in Latin America.

Power depends in considerable measure, as in the United States or elsewhere, on positions. This inevitably means a spoils system but one traditionally based more on an almost institutionalized nepotism than on rewarding loyal Liberals or constant Conservatives.

Not only the organization of a Latin American party but in addition its general place in the political life of the country will also be conditioned by the kind and degree of party opposition which it has. This leads us back to the useful Ranney-Kendall scheme of classifying party systems. Of the five types they propose we can find good examples of each in Latin America. Chile gives a wonderful illustration, perhaps the world's best, of a multiparty system.[4] Colombia—during politically normal times—provides a valid illustration of a biparty system, Uruguay presents a "modified one-party" picture, Mexico a traditional one-party scheme, and the Dominican Republic a "totalitarian one-party" type.

The highly complex picture in Chile is a relic of that country's rather unfortunate experiment with parliamentary government in the third of a century following 1891. An eminent political scientist commented almost fifty years ago on the fluid and confusing consequences of this situation:

> Looking at the events of the last ten or fifteen years, it becomes plain that if the Liberal Democratic party [which has as of now, 1957, long since disappeared] had deliberately set about the work of undermining the credit and authority of

parliament, it could not have succeeded better than it actually has, through forcing upon the various groups and parties of parliament the necessity of making shifting and temporary alliances and coalitions. . . . It has not gained this success by consistently following any definite policy of government, but rather by making opportune arrangements with this or that party or faction.[5]

A discerning Chilean president of a few years ago, Gabriel González Videla, put a finger on certain of the results when he wrote to the Social Christian Conservative party that "Political cabinets are the consequence of a combination of parties which. . . place themselves in agreement to bear governmental responsibilities and to lend their support, within and outside of the parliament, to the chief of state." The same president less than a year later wrote a footnote to that observation when in a letter published in *La Nación* on May 26, 1949, he said that

> Unfortunately the principles [of presidential government] established in the Constitution of 1925 have not been embodied yet in our political customs. We continue in essence maintaining the parliamentary spirit in our forms of being and acting; and for some time in this direction the ministerial stability that formerly depended on the votes of a responsible body, as is the parliament, has been placed in the agreements or attitudes of political organisms [that is, parties] lacking any legal or constitutional authority and many times totally irresponsible.

Power that a Chilean party has lacked because it could not, in view of the proliferation of groups, become a majority party it gained in another direction by its sometimes autocratic control over its members. So far has

---

[4] Duverger would doubtless dissent: "A country in which opinion is divided among several groups that are unstable, fluid, and short-lived does not provide an example of multipartism in the proper sense of the term: it is still in the prehistoric era of parties. . . ." *Political Parties*, p. 228. But Duverger admits that some such countries may be in an intermediate stage.

[5] Paul S. Reinsch, "Parliamentary Government in Chile," *American Political Science Review*, III, No. 3 (1909), 521.

this control gone in recent years that one or another party has on occasion forced the withdrawal of a cabinet member from his governmental post because it refused him its *"pase"* or certificate of approval, based of course on its disapproval of presidential policies and its unwillingness to provide political support for the administration.[6] A climax of sorts was reached under González Videla himself when he was forced to ask certain parties which of their members they would nominate for him to appoint to particular cabinet posts in the kaleidoscopic reshuffling which he more than once had to undertake.

The development of a strong party consciousness on a multiparty basis in such a situation as the Chilean has had two incidental but important effects. It has (1) increased the accuracy of democratic popular representation, and (2) decreased the incidence of *personalismo*. In the congressional election in 1953, for example, thirty-four parties nominated candidates, thus permitting almost every conceivable shade of opinion to be reflected. And, in recent years, only in the atypical presidential election of 1952, when the magnetic figure of General Ibáñez monopolized attention, did the element of charismatic support of a candidate take precedence over the domination of the campaign by party organizations.

We do not normally associate a multiparty system with presidential government but such countries as Chile, Cuba, Panama, and at times others, have given us Latin American examples. In part the anomaly, if it be that, can be accounted for in terms of provisions in the election laws, especially the existence of proportional representation; in part it is due to the persistence o political tradition (as in Chile) or to the relatively rudimentary state of social organization and political responsibility.

The multiparty system is not normally a product of geography, though it may be. Brazil's parties, for years organized primarily on a state basis, provide the best illustration of the exceptional situation. In Ecuador, though that country is not a good example of multipartism, the Conservative party has been largely confined to the Sierra and the Radical Liberal party to the Coast. Nicaragua's Liberal and Conservative parties were traditionally geographically oriented, with centers of gravity respectively at León and Granada.

Colombia—again with the qualification "in normal times"—provides an excellent example of a biparty system. In the period since 1927 only one party other than the Liberal and Conservative, the Communist, has had national legislative representation and then for only four years and with never more than six members. Why is this? An important part of the answer is doubtless to be found in the fact that Colombia's major parties possess excellent and realistic mechanisms for gaining and retaining power. Political consciousness is well developed and Colombian parties come almost as close as any in carrying their organization down to the grass roots. The simple and yet significant differences separating "outs" from "ins" are illustrated in Colombian politics virtually as well as anywhere in Latin America.

Many persons in the United States are mystified by a phenomenon which occurs especially in biparty Latin American countries, occasionally in multiparty. It is the boycotting of elections by one or more parties. Is that not cutting off a party nose to spite a party face? Not in the estimation of

---

[6] This autocratic control may backfire if one or more rebellious leaders decide to secede and form a splinter party.

he leaders of an "out"
nvinced that a particu-
will be fraudulent and that
ss of the voting their group will
be allowed to win they may with-
draw their candidates and adjure their
followers to stay away from the polls
for several reasons: (1) by this self-
abnegation they avoid for their party
any involvement in what they regard
as a tainted political act, and (2) they
therefore arrogate to themselves and
their party some indeterminable measure of added political virtue by their
martyrdom. (3) They also assume that
at least on moral grounds the way is
cleared for resort to bullets to replace
the ballots of which they would al-
legedly have been robbed.

Uruguay might be said to have a
conventional biparty rather than a
"modified one-party" system but for
the fact that for more than ninety years
the *Colorado* party has regularly controlled the executive branch of the government. That country has conducted
some of Latin America's most novel
governmental experiments, both in the
executive and the legislative branches,
but for more than a hundred years
parties have been an effective and
highly conscious part of the political
apparatus of the country. Indeed, the
subtle impact and weight of parties as
such were doubtless increased rather
than decreased by Uruguay's shift a
few years ago from a conventional
unipersonal presidency to a collegiate
type of executive on the Swiss model.

Mexico provides an excellent example
of a one-party state with all of the consequent effects that such a situation has
on the political operation of the country. Since 1929 the "government party"
in Mexico—successively the *Partido
Nacional Revolucionario* (PNR), the
Partido de la Revolución Mexicana
(PRM), and the *Partido Revolucion-*

ario Institucional (PRI)—has blan-
keted the politics of Mexico with
consummate effectiveness. Not even the
Colorado party in Uruguay has dominated the political scene as completely
as has the PRI—and both operate within a democratic framework. For Mexico
is to be classed as a democratic country
despite the fact that that democracy is
somewhat vitiated by the absence of
genuine party rivalry. The democracy
which is lacking in interparty competition may in part be supplied by the
intraparty operation of the PRI. That
party is almost unbelievably well organized; probably no other political
group in Latin America, not even the
unlamented *Peronista* party of Argentina, can equal it in the completeness
and effectiveness of its organization.

One of the things one looks for in
the context of a one-party system is
the degree and nature of the identification, or even the amalgamation, of
party with government. Nazi Germany,
Fascist Italy, Communist Russia, and
Falangist Spain, with interestingly varying details, provide us with examples
of what seems inevitable under such
circumstances. It must be remembered,
of course, that, unlike the four countries
just mentioned, Mexico freely permits
the operation of other parties, and
sometimes they have been legion. But
it must also be recalled that one effective method of financing the early PNR
was the official deduction of one day's
pay from each government employee's
salary in those months which had
thirty-one days—in other words, the
party treasury was the automatic
recipient of seven days' salary per employee per year.

There are certain other questions
which should be asked with regard to
a one-party picture. Does the party,
because of its noncompetitive hold on
power and positions, tend to lose an

earlier vigor and sharpness of ideological expression? The Mexican PNR and its successors were the more-or-less— that phrase *más o menos* is inevitable at some point or other in referring to Latin American politics—self-appointed custodians of the principles of "the Revolution," whatever they may have been defined to be. But concern with principles is often in potential conflict with concern with positions, and so it happened in Mexico. With almost undiscernible gradualness the early revolutionary fervor, again kindled in 1934 because of the president's personality and due to somewhat fortuitous circumstances during the Cárdenas administration, has become diluted until the impact of the PRI on politics in recent years is little other than bourgeois. Indeed, when a literal-minded congressional deputy some years ago suggested in reply to a president's address to congress, that the party should get back to revolutionary first principles, he created an uproar because he was so revolutionary! This same dulling of original ideological fervor was noticeable in Uruguay's *Colorado* party, Argentina's Radical party, and others.

Another important question is as to whether, in a one-party situation, the process of actual decision-making passes wholly or partly from governmental to party machinery. With regard to Mexico's PRI insufficient evidence precludes a complete answer. (Party participation in governmental decision-making is not limited, of course, to groups in one-party countries.) Another question relates to the mechanism devised for transmission of party control or maintenance of continuity beyond the impact of a single personality who may for the time exercise some degree of charismatic hold over the party. In this respect Mexico's dominant party has been notably more suc-

cessful than was the *Peronista* pa. in Argentina.

The *Partido Dominicano* in "the land that Columbus loved" gives us, so far as I am aware, the only modern Latin American example of a formal "totalitarian one-party" system, according to the Ranney-Kendall classification, although the position of the *Colorado* party in Paraguay resembles that on a *de facto* basis. During much of the last quarter-century the one party has been the only one legally permitted to operate in the Dominican Republic. It goes without question that its hold, in party terms, has been absolute: if all legislative and cabinet members at a given time have not been members of the Dominican party the only exceptions have been a token minority of completely ineffective proportions. In November 1940, the inner and most loyal core of the Dominican party was organized as the *Partido Trujillista* but this typical gesture toward party elitism apparently soon served its purpose and the inner circle disappeared as a separate group. Two groups labeled by some as "stooge" or "front" parties appeared in 1946 but no one has assumed that they provided even a symptom of return to democratic procedures and free party competition.

Discipline in Latin American parties is perennially threatened by the deep-rooted Latin American individualism and the innate resistance to regimentation. Not even the Communist parties, with their peculiarly effective apparatus and techniques of internal control, find this problem an easy one. In those parties in which no or little class base or economic interest is present the problem is compounded. The adoption of a party cedula or *carnet,* with space for a small picture and other identification, used by Colombia's Liberal party and various others, confers in some small

...s on members and
...ords the issuing
... theoretical control,
...eness for such a purpose
...e.

... whole broad field of Latin Amer-
...an party financing is in many respects unsystematic to the point of being almost anarchic. It is also a virgin field for further research. The gamut of methods used to fill party coffers is a wide one, including party dues, "kickbacks" from office-holders, forced contributions from those with economic axes to grind, sale of literature, open or disguised subsidy from governments, and many others, and resembles for the most part what would be found in other countries, but with various refinements largely peculiar to Latin America. Collection of party dues, traditional with Communist and Socialist parties, is the easier if the party uses a cedula on which to stamp or punch the fact of periodic payment, but it is a device whose psychological value for Latin American parties is greater than its financial return. Percentage salary assessments against party members who have been helped into office is common, and even in a country as advanced as is Uruguay it has become almost institutionalized. The *mordida* or "bite" put on contractors, merchants, and others who hope to profit from party or government favors is a lucrative source of income; the fantastic propaganda decoration of Buenos Aires' main shopping street, Avenida Florida, which I saw at the time of the presidential campaign in 1951, was financed by the *Peronista* party by levies against the merchants fronting on the street, running, in the case of the city's main department store, as high as 100,000 pesos. Party newspapers and pamphlets bring in small amounts though as business ventures they usually operate in the red. Labor unions, especially those

which the Communists have infiltrated, often have sums from their treasuries diverted to party purposes, sometimes secretly. Government regulation of party financing, as of other aspects of party operation, is rudimentary or nonexistent; it is essentially where it was in the United States 75 or 100 years ago.

The more a party has solved its internal problems of discipline and financing the more likely it will be to develop a breed of permanent professional party personnel. The *Peronista* party in Argentina on a temporary and the PRI in Mexico on a permanent basis are good cases in point. In each case a party bureaucracy developed, with all of the ponderousness, the vested interest in jobs, and the emphasis on organization for organization's sake which are normally characteristic of such situations. Colombia's Conservative party and the *Blancos* in Uruguay give good examples of the tightly knit structure which conservative parties have frequently developed even if they have not always been in power.

As Latin American countries move toward a more complex social and economic structure and as they ultimately become more democratic (which will inevitably be the case), they will necessarily develop a more involved party picture. Party progress is erratic but there is ample evidence in many directions that parties are becoming more mature and sophisticated, more responsive and responsible, and a more significant part of the broad political landscape. What I have attempted to suggest as some of the aspects of the past and present party scene is at most a fragmentary indication, a mere prolegomenon as it were, of the complex and fascinating, the vital and fluid picture of political parties in Latin America. The field is one which needs a vast amount of spade work of a primary sort and on top of that additional synthesis in order to put the raw materials in proper arrangement and perspective. The study would necessarily lead us to probe deeply into the sociology and the economy, the psychology and the religion—in other words, all aspects of the culture—of the Latin American states. I commend the field of Latin American political parties to a whole generation of prospective graduate students in political science.

20

Responsible Parties in Latin America

Federico G. Gil

...In establishing a proper and usable definition of a "responsible party" it is doubtless wise to turn to the peoples of Latin America themselves in search of the qualifications that they would impose on a political group aspiring to deserve the adjective. The convention called in 1892 in Argentina by Leandro N. Alem to establish the foundations of the *Unión Cívica Radical* party furnished a good definition of such requirements. The convention pointed out, as essential features of the party to be founded, the following:

1. Nonidentification of the party with any person.
2. Priority of party principles to personalities.
3. Unity on a national basis.
4. Periodic renovation of party officers.
5. Separation of the executive functions of committees from the deliberative functions of conventions.
6. Subservience of programs and candidates to the following:
   a. honest fulfillment of the law;
   b. morality in administration;
   c. effective exercise of popular sovereignty;
   d. recognition of provincial and municipal autonomy.

There is a voluminous literature exhibiting Latin American interest in the institution of the party, and there is to be found in it sufficient evidence of agreement as to the need for responsible parties in the democratic scheme of government. "Political parties," as stated by the Argentine jurist Linares Quintana, "constitute essential elements in the dynamics of the juridico-political structure of a representative democracy. The efficient operation of such a government is not possible without the existence of two or more partisan associations which develop their activities through certain channels defined through regulatory legislations."

And yet as it is often pointed out, a real party system implies more than the fact that political parties are in operative existence, and reference is made by many observers to the lack of that certain "climate" of political party government in Latin America. Limitations of franchise, if not of a constitutional, of a practical order; lack

From Federico G. Gil, "Responsible Parties in Latin America," *Journal of Politics,* Vol. XV, No. 3 (August 1953). Reprinted by permission.

of availability of political information; social-economic patterns which tend to prevent free expression of opinion; defects of the systems of electoral administration as well as of party organization; and lack of sense of fair play or sportsmanship are some of the faulty elements which are cited as components of the Latin American political climate. Emphasis is also placed on a supposed lack of "discipline" in political organizations on the frequent changes of party affiliations, and the question of whether there exist real differences among them is often posed. Without attempting to give an answer, it may be said that such differences were probably real in Colombia, Chile, and Argentina. . . .

The two great issues which determined party alignment during the first half of the century of independence were the separation of Church and state, and centralization. These controversies of deep social and political significance divided the ruling and nonruling groups into embittered and hostile factions. All other issues were purely personal and factional. Parties hurriedly organized around one *caudillo* or a nucleus of political chieftains had no degree of permanence beyond the prestige of the leader. . . .

The relatively simple partisan divisions of the early period following the conventional formula of conservatives and liberals, however, is now slowly disappearing in some countries, and they are being supplanted by a system of multiple parties. Cuba, for instance, "came of political age" with only two parties, Liberal and Conservative, but today a far different picture is to be drawn with some six major parties: *Auténticos, Ortodoxos,* Democrats, Republicans, Liberals, and Socialists. Chile furnishes also one of the more typical examples—here the Conservative party represented the most powerful of the old landowner class, sometimes tinted with clericalism, and except for a short period of Liberal rule, it dominated the political scene until the 1880's. During this period, the party gradually relinquished some of its so-called principles, since some groups favored various degrees of liberalism. By the turn of the century, Chile had acquired a complex set-up of parties with at least six groups clearly defined. As a result, Cuba, Chile, and other countries have had to resort to blocs or combinations of parties, thus making coalition governments a common thing.

The minor parties have their bases resting upon a variety of social groups or issues, with little cohesion or discipline. The shifts and machinations of these various political groups almost defy analysis and at times politics is little more than a struggle for the spoils of office with personal or party interests prevailing over national interests. The creation of these fluid organizations in order to achieve short-ranged political objectives is a common occurrence, as elsewhere. It was with reference to this type of organization in Bolivia, Ecuador, and Peru that a writer made this observation: "In these times, nothing is simpler than to found a political party. To form a political party only three people and one object are necessary: a president, vice-president, and a secretary, and a rubber stamp. The party can get along even without the vice-president and the secretary. . . . There have been cases in which the existence of only the rubber stamp has been sufficient."

All students of Latin America will agree that today, however, there is more popular participation in the political processes than at any other time of its history. This increased activity of the masses, they agree, is due, at least partly, to the astounding rise of labor as a political force and to the appearance, in some countries, of parties which seek to correct certain economic inequalities by appealing to the working class, the peasant, and the intellectual class. These new parties are given their strength by a middle class that has political ambitions and by a slowly awakening industrial proletariat. These new competitors of the old and strong traditional parties are causing a profound change in the political pattern of Latin America. In some cases, they are engaged in a decisive struggle with the more conservative groups, a fact which may contribute to the aggravation of the century-old ailment of political instability. In other countries they have been successful in their efforts to capture the reins of power and are attempting to carry out their programs.

A student of the labor movement in Latin America, Robert J. Alexander, observed that some of the new parties are inspired by European models, such as Socialists and Communists, but that others, the more significant perhaps, were indigenous and reflected the peculiar economic conditions of specific countries. Such native movements are the *Peronista* and *Aprista* groups of parties, which he named respectively as the controlling force of Argentine politics today and as the older Peruvian party created by Haya de la Torre. The People's party of Peru was formally organized as a political party in 1931, but it actually originated shortly after World War I. The *Aprista* group of parties includes the Cuban Revolutionary party *(Auténticos),* the Cuban People's party *(Ortodoxos),* the *Acción Democrática* party of Venezuela organized in the late 1930's; and more recently, the *Partido Social Demócrata* of Costa Rica and the *Partido Febrerista* of Paraguay.

Although all of these parties have risen independently in their respective nations with little or no contact with one another and their programs grew up as products of the peculiar domestic conditions, they are, nevertheless, strikingly similar in development and in ideology. These similarities could well result from the fact that conflicts of social and economic interests are slowly replacing political or religious issues as a basis of politics in those countries. The emphasis placed by this group of parties is one of a concept of democracy not exclusively political but socioeconomic, with appeals to nationalism and endorsements of state intervention in the domestic economy. And it should be kept in mind that in this new conception various other social-reform interests should be added to "labor" as motivating forces. Innovations of the new constitutions embrace not only many aspects of labor regulation and protection but extend to assurances of justice in many other areas of social relations, by assertion of principles of social security and by establishment of social-welfare services, protecting the family, promoting cooperative enterprises, and providing low-cost housing.

The so-called *Peronista* group includes three significant labor parties which deserve special notice here: the *Peronista* party in Argentina, the *Trabalhista* party in Brazil, and the *Movimiento Nacionalista Revolucionario* in Bolivia. It is a common characteristic of these parties that they rest primarily upon the support of the working class, long-neglected by political leaders, and which had in these countries, until recently, little or no political organization. In Argentina the backbone of the *Peronista* party is the large mass of workers, the "neglected ones" overlooked by politicians, whose support was gained by Peron's labor legislation. In Brazil, Vargas was able shrewdly and adroitly to weld the *Trabalhistas* into an effective party. In Bolivia through the MNR the miners' union, unorganized until 1943, are a controlling power in support of the administration of Paz Estenssoro. In this labor faction, a rising influence is that of Juan Lechín. It should be noted that it is possible that these new parties may use dictatorship under or outside the law and that they may, just like their older counterparts, commit many indiscretions and abuses.

The party picture in Latin America is completed by the Socialist parties, some of them dating back to 1896; the Communist group of parties including some which were formed after World War I in Argentina, Mexico, Chile, Uruguay and Brazil; and the group of social-reform parties which show evidence of Church interests and attachments.

A sampling of these party groups, followed by closer examination of some, seems the logical and most fruitful approach in the attempt to appraise Latin America's political party system.

Let us take as an example of the so-called *Aprista* class the *Partido Revolucionario Cubano* of Cuba. The party was born in 1934, shortly after the fall of the Machado dictatorship, as a result of a combination of a good number of revolutionary organizations. The program, published also in 1934, featured political democracy, economic nationalism, agrarian reform, industrialization, social security, and education. From its inception it became the standard-bearer of the "Revolution" to carry out a program of economic and social reform. After some vicissitudes the party eventually gained power through an impressive electoral victory in 1944 and remained in office until the military coup of March 1952. The PRC record while in office in Cuba is the subject of appraisal. Undoubtedly it carried out a considerable part of its program with some success, although it did not live up to the full expectations of its followers. It was a firm exponent of political democracy, and while in power it maintained scrupulous respect for freedom of expression and civil liberties. It attempted, although timidly and much less vigorously than other *Aprista* parties, some reforms of the agrarian system and some ventures in government planning. It established a firm policy of stabilization of the price of sugar and of better distribution of the wealth derived from this product; and by making efforts to develop other industries it constructively sought to reduce the dangers of a one-crop economy. It has given impulse to a social-security system and generously financed a vast educational program. Economic nationalism is perhaps less evident in the *Auténtico* party than in others of this group. It has strongly advocated and practiced while in office close relations with the other American republics and especially with those with regimes which were akin to it.

Other parties in the group supply better examples to illustrate certain phases of their common ideology. The Peruvian *Apristas* are significant for their advocacy of agrarian reform and their active defense of the Indian communities. Their short period of participation in the tasks of government in Peru, from 1945 to 1948, was marked by active support of reform measures of this kind. Government economic planning is given perhaps a more prominent place in the program of the Venezuelan Democratic-Action party than in those of other *Aprista* parties, although the Social Democratic party of Costa Rica has also favored it. Nationalization of industry is not advocated to the same degree by these groups, although generally included in their programs. While the issue is not pressed, at least for the present time, by the *Apristas* of

Peru, other parties have carried out nationalization if they considered it necessary. Such was the case of the nationalization of the banks in Costa Rica. On the issue of nationalism, the positions of these parties have been modified in recent years. It is somewhat more conciliatory to foreign capitalists but in return demands strict observance of local social legislation. The *Acción Democrática* government in Venezuela and its policies toward the oil industry furnish a good illustration.

The great weakness of the Cuban *Auténtico* party is the charge, publicly made and widely believed, of corruption and personal dishonesty. In fact, it was this situation which resulted in the establishment of a rival party, the party of the Cuban People (*Ortodoxos*), an offshoot of the PRC in 1946. The break with the *Auténticos* was justified by three factors: first, corruption; second, slowness in the reform program; and third, the belief that the party leader, Grau San Martín, intended to handpick his successor. By 1951, this offshoot of the PRC, which clearly falls into the class of the *Aprista* parties, had become a formidable political force and was making the strongest bid for the presidency in 1952. The party's program of "economic independence, political liberty, and social justice" includes also an insistence on keeping it free from political pacts of any sort without ideological content. In spite of the radical change introduced by the military *coup d'état* in March 1952, these two parties, the PRC and the Orthodox, remain as the key forces in the Cuban political party picture.

The voters to whom the *Aprista* parties make their appeal are approximately the same. The intellectuals and the middle class are faithful followers and in most cases supply the leadership.

The urban working class is heavily relied upon especially if the party has control of the organized labor movement. In Cuba, the agricultural worker who benefitted in large measure from the PRC policies, supplies a considerable bloc of voters, while the Peruvian People's party makes a special appeal to the Indian and mestizo classes. Native industrialists show an inclination to support these parties while landlords and big merchants generally throw their lot to the opposition.

Of the group of parties labeled by Alexander as *Peronista* the most significant is the senior *Partido Peronista* of President Perón in Argentina. This controversial figure of Latin American politics was elected in 1946 with the support of the *Partido Laborista,* an organization established by Perón's followers among labor leaders, and with the assistance of a dissident group in the *Unión Cívica Radical,* the "grand old party" of Argentina. It was not until after his election that Perón decided to consolidate his supporters in one strong political organization to be formed of the *Laboristas,* the pro-Perón Radicals, and the independents. There were serious objections to the proposed liquidation of the *Partido Laborista,* but Perón's plan was put into effect and the *Partido Peronista* was formed.

It is generally accepted that the Perón government rests upon three elements: the army, the Church, and organized labor. The last is the real strength of the Perón regime. Whatever Perón and the party have done to make the labor movement effective and to consolidate its position—and it has been a great deal—has come about with a price to be paid—that of subservience to personal rule. A process of ruthless liquidation of anti-*Peronista* unions was accompanied by a tightening of a rigid control of the *Peronista* labor groups themselves. The fate of the Argentine labor movement is linked, at least temporarily, to the fortunes of the Perón government.

Charges of Fascist tendencies have been frequently made against these parties. Such charges are, in my opinion, unfounded, in spite of superficial and apparent affinities. These three parties are unquestionably genuine Latin American products which have originated from peculiar local conditions. They have led to an awakening of economic, social, and political ambitions of large numbers of the populations in the countries concerned, and they are really indigenous.

The question of whether the *Peronista* party fills the role of a responsible party is, of course, a debatable one. No matter what the answer may be, it is not open to question that the *Peronista* group in spite of the inconsistencies in profession of faith, in spite of the appearance of totalitarianism, the irresponsible nationalism, and the disregard for civil liberty, performs an impressive role in adding a new chapter to the social history of Argentina. It is not too much to say that the traditional parties, including the Socialists, have failed equally to supply the worker with a positive program of social and economic reform. Until another party is able to make an effective appeal of this nature to the masses, the position of the *Peronista* party might not be successfully challenged.

The *Peronista* ideas have been making headway in Chile, Peru, Bolivia, Paraguay, and Brazil. The *Movimiento Nacionalista Revolucionario* has recently returned to power in Bolivia by means of a successful civilian revolt after several years of forced exclusion from Bolivian politics. It was this party which served as the main civilian support of the Villaroel government from 1943 to 1946. This group claims to be representative of the generation of Bolivians who fought the tragic Chaco War and who returned from the battleground with a deep-rooted desire for reform. It also claims to be the instrument that will give substance to the great reformist, nationalist, reconstructive drive born out of that conflict. In the economic field, the MNR challenges the influence of the big tin interests and of the landowning class. The feature of its program is advocacy of government powers of regulation and control over the tin industry. The recent nationalization of that industry was a definite objective of such a program. In the case of the petroleum laws, an issue for many years in Bolivian politics, reforms proposed by the party supplement what is described as a broad and ambitious plan to achieve economic and social reform simultaneously on various fronts.

From what has been said, it may be concluded that the political strength of the MNR is closely related to the large mass of tin workers and Indian peasants. The party strives to attract and build up a firm foundation of labor support, just like the Argentine *Peronista* party has done, so as not to be forced to depend exclusively on the support of the young officers group of the army which first made possible its entry into politics. Charges of fascism, arbitrariness, and irresponsible nationalism have also been hurled against the Bolivian MNR adding to the resemblance between the two parties in question. And again, its rapid rise may be explained by the fact that it seems to offer an attractive program of reform to redress the grievances of the long-forgotten and now restless segment of the nation.

The history of the other groups of parties, which we have chosen for this brief discussion, is closely linked to the history of labor movements in Latin

America. Although labor movements developed independently and in a particular way in each country, there have been certain common features in the processes. The pattern has been one from mutual-benefit societies and anarcho-syndicalism to an organized and more stable labor movement with influences sometimes exerted between countries. A tradition of anti-imperialism and nationalism seems to have been also a common feature in the labor movement. The cycle as we examine several countries takes the pattern of progression from mutual-benefit societies and *uniones de resistencia,* struggles between these and new Socialist and Communist ideas followed by the predominance of the latter in the 1930's to the final crystallization of a strong political party with appeal to the working class.

The Socialist party of Argentina is perhaps the most interesting, being the oldest and strongest of the group. Utopian socialism was introduced to the country in 1837 and was developed by the wave of European refugees later. French, Italian, and Spanish Socialist groups were organized in Buenos Aires but operated separately until they joined to launch the *Partido Socialista* in 1896 under the leadership of Juan B. Justo. The influence of Argentine socialism was soon to be felt almost all over Latin America. After a period of rapid growth in the prewar period the party began to endure dissension in 1914 and 1915, but it continued to gain strength during the 1920's and socialists controlled successfully all major labor organizations until 1942. During the same period they scored some major electoral victories such as winning control of five of the country's largest cities and electing forty-four deputies in the 1931 elections but, with the rise of the *Peronista* party, the socialists lost labor control

with the exception of a few unimportant unions. Their electoral fortunes began likewise to decline sharply. This decline has been attributed to the failure of the party in supplying leadership to the trade unions and in giving attention to long-range objectives. The constant reluctance of the party to take any strong position on important issues that affected labor interests and its responsibility in the so-called bureaucratization of the labor movement have been contributing factors.

A more graphic criticism, made on one occasion by a prominent leader of Venezuela's *Acción Democrática* to the writer, related the present deterioration of the Argentine Socialists as resulting from their lack of contact with the worker and the emphasis on intellectuals and theoreticians.[1] Whether these views are correct or not, the fact remains that the *Socialista* party has failed, so far, to evidence the type of dynamic leadership and driving force which will be necessary to challenge the *Peronista* forces with any measure of success.

A brief reference should be made to the various Communist parties although the writer cannot be convinced that they can ever fall in the category of responsible parties. Active in the labor movement since the early 1920's and having at one time or another influenced labor organizations in some countries, the Communists became a factor of some party significance in the period of World War II. For a time they controlled important groups in the labor movements of Chile, Panama, Guatemala, Colombia, Uruguay, Cuba, Brazil, Venezuela, and Ecuador. Since 1945 there has been a marked decline in their influence in countries

---

[1] Interview with Rómulo Betancourt, August 23, 1945. Betancourt referred to a *socialismo de catedra.*

such as Cuba, Venezuela, Ecuador, and Brazil. The healthy development of new political groups, such as those already described, was a significant factor in the weakening of the Communist groups. The decision of several Latin American governments to place these parties outside the law has served as a further deterrent to their growth and has provided some interesting examples of legal action against their activities. . . .

There is in Latin America one party which stands in a class by itself. It is the *Partido Revolucionario Institucional,* the cornerstone of Mexico's one-party system. A creation of President Calles in 1928, the then called *Partido Nacional Revolucionario* was a combination of regional machines claiming to represent the total revolutionary segments of the country. The component parts, labor unions, agricultural leagues, professional organizations, and even military associations retain their identity but are under the authority of a national executive committee. A process of absorption of other parties was immediately begun and the PNR became a formidable political machine with effective electoral power. The Cárdenas administration undertook the transformation of the Calles machine into a "functional" party by inducing organized laborers and peasants to pour their ranks into the PNR. In March 1938, the PNR was transformed into the *Partido de la Revolución Mexicana* and four autonomous sections—labor, peasant, popular, and army—were fused into a single instrument. The inclusion of the army was hoped to discourage military coups and to effect a revolutionary indoctrination of that element. The fundamental task, the PRM stated, was the preparation of the people for the establishment of a worker's democracy as a step toward socialism. Further reconstruction of the

party and change of its name by Avila Camacho in 1945 did not really affect the political tradition, although it inaugurated a shift toward moderation in governmental policy. Membership of the party is claimed at over four million. It includes all the political and unionist branches of the "Revolution," the majority of the rank and file of the army, and the total number of office holders. The party elaborates plans and programs for the administration. Technicians and specialists study national problems and submit plans which are first approved by the executive committee and then submitted to the party's national convention. Today this formidable electoral machine, vehemently criticized by its opponents as a nondemocratic organ in every sense of the word, makes Mexico effectively a one-party country. While any party may be constituted in Mexico (except religious organizations) with the same legal privileges of the PRI, an opposition party has little chance of electing candidates, and state governors and other high officials are often elected in the PRI national headquarters. It must be noted, however, that within the giant PRI there exist various tendencies or wings which, in the internal struggle for power, do serve in some measure to mitigate this situation by giving a semblance of the free play of parties in a broader system.

To conclude, we must point to noteworthy trends in the development of political parties in Latin America. An enumeration of these would include the appearance of new forces in politics, which are competing for power with the older and traditional political groups; the increasing párticipation of organized labor in politics; the rise of parties which give forceful and dramatic presentation of national socioeconomic problems; the strong nationalistic tone of postwar politics; and the possible weakening of *personalismo*, evident in some cases, with the consequent strengthening of party principles. These factors have already produced a substantial change in the pattern of political activity. Even newer political align-ments may still develop. The political stage is by no means static and it is to be expected that Latin America will continue to seek expression of its desires and ambitions in original ways.

21

Mexico's One-party System:
A Re-evaluation

L. Vincent Padgett

Because Mexican politics since the revolution of 1910–1917 have operated mainly within the framework of a one-party system and because in the past strong men have sometimes occupied the presidency, writers in the United States have tended to treat the system as authoritarian. Emphasis upon presidential rule and the corollary explanation of the role of the Revolutionary party as nothing more nor less than an instrument of presidential domination have served to create an oversimplified picture of presidential power. . . .

The Threefold Role of the Official Party

If the "official" or Revolutionary party has not been an instrument for shaping the dominant power pattern into a monolithic structure, what has been its sociopolitical function? The answer has more than one side since the party's role has in fact been three-

fold. The three aspects have formed the parts of a complete whole. But for analytical purposes they should be treated separately.

In the first place, the party has obviously had an electoral function. For election purposes it has served as a procedural device in the formalization of candidacies for public office, and it has organized the election campaigns for the persons nominated. Most important, however, has been its usefulness as a symbol of mutual interest. The party banner has become an emotional solvent for diverse economic groups and conflicting personal ambitions. As a symbol, it is the external manifestation of the rational conviction that the rewards of unity in terms of control of public office outweigh the occasional temporary disadvantages suffered from interpersonal or intergroup disagreements within the Revolutionary sector. The symbol seems to have become so venerated that it offers a reason in itself for unified electoral operations. Thus, during the election of 1952 when Avelino Navarro A., president of the District Committee Pro Adolfo Ruiz Cortines of Colotlán, Jalisco, sent a letter to the agrarian sec-

From L. Vince Padgett, "Mexico's One-party System: A Re-evaluation," *American Political Science Review*, Vol. LI, No. 4 (December 1957). Reprinted by permission.

retary of the party Central Executive Committee and expressed real dissatisfaction with party nominees for deputy and senator, the official's answer was couched in terms of the loyalty and unity of interest symbolized by the party emblem:

> ...I feel I should point out that regardless of whoever may be designated to run as candidates for deputies and senators, our obligation as members of the *Partido Revolucionario Institucional* is to uphold the party candidates. We should strive to prevent any division among the *campesinos* which might occur because none of our friends was nominated. On the contrary, we should continue supporting the candidacy of Adolfo Ruiz Cortines with all possible enthusiasm.

It is noteworthy that in answering Navarro the Secretary of Agrarian Action did not try to defend the choices that were made. Instead he appealed to the values of unity and electoral success for the Revolutionary group as a whole as reflected in the triumph of its presidential candidate.

A second aspect of the party's total function has been its liaison role within the Revolutionary association. Daily throughout the year party committees work to facilitate the flow of information and the reconciliation of conflicting interests among the various groups and leaders associated in the revolutionary circle at a given level of government. In concrete, operative terms this has meant that the party central committee has been responsible for furthering understanding and a sense of common cause among federal legislators, state governors, the president and his cabinet, national committees of labor, peasant, professional, industrial, commercial, and small property groups. On any typical weekday—between the hours of 10:00 and 2:00 in the afternoon and 4:00 and 8:00 in the evening—the central offices of the party in Mexico City teem with government officials, legislators, and interest group leaders who find there a kind of lodge or meeting place for exchanging confidences, swapping political gossip, sounding attitudes of colleagues, and patching up differences. Similarly, at the state level the party regional committees have worked for exchange of views and compromise of differences within the net of relationships involving functional groups, executive and legislature as well as the *ad hoc* groups of ordinarily apolitical persons which frequently emerge to demand civic improvements or redress of grievances. Day-to-day activity in the regional committee offices is not so great as in the party offices in the Federal District, but at election time it would be difficult to find a busier place than the headquarters of the regional committee in any one of the state capitals. The weakest point of party operation in terms of the liaison function has been at the municipal level where lack of finances and the consequent tendency to function on a part-time basis have limited the effectiveness of the party municipal committees.[1]

The third aspect of the party's threefold role has been its operation as an intermediary between government and people. In this connection the party has acted as a channel of communication and an agency of mediation between policy-makers in the executive branch of government, municipal, state, and national, on the one hand and the

---

[1] It should be pointed out that in some *municipios* which are geographically extensive, heavily populated, and economically well situated, local groups have felt the need for a liaison and communication device on a full-time basis and have contributed the necessary financial support. However, such conditions seem to be the exceptions rather than the rule.

majority and minority points of view at the grass roots on the other. . . .

The Role of the Party and the Ideological Bias of the Political Elite

When a party system of government —two or more parties or coalitions of parties approximately equal in strength and share of electoral success—is lacking, the choice of means by which the political elite seek to maintain their power position becomes extremely important. The vital question is whether reliance will be placed primarily upon physical and psychological coercion or upon persuasion and compromise. In Mexico there has been a growing tendency toward the latter. This tendency has gathered strength from the expansion of literacy, the private ownership of mass media of communication, the constantly improving highway network —and particularly from the way decision-makers have interpreted their role, the value system of their countrymen, and the history of the Mexican nation since independence. These ideological factors are central to an understanding of "why" the party's role has developed as it has.

In the first place the self-ideal of those holding power has not been essentially authoritarian in character. The concept of an elite meriting unlimited discretion as the right of total omniscience has been lacking. Claims to legitimacy, in other words, have not been advanced in terms of a political theology centering upon revealed, universal truth as the single means for achieving social salvation. Instead, those who have aspired to and held power have emphasized the principles of free choice and majority rule as determined by elections. Practice has sometimes fallen short of ideological prescriptions, but theory has not been devoid of signif-

icance on that account since accepted norms have made room for political pluralism as a social value to be sought rather than stamped out.

Of particular significance has been the sense assigned the symbol "democracy" in the value system of the average Mexican. Democracy has not signified the institutions of party government nor the elaborate procedural-judicial arrangements for guaranteeing individual rights so characteristic of Anglo-Saxon political organization. As defined in Mexico, democracy has been less concrete, less rationalized, and less closely tied to the institutional context. Primary emphasis has rested upon liberty in the more general and very basic sense of the capacity of the individual to move about, to associate freely, to discuss, to criticize—in summary to assert that independence without which there can be no dignity for the person. Liberty has been an ideological current running side by side with that of authoritarianism in the heritage of Spanish thought which has molded the Mexican value system. The institutional patterns by which rights for the individual have been secured in the United States and western Europe have not taken root in a large way, but this should not obscure the fact that the concept of personal liberty has been familiar, deep-bedded, and emotionally potent.

A second emphasis evident in the Mexican definition of democracy, particularly since the revolution, has involved the execution of social and economic reforms for the purpose of raising the living standard of the poverty-ridden rural and urban masses. The rights of urban and rural labor to organize and strike, the land-reform program, the social-welfare and security measures, and the efforts to reduce illiteracy all have been manifestations of the social justice bias of revolutionary democracy. But it has never been assumed that social justice precludes individual liberty, as has been the case with the political doctrine of some other revolutionary regimes of the twentieth century.

As a matter of fact, a prime conditioning factor in the development of the political institutions of Mexico has been the close interrelationship of these two emphases in Revolutionary ideology. Both facets have been treated as necessary parts of a whole. This was clearly pointed up by Adolfo Ruiz Cortines when he spoke to the people of Puebla as the candidate of the Revolutionary party during the presidential campaign of 1952:

> ...reaffirming our purpose to take care ...that Mexico shall follow without pause the path of dignity, of social justice, and of unceasing progress... the Revolutionary administrations consolidate more each time the public liberties which are the root of our *Mexicanism:* the liberty of belief, of thinking and of writing, of criticism of government, of association, and all the rest which dignify man and the citizen and which our Great Charter consecrates. Such liberties we shall never set aside.

The ideological commitment with regard to liberty, particularly important for purposes of this study, has interlocked with the interpretation of Mexican history officially set forth and widely accepted in terms of personal conviction on the part of the political elite themselves. On the one hand the Revolutionary regime has been presented to the people as the logical, historical link in the heritage of popular revolutions led by heroes of other eras —such giant symbols of the folk struggle for liberty and self-determination as Padre Hidalgo, José María Morelos, and Benito Juárez. Also included have been such latter day prophets as Francisco Madero and Emiliano Zapata—

even Lázaro Cárdenas. The stories and myths surrounding these leaders have formed the historical bases of the argument for legitimacy. On the other hand, in the process of forging the institutions of the Revolutionary regime the members of each succeeding administration have themselves been affected in their thinking and in their actions by the historical symbols which have been invoked as instruments for achieving and maintaining power.

This latter factor has been central to the creation of a widespread conviction in Revolutionary circles to the effect that the ideal of liberty in the Mexican system of values has made it difficult in the past to establish a lasting system of rule based upon organized, arbitrary coercion of the Mexican masses. It has been accepted as gospel that the Wars of the Reform and the defeat of the French puppet Maximilian in the nineteenth century as well as the overthrow of the Porfirio Díaz regime in 1910 and the ensuing years of bloody revolution all had among their primary causes the Mexican sentiment with regard to liberty.

Taken from this point of view, the lesson of history for those who wish to maintain their dominant power position in the Mexican political system has been clear enough, namely, ways and means must be found to prevent a sense of discontent and personal injustice from becoming widespread among Mexican citizens. In metaphorical terms, one way to remove the fuse from the political dynamite has been to institutionalize devices by which dissident groups can articulate their grievances and aspirations and have them considered.

Under the stimulus of this felt need the Revolutionary party has been developing into something more than an electoral mechanism, symbol of unity for diverse groups, and agent of intra-association communication for the various elements of the dominant power group in their relationships with each other. The party has become all these things; but, from the standpoint of stability within the Mexican political system and citizen participation in the molding of policy, the emerging function of the party as an instrument of mediation between government and people has been most important. For this latter aspect of the party's role reflects the understanding of Revolutionary leaders as to the importance of individual liberty, dignity, and differences in the minds of the Mexican people. It reflects the recognition of the fact that the only course by which the existing power pattern can be maintained without threat of rebellion on the one hand or resort to organized control of social action in a total sense on the other must be the development of multiple points of access by which citizen and official can meet to adjust differences and reach new understandings. An "official" party need not necessarily be an instrument of imposition. It may be a device for bridging the gap between authoritarianism and representative democracy.

22

The Confrontation
with the Political University

John P. Harrison

The revolution of aspirations that has provided so much of the driving force behind Latin America's urge for social change and economic development has had, perhaps, its longest continuous expression through a university-centered movement, the *Reforma Universitaria,* that took shape in Argentina and Uruguay during the second decade of this century. The highly publicized letter of the Chilean students to President Eisenhower in 1960 is woven from the same ideological strands as the proclamations, articles, proceedings, and decrees issued in Cordoba, Argentina, where the first dramatic expression of the reform movement occurred in 1918. Responsible and irresponsible, effective and ineffective national leaders both in and out of government who give expression and direction to these aspirations have all been touched by, and many directly involved in, this movement. It has helped create the climate of opinion in which not only the response of the United States universities must be made, but also the moral and intellectual climate that has helped form the uneven, spongy sod that all responses by this

From John P. Harrison, "The Confrontation with the Political University," *The Annals,* Vol. CCCXXXIV (March 1961). Reprinted by permission.

country to present conditions in Latin America must walk on.

The response of the scholarly community in this country to the present active climate of social change in Latin America can be made through a variety of institutional channels both here and there. My concern is solely with that response which operates in Latin America through the structure of its universities. This is because, as long as basic technical and professional services are provided in the form of assistance from elsewhere, the response can have no permanent effect. The situation ceases to be temporary when the graduates of Latin American institutions of higher learning meet the expanding needs of their society for professional and technical services. The solution to research as well as training requirements ultimately will have to be reached within the regular structure of Latin American universities. For the North American scholarly community to work to any purpose within the framework of higher education in Latin America, it needs, I believe, a more precise understanding than most of its individual members now possess of how the Latin American *universitario*—student, professor, alumnus—conceives of his function and duty in society.

The old Spanish university was a place of privilege for privileged people and, as such, was reproduced in the principal administrative centers of colonial America. Once accepted—his blood line having been officially approved—there was no question of the student's standing in the community. He was possessed of special rights and privileges not otherwise available to him. After the Wars of Independence, these older universities continued to recruit their students from the upper classes. The prestige and even the sanctuary that went with being a *universitario* continued and were often used by the intellectual leadership to further their own political careers. During the early years of this century, the university was an integral part of an essentially static social structure. Against a background of a century of general poverty and corruption as independent nations, the secondary and university students of this period had made available to them in a concentrated dose the first Spanish translations of the most important writings of modern Western civilization. The books of Descartes, Rousseau, Locke, Spinoza, Darwin, Marx, and Tolstoy were widely sold throughout Spanish America at very cheap prices. Professor Herminio Portell Vilá has pointed out that this injection of new ideas was decisive in setting the tone and scope of the intellectual revolution that took place among the university generation of 1910–1920. Under the influence of this heady literature, the students, from their position of relative immunity, challenged many of the existing institutions. Among these was the old Spanish university itself.

The basic concern of the university reform movement has never been with the university as an institution, but rather with the orientation of the national, and ultimately continental, conscience. Within the university, the effect of the reform movement has been typically administrative rather than academic. Here I will deal first with this secondary aspect—the means rather than the end. From its starting point in the Rio de la Plata in 1918, the movement spread rapidly throughout Latin America, its first international congress convening in Mexico in 1921. The specific reforms demanded varied from country to country, as did the reception given them.

One constant feature was the democratization of the university, which meant direct participation by the students in university administration. At the start of the reform movement, the faculties of the universities were largely limited to law, medicine, and engineering, and each faculty was, in effect, a separate entity run by its directive councils with but scant interference from the superior council of the university or the rector. Then, as in most instances today, there was no general liberal arts and science faculty or courses that served the university as a whole. The students wanted to elect one or more of their own number to voting status on the directive council of each faculty. These demands have expanded until today reform in many universities means *co-gobierno* or equal representation of students and faculty on the directive councils.[1] With the addition of new faculties to meet expanding professional needs the superior council has taken on added importance for the realization of

[1] This extreme was achieved at least temporarily in Guatemala in 1945 during the presidency of Juan José Arévalo, a former militant reformist in Argentine universities, and it is today the situation in the University of Havana, where the two principal student leaders are army majors who have neither reason nor time to attend academic classes. *Co-gobierno* is also a feature of a bitter struggle within the University of San Marcos in Lima. There is considerable evidence that Havana is now being used as a technical training ground for student leaders of other countries, a movement that cannot be stopped by offshore naval patrols.

the aims of the reform movement. Student membership on university councils has been central to all other aspects of reform because it provides a position of authority from which student-selected representatives can attack what they consider to be entrenched interests both in and out of the university.

Other elements that have usually been present in the demands of the students for reform include: selection of professors by an open competition and, occasionally, a limitation on the length of time a professor should occupy a chair without academic review; the freedom of students to attend lectures of their choice and to be graded solely on examination results—this permits students to go on strike with relative impunity throughout the academic calendar save for the period of examinations; the right of students to make the facilities of the university available to lecturers of their choice from outside the immediate academic community; the publication of all theses defended in the process of gaining a degree; the organization of a university extension program; and a well-defined program of financial assistance to students in the form of noninterest-bearing loans, meals at a reduced cost, and aid in housing. In addition to these innovations, the reform movement placed an increased emphasis on the autonomy of the university and its freedom from political interference. In this sense, the movement accentuated the privileged place that the old Spanish university had within the social structure. It has greatly facilitated the political activities of students by providing them with a forum for free political expression that could not be encroached upon without a challenge to academic freedom and a likely censure of the government involved by a large segment, if not the majority, of the body politic. Now, as before, a student takes

less risk than, say, a worker of the same age, should they both make an identical challenge against political authority.

Additional attitudes closely associated with the university reform movement are that no academic limitation to matriculation beyond completion of secondary school should be applied and that a student has the right to repeat a course as often as he wishes until he passes the examination.[2] These beliefs, along with the traditional one that a university education should be free except for minor fees, are supported on the grounds that to do otherwise would return control to the antidemocratic elite of prereform days.

While all of the aims of the reform movement mentioned above touch directly upon the university as an institution, it is readily apparent that none of them is concerned with curriculum revision or in improving the professional training of the student, unless one makes an exception of practical politics. That this neglect was no accident was evident from the inception of the movement in Argentina, when one of its leaders emphasized in 1918 that the university was not, nor should it be, a mere pedagogical instrument. Other participants in the original student revolt at Cordoba made it abundantly clear then and afterwards that the technical aspects of a university interested them only slightly. The recognition of academic excellence had no place within the reform movement, which recognized only two classifications for grades: sufficient and insufficient. It was thought desirable to

2 The Second National Congress of University Students proclaimed in Buenos Aires in 1932 that: "Every proposal for limiting entrance is an expression of the most obvious reactionary attitude inasmuch as their effect is not to correct any pedagogical deficiency but to assist in the plutocratization of the student body."

abolish the distinction of anything like *magna cum laude, sobresaliente,* the ambition for which was looked on as a bourgeois sickness.

The larger purpose that has given the university reform movement its persistent character has been the definition of a national and ultimately continental culture. Its ideology has been economic and its expression political. For the university to function as the fountainhead for the movement, it was necessary to remove the educational obstacles that impeded the authentic spiritual formation of a distinctive national culture. To this end, the movement has fought for the renovation of ideals in higher education—its members felt they had to break the sterile Creole habit of regarding the university as a place one passed through, like a railroad station, to get somewhere else; for the cultural integration of what was taught in universities; and for the democratic organization of the universities needed to put themselves at the service of the desired renaissance of national life. The new university was to be open to all spiritual currents and, thus, to sustain the fight between creative youth and peevish old age. Courses were introduced on superior culture that permitted the student to understand and absorb certain indispensable concepts needed by all cultivated men. The Latin American university was to be the institution where the emerging middle-class man was made into a cultured man and a good professional in the service of his country and, eventually, in the service of *Hispanoamérica, la América indohispana,* or, simply, *nuestro América.*

It was felt that any culture, in addition to this general base common to all men, must have something peculiarly its own, something drawn from the particular land on which the people lived. In this stance, the reform movement drew heavily from Ortega y Gasset, whose books, along with those of a few other Spanish writers of the generation of 1898, were circulated in quantity and in cheap editions by the publishers of the previously mentioned translations. He had written a book on the mission of the university in which he described the transmission of culture as the first and most important of its functions. At the same time, his other writings made known the web of thought surrounding his famous phrase, "man in his circumstances." National culture on this basis could be a reality only insofar as it was incorporated into the life and goals of a particular people. This, in turn, must involve the problem of their freedom, which was intimately tied to political and economic questions. The people must know that they constitute a new world. This culture and the limits of their world, the university reform group set about to define. This effort continues to the present and has expanded considerably beyond those whose main interest is university reform. The process clearly excluded any discernible foreign influence and stimulated a strong nationalism aimed principally against the United States but, to a considerable degree, against Europe also. The over-all emblem of Ibero-American "man in his circumstances" was the *Día de la raza.* This race was distinguished by its spiritual rather than its physical characteristics, and the concept began to appear in university mottoes, such as *Alma mater de la raza* for the University of Antioquia and *Por mi raza hablará el espíritu* for the National Autonomous University of Mexico. The politician turned philosopher and educator, José Vasconcelos, an active member of the university reform group after 1920, gave the word its ultimate flavor with his lengthy discussion of the *raza cósmico.*

In developing the particularity of their culture, the exponents of the university reform movement went to considerable pains to denigrate the university student in the United States and the system that produced him. They consider that the North American student is illiterate about the social problems of his country, for which he assumes no responsibility, being concerned solely with his own financial or professional betterment without regard to national needs. The political university is not part of the educational pattern in this country, but its importance in Latin America is indicated by the fact that the outstanding topic of deliberation at the 1959 Conference of the Union of Latin American Universities was political university. Germán Arciniegas, a major figure in the reform movement and later a professor at Columbia University, once wrote that the function of the university in the United States is diametrically opposed to the function of its counterpart in Latin America. The stimulus and definition of whatever social services the North American university provides—such as agricultural extension—come essentially from outside the university. In Latin America, the definition of the problem, together with its proposed solution, comes from the university, which conceives of itself as a synthesis of the people it serves. Speaking in 1960, the Secretary General of the National University of Mexico, Dr. Efrén G. del Pozo, stated that the most important mission of the university is "the task of creating free men, inspired with a deep sense of social responsibility." There is little doubt that the university community in Latin America would agree with this statement or that most of them would feel that the mission remains unfulfilled in the United States.

The reform movement has used the university as a vehicle for taking to the people the social revolution it has helped to foster. Given the broad use of polemics in expressing its political beliefs, it is not surprising to find that the extensive literature of the university reform movement has, since its inception, been highly critical of the United States. With half a century of constant repetition, the tone at times rising to pure invective, it has become a simple article of faith that does not need substantiation to say that it is the policy of the United States to take over Latin America for its own economic uses and, in the process, to destroy the basic values of the distinctive Latin culture. The Peruvian student leader and later founder of the *Aprista* movement, Victor Raúl Haya de la Torre, remarked in 1926 that the students were the first to comprehend and sound the alarm against the United States advance on Latin America. Only a dedicated youth, he felt, could deal with this threat, because the older generation were all personally implicated in the advance of imperialism.

Like any other institution or social attitude in Latin America, the position of university students and the structure of their universities do not present a monolithic entity. The extent to which the United States is regarded as an unquestioned enemy of national aspirations by student organizations varies, as does the extent of influence of student organizations within the different universities. The attitude of suspicion is, however, general throughout the Latin American student world, even though it is held with greatly varying degrees of intensity. This means that, although many may feel that there are threats more dangerous than the United States, the dominant attitude among students is to look with suspicion on offers of cooperation or assistance from this country. The university reform movement, with considerable direct and indirect foreign stimulation, has succeeded particularly in getting across an image of the United States Department of State that makes suspect any program supported or otherwise connected with the government of the United States. This suspicion—again, as a general rule—will be much stronger at this time in the older, larger, and more influential national universities than in the many newer, smaller, and sometimes private universities that have been founded or revitalized since the end of of World War II. The university reform movement had its greatest impact in the national universities of Argentina, Uruguay, Peru, Cuba, Guatemala, and, more recently, Venezuela. It has been influential but of slightly less strength in Chile, Colombia, Brazil, and Mexico. In a few instances, particular universities in existence during the early years of the reform movement remained aloof. Examples of this position include the Universities of Cuzco in Peru and Quito in Ecuador; the movement in these countries was felt, instead, at San Marcos in Lima and the University of Guayaquil. There has been, if anything, even less interest in reforming university curricula and professional training to meet mid-twentieth century needs in those universities that closed their doors to the reform movement than in those where it found fertile ground.

The end of World War II can be used as an approximate date for the start of a new attitude towards the form of higher education in Latin America. This trend—working towards a university different both from the generally static pattern of the old Spanish prototype and from the more political, socially oriented, student-controlled university that the reform movement has sought to create, yet drawing substantially from each—is not the expression of any clearly organized movement with a stated list of aims, nor does it carry with it any strong emotional appeal to

young or old, to proponents of the *status quo* or of social change. It has been directed almost solely to improving the quality of academic training within specific disciplines to the end that Latin American universities will produce graduates who are professional equals of those trained in the best universities of the United States and Europe and who are technically competent to resolve their own social, economic, and cultural problems. The initiative for placing an emphasis on curriculum and quality in higher education has come largely from exceptionally talented younger men, most of whom received part of their professional training abroad. Perhaps those in medicine, engineering, and the sciences have been most in evidence, but there have been leaders, also, whose own professional interests are in economics, philosophy, sociology, drama, and music. For the most part, they have operated as individuals working within the framework of one university or, even more typically, a particular faculty. They have, in some cases, been responsible for the organization of completely new universities. They have, in exceptional instances, taken the lead in establishing national organizations for devising and financially supporting higher levels of university instruction. The political affiliations of these men cover virtually the whole political spectrum, although the extremes of reaction and revolution are not compatible with the one purpose common to each: the training on a local and continuous basis of a sufficient number of all levels of skilled professionals to resolve the urgent problems confronting the welfare of their own people. While the success of their efforts has been substantial, there have been instances of failure and of only partial achievement of purpose. Among the difficulties facing these individuals is the opposition within the university, both covert and overt, by proponents of the static authoritarian university of old and of the student-reform movement. As gradual change is inherent to this process, those trying to effect it have encountered the opposition from political groups that want no change and, more importantly, from those advocating a sharp and complete break with the past. One thing is eminently clear: it is not possible today to touch any part of the university structure in Latin America without becoming enmeshed in local, national, and even international politics. This is a condition to which the scholarly community of the United States has had difficulty accommodating in its attempts to respond to the very real revolution of aspirations in present-day Latin America.

Concern for the Latin American university as an institution is fairly recent in the United States. Its earliest expression with anything resembling responsible continuity was the work of foundations such as the Rockefeller Foundation and, considerably later, the Kellogg Foundation. Recently, the Ford Foundation has begun to concern itself with higher education, and the Carnegie Foundation, by means of grants to United States organizations, is involved with the problem of the role of the university in the society of Latin America. Quite recently, also, and usually with outside funds, United States universities have assumed responsibility for operating programs in direct cooperation with Latin American universities. Much of this cooperative activity by the university community in this country is, however, still with institutions other than those of higher learning in Latin America. It is estimated by the authors of a recent study on the subject that there are now about sixty programs in Latin America for which thirty United States universities and colleges

are responsible. Of the thirteen examples they describe in detail, eight were in cooperation with educational institutions and five were with national or international government organizations. Of the eight Latin American institutions of higher learning involved, only one had been at all intimately associated with the student-oriented reform movement. In this single instance, the activity has not been incorporated into the regular university structure and, hence, cannot yet be considered a functioning part of the country's system of higher education. Indeed, of the cooperative programs described, only one shows any indication of substantially affecting the nature and quality of professional instruction within the Latin American university involved. If one accepts the premise inherent in this presentation—that, while urgent social and economic problems can often best be met by operating programs outside the university, the results can never be lasting until the Latin American university is capable of regularly educating the volume of well-trained professionals and technicians needed to respond to the social, cultural, and economic needs peculiar to each country —then it is clear that the scholarly community in this country needs to re-examine its response to the ongoing social revolution in Latin America.

Attention to the Latin American university as an institution of higher learning serving the needs of society has been almost solely the concern of foundations among the scholarly community of this country. The point of contact in Latin America has been largely with those universities or faculties described earlier where there exists a conviction that curriculum, teaching standards, library services, and equipment need attention and improvement. To achieve the standards of professional excellence required, attention has been given to such reforms as greatly increasing the number of full-time professors on the faculty and, conversely, the number of full-time students, so that something resembling a community of scholars may result. Efforts have been made to set admission standards and to bring the ratio of students to available equipment and other facilities to a level that will permit professional instruction of a quality necessary to compete at present world standards and to produce the specialists required to handle the multiple needs of rapid social change. Training in disciplines heretofore either ignored or treated incidentally within existing faculties has been helped. Some remarkable educational transformations have resulted from this cooperation with Latin American universities. Here it is necessary to emphasize cooperation, because nothing is possible where the university or faculty involved does not have a deep conviction of the necessity of the program in question and from a point of view of regional or national, not simply academic, need. It is equally necessary that the representative of the scholarly community in this country have the conviction of purpose to maintain the continuity of a close working relationship. It seems clear, also, that such programs as these, if they are to have any continental impact, must become a pattern within an increasing number of major national universities throughout Latin America. This will require the thoughtful consideration of many more institutions of higher learning in this country.

To be effective, the individual scholars working in such programs will have to bear constantly in mind the motivation and ideals of the university reform movement, which has been notably effective in determining the tone and defining the function of a university as it is understood by the mass of politically ambitious, upwardly mobile students who provide the overwhelming majority of those attending these universities. For them, reality may be closer to stimulating social change than to preparation for harnessing it for the ultimate benefit of the greatest number of their fellow citizens. The time and discipline required to become a competent economist, physician, or agronomist will strike many of these students as smacking too much of the ivory tower. To others, an emphasis on professional training will be regarded suspiciously as a brake on their fast-moving, frequently vast social schemes. North Americans often comment with dismay at the tendency of many excellent Latin American scholars to leave the university for a political career. This becomes more readily understandable when one remembers the primary political function of the large universities in contrast to our emphasis on professional training.

The United States, since World War II, has consistently used a vertical approach towards the Latin American university and technical assistance generally. It has concerned itself with specific problems such as improved public administration in one country, public health problems in a second, or increasing food production in another. Within universities, attention has been to an economics, veterinary medicine, or library science faculty. In contrast, the approach of the Communist world has been horizontal, concerning itself with student-reform movements, political attitudes such as anti-imperialism or anti-colonialism, national social programs, and value standards of major sectors of society. Within the university, there appears to be a discernible difference in the approach of China and Russia, with the latter, at least occasionally, giving attention to the professional training of students, even if they have to create a special educational institution in Russia for the purpose, while the interest of the Chinese is confined to cementing the commitment of students and teachers to a particular ideology and the support of one nation's international attitude. An invitation to students active in the university reform and other political movements to spend time in China is made on a mass basis. There is no question of academic training involved in that quite obviously none of the Latin American students could take academic work in Chinese, even assuming that Chinese universities had something to offer in the academic field not available at home. The appeal is political in terms of China's rapidly improved position as a world power.

The response of the North American scholarly community to the revolution of aspirations in Latin America can best be made in the interest of a better life for the greatest number of Latin Americans by continuing in the present vertical pattern of concerning itself with the situation of a particular faculty or university. On a university-to-university basis, any other approach is virtually precluded. Foundation and joint university programs may well touch questions that can best be resolved through interuniversity cooperation at a national and international level. The response must be greatly intensified if it is to achieve a sufficient scale to provide the technical competence needed to resolve the human needs of the area against a background of ever more strident propaganda for nonacademic, easy ideological solutions.

As important as greater volume and sharper focus is the need of the North American university to assume the responsibility for continuity of interest and intensive knowledge about the area or country involved. Without it, there seems considerable likelihood that whatever is accomplished professionally in working with a particular faculty, whether it be medicine or music, is likely to be obliterated by the broad wave of political reform in the university. The academic visitors must go about their cooperative work with a full comprehension of the function of the university in the national life of the country involved and with an adequate understanding of the relationship of any actions they may propose be taken to the tenets—perhaps conflicting—of the student organizations at the university involved and in the country as a whole. In certain instances, the representative of the North American university might find it advantageous to depart from his strictly professional role to confront students and faculty both singly and in groups to discuss with them the relationship of what they are about to such pervasive national problems as tax structure, land reform, or literacy programs, rather than confining their conversations to professional and organizational questions with university and government officials.

The strength and acuteness of the response of our scholarly community to the place of the university in Latin America's social revolution will test the structure and sense of function of our universities as severely as those with which we cooperate. To date, the response of our universities and of the individual scholar within his professional organization is so slight in relation to the mass and energy of the challenge that it amounts to a policy of nonrecognition.

23

Developing Political Orientations
of Panamanian Students

Daniel Goldrich
Edward W. Scott

The intense and relatively continuous political involvement of youth is characteristic of most Latin American political systems. Within very recent years, students have played instrumental roles in the overthrow of dictatorships in Cuba and Venezuela, which perhaps marks their greatest success in a long history of demonstrations, strikes, and other activities in behalf of social or political reform. Currently, there is much speculation about the impact of Fidel Castro's 26th of July movement and of international communism on the political orientation of youth throughout the Latin American area. This impact has nowhere been systematically assessed, though the wave of "anti-*Yanqui*" feeling sweeping intellectual groups, and university circles in particular, has been described by at least one analyst.

A study of the political orientations among youth in Panama conducted in January 1960, affords an opportunity to estimate the impact of various ideologies and movements on this group in a Latin American "problem" area. The study also projects the question: how stable and salient are the political orientations developed in the school environment? After presentation of our findings, we will devote some attention to the role of the secondary school and other factors in the political socialization process in Panama.

As part of a comparative study of political socialization, two groups of Panamanian students were given a questionnaire. The first group attends a private school operated by a Catholic order, while the second attends a public secondary school. Both schools are in Panama City, which is the capital and major metropolitan center (approximately 200,000 population), dominating the country's economic, social, and political life. According to informants, the private school ranks as one of the three most socially elite in the city. Many top government officials send their children there. The public school is the largest, oldest, and most renowned of nine secondary institutions in the city which youth can attend at nominal tuition rates. Some of the country's present political leaders

From Daniel Goldrich and Edward W. Scott, "Developing Political Orientations of Panamanian Students," *Journal of Politics*, Vol. XXIII, No. 1 (February 1961). Reprinted by permission.

and reformers have attended it, and it has developed a reputation as a "nest of eagles." "Its tradition is liberal, democratic, anticlerical, and nationalistic."[1] The student body is predominantly of middle-and lower-class status. These schools were selected because (1) the future political elite and second-level administrators will probably be recruited largely from among their former students, and (2) in the case of the public school, the students are currently a factor in national politics.

For our present purpose, the sample consists of ninety-one eleventh-grade students, half from each school. This includes about two-thirds of all eleventh-grade students in the private school and one-tenth of that grade group in the public school. Both are representative of their grade groupings in the curriculum they follow, and there was no known bias in ability. We shall henceforth refer to the private school students as UC's (upper class) and to the public school students as MLC's (middle and lower class)....

The Findings

Dissatisfaction with the existing allocation of values has been a common characteristic of students and intellectuals in colonial and modernizing areas. As we will demonstrate below, both socioeconomic groups in our present sample reflect this general orientation. However, it has also seemed to characterize past generations of Panamanian students, the great proportion of which have ceased to seek basic reform upon their attainment of adult social roles. Thus, we must go further and try to assess the strength and stability of the

orientation. Are the students expressing adolescent rebellion, are their attitudes a function of youthful idealism (in both of which cases the orientation will prove transitory); or are they so alienated as to become affiliates of revolutionary movements in the future? The pattern of responses suggests that the strength of the orientation varies with socioeconomic status, and that its stability is a function of the relationships between the latter factor, career expectations and their future fulfillment, and nationalistic movements.

Social background

The reputational differentiation of the two schools is validated by data on the material situation of the students' families. Fifty-seven per cent of the UC families possess both an automobile and a television set, compared to but 22 per cent of the MLC families. Only 4 per cent of the former lacked possession of either of the objects, compared to 54 per cent of the latter group.[2]

Comparing the occupational aspirations of male students in the two groups,[3] we find about half of both preferring professional careers. Proportionally more of the UC's than MLC's want managerial or proprietarial positions, while the MLC's are disproportionally pointed toward technical, clerical, and teaching careers. Comparing preferences for careers in science (and

---

[1] John and Mavis Biesanz, *The People of Panama* (New York: Columbia University Press, 1955), p. 158.

[2] The probability value is beyond the .001 level; the N of UC's, 28, of MLC's, 41. The tests of significance in this report are chi-square, unless otherwise noted.

[3] All of the UC's are boys, but one-third of the MLC's are girls. In this report, where sex differences affect the data, they are discussed. Where they are not mentioned, the factor has been held constant and has been found not to account for an important part of the variation between the socioeconomic groups.

engineering) and in all other fields, we finds half the MLC's (including the girls) and only one-fifth of the UC's oriented to science (Table 1). On the whole, the MLC's express a relatively high level of aspiration for professional and scientific careers. If frustration emerging from blocked mobility drives is to be prevented, the social system must expand the number of opportunities to move into such positions. We will refer to the relationship between mobility aspirations and political orientations in our concluding section.

The high correlation between social status and political power that we have described in Panama is borne out in the data. Although an equal proportion of the UC's and MLC's said that a family member or relative had worked for the government and/or a political party, the families of the UC's were

involved at a much higher level of the political system. Almost half their familial political ties involved high elective and administrative positions, such as president, legislator, ambassador, or cabinet member. Less than a tenth of the MLC's political ties were at comparable levels.

Another indication of closer ties to the government on the part of the UC's is that they indirectly express fear of the police and the judiciary less than do the MLC's. Given a list of occupations (including doctor, lawyer, policeman judge, and others), the students were asked to indicate, which kinds of men "most people fear." Three-fourths of the UC's and 93 per cent of the male MLC's checked "police." Sixty-eight per cent of the former and 83 per cent of the latter checked "judge." This fear probably also reflects the experience of some MLC's in the May 1958 riots in

TABLE 1 Occupational Aspirations

	UC Per Cent	MLC Per Cent	Prob.[a]
Boys Only			
Professional	54	50	
Managerial and Proprietarial	18	4	.20—.10[b]
Clerical, Technical, Teaching	18	35	.20—.10
Other	10	11	
Total	100	100	
N	(39)	(26)	
Boys and Girls			
Science and Engineering	21	48	
Other	79	52	
			.02—.01
Total	100	100	
N	(40)	(39)	

a Because of the small size of the sample, only differences between the UC's and MLC's of over ten per cent are tested for statistical significance. A percentage difference smaller than this is considered theoretically unimportant. In this and following tables, N less than sample size results from eliminating from the analysis all respondents who failed to answer the particular question.

b We are testing the significance of the difference between UC's and MLC's with regard to each category of occupation run against the sum of the others.

which several of their classmates were killed.

Political involvement

The pattern of political involvement of the two groups does not clearly establish the MLC's as more politicized, despite their reputation. Approximately two-thirds of each group express a great deal of interest in what the government does, and about one-tenth of each say they have actually participated in a political campaign or other political activities (Table 2). The UC's discuss "what the government does" "often" with family and/or friends somewhat more than do the MLC's. Conversely, a composite index of mentions of news stories that were "interesting," "pleasing," and "displeasing" shows more political response by MLC's than by UC's. A somewhat higher proportion of the MLC's mentioned some aspect of Panamanian politics and of international politics, while proportionally three times as many UC's as MLC's mentioned no political news.

Political efficacy

The two groups are about equally politicized, but their modes of expressing this involvement differ. The UC's are conspicuous in their abstention from the riots and demonstrations in which the MLC's gain their political reputation. As a measure of political efficacy, we asked for an evaluation of the role of students in politics. The UC's gave a much more positive evaluation of their role: 37 per cent said it was very important compared to only 18 per cent of the MLC's; 31 per cent said it was unimportant compared to 49 per cent of the MLC's. The tendency of MLC's to discount the students' role suggests the possibility that the MLC's are frustrated politically. The public activi-

ties for which they are noted do not bring them much power.

Political and politically relevant orientations

We expected that the UC's would have more traditional sociopolitical value orientations than the MLC's. The pattern of responses concerning religion tends to confirm the hypothesis. Asked "which of the following types of people are important," a much higher proportion of the UC's checked "priest" (Table 3). The occupation of priest was selected as personally desirable by one-fifth of the UC's and almost none of the MLC's. Asked to "name a person you want to be like," one quarter of the UC's and one-tenth of the MLC's made a positive reference to a religious figure.

Interest in scientific developments serves as another index of traditionalism. The MLC's are far more alert to news in the field of science, particularly rocketry. Almost half of them mentioned a news item concerning some aspect of scientific progress, compared to one-seventh of the UC's. One-third of the MLC's mentioned science in the context of the Cold War, compared to one-tenth of the UC's. This interest, then, indicates a greater awareness of factors of general social change on the part of the MLC's.

The relative traditionalism of the UC's appears again in responses to a battery of questions concerning domestic political orientations, although it is much less pronounced than we expected. The students were given a check list and asked "which of the following would do the best job in government": large landowners and big businessmen, Communists, middle class, students, ordinary people without much money, and labor unions. The

TABLE 2   Indices of Political Involvement

	UC Per Cent	MLC Per Cent	Prob.
Very much interested in what government does	65	64	
N	(39)	(45)	
Often discuss what government does, with family and/or friends	56	47	
N	(39)	(45)	
Has participated in political campaign or other activity	14	11[a]	
N	(28)	(27)	
Mention of political news stories			
Panamanian politics	44	57	.30—.20
International politics	41	59	.20—.10
No mention of politics	28	9	.05—.02
N	(39)	(44)	

[a] Data on MLC boys only.

TABLE 3   Indices of Traditionalism

	UC	MLC	Prob.
Religious Orientation			
Per cent checking "priest" as important	84	60	.02—.01
N	(43)	(45)	
Per cent checking occupation of priest as personally desirable	19	2	.02—.01
N	(36)	(45)	
Per cent making reference to religious figure as ego ideal	26	11	.10—.05
N	(46)	(45)	
Scientific Orientation			
Per cent mentioning news story in field of science	15	48	.01—.001
N	(39)	(44)	
Per cent mentioning news story about science in context of Cold War	10	34	.01—.001
N	(39)	(44)	

following question asked which of these groups would do the "worst job in government."

Unexpectedly, the two groups of students agreed in their rank order: the middle class and labor unions were ranked most favorably, the Communists least favorably (Table 4.) There was slightly more support among the UC's for landowners and merchants, and more support by the MLC's for the middle class. The only large and statistically significant differences occur in the negative responses. Sixty per cent of the MLC's believe the landowners and merchants would do the worst job in government, compared to 29 per cent of the UC's. Ninety per cent of the UC's nominate Communists as "the worst," compared to two-thirds of the MLC's.

Over-all, there is a total lack of sup-

port for communism on this index. The UC's negative orientation to that group is far in excess of that directed to any other. But the MLC's express almost as much rejection of landowners and merchants as of the Communists. If they are anti-Communist, they are almost equally opposed to the traditional oligarchical domination of the government.

The responses of the UC's were more liberal than would have been predicted from their social background and their ties to occupants of high governmental positions. A factor that seems to account for most of the UC's liberal responses on the foregoing item is distance from family. Among those UC's who say that they would rather be with their friends or by themselves than with their family, 75 per cent positively check "labor union" or "ordinary people with-

TABLE 4   Desirable and Undesirable Groups in the Government

	UC Per Cent	MLC Per Cent	Prob.
Which of the following would do the best job in the government? (Mark as many as you wish.)			
Middle class	60	77	.10—.05
Labor unions	46	54	
Students	26	30	
Ordinary people without much money	23	18	
Large landowners and big businessmen	17	7	.20—.10
Communists	0	4	
N	(35)	(44)	
Which of the following would do the worst job in the government? (Mark as many as you wish.)			
Communists	91	67	.01—.001
Large landowners and big businessmen	29	60	.01—.001
Ordinary people without much money	20	31	.30—.20
Students	14	24	.30—.20
Labor unions	11	4	
Middle class	3	0	
N	(35)	(45)	

TABLE 5   Perception of the Most Important National Problems

	UC	MLC	Prob.
Per cent referring to following problems:[a]			
Unemployment	12	30	.20—.10
Poverty	12	32	.10—.05
Minimum Wage	48	57	
Canal Zone	28	27	
Politics and Government	12	32	.10—.05
N	(25)	(37)	

[a] All responses were coded, so the percentages total more than 100.

out much money"; while among those who indicate closeness to family, only 47 per cent check these categories. Furthermore, there is a strong association between liberal response and having a family member or relative in government and/or a party. One hypothesis is that rebellion against parents is manifested in deviant political beliefs among children in families where politics is salient. Our numbers are too small, however, to make a real test of this hypothesis.

On additional indices, the MLC's express a more liberal attitude on economic and social matters than do the UC's. Ninety per cent of the MLC's favor government's giving food to the poor, compared to 75 per cent of the UC's. Asked "what are the major problems facing the country," one-third of the MLC's and one-eighth of the UC's mention unemployment and poverty (Table 5). The minimum wage issue is mentioned by a somewhat larger proportion of the MLC's than of the UC's. Approximately one quarter of both groups give recognition to the Canal Zone and sovereignty.

On this same item, we find more concern with the existing political system among the MLC's than among their upper-class counterparts. One-third of the former and only one-eighth of the latter mention some aspect of politics per se as among the most important national problems.

As this suggests, the attitude of the MLC's toward the political process is a good deal more disapproving than that of the UC's. Asked whether they "liked," "disliked," or were "indifferent" to "politicians," the MLC's expressed a substantially more negative point of view than the UC's. Sixteen per cent of the former and 29 per cent of the latter selected the positive alternative, while 42 per cent of the former and 21 per cent of the latter selected the negative alternative.

The students were also asked whether politics is "honest" or "dishonest," "work" or "play," and whether it "helps the country" or "hurts the country." The MLC's consistently more negative assessment of politics may reflect their relative inability (or their families' inability) to influence the making of public policy.[4] Differences

[4] It is interesting to note that, while they are less negative than the MLC's, the UC's express considerably more disapproval of the political process than does a socially heterogeneous sample of Canal Zone students from the same grade level. This indicates that there is a greater according of legitimacy to the United States political system by the latter than the former accord to the Panamanian system.

between UC's and MLC's take on added significance when we examine data on this orientation for fourth- and eighth-grade students attending the UC and MLC schools (Table 6). From this, we can see that, for whatever reason, the UC's become more positively disposed toward the political process at successive grade levels, while the MLC's become just the opposite. Although the direction of the change is not perfectly linear, it is substantial and dramatic. We conclude that the UC's adjust positively to the prevailing political relationships over time, while the MLC's increasingly reject them. We will project this line of development in our discussion of the stability of the reformist orientation.

Evaluation of major public officials followed much the same pattern. Three-fourths of the MLC's said the president was doing a bad job, compared to a little over half of the UC's (Table 7).

Thirty-eight per cent of the UC's said the National Assembly was doing a good job compared to 14 per cent of the MLC's. The two groups agreed that a bad job had been done by the Chief of the National Guard (resented for his part in the subjugation of the bloody May 1958 riots).

A high proportion of both groups (about 80 per cent) agree that it is important which party wins elections. Both indicate overwhelmingly that they would vote against the party in power (CPN), although there is much more opposition, among the MLC's than the UC's. Fifty-seven per cent of the MLC's oppose the CPN and 5 per cent support it, while 41 per cent of the UC's oppose it and 21 per cent support it. Because of the nature of the item, we cannot determine which opposition party or group the antigovernment students would support. The hostile orientation of the MLC's to the

TABLE 6   Evaluation of the Political Process by School and Grade

	UC Grade			MLC Grade		
	4	8	11[a]	4	8	11
Per cent responding that politics(is):						
Honest	41	32	50	59	32	19
Dishonest	41	23	25	8	23	39
Don't know	18	45	25	33	45	42
Total	100	100	100	100	100	100
N	(44)	(44)	(28)	(39)	(53)	(36)
Work	55	40	62	76	50	43
Play	20	38	28	17	22	33
Don't Know	25	22	10	7	28	24
Total	100	100	100	100	100	100
N	(40)	(40)	(29)	(42)	(46)	(33)
Helps the Country	58	51	69	80	51	38
Hurts the Country	42	28	19	16	24	30
Don't Know	0	21	12	4	25	32
Total	100	100	100	100	100	100
N	(43)	(53)	(32)	(51)	(55)	(37)

[a] Probability of the difference between UC and MLC eleventh graders is between .05 and .02 on the first item, between .30 and .20 on the second, and between .05 and .02 on the third.

TABLE 7   Evaluation of Major Government Officials

	UC	MLC	Prob.[a]
Per cent responding that :			
President			
Doing a good job	44	23	
Doing a bad job	53	75	
Don't know	3	2	
			.05—.02
Total	100	100	
N	(34)	(44)	
National Assembly			
Doing a good job	38	14	
Doing a bad job	59	75	
Don't know	3	11	
			.05—.02
Total	100	100	
N	(34)	(44)	
Chief of National Guard			
Doing a good job	23	25	
Doing a bad job	57	57	
Don't know	20	18	
Total	100	100	
N	(35)	(44)	

a "Don't Know" responses are eliminated for the purpose of testing the significance of the differences.

existing political process, however, suggests the hypothesis that they would not identify as strongly as the UC's with specific opposition parties because, as we have indicated, the latter represent only other elements of the oligarchy. Though we lack data to test this hypothesis directly, it is notable that a considerably smaller proportion of the MLC's than the UC's (64 per cent compared to 90 per cent) express an intention to vote on attainment of voting age.

Our data show that the MLC's are as highly politicized as the UC's, but they perceive themselves as less efficacious politically; they are more alert to general social change and less directed by tradition than the UC's; more liberal on social and economic issues; more negatively disposed toward the political process and the dominant sociopolitical group; and less inclined to vote than the UC's. Among these factors, the feeling of powerlessness and the rejection of the existing political order indicate the presence of a condition of political alienation. The concept is defined as "a combination of perceived lack of power in community affairs and distrust of those who hold power positions. . . ."[5] But these alienated MLC's have not withdrawn from politics. They are activists and they have a conception of changes to be made in the social order.

How do external political factors,

5Wayne E. Thompson and John E. Horton, "Political Alienation as a Force in Political Action," *Social Forces,* XXXVIII (March 1960), 195.

TABLE 8   Desired Changes Concerning the Canal or Canal Zone

	UC	MLC	Prob.
Per cent suggesting the following changes : [a]			
Nationalization	24	19	
Internationalization	3	5	
Recognition of Panamanian sovereignty;			
more rights for Panamanians in Zone	29	40	.50—.30
Economic gains for Panama	29	29	
Change in U. S. administrators or in U. S. attitudes	9	17	
No change	21	14	
N	(34)	(42)	

[a] All responses were tabulated, so the percentages total more than 100.

ideologies, and events impinge on the relatively alienated MLC's and relatively nonalienated UC's?

Orientation toward external political figures, groups, and events

Both groups of students are sensitized to the Canal Zone issue. Over 80 per cent would make some change with regard to the Zone. There is not much difference between the two groups in direction of the desired change, though the MLC's seem somewhat more concerned with "sovereignty" than the UC's (Table 8).

The two groups share a view of two United States officials. Three-fifths of both evaluate President Eisenhower as doing a good job, and only one-fifth take a negative view. Canal Zone Gov-

TABLE 9   References to Nationalist and Revolutionary Figures and Events

	UC Per Cent	MLC Per Cent	Prob.
Names in the news :			
Boyd			
Neutral identification	76	62	
Positive identification	8	38	
Negative identification	16	0	
			.04
Total	100	100	
N	(25)	(34)	
Castro			
Neutral identification	46	45	
Positive identification	36	50	
Negative identification	18	5	.07
Total	100	100	
N	(28)	(42)	
Composite mentions of Castro, Cuban Revolution,			
fall of Latin American dictators,			
and the nationalization of the Suez Canal			
Positive mentions	13	31	
None or negative mentions	87	69	
			.05—.02
Total	100	100	
N	(46)	(45)	

ernor Potter, however, is opposed by over 75 per cent, while virtually none support him. On both these indices, the two groups of students are agreed. But, asked to identify, as a name in the news, Aquilino Boyd (a prominent politician who played a role in the November 1959 riot in the Zone), the MLC's express both more sensitivity on the "sovereignty" issue and more positive identification with an extremely nationalistic politician. Thirty-eight per cent of the MLC's made a positive reference to Boyd, compared to 8 per cent of the UC's. None of the former made a negative reference, compared to 16 per cent of the latter (Table 9).

The students were asked whether they "liked," "disliked," or felt "indifferent" toward North Americans, Cubans, and Russians. Overall, the MLC's and UC's made the same rankings among the three nationality groups: they favored Cubans, North Americans, and Russians, in descending order. The MLC's, however, made less of a differentiation between North Americans and Russians and are a great deal more favorable toward Cubans than are the UC's (Table 10).

The MLC's strong identification with Cubans may be an expression of Latin American solidarity and/or an affirmation of sympathy for recent political developments in Cuba. When they were asked to identify Fidel Castro's name in the news, the MLC's responded considerably more positively than did the UC's (Table 9). From responses to another series of open-ended items on news stories and ego ideals, a tabulation was made of positive references toward Castro, other leftist Latin American revolutionaries and revolutionary events, plus such relevant events as the nationalization of the Suez Canal. Over twice the proportion of MLC's as UC's (31 per cent to 13 per cent) made a positive reference to these revolutionary figures or events.

TABLE 10   Attitudes Toward Cubans, North Americans, and Russians

	UC Per Cent	MLC Per Cent	Prob.
Cubans			
Like	23	51	
Indifferent	56	47	
Don't Like	21	2	
			01—.001[a]
Total	100	100	
N	(34)	(43)	
North America			
Like	21	32	
Indifferent	61	39	
Don't Like	18	29	
Total	100	100	
N	(33)	(44)	
Russians			
Like	18	26	
Indifferent	43	36	
Don't Like	39	38	
Total	100	100	
N	(33)	(42)	

a "Indifferent" responses are eliminated in the test of significance of differences.

In sum, these findings suggest that alienation from the domestic political system is associated in some degree with a positive attitude toward new symbols: Castro, Cuba, Boyd. Whether this displacement of political identification will facilitate the rise of a new Panamanian counterelite with ideological bases in social reconstruction and nationalism, as in Cuba, cannot as yet be determined. However, the existence of a set of positive symbols about which to rally a political opposition movement is probably a necessary though not sufficient factor in the success of the latter.

The Stability of the Reformist Orientation

In our introduction to Panamanian politics, we stated that students have been virtually the only continuously active reform-minded group in the society. This, of course, suggests that students have discarded their roles as active dissidents as they assume adult roles. Does it matter, then, for the Panamanian political system that its educated youth is reformist?

Let us take first the case of the UC's. Though many are cognizant of economic and social problems facing the country, though a large proportion believe that new economic and social groups would do a good job in the government, and though many oppose the party in power, there are several factors that suggest that this group of students will probably not actively express nor perhaps even maintain these orientations as they assume adult roles in the society. They are the sons and relatives of men who hold high positions in the government and in the social and economic structure. This alone assures many of easy entrance to white-collar work and *"botellas"* should they desire it. Their connections will facilitate the movement of others into choice commercial operations. Others will be able to acquire professional status because their families can afford to sustain them through extended university training. Aside from these "social background" factors, there is the fact that the UC's tend to accept the present political order as legitimate. Most of them like or feel indifferent to politicians as a group. Most of them perceive the government as honest, hardworking, and helpful to the country. Furthermore, the incidence of this positive orientation among the UC's seems to increase with age. Because of all these factors, it would not be surprising if their reformism declined in salience as they become more immersed in adult social, economic, and political roles.

It is more difficult to speculate about the MLC's as they leave their second-ary-school environment. They are so disdainful of the leading politicians, so desirous of social and political reform, and so renowned for their overt demonstrations of discontent that one might expect them to continue to manifest some of these same orientations and behaviors in adult life. Indeed, some of the past generations of MLC's who have gone on to the university have manifested those attitudes through participation in student political associations. But the most significant fact about these former MLC's is that the great bulk cease to make demands for reform after highschool or university graduation. How does the social system absorb them? The following hypotheses, developed from conversations with Panamanian students and from analysis of the literature on the subject, will be tested in future research.

Many of the MLC's upon graduation go immediately into the job market. Seeking white-collar positions, many go to work for the government, whose swollen bureaucracy is one of the major sources of such employment. Though overt adherence to the governing party may not be a condition of public employment, active support of reform movements appears to serve as an informal disqualification. Since many of the MLC's are poor and must contribute to the support of their families, and since white-collar positions confer much-desired middle-class status, these MLC's appear to accept the political requirements of the job. That is, the occupational situation becomes a primary agent of political socialization, and the former role of student-reformer is held in abeyance, if not sloughed off.

Of those MLC's who go to the university, many attend as part-time or evening students, holding a job during the day. Thus, their time and energy is a resource in short supply, and for many, politics is not as important a consideration as academic progress, maintenance of income, and expectation of future mobility. This is particularly true for those in this category who work for the government.

Another factor that may contribute to the decline of political activity among some MLC's at the university is that this environment is not as politically homogeneous as their high school had been. Because there is an admixture of social classes and urban and rural residents, there is more likelihood of being exposed to different political points of view. Furthermore, the cohesion among students at the high school is weakened at the university. Former friendship groups are dispersed among day and evening classes and among several curricula; some of the members will have gone to foreign universities, while others will not have chosen or been able to choose higher education.

This analysis suggests that the process of political socialization must be broadly conceived, so as to relate the development of orientations and behavior to role acquisition in the larger social system. Despite the intensely political, reformist orientations developed by the MLC's in the secondary-school environment, such orientations have not served as stimuli to political action in the adult lives of past MLC generations. Social mobility and security in employment appear to become paramount values with the acquisition of adult roles.

Under what conditions might the MLC's reformist orientations continue to be expressed in adult life?

A large proportion of the MLC's expressed aspirations for professional and technical employment. Their high school stresses scientific preparation, and many seek careers in science, engineering, and medicine. One condition that might promote radically-oriented

political activity among MLC graduates would be the closure or limitation of opportunities for entry into professional careers, a situation that may be developing in Panama.

A recent official report indicates that Panama now devotes 23.9 per cent of its annual budget to education, which is probably among the largest percentage investments in education of all the Latin American countries. Another report shows Panama's high ranking among the twenty Latin America republics in teachers per thousand population (third), primary-school enrollment (second), secondary-school enrollment (second), higher-education enrollment (fourth), and literacy (fifth). A rapidly increasing number of students is filling the public high schools and the university; thus the number of people educated for white-collar, technical, and professional employment is growing. Economic growth, however, is not occurring at a substantial rate. Consequently, the situation may be one of imbalance in the process of "modernization." It has been hypothesized that the elements of modernization are functionally interdependent, and that imbalance among them tends to accelerate social and political disorganization. In this case, overproduction of people trained for professional and technical positions may generate frustration that will find an outlet in revolutionary political activity, particularly since many of the frustrated are also politically alienated.

Frustrated mobility aspirations may also promote further identification with and support for those extranational political movements which promise rapid economic development and a hastening of a new social order. Fidel Castro clearly has a positive image among the MLC's. To the extent that he can continue to cast the aura of success around the Cuban Revolution, he and his revolution may become an even stronger reference point among alienated Panamanian intellectuals, particularly as the Canal Zone issue waxes ever more inflammatory. The same phenomenon may also occur with regard to the Egyptians flaunting the "imperialists" and nationalizing the Suez Canal. The single and combined efforts of the Cuban and Egyptian diplomatic corps in Panama seem designed to elevate these nations' recent experiences as a model for Panamanians. The MLC's alertness to scientific advance and Russian success in missile development suggests that one potential basis exists for identification with Russia as an agency of general social change.

On the other hand, there is over-all a negative orientation toward communism among both groups of students presently. Furthermore, the MLC's assume in many respects the classic stance of those seeking middle-class status rather than a social revolution. While these students tend currently to express some support for Fidel Castro, his increasingly threatening posture toward middle-class values in his own country may, in time, abate his attraction for these Panamanian middle-class aspirants. The abatement may the more readily occur should the latter come to associate Castro with communism. However, there is a perception, widespread in Latin America, that United States policy-makers are irrationally pre-occupied with communism. Consequently, current attempts in the United States to link Castro with that movement will probably lessen the likelihood that Panamanians will see him in this manner.

Summary

A picture has been presented of two student groups in Panama. The groups differ in socioeconomic status, and each has a relatively high probability of acquiring elite political roles, depending on developments within the social and political systems. The students' political orientations have been analyzed and related to social background, the political system, and the process of acquisition of adult social roles. We have found the upper-class group to be more liberal than was expected. However, inasmuch as these students (1) tend to accept the existing political process and (2) have relatively easy access to desirable social and political roles by virtue of their social background and familial political connections, it is unlikely that their current reformism will continue as a stable, salient orientation.

The middle- and lower-class group express more liberal and more reformist orientations. Past generations of graduates from this politically renowned secondary school who, as students, had gained the reputation of reformers and dissidents have since been absorbed, coopted, and neutralized by the political and social systems. Since the present group of students from this school are (1) upwardly mobile, (2) aspirant to careers in science and related fields, (3) but face stiffer competition for such positions as a function of a growing imbalance in the factors of social modernization, and (4) since they tend to reject the existing political process, it is likely that their current orientations may prove both stable and salient. The probability of this is heightened, to an undetermined degree, by the fact that these students have available and tend to identify with new, revolutionary figures and movements. The latter, in turn, are seeking to activate Panama's alienated intellectual and youth groups. This is occurring at a time when relations between Panama and the traditionally resented United States are seriously deteriorating, so that nationalism is accelerating the pressures for social change.

24

Labor and Politics:
Problems and Prospects

Moisés Poblete Troncoso
Ben G. Burnett

Although the nature and degree of trade-union development varies greatly among the Latin American nations, organized labor enjoys an increasing vitality and importance which place it squarely in the center of social elements competing for power. The aristocracy, clergy, and military are losing their near monopoly of political supremacy. Indeed, labor's influence in some countries —perhaps best typified by Argentina, Chile, Cuba, and Mexico—is so considerable that the traditional triarchy has been obliged to alter its methodology appreciably in order to contend with the young giant. This changing pattern is similar in its intensity, if not in its scope, in several other nations. And whenever basic freedoms widen, a sizable middle class arises, and the army and police assume apolitical roles, organized labor emerges as a vital, if not always welcome, sound in the voice of the electorate.

If organized labor is to play an ever more important role in national politics —as seems to be the case—it is only

From Moisés Poblete Troncoso and Ben G. Burnett, *The Rise of the Latin American Labor Movement* (New York: Bookman Associates, 1960). Reprinted by permission.

the logical outgrowth of many conditioning factors which have imbued the Latin American trade-union movement with a political coloration almost from its inception. Much of this emphasis is a legacy of the early leaders, the European radicals. Anarchists, Syndicalists, Socialists, and, later, Communists preached doctrines which emphasized a different function for government from that conceived by the conservative triarchy. According to the liberal trade-unionists, government would be instrumental in altering society to their desired images—an end which put them in direct contention with the conservatives for state control.

As has been discussed in earlier chapters, the history of these liberal elements coincides with the growth of Latin American trade-unionism itself. Anarchists wielded notable influence in labor's early efforts to organize in Argentina, Chile, Mexico, Peru, and Uruguay. The Syndicalists acquired a certain following in these and other countries. In time, however, the Socialists staked out the strongest claim to speak for organized labor in most areas of Latin America, though they suffered numerous reversals during the 1930's and 1940's at the hands of their major rival,

Communists, and by the 1950's were beset with impressive competition from Catholic, Peronist, and other newly formed groups. But irrespective of the doctrinal inclination of these rival elements, they almost universally kept at least one foot in the political process.

In many instances, especially before World War I, trade-unions inserted in their bylaws an announcement that they would remain aloof from politics and that none of their leaders could hold public office. Nevertheless, in order to counterbalance the triarchy's political hegemony, more than one labor official chose to champion his companions' cause in government. CROM's Luis Morones, who rose to cabinet responsibility in the Mexican government, is an outstanding example.

Latin American trade-unionism also has become embroiled in politics because of a rather general consciousness of class status. This is not surprising in lands where great differences in wealth prevail. As the working classes formed into organized groups seeking a greater share of national income, their class-conscious feelings were intensified. Thus, even when a union's basic policy eschewed intervention in the political process, it was drawn into politics in order to attack a conservative coalition which held the bulk of personal wealth and which could subvert labor's efforts to attain or enlarge their freedom to strike and to bargain collectively.

Such political overtones lend a certain uniqueness to the Latin American labor scene, while serving trade-unionism with some of its most perplexing problems. For at the same time that labor's demands become interwoven with political questions, the interests of its leaders tend to transcend such day-to-day matters as contracts, choosing instead the fame or associated rewards attainable at the political level. Of course, this partially explains the gen-erally primitive nature of collective bargaining in Latin America and, coupled with the general awareness of class status, only widens the gap between the working and upper classes. Thus, to negotiate a working arrangement directly with management is often viewed with disdain as an example of collaboration with an enemy group.

Another aspect of labor's problematic entanglement in politics is the propensity to stress rights and achievements and to ignore duties. Such an absence of the concept of responsibility—whether to the nation or to the industry —often finds organized labor seeking wage increases and other benefits at a time when the government is earnestly attempting to curb inflation and related difficulties to the ultimate benefit of the working classes as well as the rest of society. In several countries, Bolivia being a good contemporary illustration, labor's insistence upon pursuing major gains at a time when the nation is experiencing chronic economic crises only serves to tarnish the name of trade-unionism and to accentuate the critical hardships already prevalent in these nations. This is not meant necessarily to deny the legitimacy of labor's demands, but merely to question the timeliness and emphasis of the workers' insistence upon their rights in many instances.

Still another problem which labor often faces because of its involvement in the political process is its participation (or the danger of its participation) in extremist or demagogic movements. Every society experiences its Pied Pipers, who seek to lead the gullible and the discontented along devious roads to power. And in Latin America, where labor ordinarily is inextricably enmeshed in political machinations, the possibility of nefarious or, at the very least, unfortunate associations, detrimental to labor's best interests, presents an ever present problem. Certainly Perón's rise to political power in Argentina and his striking proficiency in convincing the workers that the aspirations they espoused were his own underscores the currentness of this dilemma.

By the same token, there is always the figure of alien extremism lurking on the horizon—today attired in the cloak of communism. It goes without saying that a principal target of international communism is organized labor. And the Latin American working classes have been no exception. Indeed, communism has scored impressive gains at various stages of trade-union evolution —even to the point of dominating given national labor movements.

Compounding the problematic aspects of labor's involvement in political processes is its relationship to government. For in most instances, government constitutes a major, if not the most important, external influence on trade-union organization and activities. Thus, labor groups seeking recognition may be obligated to turn to government for such acceptance, being compelled to meet certain requirements established and enforced by government. Even after recognition, organized labor generally must subscribe to certain government-dictated practices which spell out the proper uses and handling of their funds, union elections, internal structure, and countless related matters. And sometimes as a practical matter, other times in accordance with law, the labor ministry or the president's office itself provides the facilities for collective bargaining between workers and management. Finally, governmental mechanisms are even responsible for precluding certain categories of workers from union membership. Occasionally, agricultural workers fall under this classification but more often it is the government employees who are forbidden participation in trade-unions.

This dependence of organized labor upon government, a situation which is widely prevalent throughout Latin America, has led numerous observers to consider the merits and defects of such a relationship. Unquestionably, there is much that can be said in favor of governmental ministration. First of all, some labor movements were created out of whole cloth by a governing regime. Mexico furnishes a notable example of this. An agrarian nation with no important labor organizations until the end of World War I, it witnessed an overnight transformation on the labor scene as trade-unions were formed under governmental tutelage to serve in the vanguard against foreign-held industry. In the ensuing decades, labor prospered under a friendly government and, at the same time, provided the ruling regime with its principal organizational strength.

A second advantage which labor has derived from a sympathetic government is in the area of labor and social legislation. The Vargas regime in Brazil and Peronist Argentina, among others, enacted an impressive array of statutes and decrees aimed at improving the working and living conditions of the working classes. Minimum wages, maximum hours, pensions, paid vacations, severance pay, medical aid, and similar benefits accrued to the workers as recompense for their support of the state. In other countries, too, governmental initiative, rather than any struggle on the part of the workers, brought about such major economic and social achievements.

Finally, perhaps, something can be said for the government-labor alliance on democratic grounds. That is to say that the very existence of an organized labor movement, which in many instances would not have appeared when it did without government patronage or assistance, offers a new mass organization to challenge the traditional oligarchy. In many instances, economic, social, and political power had resided in the hands of a few conservative elements for centuries. Now, often for the first time, the basis of power was broadened. And even in those countries where political freedoms were sacrificed for immediate economic gains, the very fact that the working classes were brought into the political picture—voting, running candidates for office, and performing similar active roles in the political process—enhanced their political literacy and portended well for the time when civil liberties would be restored. Just as this new political awareness gave the working classes an ability to articulate, it is to be hoped that political maturation will wean them away from the authoritarianism which nurtured them and into democratic processes.

Of course, there are at least as many hazards in the government-labor partnership as there are benefits. For one thing, as mentioned above, trade-unionism may lose the right to determine its own course of action by being denied, often with the rest of society, basic civil liberties. Again, Vargas' Brazil and Perón's Argentina exemplify this dilemma. Furthermore, not only did the government-supported unions become little more than appendages of the state, but those labor groups which had the temerity to oppose the ruling clique soon found their treasuries plundered, their leaders imprisoned or exiled, and their normal activities severely curbed or halted. Legitimate functions were perverted to the will of the governing mechanism and even when in the long run a more widely organized labor movement evolved, the immediate effect was disastrous to ordinary, day-to-day operations.

Another danger stems from the fact that when labor aligns itself with a political movement it must face the inevitable possibility of loss of governmental control. Moreover, the new regime may be unsympathetic to organized labor and, in fact, may view trade-unionism with especial harshness because of its political ties. In large measure, the *Confederación de Trabajadores de Colombia,* which despite internal dissension had dominated Colombian labor under sympathetic Liberal governments, collapsed completely late in the 1940's in the face of an unfriendly Conservative regime.

Finally, labor's fealty to political causes tends to obscure its normal economic functions. Instead of pursuing gains by means of negotiation with management and seeking to put its own house in order, trade-unionism assumes a curious standard of values, blending its demands for economic and social achievement with the fortunes of a political cause. Too often, what is good for the working classes becomes distorted into what is desirable for sustaining a clique in government. In addition, splits on the political level frequently are transmitted into factionalism among union leadership. Power struggles ensue, cleavages develop, and the legitimate ends of labor are reduced to secondary or tertiary importance.

Clearly, there is much to be found on both sides of the ledger of government-labor relations. However, one fact stands out and that is the expanse and constancy of government's penetration into trade-union matters in Latin America. And whether it is good or bad in the long-term view, few labor movements are able to avoid becoming embroiled in political processes.

It seems notably true, then, that any conclusion regarding the future of Latin American trade-unionism must be based upon a recognition of the inordinately strong political currents in which it has run and is running in these countries. But at the same time, there are intriguing signs to indicate that a new development in labor's evolution is now underway in several areas which may alter this traditional entanglement with politics. For there are earmarks in certain nations—Mexico stands out—that the phase in labor-government relations where the state fosters, controls, and enjoys the support of organized labor is passing into a stage where unions are seeking freedom from the dictates of government and are stressing collective bargaining and related activities. This phenomenon is particularly observable in those nations which have experienced a wide social and economic revolution.

Thus, at the same time that progressive legislation is enacted and fully operative, the standard of living is improved, and unions become financially independent, there is a lessening inclination on trade-unionism's part to take up the cudgels of a political cause.

Should such a transition become more widespread and substantial, future chroniclers of hemispheric unionism may mark this as a tremendously important new phase—one in which organized labor in Latin America will have approached a measure of maturation commensurate with its counterparts in western Europe and the United States.

25

Civil-Military Relations in Latin America

L. N. McAlister

It is hardly necessary to assert that the armed forces have been important factors in the historical development of the nations of Latin America. By bringing into association men from all parts of the national territory, by posing as the incarnation of the national spirit, and by teaching patriotism and exalting national virtues, they have been a significant influence in overcoming regionalism and localism. By providing an avenue for advancement for members of lower social strata, they have encouraged social mobility. In many countries they have contributed to the transition from traditional to modern societies through their work in constructing communications systems, their emphasis on general and technical education within their ranks, and by their demands for industrialization. In the political sphere they have repeatedly overthrown the governments that created them; generals have employed the forces entrusted to them to make themselves heads of state; military fac-

tions have intervened in the political process in support of specific economic objectives or of broader ideologies. In a less spectacular fashion, the armed forces acting through political parties, as in Mexico, or through officers occupying cabinet posts have exerted powerful influences on public policy.

These facts are generally recognized and a great deal has been written about Latin American "militarism." Existing literature, however, raises some serious conceptual and methodological problems. These may be defined by posing and commenting on a series of questions. In the first place, do the interrelations between the military and society at large constitute a discrete sociological and historical problem susceptible to systematic description and analysis? Some scholars concerned with general principles of social organization and with the history or sociology of regions other than Latin America have conceived of them in this fashion. Max Weber and later Gaetano Mosca recognized the importance of military factors in shaping societies and developed concepts and methods for dealing with the problem. Subsequently historians and social scientists have refined

From L. N. McAlister, "Civil-Military Relations in Latin America," *Journal of Inter-American Studies,* Vol. III, No. 3 (July 1961). Reprinted by permission.

and expanded the ideas of Weber and Mosca and produced a substantial body of literature dealing with these interrelationships in general and with their manifestations in the United States, Germany, Japan, the Middle East, and Southeast Asia.

Perhaps because of their more obvious and immediate nature, the political and administrative aspects of this problem have been stressed, that is, the distribution of power within the state between civil and military elements. This area of study is commonly called "civil-military relations." The range of civil-military relations extends from situations in which civil authority is supreme to the direct and forcible usurpation of power by the military for nonmilitary ends.

The political role of the armed forces has likewise been stressed in Latin America. In general, however, Latin Americanists have been unwilling or unable to face up to the nature of interrelations between the military and civil elements of the state. The recent publications of Edwin Lieuwen, Víctor Alba, and Theodore Wyckoff are exceptions to this generalization. Much of Latin American history has been written in terms of "Progress toward Democracy" or "The Struggle for Democracy." Within this teleological system the armed forces are regarded as "Obstacles to the Achievement of Democracy." Now no right-thinking person would deny that democracy is a desirable goal and it would be mean-spirited indeed not to wish the Latin Americans success in their struggle toward it. Yet, this conceptual framework encourages simplistic interpretations and explanations. The military is conceived of as a force external to and interfering with "normal" historical processes rather than as an integral element in them. In this position it can conveniently be regarded as a constant whose importance is recognized and accepted but which need not be described or analyzed systematically.

Second, if the importance of the military as a power factor in Latin America is accepted and the nature of its relations with the civil elements of the state can be regarded as a discrete historical and sociological problem, what is the scope of the problem and how may it be defined? The most commonly used term to describe the role of the armed forces in Latin America is "militarism." In the sense that it means the use of military force or threat of force to achieve nonmilitary ends, it is adequate. It has, however, two disadvantages. To many scholars it has a more specific usage, that is, a system or way of life which glorifies war, in which the military is a high-status profession, in which an entire nation is oriented toward military virtues and mores, and which has strong imperialist overtones. Such a system may have existed in Paraguay during the dictatorship of Francisco Solano López, and the GOU in Argentina may have aspired to it. It has, however, been atypical of Latin America. Also, it does not cover instances in which armed forces have been nonpolitical and, if the problem is to be viewed broadly, such instances also require description and analysis. Another commonly used expression is "the army in politics," but this term also excludes situations where the military has been nonpolitical. Moreover, it seems rather too mild an expression with which to describe the praetorian excesses of some Latin American armies in the nineteenth century. "Civil-military relations" is also open to the latter criticism. It is, however, comprehensive enough to cover the range of phenomena involved in the problem and its accepted usage elsewhere is an argument for its adoption by Latin Americanists.

Third, what is the structure of the problem? As H. Stuart Hughes remarks, historians are reluctant to make distinctions and tend to view their problems as all of one piece. Thus *pronunciamientos, cuartelazos, golpes de estado, machetismo,* militarism, praetorianism, and all other instances where armed forces transcend their purely military functions tend to be viewed as phenomena of the same order and explainable with more or less the same formula. Sometimes these phenomena are even confused with military history. This is equivalent to regarding the Assumption of Mary and the exercise of the ecclesiastical patronage as belonging to the same order of things or of teaching surgery and medical sociology in the same course. In fact a diversity of patterns or systems of civil-military relations has existed in Latin America and each pattern consists of complex interactions involving the structure, status, and power of groups, both civil and military, and the motivations of individuals, as these several elements are influenced by the political, social, and economic environment. Thus the role of the Brazilian officer corps in the overthrow of the Empire, the institutionalized gangsterism prevailing in the contemporary Dominican Republic and the *pronunciamientos* of Antonio López de Santa Anna are sharply different examples of civil-military relations involving different types of civil and military elements interacting in different environmental situations.

At a schematic level several types of civil-military relations in Latin America may be defined. The first might be called the "Praetorian State." It is characterized by the frequent overthrow of governments by military revolutions or *coups d'état* for nonmilitary purposes. It tends to be associated with a high degree of social and political disorganization and a low degree of profes-

sionalism within the armed forces. Examples are Mexico during the first thirty years of the republic and Venezuela before and after the dictatorship of Juan Vicente Gómez. The second might be described as the "Gendarmist State." It emerges when a single individual, generally but not always a military man, uses a mercenary army to make himself master of the state, imposes social and political order, tames the army, and uses it as a gendarmery to maintain himself in power. The dictatorships of Gómez in Venezuela and Anastacio Somoza in Nicaragua are examples. The third type, after Harold Lasswell, is the "Garrison State." In it the military not only dominates or strongly influences the political system but it attempts to militarize the state and society at large. It occurs in connection with deep fears of aggression from the outside or strong aggressive tendencies within and is associated with a relatively high degree of political and social stability and a professionalized military establishment. Paraguay under Francisco Solano López might be taken as an example of this type. As noted above, it is atypical of Latin America. Fourth, is the "Civilist State." It is characterized by civil supremacy over the military and exists in relatively stable societies with professionalized armed forces. Examples are Argentina between 1861 and 1930 and Uruguay since the turn of this century. A fifth type may be emerging in Cuba but it is as yet difficult to identify.

It should be added that these are ideal types in the Weberian sense. They do not exist in pure form and may shade or metamorphose into one another. Thus a strong *caudillo* may in certain circumstances transform a praetorian state into a gendarmist state as in the case of Porfirio Díaz and Rafael Trujillo, or the weakening or death of a leader or pressures within a society may turn a gendarmist state into a praetorian state as, for example, Mexico after 1910. Changes in the social or economic structure within praetorian or gendarmist states may result in the emergence of a civilist pattern as in contemporary Mexico, while conversely political, social, or economic strains within a civilist state may result in the emergence of praetorian or gendarmist patterns as in the case of Argentina after 1930 or Colombia after 1949. These paradigms, it should be added, are not intended to present conclusions. They are devices to illustrate a point and to encourage the asking of pertinent questions.

The emphasis in the preceding paragraphs on the diversity of systems of civil-military relations in Latin America raises another question. Does Latin America itself constitute an adequate conceptual framework for the study of civil-military relations? Is it simply a convenient geographical and cultural delimitation or have civil-military relations in this region exhibited characteristic features or patterns? It is rather suggestive that Spain and Spanish America have had many similar experiences with their armed force. It might, therefore, be assumed that the Hispanic world is distinguished by typical patterns of civil-military relations. This assumption, however, is challenged by the fact that there seem to be greater structural and functional similarities between the Nasser regime in Egypt and the Perón regime in Argentina than between the latter and the dictatorships of Santa Anna in Mexico. It was recently suggested to the writer that there are certain "built-in" features of instability in the social and political organization of Moslem society which encourage military intervention in politics and that Hispanic civilization absorbed these features through its long contact and intermingling with the world of Islam. The idea is challenging. Yet it does not account for the fact that armies in Burma and Thailand appear to have acted in much the same way in much the same circumstances as armies in Spain, Latin America, and the Moslem world. This leads to the hypothesis that in general the patterns of civil-military relations in Latin America are typical of "developing areas." This might test out for the last decade when Latin America has undoubtedly shared many problems and aspirations with the emerging nations of the Middle East, Africa, and South and Southeast Asia. For earlier periods. however, it is not applicable. At the outbreak of World War II, most of the latter nations were still dependencies or colonies of Western powers while Latin America had enjoyed independence for over a century. Thus the argument comes full circle. It is quite possible that historically, Latin America or at least the Hispanic world provides a functional as well as convenient unit for the study of civil-military relations.

If civil-military relations in Latin America can be conceived as a discrete problem of considerable diversity and complexity and if it is accepted that these relationships have been important factors in the historical development of the region, historians are confronted with a challenge and an opportunity. The problem, or perhaps it would be better to say, the complex of problems, may be redefined as follows: What are and what have been the patterns or systems of civil-military relations historically present in Latin America, why has one pattern prevailed at a particular time and place rather than another, and how and why have patterns changed? These questions pose others that are still more fundamental: What are the elements or ingredients whose interaction has produced patterns of civil-military relations in Latin America in general or in particular instances? How do these elements interact to produce a particular pattern and how do they and their interactions change in time to produce different patterns?

The statement of the problem in this fashion raises a final query: What methods will be most fruitful in providing answers to the preceding questions? It is not the purpose of this paper to lecture historians on their methods. We all know what they do and how they go about it. Without committing themselves to explicit assumptions and without explicit hypothesizing, they begin with empirical data and develop conclusions, interpretations or generalizations in terms of how the data arranges itself or is arranged. Their normal procedure is, moreover, to work from the particular to the general, first the monograph, then the synthesis. Therefore it would seem that in view of the diverse character of civil-military relations in Latin America, a number of "case studies" dealing with particular countries and periods are needed before any convincing generalizations can be made. In undertaking such projects, the historian may use any one of several approaches: (1) he may describe and analyze a system or pattern of civil-military relations as it existed at a particular time and place in the past; (2) from this base he may "trace" and explain the process whereby this system changed to another; (3) without initially defining a system he may identify its elements and show how over a period of time they combined to form a system; (4) he may define a pattern as it existed at a particular time and place and then explain the process whereby it came to be what it was. In each case, if the method is narrative rather than analytical, patterns may remain implicit. These approaches and methods have and will

yield sophisticated explanations and interpretations of civil-military relations as, for example, Gordon A. Craig's *The Politics of the Prussian Army, 1640–1945* and Yale C. Maxon's *Control of Japanese Foreign Policy; a Study of Civil-Military Rivalry, 1930–1945*. Without abandoning their humanistic and literary traditions, however, historians can profit from a selective and cautious use of the theory and methods of the social sciences. The potentials and dangers of this kind of borrowing have been explored at length by Social Science Research Council, *Bulletin 64* and by H. Stuart Hughes, Richard Hofstadter, Sir Isaiah Berlin, and others, and it is unnecessary to review the argument and conclusions here. Instead certain general approaches and several specific methods will be discussed.

First, the sheer volume of sources now available and a growing awareness of the complexity of historical processes suggest that in many situations a more explicit definition of problems and assumptions would be a valuable aid to research. This entire paper is, in fact, an argument for such a procedure. Second, Lord Acton notwithstanding,[1] it would be useful for research purposes to regard Latin American armed forces "scientifically," that is, as social phenomena rather than as disasters and their relationships to civil society as a problem properly belonging to history and the social sciences rather than to demonology. It would, of course, be inhumane and illiberal not to deplore military excesses, but if "militarism" is to be regarded as a social disease, some knowledge of its pathology is necessary before remedies can be prescribed.

---

[1] Reference is to Acton's complaint that von Ranke sometimes spoke of "transactions and occurrences" when he should have spoken of "turpitude and crime."

Third, the functional approach to political systems evolved by that new hybrid, the political sociologist, helps put the military in proper perspective. James S. Coleman, *et al.* in their search for "a genuinely comparative and analytical approach" to comparative politics *(The Politics of the Developing Areas)* postulate that all societies from the primitive tribe to the modern nation state have political systems which perform the same set of functions although in different ways and through different structures, that is, associational and nonassociational interest groups, parliaments, bureaucracies, and the like. These functions are: political recruitment and socialization, interest articulation, interest aggregation, political communication, rule-making, rule-application, and rule-adjudication. In this system, when armed forces cease to be neutral instruments of policy, they may be regarded as actively performing one or more of these functions, and civil-military relations involve how and to what extent they do so.

The trend of this discussion leads to an examination of the possible value to the historian of theoretical frameworks and models. Social scientists concerned with Latin America have by and large been of a traditional turn of mind and cannot provide us with models of political systems or of civil-military relations in that region. There are, however, some general models available for examination. Samuel P. Huntington in his *The Soldier and the State* identifies six elements that in various triangular combinations shape universal patterns of civil-military relations. These are: antimilitary ideology (within the society at large), promilitary ideology, low military political power, high military political power, high military professionalism, and low military professionalism. He states that the pattern most common to the Near

East, Asia, and Latin America combines antimilitary ideology, high military political power, and low military professionalism. The systems of civil-military relations in Latin America which were constructed earlier in this paper are based extensively on Huntington's work and might themselves be regarded as primitive models. Stanislaw Andrzejewsky *(Military Organization and Society)* builds much more complex systems. He postulates various types of military organization deriving from triangular combinations of six elements: high military participation ratio (the ratio of the number of men under arms to the total population), low military participation ratio, high military subordination, low military subordination, high military cohesion, and low military cohesion. The several combinations are identified by neologisms. These models are then related to types of social organization. Although none of the examples given is drawn from Latin America, the type of military organization which appears to most closely fit that region is the Ritterian which is based on low M.P.R., low cohesion, and low subordination. The society in which such a type exists is characterized by steep social stratification and egalitarianism within the elite. The accompanying political form is a decentralized nobiliary republic.

This kind of conceptualization is uncongenial to most historians. It violates their highly particularistic and humanistic view of the social universe, and evokes among them emotions ranging from hilarity to deep hostility. These reactions derive in part, at least, from a misunderstanding of the use of models. They are intended not as the conclusions of prolonged and painstaking research but, as remarked above, are devices to facilitate the asking of pertinent questions and the ordering of data. It is not suggested that historians become model-builders but those constructed by social scientists can be stimulating if employed with caution. For example, by pointing out the significance of military professionalism and ideology in any system of civil-military relations, Huntington's theoretical frameworks suggest lines of research that might illuminate this relationship in Latin America.

Finally, traditional historical methods are inadequate to eliminate the greatest single obstacle to the systematic study of civil-military relations in Latin America. As Huntington points out, the principal focus of any system of civil-military relations is the relation of the officer corps to the state. Without commenting on the adequacy of our knowledge of the structure of Latin American states in general or particular, we have little except impressions based on random samples about those military groups in Latin America loosely and often interchangeably referred to as the "officer corps," the "officer class" and the "officer caste." Until more precise information is available about these elements, even the sociological validity of terms such as corps, class, and caste is doubtful. The techniques of group and elite analysis developed by social scientists can be of assistance in solving this problem. Morris Janowitz's careful study of the social origins, career motivations, career development, style of life, ideology, and self-image of the armed forces of the United States is an example of what can be done. If similar studies of Latin American officer corps in several countries at different periods were available it would no longer be necessary to rely on vague generalities.

It would be convenient if Janowitz or others would do the job for us, but inasmuch as social scientists are concerned primarily with contemporary phenomena, it is likely that historians will have to strike out for themselves. It will be a difficult task. The successful use of social science methods depends to a large extent on the availability of large masses of quantitative data systematically arranged (such as censuses) and the use of interviews, questionnaires, field work, and the like. The historian has nothing but his documents written by persons who mischievously neglected to collect and systematize the data needed and which at best have been randomly collected and stored. His task, however, is not impossible, as Woodrow Borah and S. F. Cook, Sir Lewis Namier and Marc Bloch have demonstrated in their research on other types of historical problems.

26

The Role of the Military
in Latin American Politics

Theodore Wyckoff

There are three types of Latin American countries in which the military plays three distinct types of role: first, the country in which the military *always* plays a role in politics, year in and year out; second, the country in which the military *never*, or almost never, plays a political role (since perhaps 1900, to set an arbitrary limit); and third, the country in which the military *occasionally* plays a political role. The twenty republics of Latin America may be arranged along a spectrum in which these three types mark the two extremes and an approximate mid-point. Such a spectrum set up for analytical purposes might show six countries at the "always" end: Dominican Republic, Guatemala, Haiti, Honduras, Nicaragua, and Paraguay. Only two would appear at the "never" end, Costa Rica and Uruguay. The remaining twelve "occasionals" would range somewhere between the two extremes: Argentina, Bolivia, Brazil, Chile, Colombia, Cuba,

Ecuador, El Salvador, Mexico, Panama, Peru, and Venezuela.

In each of the following studies, analysis of the problem hinges on the answers to two questions: first, what *nonmilitary* conditions characterize the type of state under discussion—social structure, geographic factors, economic conditions, political institutions, and historical traditions—and second, what conditions characterize the *military* in this type of state?

States in Which the Military Is Always a Factor in Politics

Most states in this category are small and relatively isolated from the main currents of world political action. Being small, they are physically easy to control by military force, and being isolated, the rest of the world is little concerned with their internal troubles. Their social structure is generally simple and clearly stratified. At the base of the social pyramid frequently are unassimilated Indian or Negro groups which have absorbed very little Western culture and which possess almost no political consciousness. Basically rural populations, such non-Europeans gen-

From Theodore Wyckoff, "The Role of the Military in Latin American Politics," *Western Political Quarterly,* Vol. XIII, No. 3 (September 1960). Reprinted by permission.

erally form a group quite apart from the rest of the national society. A second major segment is usually the social group of European origin which considers itself to be the elite of the nation occupying the apex of the social pyramid. A third group takes a position between the first two, and is comprised of persons of mixed descent. This last segment finds frequently that it has lost identity with the Indian (or Negro) culture from which it is in part descended while at the same time it is not able to feel a complete identity with its other forebears, the European group. It is often urban rather than rural, and is frequently characterized by a distinct political consciousness and by a certain sense of grievance against the European elite group.

Roughly paralleling the racial structure is an economic stratification in which the poorest are very poor, the wealthiest very wealthy, with a small middle class between the two extremes. Only a small minority of the Europeans can properly be considered wealthy, the majority constituting a "middle class." In such societies inadequate schools result in a high rate of illiteracy, and a general indifference to social welfare aggravates the economic imbalance.

Economic backwardness frequently reflects conditions of chronic political instability. Large landholdings characterize the economy, while the agricultural workers live in a state approximating peonage. One-crop agriculture is normal and a single export commodity —agricultural or mineral—frequently dominates the country's foreign exchange. The few large industries are often foreign-owned and, since they pay heavy royalties, must be lucrative. The few small industries—matches, cigarettes, flour milling, salt—are often state monopolies or the personal property of the chief of state. Urban workers are few, their wages are low, and among

them there is general irritation at the conspicuous consumption of the wealthy. The labor-union movement is often weak, underground, or controlled. Rural workers, economically and politically apathetic, are ignorant of any better life than survival at a subsistence level. With chronic political instability, high risks attend any capital investment; interest rates are high and dividends are expected to be high. The risks are such as to discourage most capital investments.

Politically, power is concentrated in a small group of influential individuals drawn from the better-educated upper classes. In addition to the wealthy families, components of this upper-class power structure include the Church, with its strong influence over mass opinion, and the military, representing the power of physical coercion. The general orientation of the power structure is toward the welfare of the privileged social classes represented in it, and on this goal there is normally general agreement.

Normally there is opposition to the regime actually holding the reins of government at any particular moment, but this generally comes from *within* the better-educated, politically conscious elite, and is bitterest among individuals who have been hurt by the regime. Political opposition is certain to exist among university students who come from disaffected families. Insofar as possible the regime may be expected to attempt to isolate, silence, or exterminate the opposition, with the result of driving it underground or into exile.

The lower and middle classes until very recent years have held virtually no political power, except as individuals have risen to power through the army. While this was the pattern of the past, these groups are undergoing a process of rapid political acculturation and are certain to be a force to reckon with soon. This sector of society has been aptly characterized as the rising "middle mass." Political acculturation in the less-favored classes, originally a by-product of this century's rising standard of economic expectations, has been tremendously accelerated by the feverish activities of Communist as well as non-Communist political movements, which in the lower classes of society have found fertile fields to till.

With this exception, partisan political action extends generally only to the educated and elite groups, while the same is true of any rational belief in any form of political ideology. Elections are a superficial contest only. Nominations and appointments are made from within the social and political elite groups. Irregular practices both in elections and between elections are normal and assumed, while the legal system and the courts are set up to keep peace among the wealthy only.

Police-state methods are frequently used to discover political opposition and to render it ineffective. The opposition is on occasion brutalized and persecuted; innocent persons may be hurt. Frequently only Communist-led opposition groups possess the "know-how" to survive such political persecution. The non-Communist opposition is the most likely to die or disappear. The obvious consequence of the use of police-state methods is a feeling of intense hatred for the regime using them. This hatred may spread over a period of years to a large enough portion of the politically conscious populace that it may erupt in mob action, riot, arson, and murder, extending even to civil war and overthrow of the regime.

Historical traditions are generally authoritarian and/or oligarchic, reflecting social and political conditions which have prevailed generally from the time of Spanish colonial rule. Since independence in the early 1800's a strong sense of patriotic nationalism has developed among nationally assimilated groups into almost fanatical pride in the *patria*. There is frequently a strong military tradition, in part at least resulting from the fact that for over a century the only avenue to high achievement, fame, and fortune, has been through a military career. There is some intellectual tradition of aspiration toward a democratic and open society, but this is confined exclusively to the educated and "Western-oriented" groups.

In states where the military is always a factor in politics, armies, although "small," are usually large in comparison to the country's population. For the most part they consist of combat troops with relatively minor provision for the technical services providing logistical support. They are not built for modern war and may be expected to encounter difficulty when forced to operate at a distance from their bases. More correctly characterized as a "police force" or *"gendarmerie,"* their primary function is to be prepared to provide a show of force, rather than an actual fighting potential. For example, it may not be necessary for a tank's guns to be loaded with ammunition, if the noise and mass of the tank itself is enough to instill respect and fear. Air forces are generally considered to be arms of the army, subject to army control and utilized in pursuance of army objectives, as are the miniscule naval forces.

In social origin, enlisted men of the army are normally drawn from the groups at the lower end of the social scale. Noncommissioned officers are usually mestizo or mulatto, or outstanding Indians or Negroes. Officers are usually drawn from the white sector of society or from better-educated mestizo or mulatto families.

Officers are in almost all cases graduates of the military academy of the nation in question. Appointments as cadets are usually available (1) to youths from the educated classes who may desire to pursue a military career or (2) to outstanding individuals from the enlisted ranks recommended by their officers. In not a few cases the nation's military academy may offer the best education available in the country. There is evidence of a rather wide range of competence in the officers graduated from the academies, reflecting in some degree the widely divergent educational and social backgrounds of the two types of cadet.

Military service, despite some drawbacks, may offer to both enlisted soldiers and officers many advantages over normal civilian life. For a civilian conscript, military service may mean his first adequate suit of clothing or his first pair of shoes (though, to be truthful, not all soldiers in these countries wear shoes). For many, military service brings life's first introduction to a classroom, for one of the army's important functions is to return *literate* citizens to the nation.

Discipline in the army is severe, but this contributes to a high level of social prestige. A man has to be good to "stay in." For regular army enlisted men, a lifetime of relative prestige, economic security, and assured retirement offers much to be desired. For both officers and enlisted men base pay is usually low, but added emoluments usually make military service financially attractive. These may include housing, medical care, recreational facilities, and foreign exchange privileges—and may be extended beyond the military man's immediate family even to include in-laws. There are in certain situations other ways in which the individual may add to his income. While promotions are slow, a career as an officer may

nevertheless provide opportunities for travel to the United States or to other countries on training missions or on attaché duty. Physical conditions vary widely—from desirable service in the national capital to very undesirable service on the frontier or in the jungle. Desirable assignments are usually reserved for political favorites or "ins"; undesirable posts go to less fortunate individuals or political "outs."

The political orientation of military personnel varies with the grade, age, and experience of the individual concerned. The primary orientation of the enlisted man is loyalty to his immediate commander, usually (but not always) coupled with a feeling of intense patriotism. Patriotism and loyalty unto death are the first and most basic lessons taught in the military classroom. The enlisted man only rarely gives evidence of any deeper political consciousness, although the political acculturation of enlisted men is a very significant development.[1]

In contrast to enlisted men in the army, junior officers—young graduates of the military academy—normally reflect their own social background and its particular political orientation. These young men are superficially familiar with modern ideologies, they are inveterate optimists, and they frequently possess genuinely high ideals and high hopes for the future of their country. Their loyalty is given unquestionably to their immediate commanders, although they may be disillusioned with top military and governmental policies and leaders. Junior

---

[1] Cuba's "Sergeant's Revolution," led by Fulgencio Batista in 1933, was a rare exception to the general rule, reflecting the accelerated political acculturation, even a quarter-century ago, of the middle and lower classes in Cuba.

officers are normally assigned to duty with troops and have little opportunity for personal contact with political events.

As officers attain the rank of major or lieutenant colonel, they approach a phase of their career in which they develop a strong political consciousness: there is usually a break with troop life, and assignment to staff duties is to be expected. The officers will go off to the nation's command and general staff school or to similar schools in the United States, France, Brazil, or Argentina for advanced training.

As the officer in mid-career travels and studies, he becomes aware of his nation's political and international position. He may become aware of conditions which he believes to be wrong, and he may develop a certain disenchantment both with his military superiors and with the political leaders of his country. On the other hand, if his country is in capable hands and things are going well he may be pleased with the *status quo.*

At this stage, an outstanding individual known for his personal loyalty to the regime may be given command of important troop units in the vicinity of the capital city: the cavalry division, the presidential guard battalion, the armored regiment. He may become the target of pressures from nonmilitary "out-groups" and political parties and cliques aspiring to power. Also, he will cement personal friendships which he may have formed years before. Occasional interpersonal rivalries may develop as the competition gets stiffer. Cliques may form based on prior service in elite units, on the army general staff, or elsewhere.

As he passes beyond mid-career and becomes a senior officer—a senior colonel or a general officer—his political

activity (and for that matter all his activity) will depend primarily on his age, vigor, and health. Promotions are slow and a large percentage of officers retire and disappear from the active scene. Vigorous, healthy senior officers who continue to enjoy favor are promoted to the top general officer positions, and the most senior of these may be named chief of staff or minister of war. Often the top position will have been pre-empted for especially favored individuals with unique family or other connections. Lines of loyalty at the top echelons of the army are often blurred and there is apparent a marked tendency for senior officers to build themselves personal positions of power in the localities or military districts to which they are assigned. There may be evidence of jealousy and some sort of jockeying for position.

Military participation in political action may take one of three possible courses: individuals in a position to make decisions for themselves may either defend the *status quo,* be prepared to overthrow the *status quo,* or stand aside without becoming identified with either side. Action to defend the *status quo* will be the normal course, although in times of crisis or grievance its overthrow may appear to offer a solution to difficulties. Ambitious key individuals or groups either among the senior or mid-career officers may be attracted by the possibility of accelerated advancement, and may be tempted to use a crisis as an excuse for political action. They may have reason to fear action by antimilitary groups to undercut the military's status and jeopardize its future. Individuals who decide to remain aloof from political action are usually unwilling to risk reasonable security and comfort for the sake of chancing success. Such prudent officers are generally reluctant to get involved in any type of trouble which could hurt their families or their future and prefer to lie low until the trouble blows over. . . .

States in Which the Military Is Never a Factor in Politics

Costa Rica and Uruguay, the two states in this category, are geographically small: size has not made the problems of government too complex, nor has it imposed too severe a strain on the political system. Small size has also made possible conditions of relative social homogeneity which tend to be conducive to a viable and open social system and to some social mobility. Both states have, for the most part, a single racial strain, generally European. The bulk of the population has at least a primary-school education; the overall literacy rate is high. The spread between poor and wealthy is not excessive: there is a large middle class. A fair degree of social mobility prevails and a general regard for the values of social welfare is apparent.

Economically, there is evidence of relative well-being. Labor is generally more productive than among non-European populations and wages are higher. There is more security for business, the risk is less, and interest rates and dividends are lower. With greater political stability and smaller economic risks, capital is more available for economic development than in most other areas of Latin America. There is general evidence of moderate economic progress.

Political life is characterized by a relatively effective constitutional system, personal political freedom, the existence of a political opposition which is not persecuted, a workable legal structure, and a system of operating courts. Corruption and public scandal are relatively minor and elections, under the watchful supervision of effective political parties, are generally honest.

Although political conditions prior to 1900 in Uruguay and Costa Rica bore little resemblance to those of today, there is now a real tradition of fifty or sixty years of relatively effective constitutional democracy. Although both countries have seen deviations from the pattern, the influence of the military on politics since 1900 has been generally negligible.

Since the armed forces of Costa Rica were formally abolished in 1948, necessary police functions being assumed by a small *Guardia Civil,* Uruguay remains the only example of a country with a military which almost never assumes a political role. Here the role of the military in relation to political institutions has had a very interesting development. While the armed forces occupy a vital position in Uruguay's governmental structure, they are small in size and are emphatically apolitical in the sense of being nonpartisan. Total defense expenditures account for less than an eighth of the national budget.

If the Uruguay military man is nonpolitical, how then does he regard his role in society? He knows that he inherits a long tradition of military participation in the life of his nation, a nation whose independence was won on the battlefield and whose freedom was only assured after decades of fighting. He knows that his is a nation in which in its younger days all men bore arms, in which the army and the nation were synonymous, and in which even the most humble *gaucho* was a noble fighting man.[2]

---

2 Most of the comments in this section are from an interview with General Horacio A. Pinto, former Uruguayan military attaché in Washington, an officer with thirty-five years of service in the Uruguayan Army.

With this tradition, the professional soldier explains, it is impossible for the army to be against the nation; it is unthinkable, for example, for a soldier to fire against unarmed citizens. It is impossible for the army to be in league with oppression. Military men today remember that "when Artigas in 1815 and Lavalleja in 1825 and even Galarza in 1904 found power to be in their hands," they "gave it back to the nation," voluntarily relinquishing their personal position of supremacy. Not one of the military leaders remembered as national heroes today is remembered as a *caudillo.* . . .

The resolution of the problems of party strife at the ballot box, in the law courts, and in the halls of government made possible the end of armed partisan strife. It became apparent that civil power exercised through the parties had been able to succeed where military power had failed, and while the army still retained the prestige of its historical tradition, recourse to arms was thoroughly discredited as a solution for national problems. When peace, prosperity, and social justice followed in the wake of this political reorientation, the prestige of civil supremacy in government became unchallengeable. There is no Uruguayan today who disputes the wisdom of the democratic solution of his country's problems. The military man is brought up to believe heart and soul in this national philosophy and he holds the belief as fervently as do his civilian countrymen.

As every Uruguayan is "born either a *Colorado* or a *Blanco,*" so every military man holds his own political views to which he is passionately attached. The professional soldier explains that his partisan passion is the same as that of his fellow citizens, every one of whom he considers his equal. But political passions are to be fought out only at the ballot boxes, and thought of recourse

to violence is abhorrent. The military man votes in his country's elections and is passionately proud of his right to do so. There is no feeling that he is "above party." A man's opinion is his most sacred possession, and any action to coerce that opinion is tantamount to betrayal of what is now the Uruguayan way of life.

The Uruguayan armed forces today have the sole mission of defending the nation against the encroachment of powerful neighbors (who, fortunately for Uruguay, act as deterrents to each other). Military force in the solution of domestic political problems is now a concept totally alien to Uruguayan mentality. In truth, the role of the military has been so reduced that many Uruguayans tend even to forget that they have an army.

States in Which the Military Is Occasionally a Factor in Politics

The picture changes in states in which the military is only occasionally a factor in politics. Although here the military only upon occasion steps into the limelight, the actors on the political stage are well aware that but one step off-stage the military stands—an attentive and critical observer of everything that goes on.[3]

It is significant that many such states are geographically large, both in population and in area. Large size brings with it a diversity of economic interests and social groups—groups which are jealous of their autonomy and freedom of local action. These are groups and interests which frequently by their very physical distance from the seat of

---

[3] Most generalizations which follow are drawn from the author's experience as a member of the U.S. military mission in Brazil, although in most cases they apply equally to other states of the type being discussed.

central government cannot easily be controlled by it.

The social structure in such large states is often complex and characterized by wide variety. Different areas may have different social systems, some stratified and immobile, others egalitarian and in continual ferment. In some the population is primarily Indian, in others Negro, in still others European. In certain areas all three racial and cultural strains are found together, plus a variety of mixed strains.

Economically, there is a diversity of crops, occupations, and industry. In regions centered around large cities, agriculture, industry, and commerce all have political as well as economic importance. Agriculture may be characterized in one place by large estates and in another by small landholdings. Industry may be represented by both foreign and domestic capital and may be very varied, including producers' as well as consumers' goods.

Economic power in such a large country is diffused. Holders of economic power are certain to be active in their own self-interest, and are not likely to be completely united in their approach to national problems. Specific measures good for one may not be good for another. There is competition within the industrial community. The labor movement is characterized by differences between areas, unions being strong in one and weak or nonexistent in another. The lower economic classes may be politically powerful in one spot and negligible in another.

The geographical, sociological, and economic diversity is reflected in the quality of educational facilities, and consequently in varying levels of literary and degrees of political acculturation. Politically, these states are characterized by several features distinct and different from those of the smaller states discussed above. Local

political units are much more important to the average citizen in his daily life than is the relatively distant national government. Although the citizen may accept many of the functions of local government unconsciously, the public works, utilities, roads, taxes, and corruption of state and local government affect him directly. On the other hand, the national government is a force which directly affects the average citizen in outlying areas much less than in smaller countries. Normally his only contacts are with the post office, the railways, national taxes, occasional election campaigns, and military conscription. All other evidences of governmental authority are state and local.

Local and state governments can rarely be despotic because the national government is always implicitly recognized as a higher authority. Not only can national troops move in to enforce a national policy in an extreme instance, but national monies raised through federal taxes usually provide a large part of the financial support of local and state governments. Although they possess a good measure of autonomy, actually the national government exercises an important and implicitly recognized veto power through control of the purse strings.

Political parties are important, but they may differ in character and in composition from one geographic area to another. Even in cases where there is a virtual one-party system (as in Mexico), the parties in different areas of the country serve as channels for the representation of local interests in the national councils.

Personal political freedom generally prevails in part, at least, because its effective denial in large and populous countries would require a political police force too large and expensive to be practical. The diversity of interests plus the prevalent personal political freedom results usually in the creation of a two-party or a multiparty system.

If a dictator presumptive actually does capture power, he generally finds that to eliminate the effectiveness of the opposition he has to create a party apparatus or other similar structure of civil control with branches throughout the nation. Neither the army nor any military force can control a large population on his behalf; a civilian totalitarian party must be founded to perform this function for him, and a system of nationally appointed "interventors" or state governors must be instituted. He can then retain his control by exercising a veto power over appointments inimical to him. This results in practical political freedom for the vast majority of the population.

The spoils of high office may be as great as or greater than in smaller states, but the public only knows as much about the doings of the national government as the press tells it. National scandal and corruption may be extensive, but they only affect the individual citizen as he pays indirectly for such spoils, and as the circumstances reported in the press offend his individual view of the proper standards of official conduct. Freedom of the press is thus frequently one of the major political issues in such countries.

The national government is confined largely to the capital city, and decision-making is in the hands of a relatively small group of people in the legislative and executive branches of government. While the executive branch includes a large bureaucracy concerned with many problems, major decisions are usually made only at the very top level of the bureaucratic pyramid. This is significant for the following reason: If and when the military forces intervene in political activity, all they can do physically is to seize control of the decision-making machinery. They can also seize control of the public information machine through which the government has primary contact with the mass of citizens. Beyond this, the effect on the rest of the country is negligible, being apparent only insofar as use is made of propaganda and the public information services and insofar as new bureaucratic institutions are set up.

Unless the military group seizing power has a major positive political program of its own it will be forced to turn back most of the functions of government to the bureaucracy and even to the legislative branch, retaining only veto power over specific actions to which it may have objection. The fact that the government of a large country is a big business requiring the services of many thousands of trained bureaucrats puts it effectively beyond the reach of anything more than nominal military-political control. Only rarely in Latin American history has the military seizure of power in such countries been extended to a real system of national control.

Historical traditions developed as a result of the political conditions described have served to perpetuate most of the established forms of political action, many of which date back to colonial times. Truly basic society-shaking revolutions against historical tradition have been rare, the Mexican Revolution of 1910–1917 and the Cuban Revolution of 1958–1959 being practically the only instances. Vargas' semi-Fascist *Estado Novo* and Perón's *Peronismo* were semirevolutionary breaks with tradition, but in each of these cases, the innovations eventually were overthrown and traditional patterns reinstated. It is worth commenting that a civilian can be every bit as much of a dictator as a military man, as was Getulio Vargas from 1930 to 1945.

Generally armies in these states are large and include important technical and logistical services. Members of the military service are professionally competent and the military forces are organized on a scale large enough to engage in modern war. There is usually a navy, and an air force, with definite and separate traditions. Both are strong enough to act in some measure as counterforces to the army— counterforces which on occasion may assume critical significance.

Enlisted men in the military forces reflect generally the areas from which they are recruited, and they usually serve in units near home. Cattlemen serve in cattle country, urban workers in their home cities, plantations laborers in nearby plantation districts. Officers are almost entirely professional career officers, graduates of the nation's military academy. Initially they reflect the society from which they were drawn. Cadets are usually chosen in nationwide competitive examinations, frequently from graduates of the local or national public high schools which are open to all classes through their own system of competitive entrance examinations. But here urban students outnumber rural ones. This system of competitive examinations on several levels gives a high degree of selectivity and a broad base from which to draw, and results in the emergence of outstanding officers of singular ability. They represent for the most part an urban, professional middle- or lower middle-class social background. Naval officers tend to represent higher economic and social backgrounds than army officers; the latter are generally comparable to those of the air force.

In political orientation, the attitudes of enlisted men are again primarily dominated by a spirit of loyalty to the immediate commander. Patriotism is also again present as an undeniable factor, but in large countries it inevitably is diluted by a spirit of loyalty to the individual's own region, province, or state. The level of political acculturation among enlisted men is low, but—most significantly—is rising.

The attitudes of junior officers are likewise generally nonpolitical—a fact resulting from the large size of the country and from the fact that the young officer considers himself to be a very small cog in a very large machine. Officers possess a strong sense of loyalty to their branch of service, and they evince a strong technical and professional interest. Young officers normally serve in small units far removed from the center of national power and may be expected to have no concept of any influence that the military may exert on politics other than the news which they may read in the headlines of the political actions of a minister of war thirty years their senior—a person so remote as to seem almost unreal.

However, an exception to this generalization is a phenomenon—almost an aberration—which appeared in Brazil in 1922, and which on other occasions since has reappeared, that of *tenentismo*. In this "lieutenantism," a few politically alert and idealistically motivated junior officers, disillusioned with the failings of their elders and feeling that by dramatic and bloody— though foolhardy—actions they can force reforms in the government, decide to chance a revolt—hopeless though it be—on their own.

The officers who conform to the norm, however (or *tenentes* who are amnestied and returned to duty), proceed to mid-career, to the grades of major, lieutenant colonel, and colonel, where the majority of officers look forward to serving out their time and retiring in peaceful security. Officers in mid-career are dependable, solid citizens enjoying a moderately comfortable family life fighting the struggle against inflation in some middle-class community. Promotions in this phase are very slow and fifteen years may pass before the handsome young major becomes the distinguished, gray, senior lieutenant colonel or colonel. Only a small minority can see "general's stars" in their future.

The officer in mid-career will probably have had some contact with United States training missions and United States military schools. This contact with North Americans and their ways of thinking may have very important by-products insofar as the individual's democratic and progressive political acculturation is concerned. While mid-career is the period when outside influences, such as economic crisis, political chaos, or executive indecision, may give rise to strong political feelings, the officer is careful to proceed with caution, since his personal security, in the form of retirement, has not yet been assured through sufficient years of service, while his family responsibilities are probably heavy.

Vastly different, however, is the personal situation of senior officers, who through sufficient length of service have earned the right to retire at will. The worst that can happen to such an individual who expresses his opinions bluntly is that he can be forced to retire—and life as a retired general or colonel is really not too undesirable. The critical factors pertaining to the individual's personal activities in this late-career period are again age, vigor, and health. The individual of only moderate vigor may prefer to "take life easy," letting other people worry about the world's problems. But active and vigorous senior officers can afford to be very independent in their opinions and they do not hesitate to assume a political role. The most senior vigorous general is usually the minister of war and he is surrounded usually by other like-minded officers just as vigorous as he, but less senior.

In contrast to the situation in countries of less political maturity, the chain of command within the higher uniformed echelons is usually strong. Insubordination is rare. There is usually an identity of viewpoint among the group of senior generals who have political opinions. They discuss politics and their political role among themselves, and they may be expected to decide on courses of action generally agreeable to the group. The normal line of political action to which they will agree is the support of the constitutional government, of the *status quo*. This is the situation when conditions are normal and the nation faces no serious crises. But if the situation is not normal, if a feeling of crisis, grievance, or danger is in the air, the situation can change drastically. Should danger threaten with which the civilian government appears unable to cope, the top military group may be persuaded that it should take over. This top group may even feel that it has a *constitutional duty* to give the nation a government competent to cope with these apparent dangers....

Conclusions

The above three examples of the role of the military in contemporary Latin American politics represent only three points on a continuum. Many intermediate points are referred to only by implication. Peru, Bolivia, or Venezuela, for example, would show many elements of similarity to both the "always" and the "occasional" states cited. Likewise, a study of Chile, or perhaps now Mexico, would show elements of similarity to both the "occasional" and "never" states cited. The examples given have referred only to the role of "regular army" officers in politics—military professionals, that is. Excluded from consideration are the irregular military movements of armed civilians which played such a large part in the Mexican Revolution of 1910–1917 and in the Cuban Revolution of 1958–1959.

Bearing in mind the continuum, it is believed that a comparison of factors in the three types of countries which have been analyzed may serve to point up some conclusions concerning the role of the military in Latin America and the possible solutions to the problem—if problem it be.

In the first place, it would appear to be a valid hypothesis that the underlying social and political conditions are more significant in the political life of a country than the actual role of the military. The military follows courses of action adapted to the political conditions of the country in question, and is not by itself primarily responsible for the absence or presence of democracy or democratic institutions. Although it may frequently be true that "although the army does not govern, in the last analysis it determines who does," the army is not responsible for the conditions which make this situation possible. The political role of the military is not a "political disease"; rather it is but a symptom of a condition of political immaturity.

In the second place, it would appear that where democracy flourishes—and even where it flourishes with occasional military intervention—there also is to be found the conditions of *powerful countervailing forces*. In homogenous Uruguay, the countervailing forces are the *Colorado* and *Blanco* parties, neither powerful enough to suppress the other. In the larger and more populous countries, different sections

are opposed to each other, and no one is powerful enough to impose its will on the others.

The corollary of this second hypothesis is that in the countries where the military is always a factor in politics (where there are the least democratic social, political, and economic conditions), there also is to be found an *absence* of countervailing forces. This is not to say that there is no opposition in such countries; rather, the nature of the country is such that the opposition can be suppressed.

This second hypothesis is sometimes expressed in terms of "political maturity." This term usually means a society's ability to govern itself according to certain accepted rules and regulations, with the added proviso that adaptability to changing circumstances, provision for both a majority and minority, and opportunities for continuing democratization and political acculturation are all built into the system.

A third hypothesis is that the political acculturation (or the attainment of a good degree of political consciousness) of the "lower" classes in the less democratic countries will turn them into a political force which will challenge the supremacy of the presently dominant "upper" classes. If the lower classes can do this without going so far as to suppress the upper classes, there should be established a system of countervailing forces within the society which could serve as the framework for a democratic party system. This, in fact, is what seems to have happened in Costa Rica.

Should the lower classes develop the power to *suppress* the upper classes and thus overturn the social order, a new despotism will simply be substituted for the old, since there will again be an absence of countervailing forces. It is well recognized that the danger of Communist or Communist-type revolutions is very real and very serious in several areas of Latin America.

A fourth (and final) hypothesis is that under certain conditions the military—far from being a threat to democratic institutions—may serve as a force to uphold and safeguard them. Constitutional provisions might even be rewritten so as to formalize this arrangement, making of the top uniformed officers a sort of *judiciary,* with power to interpret the rightness or wrongness of acts of the executive and the legislative branches of government. If this hypothesis should prove to be correct, democracy in such countries would have nothing to fear from the political role of the military. It is suggested that this step might fruitfully be added to the thoughtful and constructive suggestions with which Victor Alba concludes his perceptive study of Latin American militarism.

Where democracy flourishes it is because the society has reached a level of political acculturation such that the safeguards of democracy are institutionalized and the teeth are drawn from the forces which might imperil it. The social system includes countervailing forces institutionalized as effective political parties, jealous of their freedom of action and expression, and zealous in guarding it. They know the truth of the democratic maxim that "the price of liberty is eternal vigilance." Military force is employed to strengthen, not to weaken, democratic institutions.

One last comment is appropriate. Successful government has always depended on strong and skillful leadership—a fact as true of democratic as it is of undemocratic governments. In 1930 and 1931, under the stress of economic crisis, almost every government in Latin America fell, a victim to violence. The military simply took it in its hands to set up governments which could *act* in the face of crisis. If democratic regimes are to succeed, they must be able to bring forth strong, intelligent, and progressive leaders who can *act* in time of crisis and who can command the respect of both the general public and the military. Such leaders must come from somewhere. One of the major concerns of forward-looking Latin Americans should be to develop avenues besides the military through which promising and ambitious young men can reach political office. In this search for the leaders of tomorrow as well as the solutions to the problems of today there may be much that the discipline of political science can contribute.

27

Dichotomies in the Church

John J. Kennedy

Questions concerning the role of the Church in society and its relation to the state have persistently formed one of the central issues in the politics of Latin America. As the Latin American nations move through a period of accelerated social change and transition, it is unlikely that these questions will disappear. In the process of a profound social transformation, however, it is probable that they will be restated and re-examined. This paper does not presume to anticipate any precise formulations of restatement and re-examination. Its purpose is to identify some prevailing trends and to evaluate them in the light of historic precedent and influence. Appraisal along these lines can probably best begin with a general acknowledgment of the evidence indicating that, between the late 1920's and the late 1950's, a change took place in the fortunes if not in the attitudes of the Church in Latin America.

The Church circa 1930

The observer of a generation ago could not unreasonably conclude that,

From John J. Kennedy, "Dichotomies in the Church," *The Annals,* Vol. CCCXXXIV (March 1961). Reprinted by permission.

in the social evolution of Latin America, the Roman Catholic Church was destined to play an increasingly restricted role. On the one hand, religion itself seemed to be losing its luster as a guide to human conduct. The educated urban classes sought to find the answers to the important ethical and moral questions at least as much in university lecture halls and in philosophical reviews as in church. It was not inconsistent with a long tradition that exposure to the higher learning should loosen the bonds of religion over the individual, but the number of individuals thus emancipated was larger than ever before. If urbanization had increased the number of the educated, it was also expanding the ranks of the proletariat. In many cities, the economically deprived and insecure workers were undergoing that process that the French call de-Christianization, and many of them were coming to believe that Marxist values more realistically represented their aspirations than did Catholicism.

On the other hand, where the Church was surviving as an influential body, it appeared to have obtained a dubious short-term lease on life through alliance with a political conservatism to which the future clearly did not belong. This circumstance seemed to compound the precariousness of Catholicism. Religion *qua* religion was becoming obsolete, and this meant that the Church could claim no significant place in the future. But even if religion faced other prospects, the position of the Catholic Church was hardly better: its leaders had made its survival a question of politics, not religion.

Many specific developments of the day would have offered much to confirm these—for the Church—rather cheerless auguries. The contemporary experience of Mexico suggested that a dynamic social revolution must necessarily bring adversity, or worse, to the Church. In Chile, the recently disestablished Church had found its champion in the Conservative party, and, for many years to come, *Partido Conservador* and *Partido Católico* were to remain synonyms in ordinary speech. In Colombia, the party of the Church was again the Conservative, whose minority position was shortly to be demonstrated. Elsewhere, lawless, repressive dictatorships provoked occasional pulpit criticism from individual clerics, but the Church as a whole seemed, at best, powerless against the evils of the system; at worst, it was tolerant to the point of indifference. Adversity in revolution, alliance with reaction, impotence in the face of dictatorship, such were the alternatives that seemed to confront the Church in Latin America in the late twenties and early thirties. None of them promised a happy future.

Theological and social lag

Catholic apologists of the period would, of course, have resisted the implication that the future of the Church in Latin America was necessarily bleak. Some of them would acknowledge the existence of grave difficulties, but would, at the same time, argue that the well-tested vitality of the Church was, for the moment, engaged in the search for new outlets. Channels through which the influence of Catholicism had run for more than a century were being closed by social upheaval or had become clogged with the accumulated debris of the years. The Church of the future would have to find others, and the course of some of these could already be mapped out. In Brazil, Argentina, Chile, and even in Mexico there were promising signs of new Catholic intellectual movements. Stressing the autonomy of philosophy and science, these movements nonetheless professed to find inspiration in Catholic doctrine. In part, these developments could be regarded as the somewhat tardy responses of Latin American Catholicism to the Thomistic revival which had been inaugurated a half century earlier in the universal Church under Leo XIII. Similarly, Catholicism did not have to be an obstacle in the path of fundamental social change. The social encyclicals were authoritative indications to the contrary. If the impact of these papal pronouncements was somewhat belated in reaching Latin America, this, like the delayed start in the Thomistic revival, could be explained in terms of a rhythm of world history, the dislocations resulting from World War I, or of any number of other causes. At any rate, the tardiness in general acknowledgment of papal teachings was not due to an indissoluble union between the Church and the old order. The underdog, the proletarian, the piecerate worker, and the landless peasant had found or would soon find active champions in the ecclesiastical hierarchy, as exemplified by Bishop Andrea in Argentina and, later, by Archbishop Sanabria in Costa Rica.

While the hypothetical observer who appeared at the beginning of this account might concede the factual validity of these assertions, he would probably refuse to credit them as indicators of basic trends within the Church in Latin America. Were not the foregoing citations special cases rather than examples of general commitments? How many episcopal allies could Andrea count on in his own country?[1] If Andrea himself truly represented the contemporary mind of the Church, why had the Holy See persisted in rejecting his nomination for the Archbishopric of Buenos Aires in 1923 and 1924?[2] Was not the orthodoxy of the progressive clergy suspect? Moreover, did the new Catholic intellectuals represent anything really significant? An occasional priest like Octavio Nicolás Derisi might establish himself in the forum of the philosophers. The exceptional layman like Alceu Amoroso Lima might achieve distinction in scholarship and literature. Were these not, however, the voices of a minority, no less atypical within the intellectual world than in Catholicism itself? Individual accomplishment could be honored without conceding that the accomplishment was symptomatic of a general vitality of Catholicism as a whole.

The Church Today

The foregoing considerations do not readily lead to hard and fast conclusions about the situation of the Church of three decades ago. It is not unusual for the Catholic Church to command a diversity of resources in countries where it has had a long history. It may be that there was a general tendency to underrate the importance of this diversity in Latin America at that time. In terms of its traditional sources of strength and influence, however, it is not unreasonable to regard the Church of thirty years ago as a waning power.

New Church alignment

There is little doubt that the situation of the Church today is radically different. Contrasts between 1930 and 1960 establish the difference. At the earlier date, rightly or wrongly, the Church was widely regarded as exerting what pressure it could on behalf of the *status quo* in opposition to incipient social change. Now, when pressing social demands portend yet deeper and more far-reaching transformation, the Church appears to have given a vigorous endorsement to those demands. Most of the alliances with reaction have long since disappeared. Conservative and Catholic are no longer interchangeable symbols in the language of party politics. The Christian Democratic movements that have developed in Chile, Venezuela, Brazil, and Argentina have not inherited the function once attributed to conservatism. That is to say, they do not claim to be the political spokesmen of a political and religious combination. Moreover, Christian Democratic leadership has taken pains to emphasize the nonconfessional character of these parties.

The contrast also emphasizes the vigor with which the Catholic episcopacy in several countries has, in recent years, been willing to speak out officially and collectively. A generation ago, the Mexican bishops were engaged in an unequal contest with Calles and Obregón. In the 1950's Perón, Rojas Pinilla, Pérez Jiménez, and Batista provoked statements of condemnation, criticism, or

---

[1] It should probably be noted that although Bishop Andrea was a conspicuous figure in the Church for fifty years, he was never in active command of a diocese. His authority was never more than that of a titular bishop *in partibus*.

[2] Since the Vatican does not normally publicize the reasons for its decisions in cases of this sort and specifically refused to do so when it rejected Andrea's nomination for the second time, it is impossible to ascertain definitely why he was rejected.

stern counsel from the Argentine, Colombian, Venezuelan, and Cuban hierarchies. In each case, these pronouncements had the effect of linking the Church with other groups which disapproved and opposed repressive regimes. When these regimes shortly came to an end, the Church, in the aftermath, seemed to stand conspicuously with the victors who had destroyed unappetizing dictatorships and to have won, thereby, sympathy and cordiality in quarters where such would not normally have been expected. According to the latter point of view, it might be claimed that in a certain sense the several episcopacies had redeemed the Church in their respective countries.

Needless to say, this is not a view which will be shared by churchmen, who see the justification of the Church not in terms of its response to progressive norms but rather in accordance with the measure of zeal with which it fulfills a divine mandate. To seek on this latter basis alone, however, an explanation of current ecclesiastical attitudes will hardly prove more helpful than that which sees the Church as a late convert to liberalism. For if the real goals of the Church are not of this world, the historical truth of Western civilization, including the Latin American segment, is that the Church has been very much involved in the things of this world.

Permanent Involvement

The standing features of this involvement in Latin America offer a key to understanding both the presently prevailing attitudes of Catholicism and the seeming contrasts between these and those of an earlier period. These features chiefly result from the long search for means of adjustment and adaptation between the self-defined requirements of an ancient transnational religious body preaching a dogmatic creed and the demands of relatively young nations whose turbulent chronologies mark an unending quest for effective social orientation. This search has produced at various points in Latin American history both conflict and mutual accommodation. At hardly any point in that history, however, has it been possible for the Church and the state to go their separate ways. Even where certain nations, in imitation of the example offered by the United States, have legislated an official separation, such action has rarely taken the religious question out of the political arena, and less rarely, if ever, has it produced a duplication of the conditions obtaining in the United States.

Series of crises

The permanent involvement of the Church in Latin America can, at least partially, be delineated by reference to the series of crises through which it has passed in its relation to the state. This series undoubtedly begins in the period following liberation when two important and related problems were Church patronage and recognition by Rome of the new governments. In connection with the latter, papal hesitancy or reluctance to deal with the new and unstable authorities probably gave rise to a certain tension between a nascent nationalism and the Church, which was not entirely dissipated by the eventual extension of recognition. This problem was, however, less important and less enduring than that of the *patronato*. If the state could approach this question in terms of national interest and authority, the Church viewed the matter against the background of traditional Spanish regalism which represented a potential encroachment on its own authority.

The important consideration here, however, lies less in the conflict over the appointment of bishops and other ecclesiastical officials than in the fact that neither side could produce a solution without the other. It was not in the logic of the times for public authority, on the one side, to regard the authority which a bishop possesses as being beyond the scope of concern of the state. The implications of such authority for public order were too obvious to be ignored. It was equally impossible for the Church to forego or abandon an official recognition of its functions by the state. In what other way could it secure assurance that its functions would be tolerated?

In the course of a century and a half, the Church, in many countries, has, of necessity, learned that it can function without this recognition, but there is no denial of the fact that, in certain cases, the circumstances of withdrawal of this recognition confirmed the earlier fears of the Church. Within the same period, many Latin American governments have modified or given up their regalistic positions. The most notable survival of pure regalism, however, is in Argentina. Its history shows the two powers, Church and state, on a figurative seesaw where the pressures of each have kept a kind of rhythm and balance which apparently would be lost if either abandoned the apparatus. More than a century ago, the drafters of the Constitution of 1853 believed that their document had settled all questions between the two entities. Yet, in 1856 Juan B. Alberdi, the chief of the constitution-makers, was astounded by the attitudes he encountered on a diplomatic mission to Rome. He was presented with demands which, without specifically challenging the constitutional provisions, would, he judged, make the Argentine Church economically independent in a way that the state could not tolerate. He urged his government not to accede to the demands. Thirty years later the Argentine government attempted to dismiss certain diocesan heads, but this drastic move did not establish a precedent which has since been invoked. Thus, within the nineteenth century, Church and state in this particular country seemed to find the permissable limits of pressure one on the other. These limits clearly did not exclude the Argentine Church from involvement in the crises of 1943, 1946, and 1955.

Regalism per se raises questions that are truly political in nature. Some of the crises through which the Latin American Church has passed, however, have posed issues that have been less strictly political than they have been sociological or even—in the view of the Church—theological. Some general questions in these areas relate to the effort to laicize certain functions which the Church has claimed as primarily within its own sphere of authority. The most important have centered in legislation concerning marriage and education.

Marriage

In regard to marriage, modern formulation of Catholic doctrine does not deny the competence of the state to regulate the civil effects of matrimony. It does not, for example, oppose the issuance of a marriage license. Catholic teaching does, however, regard marriage as a sacrament, and the Church claims authority over the administration of sacraments—even though, in this case, the ministers of the sacrament are the parties to the marriage contract, not the clergyman officiating at the ceremony. Basic regulation of the conditions of marriage, then, is claimed by the Church. In many parts of Latin America, the Church has seen its claims threatened and opposed by the state in two respects. The more important one so far is the requirement of civil marriage to validate a union between man and wife. The other is the authorization of civil divorce. In connection with the first, it is probably important to emphasize that what is at stake is not permissive civil marriage, but a required one. The Church's reasons for opposing are obvious, but what has led the state to impose this requirement is not always so apparent. Anticlericalism may be an influence in some cases, but it is not the only one. It is not impossible that the requirement arises from a theoretical concept of public authority which simply cannot acknowledge that a matter so fraught with social consequences, as is marriage, does not lie within the competence of the state. Or, in terms of an attitude roughly parallel to that shown in the regalistic conflict, an assertion of state power is not so much to deny the competence of the Church as it is to make the Church recognize the effective interests of the state in matters of common concern. Apart from theory, however, it is obvious that the proponents of civil marriage legislation have often sought to combat thereby a widespread tendency to concubinage and common-law unions. And they have proposed a legalistic solution for a problem for which, in their judgment, a sacramental remedy has proved inadequate. At the same time, of course, the Church can not admit that there is a legalistic solution without retreating from a fundamental theological position.

Education

Conflicts in the field of education have, on the whole, been less clear-cut but probably no less prevalent. Three areas of possible discord may be noted: the maintenance of schools under religious auspices, religious instruction in the public school system, and the existence of universities under Catholic aus-

pices. Conflicts in any one of these areas may, of course, arise out of the directly opposing claims of Church and state. Generally, however, the problem is not so simple. Where the maintenance of Catholic schools has been in question, the question has often appeared in the context of a more intricate problem, such as the legal status of a religious order or a general breakdown of relations between Church and state, as happened in Mexico.

The introduction of religious doctrine classes into the public school system may appear as a drastic and, to many, an unpalatable settlement of the competition between Church and state in education. The Argentine experience, however, between 1944 and 1954, strongly suggests that this arrangement provides no real solution. In that case, Church spokesmen professed originally to regard the decree of December 31, 1943, as a governmental response to a single and isolated Church demand that had been reiterated for some sixty years. A case was also made subsequently that the decree did not infringe on freedom of conscience, since it contained provisions under which non-Catholics were exempt from attending the religious doctrine classes. It is apparent, however, that the Peronist government took no such simple view of the matter. Rather, it regarded the school question as merely one factor within the complex of pressures through which it was hoped to involve the Church and Catholic sentiment in general in political support of the regime. On this basis, it was probably inevitable that the two parties would clash, as they began to do several years before religious instruction was dropped from the curriculum.

Professional certification

A Catholic university presents problems of a different sort. Moreover, since the history of the universities in the six countries where they have some importance is still relatively brief, generalization must be limited. One prevalent issue between Church and state, however, is the question of professional qualification by a university which is not responsive to public authority. Lacking a tradition of private universities, Latin American society has customarily relied upon the public universities not only for instruction but also for certification of competence to pursue a profession. The question for public authority then becomes how a non-public university can be related to this general function. The matter is obviously not beyond the possibility of practical settlement, but, whatever adjustment may be made, it must take into account not only Church and state interests, but also those of professional groups. In this latter connection, intraprofessional tensions and rivalries may complicate the settlement.[3]

The foregoing paragraphs are not intended to serve as an inventory of all the factors of the involvement of Church and state in Latin America. In general, however, they support the idea that human behavior, along with the standards by which it is weighed and the influences by which it is conditioned, is the broad and inclusive concern of both parties. Economic issues, especially the question of the Church as a landowner, have, from time to time, involved Church and state in conflict or cooperation, but these issues, while important in a given historical context, have not formed the steady and perpetual problem of Church and state in Latin America. Abuses of ecclesiastical office and corruption within the Church have similar significance. The abiding problem, however, lies both in the conduct which the two powers undertake to enjoin on man in society and in the means which they respectively employ towards this end.

Expectations

In evaluating the Church, there is always the danger of oversimplification of a most complex organization. Taking that risk for the moment, may one not discern a single element pervading the whole involvement of Church and state over human conduct? This element is the authority claimed by the Church. This is an authority which, by definition, cannot be determined by the state. Yet the state is asked to recognize it. The recognition originally demanded was an official endorsement of the necessity of the Church in society in accordance with its own credal concepts of the nature and destiny of man. Up to this date, the Church has not revised its creed; nor is such an eventuality at all likely. The Church has, however, undoubtedly learned from experience that, in practice, official recognition is not quite the *sine qua non* that it is in theory. The important consequences of this lie in the greater possibility of flexibility in the Church's adjustment to society as managed by the state. It would be a serious error, however, to interpret flexibility as relinquishment or abdication of authority.

An emphasis on this element should not be understood as excluding other considerations from the concern of the Church. For the latter, as for any other interested party, the paramount fact today is that Latin America is in a

---

[3] In September 1958 when the legislation to authorize Catholic universities was being considered in the Argentine congress, the author gathered from his conversations with members of congress and with certain lawyers and physicians that some of the proponents of the legislation hoped that competition between public and private universities would ultimately raise rather than confuse professional standards.

process of rapid and profound social transformation. Within the Church, there may be many views and evaluations of this process as it unfolds in various countries. Collectively, however, the forces of Catholicism cannot be unaware of the opportunities to exert moral and ethical influences on this process. Such opportunities are open not only to the hierarchies as the official spokesmen of the Church, but also to the citizen as he participates in the social life of his country.

Undoubtedly, one of the stimuli to action in both the preceding respects is an ultimate awareness that social stagnation and repression may pave the way to a Marxist revolution which, acting in concert with international communism, could produce the least of all desirable situations from a Catholic point of view. Evaluation of current Catholic attitudes on this negative basis alone, however, is probably inadequate. The affirmative drive of Catholic forces, especially in the laity, is shown, if nowhere else, in the large area of identity between their professed aspirations and those of contemporary nationalism in general.

United States policy

This identity may have, it should be noted, some significance for the Latin American policy of the United States. Catholic nationalist sentiment has, on occasion, been critical of the United States, or, more specifically, critical of the form of inter-American organization which United States policy supports. Like other nationalists, these Catholics have feared that the existing organization results in an undue preponderance of United States influence. Catholic sources have urged that the ties of religion, language, and culture that unite Latin America would be the logical basis for the construction of an Ibero-American organization to correct the present imbalance. Serious action along these lines could have grave consequences for the future of the hemisphere, and, in the long run, this possibility should not be overlooked. For the time being, however, the idea itself must be appraised in the light of basic Catholic concerns in the Cold War, which tend to minimize its immediate influence. At least, they add to the unlikelihood that a movement along these lines would receive official Church endorsement.

The immediately foregoing evaluation suggests that all the forces embraced by Catholicism may not be in complete agreement at all times. This is a possibility that should always be taken into account in evaluating Catholicism in any social context. Particularly is this necessary in connection with contemporary Latin America. For the conditions are such as to stimulate a wide variety of responses within the ranks of the Church. It should be borne in mind that the perimeter of the area of diversity is, from a Catholic point of view, established by the Church's official concept of its own authority. The outstandingly important indication of today, however, is that the area thus delineated is a broad one allowing a generous scope for the interplay of the dynamics of social change.